Ernest John Moeran

Ernest John Moeran

His Life and Music

Ian Maxwell

THE BOYDELL PRESS

First published 2021
The Boydell Press, Woodbridge
ISBN 978-1-78327-601-1

The Boydell Press is an imprint of Boydell & Brewer Ltd
PO Box 9, Woodbridge, Suffolk IP12 3DF, UK
and of Boydell & Brewer Inc.
668 Mt Hope Avenue, Rochester, NY 14620-2731, USA
website: www.boydellandbrewer.com

A catalogue record of this publication is available
from the British Library

This publication is printed on acid-free paper

Contents

Illustrations

Music Examples

Preface

I have been examining and researching the life and work of composer E. J. Moeran for more than fifteen years. During this time, my view of him as a person has transitioned through many stages. At the outset, although I had a liking for a couple of piano pieces that I had played, and I was familiar with the Symphony in G minor and the cello concerto, I knew little about the other music and almost nothing about the man himself. While Lionel Hill's *Lonely Waters* and Geoffrey Self's *The Music of E.J. Moeran* were on my bookshelf, I confess that I had not read them. Investigating Moeran's life and work had been the suggestion of Professor Jeremy Dibble, to whom I had originally proposed an entirely different subject for research. After reading Hill and Self and listening to much more of the music, a natural sympathy for Moeran was immediately established. He had suffered dreadfully, but was, nonetheless, a very personable chap, and, despite his appalling experiences, he had composed such wonderful music. However, and most significantly, there appeared to be unanswered questions about his life: how did he support himself? Who were his family? What was the truth about his wartime injury? What happened to his uncompleted second symphony? It was a visit to the National Archives at Kew to examine the composer's military record that unlocked the chest of discovery. The information I found there did not correspond with the biographical material that I had read, and it was apparent that Moeran was not who I had been led to believe he was.

As I unearthed more data, Moeran the man became more complex and, as I eventually realised, more human and more real. He was not just a composer of music. He was a person, with everything that entails for every one of us. He made decisions: some wise and some less wise. He experienced emotion: some of which we all may experience and some of a kind that most of us could not imagine. He succeeded and he failed. He dissembled and he was truthful, and he could be either pleasant and personable or thoroughly objectionable. While all this may seem self-evident, it is often the case with composers that, in the minds of enthusiastic admirers, their realities are obscured by an imagined personality that accords better with the splendour of their creation. Images of Moeran as an agreeable chap have abounded since his reinstatement as a 'scandalously neglected composer' by British music aficionados in the 1970s. However, this is an oblique perspective, informed by the beauty of the creation having been conflated with the creator, and Moeran was so much more than that. Whether what emerges, as readers progress through the book, is to be admired, pitied, loathed, adored, empathised with, or simply accepted, is ultimately the decision of each reader. My own conclusions will gradually become apparent.

The form I have employed for the book is that of a biographical narrative, beginning with Moeran's ancestors and ending with his residual family. The narrative is interspersed with writings about the compositions presented chronologically, as far as can be determined. While I have endeavoured to at least mention everything that Moeran is known to have composed, the depth of examination necessarily varies, from a brief comment to a more extended assessment. Had I devoted equal attention to every work, with thorough-going technical analyses of each major composition, the book would have been three to four times its present length and would have run the risk of the reader drowning in detail. So, perhaps counter-intuitively, I have chosen to focus more attention on what some might consider to be minor compositions, and I have emphasised works that have either received less consideration in past writings or have acquired a previously unrealised importance through the biography. Since Moeran composed relatively smaller works throughout his career, a more detailed study of these enables better granularity in the tracking of his stylistic evolution. Moreover, some of what I believe to have been Moeran's most significant creations have hitherto been dismissed as inconsequential, and it has been my intention to illuminate their importance. If readers familiar with Moeran's music feel that their favourite work or works has or have been given less attention than they would wish, I can only apologise, and express the hope that the discovery of equally compelling other music will be sufficient compensation. Most of Moeran's major works have previously received detailed analytical examination and comment in several pieces of writing, including Geoffrey Self, *The Music of E.J. Moeran*, Rhoderick McNeill, *A Critical Study of the Life and Works of E. J. Moeran*, Fabian Gregor Huss, *Inspiration, Influence and Stylistic Development in the Symphonies and Concertos of E.J. Moeran*, Bruce Polay, *Selected Orchestral Compositions by Ernest John Moeran* and Christopher Pidcock, *An Exploration of the Compositional Idiom of E. J. Moeran with Specific Focus on his Cello Concerto*. The interested reader is referred to these.

Whatever additional purposes may be asserted for music, it is surely for listening to and enjoying, and Moeran's music is indeed enjoyable. Whether or not one is interested in the circumstances of its composition, or the technical aspects of its construction, it is something that may be experienced for itself alone. Nonetheless, I hope that this book will enhance that experience – after all, there is little point in reading the book and not listening to the music – both for those who believe they already understand Moeran, and for those for whom he remains to be discovered.

Dr Ian Maxwell
Wigton, Cumbria
November 2020

Notes on Archival Sources and Citations

To avoid proliferation of footnotes, citing of sources throughout this book has been restricted. Much of Moeran's life is represented in the contents of several hundred letters that he wrote and that were written to him, and in third party correspondence. Many of these letters are in private collections, or, in some cases, have been lost, but over the years copies were made for the Barry Marsh Collection and are now available for examination. The author expresses his thanks to Rachel Marsh for providing access to the items in her late father's collection. This correspondence includes many letters between Moeran and Douglas Gibson of J. & W. Chester music publishers.

Rhoderick McNeill transcribed hundreds of letters from and to Moeran in Appendix I of his 1982 doctoral thesis.[1] In particular, he transcribed the 175 extant letters that Moeran wrote to Peers Coetmore between October 1943 and March 1950 and which now form part of the *Coetmore, Knott, Moeran Family Collection* at the library of the Melbourne Arts Centre, having been bequeathed by Coetmore's fourth husband and widower Maurice Walter Knott on his death in 2004. Correspondence between Moeran and Lionel Hill was transcribed in Hill's 1985 book *Lonely Waters*.[2]

Quotations from letter copies in the Barry Marsh Collection are not individually cited except for clarification, and neither are quotations from McNeill's transcriptions of letters from Moeran to Coetmore. Quotations from letters transcribed by Hill and letters to recipients other than Coetmore transcribed by McNeill are cited with page number only. Quotations from letters in all other sources are fully cited.

The research for this book has drawn extensively on the archives of the Oxford & Cambridge Musical Club. Again, these references will not be cited individually. The sources for quotations and references have been: *Oxford & Cambridge Musical Club Archives*, Oxford University Library Dep.c.958, Dep.c.961, Dep.c.962, Dep.c.966, Dep.c.967, Dep.e.487, Additional Deposits Dep.2.3, Additional Deposits Dep.3.2, Additional Deposits Dep.4.1, Additional Deposits Dep.5.1.

Information pertaining to Moeran's military service between 1914 and 1919 and his army medical record has been derived from documents in the National Archives: WO 374/48245 C457620: Lieutenant Ernest John Smeed MOERAN, The Norfolk Regiment and AIR 86/352/471: E. J. Moeran RAF Record. Individual citations will not be included except where clarification is necessary.

---

1   Rhoderick McNeill, *A Critical Study of the Life and Works of E. J. Moeran*, (University of Melbourne, PhD Thesis, 1982), available on open access at the University of Melbourne Institutional Repository (https://minerva-access.unimelb.edu.au/handle/11343/35509 accessed 31 August 2020)

2   Lionel Hill, *Lonely Waters: the diary of a friendship with EJ Moeran*, (Thames Publishing, London, 1985)

War diary information has been extracted from National Archives: WO 95/3082/3: 2/8 Battalion West Yorkshire Regiment: War Diary. Again, individual citations are given only for the more significant entries.

Acknowledgements

A research project of this nature that has spanned sixteen years and several countries and even continents can only be completed with the generous assistance of many people and on many levels. If I have missed anybody in this list of acknowledgements, I apologise for the oversight.

I would like to thank the librarians and staff of Durham, Oxford, Cambridge, Melbourne and Sydney University Libraries, and of the British Library and Trinity College Dublin Library. I would also like to thank the staff and archivists of The National Archives in Kew, the London Metropolitan Archives, Uppingham School, Britten Pears Arts, Lambeth Palace, Lincoln Cathedral, Clare College Cambridge, The Inner Temple Library and the Police Service of Northern Ireland.

Special thanks are due to the Leo Baeck Institute Center for Jewish History in New York for permission to include quotations from the Arthur Willner Collection, to JPI Media (Belfast News Letter, http://newsletter.co.uk) for permission to include a scan of an article relating to Moeran's 1935 driving conviction, to Óglaigh na hÉireann (Military Archives) for permission to include a quotation from the Bureau of Military History witness statement and to the committee of the Oxford & Cambridge Musical Club for permission to include many references to the Club archives. The photograph of the Norfolk Regiment Cyclist on page 56 is reproduced courtesy of the Trustees of the Royal Norfolk Regiment Museum Collection. The extract from the Freemasons of Ireland Membership Registers on page 80 is reproduced by permission of The Grand Lodge of Freemasons of Ireland. The Stuart Hall Norwich concert programme on page 190 is reproduced by kind permission of Britten Pears Arts, and the quotations from Britten's diaries are © Britten Pears Arts.

I would also like to give thanks to the following individuals who have made their time generously available to answering my questions and enquiries: Helen Allinson (Sittingbourne Museum), Robert Atholl (Clare College, Cambridge), Sarah Batchelor (Royal College of Music Library), Dr Ita Beausang, Barry Sterndale Bennett, Georgina Binns, Mark Bostridge, Stephanie Browne, Mariarosaria Canzonieri (Royal College of Music Library), Dr Nicholas Clark (Britten-Pears Foundation Librarian), Patricia Convery (The Performing Arts Centre, Melbourne), Dr Michael Crowe (Oxford & Cambridge Musical Club), the late Gordon Cumming, Michael Dixey, Dr Ruth Fleischmann, Hugh Forrester (Curator, Police Service of Northern Ireland), Ann Francis (Clare College, Cambridge), Claudia Funder (Research Service Coordinator, Arts Centre Melbourne), Chris Garrod, Caoimhe Ni Ghormain (Trinity College Dublin Library), Dr Rosemary Golding (The Open University), Helen Hawes (Parish Assistant, St. Mary's, Spring Grove), Merlin Holland, Anna Hollis, Dr Peter Horton (Royal College of Music Library), Dr Ronan P. Kelly (Royal College of Surgeons in Ireland Library), Dr Axel Klein,

Rev. Michael Kneen, Susan Leyden (Royal College of Surgeons in Ireland Library), Stephen Lloyd, Calista Lucy (Dulwich College), the late Barry Marsh, Rachel Marsh, Professor Rhoderick McNeill (University of Southern Queensland), Professor Brian Moeran, Monica McCabe, Suzanne Mendel, Jack Moshakis (Wesley College, Melbourne), Aidan Murphy (Met Éireann), Lyn Parkyns (Oxford & Cambridge Musical Club), Dr Thérèse Radic (University of Melbourne), Hannah Rogers (York Army Museum), Andrew Rose, Jerry Rudman (Uppingham School), André Saubolle (Cork Ancestral Archive and Genealogical Research), Diana Spelman, the late Colin Scott-Sutherland, Bernard Spillane (the Cathedral of St. Mary & St. Anne, Cork), Professor Bill Sweeney (University of Glasgow), John Talbot, Alun and Barbara Thomas (Norwood Society), Dr Malcolm Tozer, Andrew Westlake (Oxford & Cambridge Musical Club), Richard Westwood-Brookes, Bridget Whittle (Digital Archives Librarian at McMaster University), and Darrin Winter (The Fisherman's Return, Winterton).

I would like to thank Dr Michael Middeke, Dr Elizabeth Howard, Julia Cook and Dr Megan Milan of Boydell & Brewer Ltd. for their enthusiasm for the project, for help and understanding during the writing phase, and for guidance for a new author as he (sometimes) floundered his way towards a completed book.

I would also like to thank my friends Simon Fenwick, Dr James Reid Baxter, Professor Bill David and Graeme Herrington for invaluable advice, and special appreciation is due to Professor Jeremy Dibble of the University of Durham, on whose suggestion I began this study of Moeran, and whose interest in and enthusiasm for my research and discoveries have only been matched by my own.

My personal thanks go to my three daughters, Catherine, Clare and Nicola, for putting up with my Moeran enthusiasm for so long, and to my wife, Jane, who has supported and helped me over the years of this project in more ways than I can count.

Finally, this book is dedicated to my mother and late father. My love of English music was awakened at an early age through hearing my mother play and sing the songs of Finzi, Quilter, Ireland, Michael Head and many others, and that characteristic sound has been a part of my identity for as long as I can remember.

Thank you all.

Barry Marsh

This book could not have been completed without the benefit of access to the comprehensive archive of information collected over many years by the British Music enthusiast Barry Marsh. I would like to express my appreciation to Mr Marsh's family for their generous decision to make this archive available to me during the latter stages of the writing of this book. The following is their tribute to their father:

> In loving memory and in honour of our late father Barry Marsh; a true inspiration to us as children. Barry was a man who had an endless passion and enthusiasm for all classical music but with a particular interest in English music. As a choral singer and writer originally based in Norwich, he discovered and fell in love with the music and life of Ernest John Moeran and eventually dedicated himself to a

lifetime of research into this lesser-known English composer. Moeran was part of our family when we were growing up, and he continued to be so as we both took our careers and studies further into the music world, where Dad encouraged us to include songs by Moeran in our public performances. Although it was Barry's intention to complete a biography of Moeran, this, sadly, did not come to pass—due to his sudden and tragic death in March 2016. While it is disappointing that his version of the book was never finished, we are both delighted to know that much of his hard work and research has been used to bring the story of this remarkable composer to life.

Rachel Marsh
Simon Marsh
November 2020

Introduction

Ernest John Moeran has been one of the least written about composers that were active in Britain during the first half of the twentieth century, and who worked in the folksong-influenced pastoral style that has come to be associated with the conveniently but misleadingly labelled English Musical Renaissance. Of attempts made during the seventy years since his death to produce an authoritative and comprehensive biography, only Geoffrey Self's study *The Music of E.J. Moeran* was completed and published. Although some academic research has been undertaken, with some of Moeran's life and work being the subject of detailed scholarship, none resulted in a full biography. The seemingly intractable problem that prospective biographers have encountered has been an apparent shortage of credible primary source material about the composer's early life, in particular his childhood and years of education. This has led to an unsatisfactorily incomplete evidence-based picture of the adult composer, and it seems that there has been insufficient information to make an extended biography worth writing. Moreover, Moeran destroyed much of his work – including everything that he composed as a child or schoolboy – and his lifelong peripatetic existence ensured that many of his possessions, including manuscripts, were scattered and lost. Few family papers have survived, and the passage of time has meant that there are no longer witnesses to verify or contradict what has previously been claimed or stated. Perhaps inevitably, the place of evidence has been taken by a perceptual framework that has been constructed over the years, based on the compounding of rumour, unsupported assertion, exaggeration, and invention, some of which undoubtedly originated with the composer himself. Facts have been supplemented or superseded by a detailed and ostensibly credible mythology. The understanding of Moeran's personality and the reception of his music has become so rooted in this mythology that the task of separating fact from sometimes sensational fiction is now extremely difficult.

The most powerful and enduring aspect of the mythology has been the story of Moeran's experiences during the First World War. The life-changing head injury he is said to have suffered in France in May 1917 and its treatment by the insertion of a metal plate into his skull, residual fragments of shrapnel embedded too close to his brain for safe removal, and a physical legacy of both the injury and its treatment, are all presumed to have plagued Moeran throughout his life, eventually contributing to his early death at the age of fifty-five. It has also been assumed that he lived through several years of the horrors of the trenches of the Western Front, that what he witnessed there damaged him psychologically, and that all these experiences together defined his character and fundamentally informed the music that he composed. It may be reasonably asserted that the narrative of the injury with its supposedly lifelong effects has been one of the key factors driving the late twentieth-century revival of interest in Moeran's music. One is naturally inclined to a sympathetic response to somebody that has apparently suffered so badly yet who achieved so much. The character that emerges, if the litany of wartime dreadfulness is taken at face value, is one that sits comfortably beside those of other First World War composer victims, such as Ivor Gurney, George Butterworth, William Baines and Frederick Septimus Kelly.

The above being the case, the reader may be forgiven for wondering why the author has embarked on such a seemingly futile project as writing a biography of Moeran. Indeed, the author began his research into the composer's life with the mythology preconceptions intact, and with no notion that they might be susceptible to challenge. However, inconsistencies in the narrative, relating both to Moeran's early life and to his apparent wartime experiences, initiated a process by which much of the hitherto accepted biography was scrutinised, discredited, and discarded. It was the need to find alternatives that enabled the author to discover significant biographical evidence that had previously lain unexamined. Since Moeran's life had been regarded as understood – through the uncritical acceptance of the mythological framework – seeking such material had not been considered as either necessary or even possible. It was at this point in the author's original research project that it was decided to unearth as much information about Moeran's life as possible, confronting every aspect of the accepted wisdom since, in the light of the author's discoveries, it could no longer be regarded as reliable. Thus, the author began an investigation of the life of Ernest John Moeran with a clean sheet, and, over the course of more than fifteen years, has assembled a body of primary evidence and reasonable supposition that has dispersed the Moeran mythology and replaced it with a thorough-going and verifiable biography of the man. This has naturally also required a re-assessment of the music, now illuminated by an understanding of its composer that is underpinned by a foundation of supportable facts.

Moeran's music is straightforward to categorise. Almost every work has a recognisable tonal base and employs conventional harmony, although he occasionally tested its boundaries. He worked with established formal structures – such as sonata form – although the interpretation of these frequently exhibits inventive modification. Nonetheless, Moeran cannot be presented as having been a musical innovator. At first sight, none of his music may be considered progressive in its chronological context. Perhaps more than most of his contemporaries, Moeran was content with the relatively limited stylistic framework that his inherited musical philosophy imposed. At a time when tonality was being challenged both elsewhere in Europe and by many of his compatriots, Moeran had no time for what he called 'a new branch of academism', and the extremes of dissonance that were being explored in the music of his younger contemporaries, such as Elizabeth Lutyens and Humphrey Searle, held no fascination for him. Neither did he embrace influences from popular music genres – such as jazz – in the way that some composers – William Walton, for example – did.

Opinion has been divided as to what extent Moeran created a distinctive voice in his music, with writers being reluctant to credit him with freshness of idea or style. Indeed, discussion of Moeran has almost always taken place within the context of seemingly obvious influences from other composers, such as Ireland, Delius,

Warlock or Sibelius, and the higher profile enjoyed by these composers has ensured that when apparent similarities are identified, it is always Moeran's music that is presumed to be the derivative. The notion that he exhibited a unique style that may even have inspired other composers has never been considered seriously, and his compositional skill has been relegated to an expertise in the re-working of influences. The existence of creative individuality is difficult to establish effectively, as it ultimately requires the identification of the nebulous quality of originality. Nevertheless, if it may be reasonably asserted that Moeran's music could not have been composed by anybody else, then it is equally reasonable to assert that Moeran did have a distinct voice.

While Moeran's music, as with that of many of his contemporaries, must now find an alternative relevance in a world that can no longer remember the traumas experienced and witnessed by its creator, its appreciation can surely only be enhanced if it is accompanied by a clear understanding of its composer's life. Moeran's achievement is available for all to experience in the 120 or so musical compositions that posterity possesses, and which technology has now ensured most of which may be listened to by almost anybody at almost any time. It is the enduring legacy of a life that, as this book will show, was filled variously with promise, achievement, disappointment and despair. While bearing in mind Igor Stravinsky's admonishment that if music appears to express anything beyond itself, this can only be an illusion, it is nonetheless suggested that the sensations and emotions that much of Moeran's music still has the capacity to arouse in attentive listeners may, in themselves, be regarded as evidence that he successfully expressed himself. It is the nature of music that each response to it is an individual one, informed by the unique experiences of each listener, and it is the lasting power of Moeran's creation that it still resonates so vividly. This book presents a definitive and candid study both of Moeran (the man) and of Moeran (the composer), each finally revealed after decades of opaqueness and misunderstanding. The journey of discovery is both challenging and fascinating.

PART 1

ANCESTRY, CHILDHOOD AND EDUCATION

1

Irish and Victorian Origins

Hitherto, it has been problematic to determine with any confidence the source of the apparently Irish surname Moeran. Exhaustive searches of archives in Ireland[1] and elsewhere have located just one spurious reference that may be dated to any point earlier than the first decade of the nineteenth century.[2] A speculative legend promulgated by the present day Moeran family that the name was brought to Ireland as a corruption of the Huguenot de Meuran (or de Meuron) by exiles from Cardinal Richelieu during the seventeenth century lacks any supporting evidence.[3] Similarly, an account that the name came from Brittany during the late eighteenth century as the result of the travels of an itinerant (and possibly Dutch) musician and swordsman named Moeran is also unsupported.[4] Furthermore, transliteration of the German or Swedish surname Möran seems to be very unlikely. The first mention of anybody named Moeran in any source in the British Isles located thus far is dated March 1808, and it may reasonably be supposed that the name appeared at about that date.

A newspaper report of the death of one Edward Moeran at the age of eighty-four on 17 February 1865 in Cork suggests that a Moeran family may have been living in the city for some time, and it would seem reasonable to believe that this was also the case when Edward was born in about 1780.[5] However, as suggested above, Edward Moeran can be traced back only to March 1808: 'MARRIED: Last Saturday, Mr Edward Moeran, to Miss Busteed.'[6] While Edward Moeran is mentioned in an

---

[1] The convention adopted for convenience throughout this book is to refer to the Republic of Ireland, the Irish Free State, Eire or Éire as 'Ireland'. Exceptions to this occur where the name 'Eire' is included in quotations from Moeran's letters.

[2] References in late nineteenth and early twentieth century sources to Thomas Moeran, who as dean of Cork was executed in 1578, derive from a mis-transcription of the account of martyr Thomas Moran in John Mullan ('Molanus'), *Idea Togatae Constantiae, cui adjungitur Epitome Tripartita Martyrum fere omnium qui in Britannicis insulis nostra patrumque memoria de heresi gloriose triumpharunt*, (Paris, 1629), 66. The text mentions that Moran was buried in a marble tomb bearing his name near the choir of St Peter's Church, Cork. The tomb was removed when the church was deconsecrated in 1949.

[3] The author is indebted to Moeran's first cousin-once-removed Professor Brian Moeran for this information.

[4] This information was provided to the author by Moeran family researcher Brian Bornemann.

[5] 'Deaths', *Cork Examiner*, (18 February 1865), 2.

[6] 'MARRIED', *Cork Mercantile Chronicle*, (21 March 1808), 3.

abundance of newspaper reports from that date until the report of his death in 1865, there is no reference to his birth or childhood. A clue to resolving the mystery of Edward's identity is provided by an earlier marriage announcement in November 1802: 'MARRIED – Last Tuesday morning, at St Finn Barre's by the Rev. Henry Sandiford, Mr EDWARD MORAN, Professor of Music, to Miss NESBITT.'[7] While this may at first sight be coincidence, the many newspaper references between 1808 and 1865 to Edward Moeran as a musician, and the lack of any further mention of Edward Moran, suggest compellingly that Moran and Moeran were one and the same, his marriage to Margaret Busteed having been made possible by the death of Helena Nesbitt. The history of Edward Moeran's musical life in Cork begins with an advertisement placed in the *Cork Mercantile Chronicle* a year after his marriage to Miss Busteed: 'Grand Pianoforte Warehouse, Rutland Street. Edward Moeran has for sale and [indecipherable] all the most fashionable, newly constructed, and best patent pianofortes.'[8] Similar advertisements and reports testifying to Edward Moeran's musical talents and activities appeared in Cork newspapers during the next five decades, and he is listed in William West's 1810 *Directory of Cork* as a 'music-master'. It seems, therefore, that the name 'Moeran' was adopted by Edward Moran, at some time between his first marriage in 1802 and his second in 1808.[9]

Edward Moeran's long career as a musician is documented principally in the pages of local Cork newspapers, and these reports indicate a devoted contribution to the musical life of the city over a period of nearly sixty years. Edward was a member of the Masonic order, and he formed a glee-singing quartet that performed regularly, especially at official celebrations and Masonic events. On 10 September 1818, the Lord Lieutenant of Ireland attended dinner at the Cork Mansion House, and Edward and his colleagues provided the after-dinner diversions:

> The Lord Lieutenant – Yesterday his Excellency was splendidly entertained at the Mansion-House … Between the toasts, Messrs Magrath, Shaw, Gillespie and Moeran, assisted by some amateurs amongst the guests, gave several Glees and

7   'MARRIED', *Cork Mercantile Chronicle*, (8 November 1802), 3. The news was also carried in 'Marriages', *Walker's Hibernian Magazine*, (December 1802), 764. In 1802 there was no institute of higher education in Cork that would employ professors, so Edward Moran's identification as a professor of music necessarily denotes something other than the academic position now associated with the title. It is likely to have meant that Moran was a teacher of music. A scan of contemporary Cork newspapers reveals that several professors of music were active in Cork during the early 1800s.

8   *Cork Mercantile Chronicle*, (10 April 1809), 1.

9   The suggestion that Moeran is an alternative to Moran was originally made by Aloys Fleischmann shortly after Ernest John Moeran's death: 'The name Moeran is a variant of Moran or Morehan,' Aloys Fleischmann, 'The Music of E. J. Moeran', *Envoy*, Vol. 4, No. 16 (1951), 60). At the time, Fleischmann could not have known about Edward Moran's change of name, and his assertion originated in a book on Irish surnames (Robert E. Matheson, *Varieties and Synonyms of Surnames and Christian Names in Ireland*, (His Majesty's Stationery Office, Dublin, 1901), 56), which groups Moeran together with Moarn, Moren, Morin and Morrin, all as variants of Moran.

Songs with their accustomed talent. No entertainment could be conducted in a style of greater elegance or pass off with more harmony and conviviality.[10]

Moeran and his fellow glee-singers did not limit themselves to official engagements. The concert-promoting enthusiasm that had developed in London and provincial cities during the late eighteenth and early nineteenth centuries was also evident in Cork, and on 28 January 1823, Mr Forde presented a Grand Concert in the Cork Assembly Rooms, during which a wide range of repertoire was presented in a three-part musical extravaganza.[11] Messrs Magrath, Brettridge, Moeran and Keays sang several four-part Glees, including *Faithless Emma* by Banks and *By Celia's Arbour all the Night* by Horsley, and Edward Moeran accompanied himself on the piano in the *Spirit Song* from Dr John Clarke's setting of *Lalla Rookh*. Evidence of Edward Moeran's expertise on the organ abounds, from his participation in a charity event held in January 1827 to raise funds for the Cork Fever Hospital, to his description as 'the old and respected organist of the Cathedral' who 'presided with his usual ability at the organ' in a report of a special church service in August 1847.[12] Edward also regularly provided his services as a choral conductor: 'Edward Moeran Esq, is entitled to our best thanks for having, with his usual kindness and efficiency, conducted the Choir.'[13] He also occupied himself with teaching, periodically advertising his services as a pianoforte and singing instructor. The following announcement was placed in November 1836:

> Piano-forte and Singing – Mr Moeran takes leave to inform his friends and the Public that having recently studied under the celebrated Mons. Herz, he is induced to set apart two days in each week, for his professional avocations in Town. Any commands left for him at the office of Samuel Merrick Esq. Solicitor, South Mall; or at his residence, Wood View, Blackrock, will be attended to.[14]

Edward's claim to have been instructed by the internationally renowned Herz would have significantly enhanced his reputation.[15]

---

[10] 'The Lord Lieutenant', *Saunder's Newsletter*, (14 September 1818), 2.

[11] 'Grand Concert', *Southern Reporter & Cork Commercial Courier*, (25 January 1823), 3. As if an extended three-part concert beginning at half past eight in the evening was not enough, the concert was followed by a grand ball.

[12] *Cork Examiner*, (16 August 1847), 4. While there are several newspaper reports mentioning that Edward Moeran was organist at the cathedral, it must be noted that the main antiquarian reference work to Cork Cathedral, Richard Caulfield's *Annals of St Fin Barre's Cathedral, Cork* (Purcell & Co., Cork, 1871), which was compiled from manuscript and printed sources in such archives as the British Museum, the Bodleian Library, the London Public Record Office and the Chapter Books of Cork Cathedral, contains no mention of anybody called Moeran or Moran, either in a musical or any other capacity. Neither do the records of the Roman Catholic Cathedral of St Mary and St Anne mention Edward Moran/Moeran, and the author is grateful to Bernard Spillane of the Parish Records Office for this information.

[13] 'Peacock Lane & Sullivan's Quay Schools', *Cork Examiner*, (21 March 1842), 4.

[14] 'Pianoforte and Singing', *Cork Southern Reporter*, (1 November 1836), 2.

[15] Henri Herz (1803–1888), Austrian-French composer, pianist, teacher, and inventor. It is not known where Edward Moeran's instruction took place and over what period. During

Following the founding of the Anacreontic Society in London in 1766, similar gentlemen's clubs dedicated to the companionable celebration of music and singing were established in cities around the country, and Cork was no exception. The first mention in the newspapers of the Cork Anacreontic Society comes from March 1828, and, over the years, Edward Moeran's name appears frequently as a professional member of the society. In February 1844, the *Cork Examiner* reported:

> The Cork Anacreontic Society held their Third Meeting for the present season on Thursday last. The selection of music made for this occasion presented, if possible, more attractions than the programme of any former evening. The professional members, Messrs Orr, Keays, A.D. Roche, Moeran, McCarthy and Wheeler, were all in excellent voice.[16]

While much of Edward Moeran's life in Cork between 1808 and 1865 is recorded in local newspaper reports and advertisements, his life as Edward Moran up to 1802 seems to be a mystery. While no records of a Moran family living in Cork during the last decades of the eighteenth century have been found, the name was and remains quite widespread in Ireland, and numerous Morans are mentioned in newspaper records from the mid-eighteenth century onwards. It is interesting to discover that two musically talented Morans were active in Dublin during that period. These were Peter K. Moran, born 1767 (probably in Dublin), who was a pianist and composer and a pupil of the Dublin-based teacher Philip Dwyer, and 'Master Moran', who was promoted as a nine-year-old child prodigy pianist in newspaper advertisements between mid-May 1799 and June 1800, and who was also a student of Dwyer. Peter K. Moran emigrated with his family to the United States of America in 1817 and established a career for himself as a New York-based pianist, composer and music publisher until his death in February 1831.[17] Master Moran enjoyed a brief period in the limelight which ceased abruptly in June 1800, and the inquisitive and imaginative biographer cannot help but speculate about what happened to him. His last appearance before the public seems to have been at a benefit concert on 12 June 1800, which was advertised as taking place in the Exhibition House, William Street, Dublin.

In common with the publicity for each of Master Moran's concerts, this event was patronised by 'Ladies of Distinction'. Many child prodigies were active in Europe during the eighteenth and early to mid-nineteenth centuries – often aggressively promoted by ambitious fathers or (sometimes) unscrupulous agents – and they generally held a strong appeal for wealthy society ladies. Press notices for Master Moran include references to his female admirers, many of whom sponsored his performances. The issue of *Saunder's Newsletter* dated 13 May 1799 carries the notice: 'Master Moran most respectfully begs leave to inform those Ladies who have honoured him with their kind and generous patronage that Friday the 24th inst. May is

---

the 1830s, Herz was living in Paris and was the proprietor of a piano factory there. Since Edward Moeran was also a retailer of pianos, it is quite possible that he travelled to Paris to meet Herz and perhaps to negotiate an agency in Cork for Herz's pianofortes.

[16] 'The Cork Anacreontic Society', *Cork Examiner*, (12 February 1844), 1.

[17] J. B. Clark & E. R. Meyer, 'Peter K. Moran: Amerigrove Expanded', *Sonneck Society Bulletin*, 15 (1989), 106.

Under the Patronage of feveral Ladies of Diftinction.

MASTER MORAN's CONCERT

EXHIBITION-HOUSE, WILLIAM-STREET.

ON Thurfday, 12th June, 1800, will be a CONCERT of VOCAL and INSTRUMENTAL MUSIC. The Band compofed of the firft Amateurs in Dublin, will be led by Mr. Bianchi;

Mr. Giordanij will prefide at the Piano Forte.

A C T I.

Overture, - -	Playel.
Song, Love Sounds the Alarm,	Mr. Caldwell.
Quartetto, - -	Playel.
Duet, Harp and Grand Piano Forte, Mr. O'Hagerty and Mafter Moran.	

A C T II.

Overture, - -	Hayden.
Song, The Wolf, -	Mr. Weyman.
Concerto, Piano Forte,	Mafter Moran—Giornovichi.
Glee.	
Concerto Violin, -	Mr. Bianchi.

After the Concert will be a Ball, Conducted by Mr. Kelly.

The Room will be illuminated with Wax.

Single Tickets, Half-a-Guinea—Tickets admitting three, one Guinea, to be had at No. 3, Chatham-ftreet, and at all the Mufic-fhops.

Figure 1. Freeman's Journal, 10 June 1800, 'Master Moran's Concert'

appointed for his benefit,'[18] and in the issue dated 18 June 1799, the notice mentions: 'by particular desire of several Ladies of Distinction, Master Moran, Pupil of Mr Dwyer, will perform on the Pianoforte, Madame Krompholtz's favourite Concerto.'[19] Single tickets for the 12 June concert were half a guinea – the present-day equivalent of at least £50 – and it is probable that substantial funds would have been taken both

[18] 'THEATRE ROYAL', *Saunder's Newsletter*, (13 May 1799), 2.
[19] 'THEATRE ROYAL', *Saunder's Newsletter*, (18 June 1799), 2.

in advance (including the patronage payments) and at the door. While the claim in several of the publicity notices that Master Moran was nine years old may have been genuine, it is also possible that this was a subterfuge inspired by his having the appearance of a younger boy than he really was.[20] Exaggerating the youth of a child prodigy was an occasional practice where proof of age was difficult to establish. Although Master Moran's talent for the piano could not have been in any doubt, it would have been far more marketable as a nine-year-old than as an immature four-teen- or fifteen-year-old. His boyish looks could have enabled Moran and his agents to hoodwink the ladies of distinction and the respectable concert-going society of Dublin and Belfast, up to the point when it became physically impossible to main-tain the deception any further. Master Moran's disappearance in mid-1800 would be consistent with this. Moreover, if this suggestion is true, the amount of money invei-gled from the pianist's admirers would have led at the very least to some uncomfort-able questions being asked.

It is entirely possible that Master Moran simply stopped playing the piano in public for some reason and disappeared from history. However, if the supposition presented above has any basis, then it also needs to account for what Master Moran may have done after the deception was realised. It is possible that he left Dublin in order to escape those that demanded he should repay the money that had been extracted from them. Under these circumstances, relocating himself to Cork and establishing a new identity would be readily understandable. In which case, could the child prodigy Master Moran of Dublin and music-master and piano warehouse proprietor Edward Moran/Moeran of Cork be one and the same person? Directories and chronicles of life in Cork during the late eighteenth century include no ref-erences to a family called Moran, and although not everybody that lived in Cork was mentioned in newspapers, directories or other chronicles, the fact that Edward Moeran and members of his family frequently appear throughout the nineteenth century strongly supports the notion that their involvement in Cork life began after Master Moran's speculated arrival in 1800. Thus, Edward Moran changing his name to Moeran may have been the result of his endeavouring to obscure his origins. The only evidence that supports these suggestions is circumstantial. Nonetheless, Edward Moran/Moeran must have been born and spent his childhood somewhere, and the sparse evidence is fully accommodated by the compelling story that he led an earlier life as a fake child prodigy, who accumulated a substantial fortune by swin-dling society ladies in Dublin and Belfast, and who fled to Cork and changed his name when the fraud was exposed. Whatever the truth, after his change of name to Moeran and his second marriage to Margaret Busteed in 1808, his life in Cork as a piano-dealer, music teacher, glee-singer, pianist, organist, choirmaster and member of the Masonic order appears to have been thoroughly respectable, notwithstanding the possibility that it may have been established through ill-gotten gains.

[20] 'EXCHANGE-ROOMS, BELFAST. Grand Concert of Vocal and Instrumental Music. They have engaged the Musical Phenomenon, Master Moran, (a Child only nine years of age), whose performance has been the admiration of all the Musical World', *Belfast Newsletter*, (16 July 1799), 3.

Edward Moeran had twelve children with his second wife Margaret Busteed, two of whom were Edward Busteed Moeran, born 1809, and Thomas Warner Moeran, born 1819. Both these sons attended Trinity College Dublin and were ordained as ministers of the Church of Ireland. While no evidence of musical talent or ability has been found in the lives of either Edward Busteed or Thomas Warner, or, indeed, any of Edward Moeran's other children, intellectual drive is apparent through the achievements of members of the next generations of the Edward Moeran dynasty. After taking a Bachelor of Arts degree from Trinity College in 1845 and then being ordained, Thomas Warner Moeran served as curate of Westport, County Mayo (1845–1847) and curate of Youghal, County Cork (1847–1849).[21] In 1849, he was appointed curate at St Mark's Church, Liverpool, and in 1853 he married Frances Byrne of Dublin.[22] Although the Moeran family lived in Liverpool, their children were all born in Dublin: Edward Joseph in 1857, Joseph William Wright in 1859 and daughter Frances Anna Swift in 1861.[23] In 1857, Thomas Warner Moeran was appointed vicar at St Matthew's Church, Toxteth Park, and the family lived there until 1873 when Thomas was appointed to the living of Bacton in Norfolk.[24] The Reverend Thomas was to remain incumbent at Bacton for the next forty years.

Instead of following his father and uncle to Trinity College Dublin, Joseph William Wright Moeran established a new family university tradition by entering St Catharine's College, Cambridge, in 1879, graduating with a Bachelor of Arts degree in Theology in 1882.[25] He was ordained and, for his first clerical appointment, took up a curacy at Pocklington, a village some ten miles to the east of York. He remained in this position until 1885, when he was appointed curate at the parish church of St Paul's, Upper Norwood, where the vicar was the Reverend William Graham. It may reasonably be supposed that soon after his arrival Joseph began a courtship of the vicar's nineteen-year-old niece and ward Ada Esther Smeed Whall, because three years later, on 10 April 1888, in a ceremony co-celebrated by the bride's uncle and the groom's father, the couple were married. While the wedding was briefly announced in several national newspapers, it received a detailed report in the local Norwood magazine *The Norwood Review*, which was reprinted in the issue of *The Norfolk Chronicle & Norwich Gazette*, dated 21 April 1888. The report began:

> From the number of people travelling in the direction of St Paul's Church, Hamlet Road, on Tuesday, it was evident that something of an unusually interesting character was on the *tapis*, and on entering the sacred edifice this was at once confirmed. Need we mention to any of our readers connected with the above

21 *Register of the Alumni of Trinity College Dublin*, 9th edition, (Trinity College, Dublin, 1970), and W. M. Brady, *Clerical and Parish Records of Cork, Cloyne, and Ross*, Vol 3, (Alexander Thom, Dublin, 1864), 224 and *Crockford's Clerical Directory for 1915*, (Horace Cox, London, 1915), 1060.

22 *Cork Examiner*, (9 May 1849), 3, and Ireland, Civil Registration Marriages Index, 1845–1958, Vol. 5, Page 372, FHL Film Number 101244.

23 1 England Census, Class: RG 9; Piece: 2687; Folio: 49; Page: 35; GSU roll: 543013.

24 *Crockford's Clerical Directory for 1908*, (Horace Cox, London, 1908), 995.

25 John A. Venn, *Alumni Cantabrigienses*, (Cambridge University Press, Cambridge, 1974). Joseph William added his Master of Arts in 1892.

church that the occasion was the marriage of the Rev. J. W. W. Moeran, the senior curate, to Miss Whall. When we consider the popularity of the Rev. gentleman, we are not surprised that the members of the congregation should wish, by their presence, to express their good wishes to the bride and bridegroom. The bride, as mentioned, was Miss Ada Esther Smeed Whall, daughter of Mr. B. J. Whall of Glasgow, the bridegroom being the son of the Rev. T. W. Moeran, vicar of Bacton, Norfolk.[26]

The report of the wedding continued for a broadsheet half-column and provided details of the participants' outfits, the bridesmaids, the co-celebrants, the service itself, which was described as 'fully choral', the flowers, the wedding gifts and an extended commendation of Joseph himself as a very popular and hard-working curate in the parish. Evidence of the bride's position in society was underlined by one of her bridesmaids being Miss Chetham-Strode – a member of the prominent late-Victorian family – and the fact that the flowers were supplied by Lady Wodehouse.[27]

Who was Ada Esther Smeed Whall, whose wedding to Joseph Moeran attracted such society and press interest? The beginnings of the answer to this lie on the southern edge of the town of Sittingbourne in Kent, where there is a public park that has been known since the 1930s as the King George's Playing Fields. In the north-east corner of the park is a converted stable block, near to which may be found the base of a row of pillars and the remnants of foundations, which together provide a clue to the former use of the land. The park is the site of Gore Court, a country estate and mansion built during the 1790s. The estate was bought in 1853 by local industrialist George Smeed, both to befit his prominent social position and to provide an appropriate home for his growing family. Smeed was a proficient entrepreneur who had created a large personal fortune through the businesses of brick making and barge building that flourished in the Milton Creek area of Sittingbourne during the nineteenth century. He was a combination of fellow of the people, ruthless businessman and, in later life, philanthropist.[28]

Smeed and his wife Eliza had a family of seven daughters, ranging in age from Mary Ann, who was twenty, down to the newly born Emily Ruth. There was also a household staff comprising a groom, a cook, a governess, three maids and two gardeners.[29] The estate included several cottages, and these were occupied by estate

[26] 'Marriage of the Rev. J. W. W. Moeran', *The Norfolk Chronicle & Norwich Gazette*, (21 April 1888), 8.

[27] Probably Isabella Stracey, wife of Lord John Wodehouse. The living of Thomas Warner Moeran's Bacton parish was in the gift of the Earl of Kimberley (previously Baron Wodehouse), whose seat was Kimberley Hall, Wymondham, Norfolk.

[28] See Richard-Hugh Perks, *George Bargebrick Esquire: The Story of the George Smeed – the Brick and Cement King* (Meresborough Books, Rainham, 1981) and 'Urban Rus', *Old Faces in Odd Places* (Wyman & Sons, London, 1882). 'Urban Rus' was the pen name of George Smeed's stepson Harry Greensted.

[29] 1861 England Census, Class: RG 10; Piece: 529; Folio: 201; Page: 2; GSU roll: 542656.

workers.[30] The railway arrived at Sittingbourne in 1858, and Gore Court was just a short carriage and train journey from the metropolis. Smeed travelled regularly to London and it is also likely that his older daughters enjoyed the social life available to affluent young ladies in the mid-Victorian era. Over the years, the Smeed girls made appropriate marriages. The eldest daughter Mary Ann married Smeed's business manager George Hambrook Dean, Sarah Ann married the Reverend William Henry Graham in 1861 and third daughter Esther married King's Lynn banker's clerk Benjamin John Whall.

How Esther Smeed of Gore Court, Kent and Benjamin John Whall of King's Lynn, Norfolk met and effected a relationship that eventually resulted in their marriage at Tunstall Church on 21 December 1864 can only be speculated. Benjamin John was an employee at the King's Lynn office of the Norwich-based Gurney's Bank, and it is possible that Smeed held an account there to facilitate his business interests in Norfolk. King's Lynn was a busy port during the nineteenth century. Many of Smeed's barges arrived and departed discharging and loading a variety of cargoes. Benjamin John Whall may on occasion have been required to travel to Gore Court, perhaps to obtain a signature from Smeed on a business document, and while there he could have met Smeed's daughter and a relationship began. It is probable that conducting a courtship at a distance presented some difficulties for Benjamin John, but his persistence paid off as the wedding was reported in the issue of the *Maidstone Journal and Kentish Advertiser* dated 26 December 1864:

> Marriage Festivities at Gore Court – On Wednesday last the monotony of the parish was interrupted by the marriage of Miss Esther Smeed, third daughter of George Smeed Esq, of Gore Court, to Benjamin John Whall, Esq, of King's Lynn, Norfolk. The ceremony was impressively performed by the Rev. G. B. Moore, after which Mendelssohn's *Wedding March* was efficiently played on the organ, and the bells of the church sent forth a merry peal. The wedding breakfast was given in the large dining-room at Gore Court. Among those who took part in the festivities were Mr and Mrs Smeed and the Misses Smeed, Mr and Mrs G. H. Dean and family, Mr and Mrs W. B. Whall, &c. ... In the afternoon, the happy bride and bridegroom took their departure for Hastings.[31]

Sadly, the happiness of the bride and bridegroom ended abruptly just over one year later when, on 2 February 1866, Esther died, shortly after giving birth to her daughter Ada Esther. Benjamin John Whall had previously been widowed when his first wife, Julia Anne, died two years earlier, and he had a six-year-old daughter, Emily Whall, from that marriage. Thus, he was thrust into the position of having to care for two young children. For a time, Benjamin had the support of his large family that was living near him in King's Lynn. However, when he took his third wife, Caroline Dennis, the following year, baby Ada Esther was made a ward in chancery, and she was placed in the care of her maternal grandfather George Smeed. The reasons for this decision are not known, but it is possible that Whall's new wife found the pres-

---

30 See Helen Allinson, *The Story of Gore Court House and Estate, Tunstall* (Sittingbourne Heritage Museum, 2006).

31 'Tunstall', *Maidstone Journal & Kentish Advertiser*, (26 December 1864), 6.

ence of two children from previous marriages to be unacceptable – especially when she became pregnant herself – and she required their removal. Whatever the reasons might have been, at the age of just a few months, Ada Esther Smeed Whall was taken to live at Gore Court to be brought up in the care of her maternal grandparents.

Further tragedy was to strike a year or so after Ada Esther's arrival. In a period of a few weeks, both Smeed's wife Eliza and his eldest daughter Mary Ann died from fever. It seems though that Smeed was not consumed by grief for long, for within a year, he had married Martha Greensted, a local widow with three children from her previous marriage. The 1871 census entry for Gore Court reveals the presence in the house of two governesses, and it may be supposed that the education of the five-year-old Ada Esther, together with that of her fifteen-year-old aunt Emily Ruth, step-brothers Harry and Frank Greensted and step-sister Ann Greensted, was being done privately.[32] In 1877, at the age of eleven, Ada Esther was sent to Vanbrugh Castle Ladies' College at Maze Hill in Greenwich, an exclusive boarding school for the daughters of gentlemen. Although poorly educated himself as a child, it is evident that Smeed provided Ada Esther with the best education that his fortune could buy. Vanbrugh Castle had been acquired in 1846 by Mrs Mary Hart and her four daughters for the establishment of a school for young ladies. The building tenancy record shows that the Hart school was taken over by the Misses Henrietta, Martha and Ellen Nicholson in 1868 and re-named Vanbrugh Castle Ladies' College.

In 1881, there were several governesses teaching alongside the three Misses Nicholson, including a French governess from Bordeaux and a German governess from Minden.[33] While no archives of the college during the time of Ada Esther's residence have been located, anecdotal evidence about school life can be gleaned from items and advertisements in various local and national newspapers and occasional references in contemporary periodicals. This advertisement provides some details of the subjects offered:

> Education – Vanbrugh Castle, Blackheath, London – The Misses Nicholson have a few vacancies in their High-Class School for the Daughters of Gentlemen. A Comfortable Home, with careful Religious Training, combined with all the advantages of an English and Continental Education. Resident English and Foreign Governesses. Professors attend for the Accomplishments. Lectures are given on the Higher Branches of Literature. Terms (to fill vacancies), 50 Guineas per Annum, to include English, French, Italian, German, Music, Drawing, Singing, Dancing, Calisthenics, &c. Term commences January 25th.[34]

The curriculum would probably have followed the general pattern of Victorian schools for young ladies, so it is possible to gain some understanding of what the young Ada Esther would have been taught. In addition to the subjects mentioned in the advertisement would have been mathematics, the sciences, needlework, deportment, manners and all the social skills appropriate for a young lady of the time. An

---

[32] 1871 England Census, Class: RG 10; Piece: 984; Folio: 110; Page: 9; GSU roll: 838720.

[33] 1881 England Census, Class: RG 11; Piece: 726; Folio: 112; Page: 50; GSU roll: 1341169.

[34] 'England', *The Scotsman*, (7 January 1875), 8.

advertisement placed in *The Times* suggests that one of the music teachers was also a composer:

> Music and Singing – A lady (composer), in the neighbourhood of Blackheath, wishing to increase her connexion, will be happy to give Lessons at her own or pupils' residence. Understands harmony. For terms address E. K., Vanbrugh Castle, Blackheath.[35]

While it is not known to what extent Ada Esther's father, Benjamin John Whall, had any part in her upbringing after she was adopted by George Smeed, the facts that Whall attended Smeed's funeral in 1881, was a beneficiary of Smeed's will and attended his daughter's wedding clearly suggest that his connection with the Smeed family remained close.[36] Whall was an amateur musician of exceptional talent, and his musical career as an organist, pianist, conductor and composer from the mid-1850s to 1885 can be followed in some detail through dozens of reports of musical events in local newspapers and numerous items in the pages of *The Musical Times*. He was associated with the Lynn Musical Union for many years. In 1853 he was appointed librarian, and by 1856 he was the regular organist:

> Lynn Musical Union. The first *soirée* for the season was given by this society, at the Music Hall of the Athenaeum, on the 31st October. The music comprised various pieces from the oratorio of *St Paul*, and a selection of songs and glees; all of which were very creditably performed. The band and chorus consisted of 70 performers, under the direction of Mr J Thomson, R.A.M. The leader was Mr J. Bray; and Mr B. J. Whall presided at the organ.[37]

Whall was not only an organist, as this item from the Lynn News section of the *Norfolk Chronicle and Norwich Gazette* dated Saturday, 13 December 1856 suggests:

> *Conversazione Society* – On Friday evening last, Mr B. J. Whall read before this society a highly interesting paper, entitled 'Music in England', with vocal illustrations by members of the Musical Union. The historical and critical statements of the lecturer were well received and deservedly applauded.[38]

This was the first of many such reports that recorded Whall's close involvement with the King's Lynn Conversazione Society during the next thirty years. His organ and keyboard playing continued to be highly commended, and he assisted choral societies in neighbouring towns:

> Wells Choral Society – The second Concert of the season given by this Society took place on Friday at the British School-room ... Mr Bray, of Lynn, most ably

---

[35] 'Classified Advertising', *The Times*, issue 28984, (3 July 1877), 3. The identity of E.K. is not known.

[36] See 'Death of George Smeed, Esq. – The Funeral', *East Kent Gazette*, (7 May 1881), 5 and 'The Will of the Late Mr. Smeed', *East Kent Gazette*, (23 July 1881), 5.

[37] 'Brief Chronicle of the last Month', *The Musical Times and Singing Class Circular*, Vol. 7, No. 166 (1 December 1856), 355.

[38] 'Lynn', *The Norfolk Chronicle and Norwich Gazette*, Vol. 8, No. 170 (1 April 1857), 24.

officiated as leader of the band, and Mr B. J. Whall, organist, of the Lynn Musical Union, presided at the harmonium and pianoforte.[39]

By 1860, Whall had taken over as conductor of the Lynn Musical Union choir, and in August that year, he was recorded as having conducted a choral concert in the Lynn Music Hall.[40] The local press contains regular reports of the Lynn Musical Union and the Lynn Philharmonic Society concerts over the next decade. Particularly interesting is the report of the 43rd Philharmonic Society concert, which took place in Mr Noverre's Concert Room on Monday 3 March 1862.[41] The programme of songs, chamber and light orchestral music included a song *Love's Remembrance* composed by Benjamin John Whall. Further evidence of Whall's composing talent is provided by other local newspaper reports, including the mention of a part-song performed at a Philharmonic Society concert in April 1865, an overture for organ performed by the composer at a Lynn Choral Union concert in October 1865 and the performance of a setting of Dr Reed's *Sleep, Queen of my Bosom* in 1867.[42] Moreover, Whall's talents were not confined to music. The report of a meeting of the Young Men's Christian Association in March 1866 recounted that 'Mr B. J. Whall delivered an amusing and instructive lecture on Electricity, illustrated by experiments and diagrams'.

Whall spent more than thirty years in King's Lynn carrying out his duties during the day as a clerk at Gurney's Bank and pursuing his extensive amateur musical activities in the evenings and at weekends. However, in October 1885, at the age of forty-nine, Whall appears to have taken the decision to leave King's Lynn and to move himself and his family to Renfrewshire in Scotland. While a move so far from his family, including his daughter Ada Esther, might suggest that a rift had occurred, Whall may simply have decided to retire from his job at the bank, possibly having come into an inheritance. Alternatively, he may have been transferred to Scotland to work in another branch. Whall's departure was mentioned in the issue of the *Norfolk News*, dated 17 October 1885:

> Presentation – Mr B. J. Whall, who for many years has been the organist at the Union Chapel and an otherwise active member of the congregation, being about to leave Lynn, the members of the congregation have made him a handsome presentation of plate. Mr Whall has been for about 35 years in the bank of Messrs Gurney & Co. and has now left Lynn to reside in Glasgow.[43]

Aspects of Whall's subsequent life in the Glasgow area may be gleaned from occasional newspaper reports, and he and his wife seem to have integrated themselves

---

39 'District Intelligence', *Norfolk News*, (21 March 1857), 2.

40 'Lynn', *Norwich Mercury*, (15 August 1860), 3.

41 'The Philharmonic Society', *Norfolk Chronicle & Norwich Gazette*, (8 March 1862), 5.

42 See 'Lynn Philharmonic Society', *Norfolk Chronicle & Norwich Gazette*, (2 December 1865), 7, and 'Lynn – Concert', *Norfolk Chronicle & Norwich Gazette*, (23 February 1867), 7. A further choral work by Benjamin John Whall featured as an example in a lecture given in November 1900 concerning the 'musical doings and musical people who have been connected with Lynn from the earliest times down to the present.': 'King's Lynn – A Record of Music in Lynn', *Norfolk News*, (1 December 1900), 8.

43 'Presentation', *Norfolk News*, (17 October 1885), 8.

into local society soon after arriving. He was elected organist of the Kelburne Masonic Lodge in December 1900, and in the Scottish census entry of 1901, he is described as a Professor of Music.[44] Benjamin also married twice more during his thirty-five years in Scotland, his fifth wife Bethia (*née* Hardie) surviving him to sign his death certificate in 1921. Benjamin John Whall was clearly a musician of exceptional ability – as performer, conductor and composer – and he lived long enough to see the beginning of his grandson Ernest John Moeran's career. He would have been interested in the boy's developing musical talent and, as a composer himself, may well have encouraged the young Moeran's juvenile musical invention. Indeed, it is possible that Moeran's later habit of referring to himself as 'E. J. Moeran' was inspired by and in tribute to his grandfather: always known as 'B. J. Whall'.

The parallels between the lives and musical careers of Benjamin John Whall (Moeran's maternal grandfather) and Edward Moeran (Moeran's paternal great-grandfather) are quite extraordinary. Although the two men could not have known of each other's existence, and there was a separation of more than fifty years in their ages, the individual musical talents that they added to the family that eventually combined to produce composer Ernest John Moeran had a remarkable similarity. Both were able organists and conductors, both were passionate about the educational benefits of music, they were members of convivial societies dedicated to the celebration and performance of music, and each was a long-standing member of the Masonic order. Regardless of whether traits such as musical ability can be inherited, the biographer of a musical personality is always interested to discover that music features in the ancestry of his or her subject. Such connections reinforce the inheritance conjecture, and they are frequently proposed as part of the reason that the biographical subject became a musician. In the case of Moeran, it is evident that he had an exceptional musical ancestry; indeed, it is no exaggeration to assert that music was a fundamental part of the heritage of both his parents' families.

Moeran had other maternal relatives whose musical achievements and talents were noteworthy. Amongst these, B. J. Whall's great-uncle, also Benjamin Whall (1781–1855), was active for many years as a lay clerk at Lincoln Cathedral and was master of the choirboys and organist both at the cathedral and of St Martin's Church, Lincoln. The *Norfolk Chronicle & Norwich Gazette* noted, in an appreciation of his life:

> The late Mr Benjamin Whall – This talented gentleman, whose death appears in our obituary, was a native of this city and was, at the early age of 7 years, distinguished for his splendid voice, in which he was only excelled by his contemporary, Vaughan, another chorister, under Dr Beckwith. At the age of 19, he was appointed master of the choristers, at the Lincoln Cathedral, and subsequently organist. The above situations he held for 56 years, and was respected and beloved by all the dignitaries, and all the members of the cathedral, especially by the choristers, four of whom resided in his house, in accordance with the statutes of this

---

[44] It is probable that, as was the case with Moeran's great-grandfather Edward Moeran in Cork, the title 'Professor' was a euphemism for private teacher.

body. Mr Whall was distinguished as a cathedral organist and was celebrated for the pure style of playing the old Ecclesiastical compositions.[45]

Benjamin Whall's son William, after marrying Mary Boultbee in 1845, fathered eight children, many of whom became noteworthy or achieved eminence in the creative arts. These included William Boultbee Whall (1847–1917), Christopher Whitworth Whall (1849–1924) and Roughton Henry Whall (1862–1937). William Boultbee was a polymath who studied music under Stainer at Oxford. Under the pen name 'Alan Oscar', he wrote *Captain Kid's Millions*, supposedly the true story of the pirate known popularly as Captain Kidd. William Boultbee eventually became a ship's captain and was later elected a Fellow of the Royal Astronomical Society. Roughton Henry Whall took a Mus. Bac. degree at Durham University and was also a Fellow of the Royal College of Organists. Like Benjamin John Whall, he featured frequently in the pages of the *Musical Times* and musical reports in local newspapers. During the early 1900s, William Boultbee and Roughton Henry collaborated on a musical collection called *Ships, Sea-Songs and Shanties*.[46] William Boultbee collected the songs and wrote the text, while Roughton Henry provided harmonisations of some of the songs. Their brother, Christopher Whitworth Whall, is now renowned as having been an important founding member of the Arts and Crafts movement and was a leading artist in stained glass.[47] Christopher's daughter Veronica Whall (1887–1967) was also eminent as a stained-glass artist, creating windows for many cathedrals and churches throughout Great Britain. She also designed and illustrated the sea-songs collection for her uncles.

George Smeed died suddenly in April 1881, and Gore Court was sold. Under the ward in chancery arrangements, a substitute guardian and home had to be found for the orphaned Ada Esther. Two more of Smeed's daughters had also died by this time: Eliza Amelia in 1877 and Ellen Maria in 1878, and so it was decided that supervision of Ada Esther would be taken over by her aunt Sarah Ann, who, with her husband the Reverend William Henry Graham, lived at the vicarage of the south London parish of St Paul's, Upper Norwood. Sarah Ann was the only surviving relative who could realistically have undertaken responsibility for her niece, since Smeed's youngest daughter Emily Ruth had a family of four young children, and fourth daughter Georgiana Silvester was unmarried. It is unknown why Ada Esther's father did not resume parental responsibilities for his daughter on the death of his father-in-law. Generally, a ward in chancery order was put in place to cover the period until the ward came of age, usually on their twenty-first birthday. At the time of Smeed's death, Benjamin John Whall was still living in King's Lynn with his third wife and new family, and it may have been that their needs were sufficient pressure on him to leave the ward in chancery arrangement in place.

[45] 'The late Mr Benjamin Whall', *Norfolk Chronicle & Norwich Gazette*, (10 February 1855), 2.

[46] William Boultbee Whall, Roughton Henry Whall, Veronica Whall (illus.), *Ships, Sea Songs and Shanties*, (James Brown & Son, Glasgow, 1910).

[47] Christopher Whall glass may be found in the Lady Chapel of Gloucester Cathedral and in the south transept of Canterbury Cathedral. Other works are exhibited at the William Morris Gallery in Walthamstow.

Smeed left a total estate worth some £160,000.[48] The terms of his will and its several codicils were many and varied, but the bulk of the fortune was settled upon his surviving daughters and granddaughter in the form of a trust fund paying annuities for twenty-one years. At the end of this period, the fund was to be wound up and the residue distributed amongst the surviving beneficiaries and their named dependents. After going to live in the Upper Norwood vicarage, Ada Esther received an annuity of £150 for her education and maintenance, which would have been paid to her uncle and aunt to disburse at their discretion.[49] Ada Esther would have continued attending Vanbrugh Castle School, and it may be supposed that she remained there as a scholar until the age of about eighteen. It is probable that she took on some teaching and pastoral responsibilities towards the younger girls, as was then usual.

Upper Norwood was a magnet for artists and intellectuals during the 1870s and 1880s; the impressionist painters Camille Pissarro and Claude Monet spent time there. As a wealthy and eligible young lady in Victorian society at a time when women were beginning to assert their independence and individuality, it is probable that Ada Esther met and became acquainted with much of Norwood society, particularly after she left Vanbrugh Castle School. On returning to live permanently at the Upper Norwood vicarage, she probably adopted the role of assistant to her aunt, who would have had many duties to perform as a vicar's wife amongst the women, children and elderly of the parish. Ada Esther's annuity – the equivalent of about £15,000 in present day terms – was not immense, but it would certainly have enabled her aunt and uncle to provide comfortably for the modest needs of a young woman of the 1880s. Most significantly for Ada Esther and for the story of Moeran the composer, shortly after she went to live in the vicarage, her uncle William Graham appointed a new curate, the twenty-six-year-old Joseph William Wright Moeran, whom Ada Esther married in 1888. Joseph and Ada's first son, William Graham, was born in 1889, and their second, Ernest John, followed five years later.

---

[48] 'George Smeed of Sittingbourne ... farmer and brickmaker ... bequeathed personal estate stated to be of the value of £160,000 and devised real estate stated to produce £4,000 or £5,000 per annum to his trustees and executors ...' 'High Court of Justice', *The Times*, issue 31275, (27 October 1884), 9. A comparative purchasing power calculation suggests that £160,000 would have an equivalent value of at least £15 million in 2020.

[49] Smeed's will also directed that an annuity of £200 be paid to Ada Esther's father, Benjamin John Whall. This annuity was to persist until his death, upon which event, it would be paid to Ada Esther, in addition to her own provisions.

2

Childhood and Early Education
(1894–1908)

The extended families of each of his parents provided a financial, intellectual and cultural framework that established an unusually privileged and creatively fertile environment into which Ernest John Smeed Moeran was born on 31 December 1894 and within which he was brought up. Intellectual stimulus was provided both by the Trinity College and Cambridge educated relatives on his father's side and by the artistic members of his mother's family. Moreover, the musicians in both ancestries would suggest that music was an important aspect of Moeran home life. Together, these factors show that Moeran grew up surrounded by a very advantaged and influencing family. However, his father seems to have been unsettled professionally, transferring every few years from one living to another throughout the south of England. After his marriage, the Reverend Joseph William Wright Moeran remained as senior curate at St Paul's, Upper Norwood for seven years until 1893, when he was appointed vicar of St Mary's, Spring Grove in Middlesex. In 1898, he was appointed vicar of St Mary Magdalene, Peckham, and the family moved to nearby Camberwell. Joseph William remained there until 1901, when he became vicar of St Simon's Southsea, near Portsmouth. This incumbency lasted until 1905, when he was installed as vicar of the joint parishes of Salhouse with Wroxham in the county of Norfolk. This was some twenty miles from Bacton, on the Norfolk coast, where Joseph William's father, the Reverend Thomas Warner Moeran, had been vicar since 1873. Joseph William had spent his late childhood years living in Bacton, so it was a part of the country that he knew well. The changeable domestic life that would surely have been the consequence of regular relocations would later find reflection in Moeran's adult life as an inability to settle anywhere for an extended time.

While the Elementary Education Acts of 1870 and 1880 had provided for universal schooling for all children in England between the ages of five and twelve, including compulsory attendance at a suitable school if one was available, exceptions to actual attendance were allowed in cases where the child could be shown to be receiving an equivalent education elsewhere. The 1901 census return for 22 St Mary's Road, Camberwell includes one Kate Hyom, described as a governess, indicating that the six-year-old Moeran was being educated privately at home.[1] At that time, Moeran's

---

[1] 1901 England Census, Class: RG 13; Piece: 506; Folio: 57; Page: 49 (name transcribed as Kate Wyom). This census return also records that the Moeran household included a cook

eleven-year-old brother William Graham was resident at 42 & 44 Alleyn Park (a dormitory house for Dulwich College Preparatory School).[2] Ada Esther's own level of education would have been adequate in the nineteenth century to qualify her as a teacher or governess, so it is reasonable to suppose that she would have also participated in her children's primary schooling. The memory of her grandfather's passion for education, together with the income from his legacy, one of the provisions of which was to cover the education of her children, would have motivated Ada Esther's own devotion to the task.

Although it is not known how daily life in the vicarage was conducted during Moeran's childhood, a plausible scenario can be constructed from a general knowledge of late Victorian households, such as may be garnered from literature and reference works. The employment of a governess by middle and upper-class households was partly a display of wealth and status and partly filled a utilitarian function. The sons of the family were often sent away to preparatory school from the age of about eight, public school from twelve to eighteen and subsequently Oxford or Cambridge. Daughters were usually educated at home, in preparation for their own eventual roles as middle and upper-class wives and mothers. Thus, the duties of the governess encompassed the nursery stage for the boys and often the entire curriculum for the girls. In Moeran's case, it seems likely that he was home-educated until the family arrived in Salhouse in 1905. The subjects expected to be provided by a well-educated governess included reading, writing, arithmetic, history, geography and foreign languages (usually German and French, but Italian, Russian and other more exotic languages could be offered). While little information about the Moeran's governess Kate Hyom can be found, other than her birth in Watford in 1857, her employment as a 'lady's companion' at the age of twenty-four and her death in 1933 at the age of seventy-five, it may be reasonably supposed that she instructed Moeran over a period of several years in many of these subjects. In common with other large Victorian houses, the St Mary Magdalene and St Simon's vicarages would most probably each have had a schoolroom, and the young Moeran may be pictured with his mother or his governess, learning his lessons, which would have become gradually more formal as he grew older. The vicarage would also have had a drawing room, in which it may be presumed that Moeran's mother would have entertained herself and her children by playing the piano and singing. Moeran's testimony, which will be presented later, about playing 'great chords' on the piano strongly suggests that Moeran himself sat for extended periods of time at the piano, possibly from an early age.

Despite the lack of primary evidence, a picture of the young Moeran is beginning to emerge. Since the experiences of childhood establish so fundamentally the framework within which the adult develops, an understanding of Moeran's early years is crucial to an informed appreciation of his musical creation, and it is music that provides the first of several conundrums, the resolutions of which underpin the narrative of this biography. While evidence has been presented here that demonstrates

---

and a housemaid as the other domestic servants.

2   1901 England Census, Class: RG 13; Piece: 492; Folio: 42; Page: 14 (name transcribed as William G Mocran).

unequivocally that music was an ever-present aspect of the young Moeran's upbringing, the composer himself in adult life seems to have gone to some lengths to obscure the reality of his childhood, especially the part that music may have played. He apparently endeavoured to present the impression that he was nurtured in a household almost devoid of musical influences. Since there is an absence of diaries, letters and any other form of primary evidence relating to his early years, the contents of three essays written about Moeran by Philip Heseltine during the mid-1920s provide the only clues revealed by the composer himself about his childhood. In the third essay, published in 1926,[3] it is stated that there were no musical activities in the Moeran household, that any interest Moeran had in music was not encouraged by his parents and that he had limited printed music sources available to him:

> Young Moeran was brought up in the secluded atmosphere of an Evangelical household, and at the age of nine he was sent to a boarding school at Cromer, where he had some violin lessons, but heard practically no music except in church. However, his harmonic sense began to assert itself at an early age, and he taught himself to read music at the piano with the aid of the only music books available in his home, namely *Hymns A & M* and *The Cathedral Psalter*.[4]

Later in his life, Moeran contradicted these earlier suggestions, and the conspicuous compositional fluency apparent from the few extant works from Moeran's late teenage years and his early twenties renders it implausible that he did not have years of development and practice in the craft. So why would Moeran have denied that music was present in his home during his childhood? Since the story originated after Heseltine and Moeran had established a close friendship, it is probable that Moeran's claims were influenced by his perception of that friendship. Perhaps he was conforming to what he believed was Heseltine's image of him, or, consciously or unconsciously, was trying to emulate the personality of his somewhat domineering friend. Heseltine had been largely self-taught in music and there was little music at home during his childhood: assertions that, unlike those in Moeran's case, are supported by strong evidence. The narrative of Moeran's life as presented in this book will illustrate how his attempts to establish and preserve friendships evolved as a result of the difficulties he encountered, and by the mid-1920s, his earlier childhood-influenced personality had undergone increasingly violent adjustment through his experiences at public school and during the First World War. It is possible he felt that claiming a shared experience with Heseltine would resonate better with their relationship as friends.

The implication of musical barrenness in the Moeran household does not stand up to scrutiny. Moeran himself said that his parents arranged for him and his brother to have music lessons: William Graham learnt to play the piano and Ernest John learnt to play the violin. This was recounted during an interview in 1947 for Radio Éireann conducted by Eamonn Andrews. When asked about the practice of musical composition and how it was that he came to be a composer, Moeran said:

[3] Philip Heseltine, *Miniature Essay: E. J. Moeran*, (J. & W. Chester, London, 1926).

[4] Heseltine (1926), 3–4.

When I was a small boy – I was about the age of nine – my parents decided that my brother and myself should learn music. My elder brother was taught the piano, and so it was decided that I should learn the fiddle, the idea being that we two boys should play together.[5]

Although the level of playing ability that Moeran and his brother achieved is not mentioned, this is anecdotal evidence that there must have been a piano in the Moeran home. Additionally, there is the strong probability that Moeran's mother both played and sang. In any case, the affluence of the family would have ensured that a piano, possibly even a quality grand piano, was readily affordable. Moeran continued:

But I found that scales and exercises – only playing one note and not playing chords was rather dull and I used to love to get to the piano and invent, as I thought, great chords with three or four notes in both hands and I used to extemporise these things by the hour.

The anecdote is interesting for several reasons, but when considering its importance, it must be borne in mind that Moeran was recalling events from more than forty years earlier and his memory is the only evidence. Most significant is his recollection of 'get[ing] to the piano' to 'invent great chords with three or four notes in both hands'. Although Moeran stated that it was his brother who was taught the piano, it is apparent that Moeran also played the instrument, if only for his own pleasure and gratification. Given the span of years between the events being recalled and the date of the recollection, it may be reasonably supposed that the radio interview is a conflation of several memories, all of which were imperfectly remembered, but each of which had some element of truth. While Moeran suggested that he was about nine years old when the music lessons began, this is unlikely to be correct, since by that time, his brother had been away during term time for several years, initially at Dulwich College Preparatory School and subsequently at Marlborough College public school. Moeran himself went away, first to Suffield Park Preparatory School at the age of ten and then to Uppingham at the age of thirteen. Thus, it is more probable that Moeran's first exposure to music took place when he was no more than about four or five. William Graham would have begun piano lessons at the age of six or seven while he was still living at home and under the tutelage of the governess. Since he apparently never showed any further interest in music during his later life and there is no evidence of his having continued music lessons at school, it may be supposed that the parental ambition for Moeran and his brother to 'play together' was never realised.

It was also absurd for Moeran, through the prism of Heseltine, to suggest that a wealthy late Victorian or Edwardian household possessed a piano, but that there was no music, other than a couple of hymn books, from which to play. If the claim that William Graham was being taught the piano is accepted at face value, then he, at least, must have been provided with instructional music, and the probability that their mother played and sang also suggests that printed music would have been

---

5   A recording of the interview was formerly at http://www.moeran.net/Writing/Radio-Interview.html (accessed 1 January 2013 – website now defunct) and the transcription was made by the author.

present. During the latter part of the nineteenth century, countless collections of songs were published for a ready market. In the pre-electronic era, the piano was the centre of entertainment in many households, and companies around the country existed to build and supply affordable pianos. Indeed, as described in Chapter 1, Moeran's great-grandfather Edward Moeran was proprietor of a piano and music business in Cork during the early years of the nineteenth century, and innumerable music publishers provided the media in the form of songs and piano music. When the facts about the musical ancestors on both sides of the family are also taken into consideration, the notion of the Moeran household being devoid of music becomes even more preposterous. Along with many books and collections of songs and piano music, the Moerans would certainly have owned a copy of the volume *Ships, Sea-Songs and Shanties* that had been compiled by Moeran's mother's cousins William Boultbee Whall and Roughton Henry Whall. Examination of Moeran's own compositions, especially the extant early works, suggests that the young teenage Moeran gained technical and extemporising fluency by playing on the piano the songs from this and similar music books. As he maintained in the 1947 interview, Moeran experimented with harmonies and thus began to develop the characteristic harmonic-based personal idiom that would find expression in his later mature compositions. It is interesting to note that the first melody in *Ships, Sea-Songs and Shanties* is a version of the song 'Shenandoah' (see figure 2).

The ease with which any number of alternative harmonisations of this melody may be devised, reveals one plausible source for Moeran's later harmonic diversity. The 'great chords' can readily be imagined. The octave-rise structure seen here from the first beat of full bar 1 to the final beat of bar 2 is also a distinctive element of Moeran's melodic style, recurring throughout his oeuvre. Since it is also a characteristic feature of English and Irish folksong – both of which were also important influencing factors in Moeran's stylistic development – it is presumptive to suggest that the idea originated from his playing of 'Shenandoah'. However, it is also significant, in the context of Moeran's later compositions, that the 'Shenandoah' melody comprises five two-bar sub-phrases. This ten-bar melodic construct frequently appears in a range of contexts in the music Moeran composed, and it may reasonably be suggested that his acquiring of a natural sympathy for this device has its origins partly in this song.

Given that there were numerous musicians on both sides of his family, it is strange that William Graham Moeran should have written, 'It has always been a puzzle from whom [Moeran] inherited his musical talent – possibly from his maternal grandfather, Mr B. J. Whall.'[6] Clearly, in the case of his great-grandfather Edward Moeran of Cork, who died in 1865, there could have been no direct influence, but some of his other musical and artistic relatives were still alive during Moeran's childhood and youth, most particularly, as suggested by William Graham, his maternal grandfather Benjamin John Whall. It is, therefore, important to understand how well Moeran could have known his relatives and how extensive was their influence on his creative

---

6   Letter from William Graham Moeran to Colin Scott-Sutherland, dated 24 August 1962; quoted in John Talbot, 'Memories of Jack', *British Music* Vol. 31, 2009 (British Music Society, London, 2009), 7.

Figure 2. Ships, Sea-Songs and Shanties, p. 1, 'Shenandoah'

development. While Moeran's early life was spent in a variety of home locations, it was also a time when almost everywhere in mainland Britain was easily accessible by railway. Moeran's exceptional familiarity with the sounds of railway engines and his apparently encyclopaedic knowledge of timetables is a recurring aspect of his life, and this could have been acquired during the numerous journeys that he undertook as a child with his family. It is also reasonable to assume that the Moeran family received regular visits by relatives from both sides of the family at their various vicarages and houses. During an interview conducted towards the end of the composer's life, Moeran mentioned an anecdote from his youth that involved his purloining a set of superfluous false teeth that he found in a spare bedroom at home and selling them in London to raise funds to attend a concert.[7] The anecdote asserts that the teeth had been left behind by a relative. Whether or not this took place as Moeran recounted is less relevant than the fact that the story provides corroborative evidence that family members visited the Moeran home. The notion of the young Ernest John being made to play or recite in front of his uncles and aunts is consistent with usual family practice at the time, and if his talents included the composition of his own music, this is also likely to have been shown off by a proud mother.

Clearly, Moeran grew up in a culturally rich environment, and his family regime encouraged the development and expression of his musical talent and interest. Indeed, the young Moeran may have been playing and inventing music from as early as the age of five. While the lack of any surviving manuscripts dating from before 1912 could be viewed as problematic, it has been shown that Moeran actively suppressed any notion that his interest in music derived from his childhood, and he is known to have disposed of almost all his juvenile work. Stephen Wild wrote: 'Moeran's widow,

7   Evan Senior, 'E.J. Moeran', *Australian Musical News and Digest* (1 May 1950), 30–31.

Peers Coetmore, has stated that he destroyed much of his earlier music.'[8] Moeran's surviving correspondence also contains evidence to indicate that – later in his life – his increasingly severe self-criticism led to occasional orgies of destruction during which manuscripts were burned. Thus, the possible former existence of even large quantities of early compositions cannot be challenged.

When the family moved to Salhouse vicarage in 1905, the governess did not go with them, and Moeran was enrolled at Suffield Park Preparatory School in Cromer, on the north Norfolk coast. The school was situated some twenty-four miles distant from the Salhouse vicarage and, according to an advertisement placed in Ward Lock's *Pictorial and Descriptive Guide to London and its Environs*, was: 'In Sheltered Situation, one mile from Cromer town' with 'Accommodation for 50 Boys in airy Class Rooms and Bedrooms'.[9] It is most likely that Moeran attended as a weekly boarder, travelling there by train from nearby Salhouse railway station on a Monday morning and returning from Cromer the following Friday afternoon. The school has long since closed, and its records have been lost. The only source that provides information about any aspect of Moeran's time there is the Evan Senior article, and this was not an exact transcription of his interview with Moeran; rather it was Senior's interpretation of Moeran's words with a few approximate quotations included to provide verisimilitude. The recollections that may be distilled from the article suggest that Moeran's interest in music was (further) stimulated while he was at Suffield Park by the arrival of a new piano teacher and that his piano and violin lessons continued during his time there:

> 'I think', Moeran told [Senior], 'that my first real interest in music came from this man, an interest that grew when I went to Cromer Pier and heard a band for the first time. Perhaps I was fascinated by the wonderful blue and gold uniforms of that band that played things like *The Merry Widow* and Beethoven's *Coriolan* overture.'[10]

Until he went to preparatory school, Moeran had spent most of his time either on his own or in the company of adults. The combination of the five-year age gap between Moeran and his brother William Graham, and the fact that William spent much of his time away at boarding school, suggests that there would not have been much fraternal engagement. Thus, Moeran spent his earliest formative years with little opportunity to develop the social skills required for interacting with his peer group. Although this was later rectified to some extent by the opportunities presented at his public school and college, the legacy of his insulated upbringing remained part of his character. However, despite preparatory school being a novel environment for the young boy, there is no indication that Moeran was particularly unhappy there. Possibly the relative proximity of his parents mitigated any loneliness or homesickness.

According to the testimony of William Graham Moeran, poor health forced the Reverend Moeran to retire in 1907: 'When Jack was about 12, his father was

8   Stephen Wild, *E. J. Moeran*, (Triad Press, London 1973), 10.

9   *A Pictorial and Descriptive Guide to London and its Environs*, (Ward, Lock & Co, London, 1919), 63.

10 Senior (1950), 30.

forced to retire from the Active Ministry of the Church owing to a breakdown in health from which he never fully recovered, although he lived to the ripe age of 85.'[11] *Crockford's Clerical Directory* shows that the Reverend Moeran and his wife moved to a house in Nutfield near Redhill in Surrey.[12] It is reasonable to assume that Moeran would have remained in attendance at school in Cromer until the end of the school year in July 1908, but, due to the greatly increased distance, he probably became a full boarder for his final year there. On leaving Suffield Park, he was awarded the school music prize – a hard-bound copy of the *Beethoven Piano Sonatas* published by Breitkopf & Härtel, Leipzig – that was inscribed to 'Ernest John Moeran'.[13] Whether or not Moeran chose this prize himself, it indicates the level of playing ability that he had achieved by the age of thirteen. It is not known whether the prize was awarded for a specific musical skill, or that it was a reward for overall achievement. As has been shown, Moeran had been playing the violin since the age of six, and some six or seven years later it would be expected that he had reached an advanced level of competence.

[11]   Talbot, (2009), 8.

[12]   Crockford's (1908), 995.

[13]   This volume is now part of the *Moeran-Coetmore-Knott Collection* (box 1M27) held at the Performing Arts Museum in Melbourne. The author is indebted to Georgina Binns of the University of Melbourne Library for this information.

3
Uppingham School
(1908–1912)

The trust fund established by George Smeed's will that had been providing both Ada Esther's annuity income and the funds for William Graham's and Ernest John's education had been wound up in 1903, and the residual capital and accumulated income was disbursed to the surviving beneficiaries. Although the exact amount received by Ada Esther is not known, the evidence of the remainder of her and her husband's lives shows that they were able to live comfortably with no income beyond that provided by their investments. Thus, they were in a favourable position when it came to the selection of a public school for their sons. Marlborough College in Wiltshire had been founded in 1843 to provide 'a public boarding school education chiefly for the sons of clergymen at a modest cost'.[1] Moeran's father's cousin, Edward Henry Moeran (son of the Reverend Edward Busteed Moeran), had attended the college between 1861 and 1867, and it was probably because of this family connection that the Moerans chose Marlborough as the school for their elder son William Graham, who was admitted in January 1903. Five years later, when it came to school selection for their second son, it is apparent that they had a different intention. Instead of following his brother to Marlborough College, Moeran was sent to Uppingham School in Rutland. William Graham Moeran suggested in 1962 that when his 'parents sent [Moeran] to Uppingham, their plan was that he should become an Engineer',[2] but this claim does not stand up to rigorous scrutiny. There is no reason to believe that the provisions for education in science, mathematics and the other subjects appropriate for a budding engineer were any less adequate at Marlborough or any better at Uppingham during the early 1900s than they were at other schools.

Moeran had left Suffield Park Preparatory School having achieved a competent playing ability on both violin and piano and probably with a portfolio of juvenile compositions. Thus, Uppingham was chosen because Moeran's parents (or at least his mother) had the intention that his obvious musical talent should be encouraged. Although music tuition was possible at other schools – including Marlborough College – none could match Uppingham's pedigree and particularly the excellence of the violin and piano teaching that was available. The music master Paul David, son of violinist Ferdinand David and friend of the world-renowned Joseph Joachim,

---

[1] *Marlborough College Register: from 1843 to 1904 inclusive,* (Oxford, 1905), vii.
[2] William Graham Moeran; quoted in Talbot (2009), 7.

had been at the school since 1864 and over more than forty years had encouraged and inspired sometimes latent musicality which greatly enhanced the education of generations of Uppingham schoolboys. The actor Boris Karloff, who attended Uppingham from 1903 to 1906 under his birth name William Henry Pratt, said in an interview towards the end of his life:

> If only I had decided to work a little harder at music. I missed a great opportunity. The music master was a brilliant man. If any boy had music in his soul, he would have brought it out … I made a great mistake there; although I had no particular aptitude for music, my mistake lay in not taking advantage of that man's great knowledge and patience.[3]

David retired in July 1908 and Robert Sterndale Bennett was appointed in his place. Sterndale Bennett clearly had a very tough act to follow, but the change did not necessarily prompt a major discontinuity. The presence of other staff members involved in the teaching of music who had been at the school for many years under David – such as Walter Greatorex, Samuel Fricker and Oskar Bedall – would have ensured that the transition was smooth. In any case, Sterndale Bennett's family musical credentials were as impressive as had been those of Paul David. Robert was the grandson of composer William Sterndale Bennett and, like David, he had been a friend of Joseph Joachim.

On his arrival at the school in September, Moeran became a member of Lorne House. The school had a system – which is maintained to the present day – of boarding houses for the pastoral care of pupils. Each pupil was assigned to one of these under the supervision of a housemaster and his wife, who took over the duties of parental responsibility. Figure 3 shows Moeran (fourth from left in the back row) and his Lorne House colleagues, probably in the summer of 1911, together with the housemaster, the Reverend F. W. Welldon and his wife, who had lived at Lorne House since 1895. To Moeran's immediate left stands Roland Perceval Garrod, and the possible significance of this will become apparent later in this chapter. The presence of a silver cup on the table in front of the Reverend Welldon and his wife indicates that Lorne House had been successful in one of the annual inter-house sports tournaments that were, and remain, an important feature of Uppingham school life. Moeran was aged sixteen when the photograph was taken, and he was coming to the end of his third year at the school. Despite the slight fadedness of the picture, his mature appearance can be distinguished, and this was a personal characteristic of which Moeran may have taken advantage during the next few years.

Moeran's distinctly wry smile contrasts with the serious expressions on the faces of the other boys, probably the result of having been instructed by the photographer not to smile (as was usual in early photography). Writing in an age when technology has enabled instant recording and broadcast of every imaginable scene and social event, it is difficult to recall the time when such a group photograph was anticipated, planned for and executed with care, taking time to set poses appropriately. That this was done is clear from the symmetrical arrangement of the heights of the boys in

---

3   Peter Underwood, *Horror Man: The Life of Boris Karloff*, (Leslie Frewin, London, 1972), 19–20.

Figure 3. Lorne House, Uppingham School, 1911 (Moeran fourth from left in back row)

the back two rows. A pleasing undulating contour has been achieved, and it may be imagined that prints were proudly sent home to parents as a lasting memento of a fondly remembered occasion. However, this photograph, along with many hundreds of similar photographs taken in public schools across the country around this time, acquired an immensely more powerful and poignant significance just a few years later, as countless boys whose youthful ambition was captured so vividly fell victim to the slaughter of the First World War. Of the thirty boys pictured here, more than a third were killed in various theatres of operation between 1914 and 1918, including several members of the successful house rugby team and at least three of the junior boys sitting cross-legged in the front row.

Biographers whose subjects spent their adolescence in one of the English public schools during the nineteenth or early-twentieth centuries are obliged to confront some now uncomfortable realities. Uppingham was part of a system whose inherent brutality – despite the reforms begun by Dr Arnold during the 1830s – was still tolerated, justified and perhaps even encouraged in the name of character-building and the development of manliness. Some details of life at the school during the late 1800s and early 1900s can be garnered from the memoirs and biographies of later eminent personalities who were there, and few of them paint an attractive picture. In his autobiography, Sir Malcolm Campbell wrote about a fags exam, which entailed brutal punishment by prefects for failure to answer correctly. He wrote: 'These weekly ordeals continued for more than half-way through my first term, by which time the series of vigorous hidings had made me so hardened that I took them as a matter of course.'[4] In an extended piece on her husband Canon Hardwicke Drummond Rawnsley's years at Uppingham, Eleanor Rawnsley chose to focus on his academic achievements, drawing heavily but selectively from Rawnsley's journals and the recollections of some of his contemporaries. Although by the time he left the school in 1870, Rawnsley had become a fine athlete and captain of both football and cricket, his early years were blighted by being: 'extremely little ... and very queer looking.'[5] In a letter to his mother, the young Rawnsley complained, 'Some fellows I think got into my study and broke open both my drawer locks and took all my nice things and jolly books that he [Rawnsley's brother] gave me, and I cannot find out who did it.' The poet and novelist James Elroy Flecker attended Uppingham for five terms from January 1901 to August 1902, and his biographer John Sherwood devoted an entire chapter to his subject's formative experiences there. Although a relatively older boy on arrival, Flecker did not fit easily into the obsession with games that he encountered, although he did his best:

> James Elroy was not a natural athlete, but his early letters reflect a proper team spirit and a dogged eagerness to improve his mediocre performance at Hockey, Cricket and Rugby. Unable to excel, he soon relaxed his efforts. But he raised no standard of revolt against Uppingham's games-worshipping set of values, and persisted with cross-country running, which required doggedness rather than the dexterity he lacked.[6]

Flecker's testimony has been extracted from the numerous letters that he wrote to his parents, some of which mention what was euphemistically referred to as 'immorality'. Sherwood wrote:

> In his letters home he took up a wholly detached attitude to a chronic public school problem, reporting that a meeting of praeposters and house captains had been held under the auspices of Dr Selwyn, the headmaster, at which: 'a resolution was passed to "stop the immorality in the school."'

The 'chronic public school problem' was undoubtedly a euphemism for homosexual relationships amongst the boys, most particularly between older boys and the younger pupils. In contrast, the novelist E. W. Hornung, creator of the character Raffles, had nothing but happy memories of his schooldays. Indeed, the impression gained from reading his Uppingham recollections is that the school in the 1880s was a paradise:

> Perfect bliss ... were those summer Saturday afternoons when school had ended at midday and there were only a few Latin verses to do before going up to the

4   Sir Malcolm Campbell, *My Thirty Years of Speed*, (Hutchinson & Co., London, 1922), 11–12.

5   Eleanor Rawnsley, *Canon Rawnsley: An Account of his Life*, (Maclehose, Jackson & Co., Glasgow, 1923), 11.

6   See John Sherwood, *No Golden Journey: A Biography of James Elroy Flecker*, (Heinemann, London, 1973), 15–26.

dormitory that night. 'A match on the Upper, where you could lie on your rug and watch the game you couldn't play; call-over at the match; ices and lemon-drinks in a tent on the field; and for Saturday supper anything you liked to buy, cooked for you in the kitchen and put piping hot at your place in the hall, not even for the asking, but merely by writing your name plainly on the eggs and leaving them on the slab outside!'[7]

The artist Christopher Richard Wynne Nevinson, whose autobiography *Paint and Prejudice* included a memoir of his time at Uppingham, recalled that the school in the 1900s was a place of '[bad] feeding ... and ... brutality and bestiality in the dormitories'.[8] He wrote that he was 'kicked, hounded, caned, flogged, hair-brushed, morning, noon and night', and while his references to sexual matters were oblique, there is no doubt as to what was implied. Novelist Ronald Firbank attended Uppingham for just a few months in 1900. His biographer Ivan Lyrle Fletcher wrote that he was a 'tall weed of a youth, entirely incapable of holding his own in the rough-and-tumble of school life'.[9] The distinguished soldier Sir Brian Horrocks arrived at Uppingham in September 1909 and looked 'back on his days [there] as being thoroughly enjoyable'.[10] Theologian Charles E. Raven won a scholarship to Uppingham in 1898 and, as his biographer F. W. Dillistone observed, 'two years at Uppingham went by without undue strain or unhappiness. Then the coming of adolescence seemed to change the whole situation.'[11] Raven wrote about these experiences in his autobiography *A Wanderer's Way*:

> Of those later years it is less pleasant to write ... on the whole I hated it; and as I grew the hatred settled into a steady ache of loneliness and fear ... the wounds are old scars now: but the marks are still too sensitive for me to touch.[12]

The writer Norman Douglas was a schoolboy at Uppingham during the 1880s and seems to have found the place tolerable only in the fact that he had a close friend in one of the older boys. The friend was called Harry Samuel Collier and was known as 'The Bug'. According to Douglas's biographer Mark Holloway, 'The company of the Bug made [Douglas's] life endurable.'[13] While the exact nature of Douglas's relationship with Collier was not explored by Holloway, there can be little doubt that their friendship was more than just companionable.

Each of these accounts has been filtered through the prism of their author's affection, or otherwise, for the school – or, at least, for the selective memories of it they

[7] Peter Rowland, *Raffles and his Creator: The Life and Works of E. W. Hornung*, (Nekta Publications, London, 1999), 17.

[8] Christopher Richard Wynne Nevinson, *Paint and Prejudice*, (Methuen, London, 1937), 11.

[9] Ivan Lyrle Fletcher, *Ronald Firbank: A Memoir*, (Duckworth, London, 1930), 20.

[10] Philip Warner, *Horrocks: The General Who Led from the Front*, (Hamish Hamilton, London, 1984), 5.

[11] F. W. Dillistone, *Charles Raven: Naturalist, Historian, Theologian*, (Hodder & Stoughton, London, 1975), 34.

[12] Charles E. Raven, *A Wanderer's Way*, (Martin Hopkinson & Co. Ltd, London, 1928), 11.

[13] Mark Holloway, *Norman Douglas: A Biography*, (Secker & Warburg, London, 1976), 40.

retained – and, thus, can only be regarded as anecdotal. The recollections considered together provide a general impression of the school during the thirty-year period from 1880 to 1910, and it is evident that life was tough, unpleasant even, for many of the boys, except for those who were particularly athletic or of a robust disposition. The public-school experience was believed to be character-building, with the weak and incapable being weeded out through a form of natural selection, producing the next generation of builders and maintainers of the British Empire, and this seems to have been successful. Most of those that were unable to be moulded or to mould themselves into what was expected in the community of the school did not remain there for long. Those that hated it but did stay developed a resilience that became part of their adult character.

It is not known how Moeran fitted into the complex life of the school, or how he conducted himself *vis-à-vis* the other boys, whether as a junior or as he became more senior. The sparse evidence suggests that he built close friendships with several of his contemporaries, but given the testimony from Flecker, Raven and Douglas presented above, the obvious question is whether any of these friendships included a homoerotic element. Hitherto in writings about the composer, no consideration has been given to the possibility that Moeran was gay or bisexual. While anecdotes relating to his residence in the Eynsford cottage during the 1920s might suggest an apparently heterosexual identity, some aspects of his character in later life could be regarded as being consistent with a latent or repressed homosexuality. The nature of his relationships during the Eynsford period and the failure of his marriage both argue for a homosexual identity, and his self-identification with an alternative culture (Celtic/Irish) and the creation of a parallel personal narrative also provide a persuasive case. Moreover, the knowledge that many of his friendships or acquaintanceships were with musicians and composers that are now either known or believed to have been gay or bisexual, such as John Ireland, Philip Heseltine, Benjamin Britten and Francis Poulenc, warrants consideration that Moeran's identity may have been homosexual. If that were the case, then that aspect of his personality would surely have manifested itself during his schooldays and would have strongly informed the relationships that he created at Uppingham and which probably persisted after he left. This subject will be revisited later in this and other chapters.

In his obituary for Moeran, published in the March 1951 issue of the Uppingham School Magazine, Robert Sterndale Bennett wrote, 'I doubt if any boy has grasped with more discernment and avidity or made better use of the opportunity which school music has to offer,'[14] and this one sentence succinctly summarises Moeran's four years at Uppingham. While his career at the school is slightly better documented than is his time at Suffield Park, it still relies heavily on anecdotal evidence, much of which derives ultimately from Moeran's own selective and unreliable recollections. No letters or diaries or other primary autobiographical material relating to the period 1908 to 1912 have been found, and there is no mention of his time at school in any of his surviving letters and articles. Any ideas about his daily life can therefore only be speculative. Apart from music, there is no evidence that Moeran participated

---

[14] Robert Sterndale Bennett, 'Obituary: Ernest John Moeran O.U. 1894–1950', *Uppingham School Magazine*, Vol. 89, No. 631, (March 1951), 36.

enthusiastically in any non-academic pursuits, the principal of which were – as in all public schools at the time – sport (or games) and the Officers' Training Corps. While there is evidence that Moeran was a keen swimmer in later life, at school he apparently had neither time for nor aptitude in any sports, although he did have some minor involvement in house cricket and rugby matches, and this is chronicled in several issues of the school magazine. He also seems to have taken little interest in the Officers' Training Corps. Although enrolling in the Corps was voluntary, it was strongly encouraged, and membership gradually increased during the immediate pre-war period, reaching its peak of nearly 100 per cent during the First World War. Although no membership records survive for the period while Moeran was at Uppingham, it may be safely assumed that he was not a member of the Corps, since, on his application form to join the Territorial Force in September 1914, he left the section about previous military experience blank, and he did not immediately apply for a commission, as did many ex-OTC former schoolboys. Headmaster Dr Edward Selwyn had instituted a rule at the beginning of 1900 that every boy in the school would be obliged to pass a shooting test, regardless of whether they were members of the Officers' Training Corps (known as the Cadet Corps until 1907) and that until they had successfully done so, they could not be awarded a school prize or take part in any inter-house competitions. Since Moeran was awarded several prizes during his school career – including the Violin and Piano Prize in 1909 and the Piano Prize in 1911 – and he was a member of his house cricket team, it may be presumed that he passed the required test.

The only primary documentary records of Moeran's schooldays are the Uppingham School magazine, of which some thirty-two issues cover the period of his time at the school, and the archived programmes of more than a dozen school concerts between March 1909 and July 1912 in which Moeran participated.[15] The principal concern of the magazine was sporting activities and achievements, and while Moeran was rarely mentioned in any connection, the pages contain sufficient anecdotal and circumstantial evidence to enable the construction of a quite detailed impression of daily school life. Alongside the concert programmes, evidence pertaining to music at Uppingham was also provided by Philip Heseltine in essays he wrote about Moeran during the 1920s, the source of which must have been Moeran himself. These reminiscences form the basis both for an article written for *The Music Bulletin* in 1924 and for a miniature essay written in 1926. In the 1924 article, Heseltine wrote that '[Moeran] learned also how to listen intelligently, how to read and absorb music'.[16] It is reasonable to assume that Moeran would have attended or participated in each concert, and an idea of the repertoire with which he became familiar with may be gathered from reports in the school magazine. During his first term at the school, monthly chamber music recitals provided him with the opportunity to hear performances of the Partita in D minor for Violin and Pianoforte by Parry, the

---

[15] Details of school activities and concerts that are mentioned in this chapter have been extracted from various issues of the Uppingham School Magazine and the archived school concert programmes, access to which was kindly provided by school archivist Jerry Rudman to whom the author expresses his grateful thanks.

[16] Philip Heseltine, 'E. J. Moeran', *The Music Bulletin*, Vol.6, No.6, (June 1924), 171.

Pianoforte Trio in C minor op. 66 by Mendelssohn, Haydn's String Quartet in G op. 64, No. 4, Beethoven's Pianoforte Trio in B flat op. 11, Mozart's Quartet in B flat, No. 3, a Sonata for Flute, Violin and Piano in G by Bach, Mendelssohn's Pianoforte Quartet in B minor op. 3 and piano music by Chopin and Handel. Except for the Parry Partita, each of the works performed comes from what Heseltine referred to as 'the classics', and Moeran's remarkable memory for music would have ensured that the sounds of these composers became intimately familiar to him. Robert Sterndale Bennett staged an end of term orchestral and choral concert on 15 December, and Moeran would have returned home for the Christmas vacation with the sounds of Cherubini's overture *The Water Carrier*, extracts from Gluck's *Orpheus*, Beethoven's First Symphony, Grieg's choral song *Recognition of Land* and violoncello solos by Simon and Popper fresh in his mind.

The schedule of monthly chamber music recitals continued during Moeran's second term, and he would have heard music by Corelli, Brahms, Beethoven, Bach, Mozart, Becher, Boccherini, Mendelssohn and the Piano Quintet in E flat op. 44 by Robert Schumann. The centenary of Mendelssohn's birth was celebrated on 31 March 1909 with a concert featuring the *Hebrides* overture, the Violin Concerto in E minor in an arrangement for violin and piano and the *Hymn of Praise*, performed by the school choir and orchestra. Moeran had joined the second violin section of the orchestra, and – apart from rehearsals – this concert would have been his first experience as an orchestral player. The 1909 annual Speech Day concert took place on Saturday 3 July, and Moeran again played in the ranks of the second violins alongside Uppingham Lower School pupil Edward Brittain. The programme was an assortment of solo and ensemble pieces, including a selection of movements from Handel's *The Water Music*, Samuel Coleridge Taylor's *Valse Rustique* and the Serenade for String Orchestra by Edward Elgar, performed by the orchestra and songs and piano solos performed by various pupils. The school choir also contributed part-songs by Charles Wood and Henry Smart and settings by George Rathbone of the traditional song 'Will ye no come back again' and of Robert Herrick's poem 'Gather Ye Rosebuds'.[17] Three weeks later, the summer term ended with the annual school concert at which Haydn's *London* symphony was performed, together with items repeated from the Speech Day concert. The participant lists for the 1910 April and Speech Day concerts include names that would be important for Moeran during the remainder of his time at the school. Alongside Edward Brittain – who had moved up from the lower school in September 1909 – were treble Victor Richardson, treble and cellist Roland Perceval Garrod and violinist Christopher Whitehead.

In addition to broadening his musical knowledge by taking part in concerts and recitals, it is also likely that Moeran would have spent time listening to recorded music on the school gramophone. By 1908, a huge repertoire of classical music recordings was available, initially on cylinders but increasingly on discs.[18] This would have been an exciting and quite extraordinary time for music

[17] 'Gather Ye Rosebuds' may have made a lasting impression on Moeran, as he composed his own setting of these words in 1924.

[18] Gramophones were in general use at the school as early as 1900, as shown by this note in the school magazine: 'On Saturday, Oct. 6th, an entertainment was held in the

enthusiasts. Ever since music performance for an audience had become commonplace during the seventeenth and eighteenth centuries, the only way to hear works more than once, had been to attend multiple concerts. Now a listener could hear the same performance repeatedly, simply by replaying the record. The gramophone would have been instrumental in expanding Moeran's musical horizons, and it is reasonable to suppose that he and his musical colleagues spent countless hours with the machine.

According to the concert programmes, during his four years at the school, Moeran participated in performances of symphonies by Mendelssohn, Schubert, Beethoven, Mozart and Haydn, played or listened to chamber music by various composers, including Weber, Beethoven, Mozart, Schubert, Schumann, Mendelssohn and Haydn, and experienced other music ranging from Bach, Gluck and Handel to contemporary composers such as Sullivan, Elgar, Charles Wood and John Ireland. He held his place in the second violin section throughout his time at Uppingham, taking over the principal position at the beginning of 1911. He also assiduously continued his piano studies, and by the time he left Uppingham, he was by some margin the finest pupil pianist in the school, and his talent was exhibited at the annual Speech Day concert on 6 July 1912, at which he performed the *Allegro* from Schumann's *Faschingsschwank aus Wien*, Op. 26. He also accompanied the school choir in John Ireland's unison choral song *In Praise of Neptune* and with Christopher Whitehead and Roland Perceval Garrod played the Schumann piano trio *Humoresque in F*, Op. 88, No.2. However, playing was not Moeran's only musical activity at Uppingham. In his 1926 miniature essay, Heseltine mentioned Moeran's composing:

> During his last year at Uppingham, Moeran formed a school string quartet, and he and his three associates thus made themselves acquainted with a great deal of classical chamber music; and it was in this year that he first attempted composition, the work in question being a sonata for piano and violoncello in four movements, which took nearly an hour to perform.[19]

It was shown in Chapter 2 that there is strong evidence to suggest that Moeran had begun his composing activities at a much earlier age and that this is supported by his own testimony. He would have composed more extensively while he was at the school. Alongside the hour-long violoncello sonata in four movements – which would undoubtedly have been for Moeran's Lorne House cellist friend Roland Perceval Garrod – Heseltine also mentioned in other writings the composition of several string quartets and at least one violin sonata. His report that Moeran formed a string quartet during his final year at the school is supported by Bryan Matthews in his 1984 history of Uppingham, although Matthews' sources must have included Heseltine's essay. In an item about Robert Sterndale Bennett, Matthews wrote:

Schoolroom, which was well attended. West Bank kindly lent their house gramophone': 'Postscript', *Uppingham School Magazine*, Vol. 39, No. 302, (October 1900), 310.

[19] Heseltine (1926), 4.

Among his earliest pupils at Uppingham Bennett found one of the greatest musicians the School has produced; this was E.J. Moeran, already at 13 a fine pianist, and an all-round performer and embryo composer from early days. Some of his first serious compositions were written at Uppingham, and he was the lynchpin of a string quartet which played in his time, another member of which was Edward Brittain, Vera's ill-fated brother.[20]

Of interest is the assertion that one of Moeran's fellow quartet-players was Edward Brittain. An examination of the school magazines, in combination with information provided by the writings of Vera Brittain, provides sufficient evidence of Moeran's close relationship with the circle of Uppingham friends immortalised in the first volume of Brittain's memoirs *Testament of Youth*.[21] Brittain's brother Edward Harold, along with Roland Aubrey Leighton and Victor Richardson – these three being collectively known as 'the Three Musketeers' – and Roland Perceval Garrod had entered the school either in April or September 1909 and had become friends, drawn together both by interests in music and poetry and through their membership of the Officers' Training Corps. Garrod was a cellist and, as a member of Lorne House, was pictured alongside Moeran in the house photograph presented in figure 3. Brittain played in the second violin section with Moeran in 1909 and 1910, moving into the first violins for the years 1911–1914. In the 1910 Speech Day concert, Brittain was treble soloist, singing one of the Uppingham school songs. Brittain and Richardson were also treble soloists in the performance of the Borth song 'The Colony' by Paul David, which was included in the annual July concert three weeks later. While the performance of the Borth song is the only mention of a musical performance by Richardson, Brittain's musical career at Uppingham is documented similarly to that of Moeran in the issues of the school magazines and the concert programmes, and his ambition to become a composer is mentioned in the writings of Vera Brittain.[22]

Heseltine's assertion that 'Moeran formed a school string quartet' implies that Moeran was the leader, playing first violin. Although Moeran played second violin in the orchestra, he was also a competent viola player: the record of the 1912 Speech Day concert mentions him as playing in both the second violin and viola sections of the school orchestra. Moreover, Moeran later selected the viola as a secondary study at the Royal College of Music, and he claimed it as a performance skill on his application form to join the Oxford & Cambridge Musical Club. It is probable, therefore, that Moeran was the viola player with Brittain as one of the violinists and Garrod as cellist. The other violinist was probably the above-mentioned Christopher Whitehead who played regularly in the second violin section with Moeran. It is reasonable to assert that this ensemble spent many hours playing music composed by both Moeran and Brittain, together with works from the

[20] Bryan Matthews, *By God's Grace: A History of Uppingham School*, (Whitehall Press, London, 1984), 221.

[21] Vera Brittain, *Testament of Youth*, (Victor Gollancz, London, 1933).

[22] The Vera Brittain Archive, which is held at McMaster University in Canada (Fonds RC0103), contains a small collection of music manuscripts by Edward Brittain.

standard string quartet repertoire.[23] As the oldest boy, Moeran would have led the quartet and was therefore the principal figure in a group of talented musicians that attended Uppingham during the years leading up to the outbreak of the First World War.

Before drawing a curtain on Moeran's years at Uppingham, an attempt must be made to situate his experiences there in the context of his later development both as a composer and as a man. While the biography presented in this chapter is based on just a small amount of primary evidence, it is confidently suggested that the conclusions drawn are the most probable extrapolations from the little that is known and that the most likely of these is that his closest friendship was with Roland Perceval Garrod. Garrod had entered the school a year after Moeran and was just six months younger. From the little available evidence, it can confidently be asserted that the Garrod household was both musical and artistic: alongside cellist Roland Perceval was his elder brother Geoffrey – a talented singer – and his artist mother Lucy Florence (*née* Colchester). It is possible, therefore, that Moeran was drawn to his new Lorne House colleague initially through a shared love of music. While it cannot be asserted unequivocally that Moeran was gay or bisexual, the evidence of his character and personality presented above is credible. The nature of his relationship with Garrod therefore acquires an additional possible characteristic. All that is known about Garrod is that he was the youngest of four male siblings and while this familial status would inevitably have had a formative influence on his personality, it does not imply a particular sexual identity. Thus, whether or not Moeran's attraction to Garrod was also sexual, it is not known if this was reciprocated or unrequited. However, it may reasonably be argued that the composition of a sonata lasting nearly an hour – which must have entailed days or even weeks of concentrated attention – suggests a devotion that transcends typical schoolboy friendship, and the fact that Garrod and Moeran evidently performed the work together at an informal recital in the school implies that Garrod accepted its dedication. Moreover, Moeran's exclusive mention of the work to Heseltine years later is surely significant.[24] Garrod is standing on Moeran's left in the house photograph shown in figure 3, and while this could be coincidence, that they may have chosen to stand together provides an additional sliver of substantiation for their relationship. Moeran's friendship with the Garrod family extended beyond Roland Perceval – as will become apparent later – and this would almost certainly have been the result of Moeran having visited their family home during school vacations. The context of homosexuality during the first few decades of the twentieth century ensures that speculation from limited evidence is frequently all

---

[23] During the interview with Moeran conducted by Evan Senior that led to the article published in the May 1950 edition of the *Australian Musical News and Digest* that was mentioned in Chapter 2, Moeran evidently asserted that his earliest completed composition was a string quartet for his school ensemble. Moeran further asserted that he had composed it after hearing the Debussy String Quartet in G minor at a concert he attended in London.

[24] Since there were no other schoolboy cellists in Uppingham at the time, the possibility that Moeran composed the hour-long sonata for somebody else can be dismissed.

that is available to a biographer, and whether Moeran and Garrod were genuinely lovers cannot be known definitively. Nevertheless, there are aspects of Moeran's behaviour during the years following his departure from Uppingham that would be consistent with such a liaison.

4

The Music Student
(1912–1914)

A favourite destination for pupils leaving Uppingham during the early decades of the twentieth century was Clare College Cambridge, and the college
Admissions Registers record several entrants each year between 1909 and 1914.[1] The
family tradition established by Moeran's grandfather's generation was, on leaving
school, to go to university and study for a career in either the law or the church.
Moeran's father and uncle were both Cambridge alumni, and his brother William
Graham had graduated with a BA degree from Emmanuel College, Cambridge in
1911. While it may have been Moeran's intention to follow their examples and apply
for a place at Cambridge, and despite having claimed to be or to have been a student
at Clare College Cambridge at least twice during the next few years, at some point
during the summer holidays, he changed his mind – the musical opportunities available in London evidently proved to be too strong to resist. He had left Uppingham
having developed into a musician of exceptional talent, and it is possible that his
teacher Robert Sterndale Bennett recommended to Moeran and his parents that
the young musician proceed to study at the Royal College of Music. The support of
Sterndale Bennett and the financial backing of his parents would have ensured that
acceptance into the college would have been a formality, and Moeran was enrolled
at the college on 26 September 1912. He selected piano as his principal study with
theory as secondary, and his father was named as fees guarantor.[2] Amongst the students who entered the college at the same time as Moeran were Marie Goossens and
her brother Adolphe, Brazilian violinist Edgardo Guerra and organist and composer
Heathcote Statham. It seems to have been decided that while he was in London
Moeran would live in Upper Norwood with his great aunt Sarah Graham, who, with
her husband, had some thirty years earlier provided Moeran's mother with a home
when her grandfather George Smeed died. As a minor living away from the parental
home, Moeran would have required the guardianship of a responsible adult relative,
and he probably moved into his room at his great-aunt's house in Auckland Road
in mid-September.

The Royal College of Music term started in early October and Moeran would
have begun his studies with enthusiasm, immersing himself in the musical life of the

---

[1] *Clare College Admission Registers 1871–1950*, Cambridge University Archives Repository
   Reference CLARE/CCAC/2/1/1.

[2] *Royal College of Music Students Register*, No. 10 1911–1914, RCM Records & Archives MS
   P35.03, 3768. Moeran's first term fees of twelve guineas were paid on 25 September 1912.

college and the city. Contemporary newspapers and music periodicals and journals chronicle a plethora of concerts and recitals around London and the suburbs. His parents would have provided a living allowance that would have enabled him to take advantage of the many opportunities to hear and experience music, ranging from orchestral concerts to chamber music and solo and vocal recitals. Moreover, in addition to public concerts, other musical activities took place in London, and Moeran also availed himself of these. In particular, he became a member of the prestigious Oxford & Cambridge Musical Club.

This club had been established in London in 1899 by graduates of the two universities who, during their student years, had been members of either the Cambridge University Musical Club or the Oxford University Musical Union. Its purpose was the encouragement of the 'practice and knowledge of chamber music' and was constituted as a gentlemen's residential club that would provide graduates of the two universities with the facilities both for making and enjoying music and for socialising that were similar to those available to them during their time as students. Membership was both exclusive and expensive. Many of the prominent men of the time, politicians, industrialists, senior officers in the armed forces and members of the professions, had attended one of the universities, and both interest in and demand for the facilities of the musical club were considerable. The first President was violinist Joseph Joachim, and there was also a provision for honorary members, amongst whom were Sir Edward Elgar, Sir Hubert Parry and Dr Hans Richter (the eminent Austrian conductor and friend of Joachim and Brahms).

The Oxford & Cambridge Musical Club Committee Meeting Minutes Book notes that Moeran was elected to membership on 7 October 1912, and the full record of his membership was recorded in the Candidates' Book. Normal membership of the club was usually open only to graduates of the universities of Oxford or Cambridge, and Moeran had provided Clare College, Cambridge, as his college and university affiliation. Thus, his election to membership is immediately problematic. While his appearance and bearing may have been more adult than many seventeen-year-old boys of the time, it is difficult to see how he could have substantiated a declaration to be a graduate of Clare College Cambridge. The fact that the 'Period of Residence', 'Degree' and 'Profession or Occupation' entries in the Candidates' Book entry were left blank, together with the proposer for membership being Roland Perceval Garrod's elder brother Geoffrey, suggests that his election was exceptional and that the rules were adjusted appropriately. Indeed, Moeran was unique in having been elected at such a young age with no apparent qualifications for membership. Garrod would have known the extent of Moeran's musical talent and ability, particularly as a pianist, and together with the recommendation of Uppingham music master and long-standing musical club member Robert Sterndale Bennett, Garrod could have made a convincing case that, his age notwithstanding, the young college student would be an asset for the club. Moeran's election at the age of seventeen into a club whose membership included such early twentieth century musical celebrities as Donald Tovey, Ralph Vaughan Williams and George Butterworth must therefore be regarded as powerful testimony to his talent. It was also a significant milestone in the evolution of Moeran the composer. His membership of the musical club during the next dozen years or so was the most important factor that under-pinned his rise to musical prominence.

Also interesting is the fact that the Membership Record listed Moeran's musical attainments as piano, viola and trombone. Moeran's playing of the trombone is not supported by any other evidence. He did not compose any trombone music, except in as much as it figured as a standard part in his orchestral works. Moreover, none of the evidence relating to his time either at Suffield Park or at Uppingham includes any reference to trombone playing or study. It is difficult to see how inventing an instrumental playing ability, which would have been obvious the first time he was asked to play, could have enhanced his membership prospects. Thus, it must be supposed that, somehow and at some time, Moeran had reached a level of proficiency on the trombone.

The principal activity of the musical club was the playing of chamber music, and this was organised in the form of fortnightly musical *soirées* in the club Concert Room. The names of members present at these recitals were not recorded, at least, not in any of the extant archives, unless they were performing in some capacity and were therefore mentioned in the programme. Since Moeran was elected to membership on 7 October, the first fortnightly programme that he would have been able to attend would have been the 300th Anniversary Programme that took place on Thursday, 7 November. The performers for this programme included the singer Gervase Elwes and the musicologist Donald Tovey. It may be reasonably assumed that Moeran attended musical evenings where he was not involved in the performance and that he made use of the practice facilities and other music-making activities that took place at the club but were not formally recorded. The programmes of the musical evenings provide an invaluable insight into some of the music that Moeran would have heard and the musicians with whom he would have regularly associated. The first recital where it is known that he participated was a Ladies' Night programme on Friday, 20 December. Moeran appeared on the programme as accompanist of a group of songs by Wolf, Brahms and Schubert that were sung by Geoffrey Garrod. The programme also included as performers several musically prominent names of the time, including the clergyman, violinist and renaissance music scholar Edmund H. Fellowes and Alexander Fachiri, barrister and amateur cellist, better known as the husband of renowned violinist Adila d'Arányi.

Dance, Fields at Harvest

On 15 October, Moeran paid his one and a half guineas half-annual subscription to the musical club, thus cementing his association with it and beginning the process of establishing himself in London musical life, and it is from Moeran's first year as a student in London that his two earliest extant compositions date. The manuscripts of the piano pieces, *Dance* and *Fields at Harvest*, which are part of the *E. J. Moeran Collection* at the Southbank Library at the University of Melbourne, have unaccountably survived when all the composer's other early material was lost or deliberately destroyed.[3] No records exist of a public performance of either piece, neither have they been recorded. Their survival is probably fortuitous, rather than due to Moeran's selective retention. The manuscripts were discovered in a bundle of Moeran's effects from his mother's home that were sent to his widow Peers Coetmore in Australia some years after the composer's death. It is possible that they were items that Moeran gave to his mother as examples of his student work and that he later forgot about. However, they have left the Moeran biographer with a problem. While the dating of *Dance* is straightforward, the manuscript being marked 'May 1913', that of *Fields at Harvest* is less so. The manuscript bears the date 'Dec. 23rd' but the year is frustratingly omitted. Writers on Moeran have been divided hitherto as to the year of its composition, with cases being made for both 1912 and 1913. The significance of establishing the year of composition is that it would determine which of these early piano pieces is Moeran's earliest surviving work. The author's examination of the two pieces suggests that, due to the presence of folksong-like idioms in *Fields at Harvest*, it was composed after Moeran's discovery of folksong, which – as will be shown below – took place probably in late 1913. Moreover, the use in *Dance* of an archaic bass clef – which probably originated in his time at Uppingham and which appears in no other surviving Moeran manuscript – also places it chronologically at the earliest stage of Moeran's oeuvre. Finally, a comparison of the forms of the two pieces again strongly favours *Fields at Harvest* as having been composed later, due to its more imaginative structure. Thus, *Fields at Harvest* may be dated with some confidence to December 1913 at the earliest. This makes *Dance* the earliest surviving manuscript by Moeran. It bears little resemblance to any of Moeran's other works, and its inexperienced character is all that is available as evidence of its composer's early development.

Little is known about Moeran's daily life at the Royal College of Music between 1912 and 1914, other than what may be gathered from secondary sources concerning the college. According to both Brightwell and Wright, all students had two weekly lessons in their principal study and one in their secondary study. Additionally, students attended weekly classes in harmony, counterpoint, choral singing, aural training and sight singing. Instrumental students were also required to attend orchestral rehearsals and practical chamber music classes.[4] As a piano student, Moeran would have had lessons either with Franklin Taylor or John St Oswald Dykes, both of whom had studied with Clara Schumann. Music theory and harmony and counterpoint were taught by Sir Frederick Bridge, although Thomas Dunhill is also listed as having been professor of harmony and counterpoint. Moeran's entry in the college students' register indicates that after his first year, he changed his principal study to composition, but somewhat indecisively changed his secondary study between

3   *E. J. Moeran Collection*, MS numbers VCA 9 (*Dance*), VCA 11 (*Fields at Harvest*), Southbank Library, University of Melbourne.

4   See Giles William Edward Brightwell, '*One equal music': The royal college of music, its inception and the legacy of Sir George Grove 1883–1895*, Durham theses, Durham University. Available at Durham E-Theses Online: http://etheses.dur.ac.uk/2611/ (accessed 12 November 2020), and David C. H. Wright, *The Royal College of Music and its Contexts: An Artistic and Social History*, (Cambridge University Press, Cambridge, 2019).

piano, viola and theory each term. While he was a very able pianist, it seems that from early 1913, composition became his foremost activity.

Together with exposure to chamber music at the musical club and in his college classes and to orchestral music through his playing in the college orchestra, Moeran's recollections over the years mention attending concerts in London from 1911 onwards. However, the incomplete and selective memories render it difficult to determine which performances these were. Most significant are mutually incompatible accounts of hearing music that evoked an almost Damascene revelation that radically changed his appreciation of British music. In an article written for *The Countrygoer* magazine in 1946, Moeran included the following story about the pre-First World War Balfour Gardiner concerts:

> [O]ne winter's evening, when I had been to St Paul's Cathedral intending to hear Bach's Passion music and failed to obtain a seat there ... I went to the Queen's Hall where there was a Balfour Gardiner concert, prepared to be bored stiff ... I was so filled with enthusiasm, and so much moved by some of the music I heard that night, that from then on, I made a point of missing no more of these concerts. Among other works I heard was a rhapsody of Vaughan Williams, based on songs recently collected in Norfolk by this composer ... it caused a profound effect on my outlook as a young student of musical composition ... [it] seemed to me to express the very spirit of the English countryside as I then knew it.[5]

Moeran's recollection was befogged by the distance in years between the events and the date they were being recalled and, in writing it, he had evidently forgotten that he had recounted a similar tale some twenty years earlier for Heseltine's 1924 *Music Bulletin* appreciation:

> Beyond Brahms [Moeran] had not pursued his investigations. He felt no curiosity about the music of his contemporaries; even Wagner was unknown to him. But chance came to his assistance one night in the spring of 1913 when, finding himself crowded out of St Paul's Cathedral where Brahms' *Requiem* was to be given, he went to Queen's Hall to hear a concert, rather than hear no music at all. This was one of the admirable series given by Balfour Gardiner – concerts that will long be remembered in the annals of British music, though they were insufficiently appreciated at the time they were given – and the programme contained the Delius Piano Concerto, which accomplished for Moeran the same sort of miracle that *Tristan* and certain works of Grieg had effected for Delius in the eighties and revealed a new world of sound to his imagination.[6]

The anecdotes are striking both for their circumstantial similarities, conflicting claims of the music that Moeran had intended to hear and for the musical differences between the works that he asserted had such an effect on him. The Delius piano concerto and the various *Norfolk Rhapsodies* of Vaughan Williams were indeed performed at Balfour Gardiner concerts between 1912 and 1913, and it is

---

5   Moeran (1946).
6   Heseltine (June 1924), 172.

probable that Moeran heard them.[7] While some music by modern British composers had been performed at Uppingham during Moeran's years there, there is little
reason to doubt that hearing the Vaughan Williams in particular would have opened
the young composer's ears. While neither of the anecdotes was an exact recollection
of events, there is no doubt that between 1912 and 1914 Moeran's musical horizons
were rapidly and extensively widened by the music that he heard in London. His
creativity would have been stimulated both by the possibility of using folksong as a
melodic inspiration, as revealed in the Vaughan Williams *Norfolk Rhapsody,* and by
the unconventional and adventurous harmonic language employed by Delius.

Moeran maintained his membership of the musical club for 1913 by paying the
annual subscription of three guineas on 30 January, and on 8 May he again featured
in the Thursday evening recital. On this occasion, Moeran took a much more prominent role than in his first appearance the previous December, playing the Fantasia
in A minor by Bach as the central solo item, again accompanying Geoffrey Garrod in
two groups of songs and also playing the piano part in the performance of Mozart's
Pianoforte Trio in B flat, which ended the evening. Moeran was again central to the
recital programme on 5 June. The programmes of the Thursday evening recitals provide a sense of the range of music that Moeran was experiencing at the club, and it is
apparent how he was absorbing a multitude of stylistic influences that would inform
his own musical creations. He was also establishing for himself a set of musical and
professional society contacts that would prove helpful as his career progressed.
Alongside those who had entered the Royal College of Music with Moeran in 1912,
his contemporaries included Arthur Benjamin, Herbert Howells, Arthur Bliss, Ivor
Gurney and Mariel and Adolphe Goossens' oboeist brother Leon.[8] It may be reasonably assumed that from 1913 he spent much of his time composing, either as exercises from his composition classes or his own work, and it is probable that the few
extant scores represent just a small proportion of the music that Moeran set down
in manuscript. Writings hitherto on Moeran have emphasised the influence that Sir
Charles Stanford would have had on Moeran during his year of composition study,
but Moeran's composition teacher may not have been exclusively Stanford. Both
Sir Hubert Parry and Thomas Dunhill taught composition at the college in 1913, and
it is possible that Moeran attended their classes. Moeran published an obituary for
Stanford in the *Journal of the Folk-Song Society* in December 1924 in which he wrote:

> As a teacher he was always insistent in pointing out that the study of folk-song is
> a most valuable aid to the acquirement of purity of style and true melodic outline.

---

7 The Delius Piano Concerto was performed by Evelyn Suart at a Balfour Gardiner concert
in the Queen's Hall on Tuesday 18 March 1913. The programme also included the first
performance of the Symphony in E major by Frederic Austin, Granville Bantock's
Symphonic Poem *Fifine at the Fair,* and works by Bax and Balfour Gardiner himself.
Vaughan Williams' second and third *Norfolk Rhapsodies* had been performed at a Balfour
Gardiner concert the previous year on Thursday 18 April 1912. However, at that time,
Moeran was still a pupil at Uppingham and was not yet in attendance at the Royal College
of Music.

8 *Royal College of Music Students Register,* No. 10 1911–1914, RCM Records & Archives MS
P35.03.

His teaching and work inspired many to become collectors of folk-music, and were responsible for the preservation of many beautiful songs.[9]

As this obituary is the only extant writing by Moeran about his former teacher, it is invaluable in that it indicates that Moeran's burgeoning interest in folksong was supported by Stanford.

The only other items of evidence for Moeran's activities during the remainder of 1913 are the October programmes of the musical club. On 9 October, Moeran took part in the programme playing the central solo item, Schumann's *Kriesleriana Nos. 2 & 6* and accompanying the *Idylle* for flute by Théodore Akimenko and songs by Warburg, Gretchaninow and Easthope Martin.[10] Although the Thursday programmes in which Moeran participated provide a good snapshot of the composers whose music he was studying in detail in preparation for performances, he would undoubtedly have attended many of the other programmes. Knowing which composers and works were represented in these adds considerably to the knowledge of the repertoire that Moeran was absorbing. New music appeared on the programmes of the fortnightly Thursday evening recitals almost as frequently as did the classical chamber music repertoire. Thus, Moeran would have had the opportunity to discover a wide range of music, greatly widening the boundaries of that with which he had become intimately familiar during his schooldays.

On 23 October, the 323rd musical club programme took place, and on this occasion, Moeran's involvement was as recital coordinator. This involved managing the programme, arranging such things as canvassing members to contribute items, securing an accompanist and the compiling and printing of the actual evening programme. As far as can be determined, this programme was the first that Moeran organised, but it seems that it was not a complete success. The printed programme in the club archives has several hand-written alterations, and it may be supposed that each of the printed programmes would have had to have been so modified. As the handwriting is identifiably that of Moeran, it is evident that he had some considerable work to do during the day of the recital.

Moeran's 1913 musical pursuits concluded with the 327th club programme, which took place on Thursday, 18 December. He performed the Toccata and Fugue in E minor by J S Bach, and he contributed the piano part in a performance of Hurlstone's Suite for Clarinet and Piano.[11] At the beginning of April 1914 he was invited – presumably by Robert Sterndale Bennett – to contribute an item to a Sunday Musical Evening held at Uppingham, and he performed Schumann's *Faschingsschwank aus Wien*.[12] Otherwise, details of Moeran's day to day life during the first few months

---

9   'Obituary: Sir Charles Villiers Stanford, Mus. Doc., D.C.L.', *Journal of the Folk-Song Society*, Vol.7, No.28, (December 1924), 199.

10   Frederick John Easthope Martin (1875–1925), best known for his popular song *Come to the Fair*.

11   William Hurlstone (1876-1906) produced a considerable amount of chamber music during his short composing career. The list of works performed in Oxford & Cambridge Musical Club programmes includes the Piano Quintet in E minor, the *Phantasie for String Quartet* in A major and minor and the Piano Trio in G major.

12   'Musical Evening', *Uppingham School Magazine*, Vol. 52, No. 410, (June 1914), 105.

of the year are not known, but there is no reason to doubt that he continued to spend time at the musical club, playing through items of chamber music with his fellow members. He also made considerable progress in his composition studies with Stanford at the Royal College of Music, and it is likely that he produced numerous works of his own. The Midsummer Term 1914 issue of the college magazine reports that Moeran 'was awarded a [Royal College of Music] Council Exhibition for Composition at the close of the Midsummer term to the value of £7'.[13]

---

[13] *Royal College of Music Magazine*, Vol. 10, Issue 3, 95.

PART 2

THE FIRST WORLD WAR

5

In the Army
(1914–1917)

Moeran would have travelled home to his parents' recently built house in Bacton-on-Sea on the Norfolk coast in late July, just as the European political situation was entering a critical phase. A few days later, on 4 August, war was declared. Conversation in the Moeran household, just as in countless other households around the country, must have centred on the prognosis for the immediate future. When it came to the question as to whether the nineteen-year-old music student should enlist, it is likely that the attitude of his family, in common with many others with sons of a similar age, would have been one of reluctant acceptance, although it is probable that Ada Esther would not have been happy to see her younger son become a soldier so soon. However, it seems that Moeran was not swept up in the immediate post-declaration enthusiasm, and it is likely that he planned to spend his summer vacation in much the same way as he had spent it the previous year, devoting himself to music and composition and probably visiting Roland Perceval Garrod at the family home in Hampstead.

Garrod and the other members of Moeran's circle of friends had left Uppingham in July 1914, after having taking part in the Speech Day proceedings so movingly recorded by Vera Brittain.[1] Although Brittain's future fiancé Roland A. Leighton had carried off most of the Speech Day prizes, Garrod was an outstanding scholar and had been awarded an exhibition at Clare College, Cambridge. Moeran may have wished to congratulate his friend, and the two would also have been eager to renew their musical collaboration. It is inevitable that they would have discussed the prospect of enlisting, and they perhaps agreed together that they would join the army. According to his entry in *De Ruvigny's Roll of Honour*, Garrod was given a commission in the 6th London Regiment on 26 August 1914. He would have had to inform Clare College of his decision and request a suspension of his exhibition for the period of his service. Moeran also required the permission of the Royal College of Music to enlist, and he would written to Sir Hubert Parry to request this.

Parry was both proud of and concerned for those of his students and staff who were volunteering to serve their country. As a musician, he fully appreciated the contribution to European culture made during the previous 300 or more years by German composers and musicians, yet he was bound by intense national pride to support what he saw as a wholly justifiable war against unwarranted aggression and

---

[1] Brittain, (1933), 86–91.

expansionist ambition. While he considered that his students were special people whose lives ought to be considered too valuable to waste in battle, they were also British men, whose willingness to fight for the honour of their country should be placed above all other considerations. In his address for the Christmas Term 1914, Parry voiced his concerns:

> The College in relation to war is in a different position from other educational institutions. Our pupils are made of different stuff from the pupils of ordinary schools. They are gifted in a rarer and special way. Some of them are so gifted that their loss could hardly be made good. It would be a special loss to the community … the world cannot afford to throw away such lives as if they were of no more account than lives which gave no special promise of a rare kind.[2]

However, Parry felt that he could not stand in the way of a noble ideal, and his compromise seems to have been to label what he saw as the warmongers as 'Prussians' and thus effectively disconnected from the undeniably great artistic, literary and musical achievements of Germany. Despite his despair at the wasteful loss of life, there is no evidence that Parry withheld his permission for any student to suspend his studies, or, indeed, to leave the college in order to join the war. On the other hand, some of the current and former students and staff, being perhaps mindful of Parry's concerns, enlisted in non-combatant or supporting roles.

Moeran presented himself on 30 September 1914 for inspection at the North Walsham barracks of the Norfolk Regiment. It is apparent that he did not seek a commission from the outset, as had many of his public-school contemporaries. Unlike most of his fellow schoolboys at Uppingham, Moeran had not been a member of the Officers' Training Corps. Many young men who had been members of school and university OTCs did apply for commissions during the first few weeks of the war, to the extent that the supply of potential officers outstripped the immediate requirements. While former OTC officers were prioritised, many were turned down and had to enlist as privates while they waited to apply again. Roland Perceval Garrod's family connections probably ensured that his commission was a formality. Having been examined and passed as medically fit for service, Moeran was enlisted with the rank of private in the 6th (Cyclist) Battalion of the Norfolk Regiment. This was a Territorial Force unit, so Moeran, during times of normality, would have remained a civilian, attending a few days per year to train and drill with his regiment. Nonetheless, war had been declared and a national emergency was in force. A decree embodying the entire Territorial Force had been issued by Parliament on 4 August and so Moeran immediately became a full-time serving member of the battalion. The peacetime standard term of service for a Territorial Force recruit was four years, but this had been changed to the duration of the war. Although by the time of Moeran's enlisting the war had been in progress for two months, it was still not expected to last very long, and Moeran might well have thought that he would serve much less than the four years that were otherwise required. Two days after enlisting, and along with many in his battalion, Moeran

---

[2] 'Director's Address', *Royal College of Music Magazine*, Vol. 11, No. 1 (Christmas Term, 1914), 5.

signed the Imperial (or General) Service Obligation, which effectively rendered him liable to be sent to serve as a soldier anywhere in the world.

In common with the battalions of all the Territorial Force regiments, the 6th (Cyclist) Battalion of the Norfolk Regiment was divided from the outbreak of war into two units.[3] Those recruits that had signed the Imperial Service Obligation were formed into the 1/6th 'First Line' or 'Foreign Service' battalion, and those that had not signed became the 2/6th 'Second Line' or 'Home Service' battalion.[4] Despite the liability of the 1/6th to be sent abroad, both units were tasked with essential home defence duties. In practice, this meant bicycle or motorcycle patrols along the Norfolk coast to observe unusual activity and to provide early warning of enemy landings. Fear of invasion by a foreign power had been a constant worry to successive British governments during the latter half of the nineteenth century, with, variously, France, Germany and Russia, or an alliance of some of these, seen as a clear and present threat. Now that a state of war existed with Germany, it was popularly believed that the enemy would inevitably mount a seaborne invasion, and the German naval bombardments of Scarborough, Hartlepool and Whitby in December 1914 greatly exacerbated public fear. Consequently, the reassuring sight of the bicycle patrols, keen and (eventually) well-armed, was welcomed in coastal parts of eastern England, and the members of the 1/6th and 2/6th (Cyclist) Battalions became regular features of the Norfolk landscape during 1914 and 1915. Along with the patrols of small groups of cyclists, regular massed rallies were held, and manoeuvres were organised both along the coast and inland. Despite the improbability of a real invasion, the presence of these patrols was so essential for public morale that reassurance was sought in Parliament that the 1/6th 'Foreign Service' battalion would not be sent overseas.[5]

Details of Moeran's day to day activities in his battalion can only be guessed at from what has been written generally about army life at the time, and a few hints from Moeran's personal recollections and his military service record. It is not known whether Moeran carried out his duties on a bicycle, or motorcycle. While most of the men in the cyclist battalions rode bicycles, some recruits were able to supply

---

3 For a detailed explanation of Territorial Army battalion organisation on the outbreak of the First World War, see The National Archives WO 95/3082/3: 2/8 Battalion West Yorkshire Regiment: War Diary Vol. 1, 2.

4 Almost inevitably, the 2/6th unit became known as the 'Half-Crown Holy Boys'. The origin of the Norfolk Regiment nickname 'Holy Boys' seems to have derived from their service during the Peninsular War (1807–1814), during which the local population are said to have mistaken the figure of Britannia on the regimental badge for a representation of the Virgin Mary.

5 In response to a parliamentary question in early November 1915 by Arthur Wellesley Soames, the MP for Norfolk South, Harold Tennant, the Under-Secretary for War, is reported to have said that '…there was no immediate prospect of the 1/6 (Cyclists) Battalion Norfolk Regiment being required in any of the war zones – Cyclists' Battalions were doing valuable work on our coasts and could not be replaced. This, it would appear, applies to all Cyclists' Battalions…', from '*Question in Parliament*', Half-Crown Holy Boys Chronicle, Vol. 2, (19 November 1915), 15, British Library General Reference Collection, P.P.4039.wbc.(2.).

Figure 4. Member of the 1/6th Battalion, The Norfolk Regiment; in riding order

their own motorcycles and were effectively enlisted together with their machines.[6] None of the documents relating to Moeran's enlisting mention that he was providing his own equipment, but anecdotal evidence suggests that he would have done. Moeran's abiding interest in motorcycles is well-documented, and the family's economic circumstances were certainly such that he could have owned a machine. His apparent ability to travel freely around the east of Norfolk to listen to folksong singing suggests that he possessed an independent means of transport. However, regardless of whether he rode a bicycle or motorcycle, it is likely that his duties would have been relatively light and, apart from the regular coastal patrols and exercises, would have been concerned primarily with practising his riding proficiency, learning how to maintain his machine and acquiring other necessary skills, such as map-reading. Additionally, as a soldier, he would also have been required to attend basic training and drills, and he would have learned to use a rifle and revolver. On 19 November, just seven weeks after enlisting, he was promoted to lance-corporal.

The North Sea Ground

Moeran remained in the 1/6th (Cyclist) Battalion for two years, and during this period, it is apparent that he could devote considerable time to music. He remained a performing member of the Oxford & Cambridge Musical Club, its records confirming that he paid his annual army subscription of one guinea on 28 January 1915. He also continued to compose, and it is likely that numerous works were written during his time in the Cyclist Battalion, although just two are extant. These are the song *The North Sea Ground* and the cycle *Four Songs from 'A Shropshire Lad'*. *The North Sea Ground* is a setting of a patriotic poem that was published without attribution in the 24 March 1915 edition of the magazine *Punch*.[7] The seven verse text refers to the use of North Sea coast fishing fleets, particularly the Grimsby fleet, as minesweepers and anti-submarine vessels during the early years of the war. The poem describes the duty felt by the fishermen crews and suggests the terrible dangers faced by the trawlers when carrying out their tasks. Many of the boats became victims of mines and submarines, and many crew members lost their lives. It is clear from the sense of the verse that there is a low expectation of survival. Nevertheless, the fishermen felt it was their duty to put out in all weathers to ensure the safety of other vessels. While *The North Sea Ground* is a minor work in the overall context of Moeran's oeuvre, its interest derives from its being his earliest surviving verse

---

6   See, for example, 'Recruiting the Motor-Cyclists', *Sheffield Daily Telegraph* (23 August 1915), 3 and 'Motorcycle Territorial Recruits Wanted', *Hawick News and Border Chronicle* (1 August 1913), 2.

7   *Punch*, Vol. 148 (24 March 1915), 230. The writer of the poem, Cicely Fox Smith, was known as a prolific writer of verse, especially that with the sea or maritime matters as the subject. She generally signed herself as 'C Fox Smith' to disguise the fact that she was a woman. The poem was eventually included in several later anthologies of war time poetry. The manuscript of Moeran's setting was discovered in 2000 in the archive of the Oxford & Cambridge Musical Club by the late Gordon Cumming and is now on permanent loan at the British Library. For the author's extended presentation of Moeran's *The North Sea Ground*, see http://www.musicweb-international.com/classrev/2010/Feb10/North_ Sea_Ground.htm (accessed 18 November 2020).

Music example 1. *The North Sea Ground*: bars 1–8

setting. The song betrays some understandable naivety in dealing with text, but the tune is an early indication of the melodic inventiveness that would eventually prove to be one of his strongest style characteristics (music example 1).

In addition to obvious influences assimilated from his mother's cousins' volume *Ships, Sea-Songs and Shanties*, the music also suggests a familiarity with the Victorian parlour song genre. The poem includes a repetitive element in stanzas two, four and seven, and Moeran adopted a verse-refrain form for his setting, casting stanzas two, four and seven as variant choruses. However, this left the problem of how to deal with stanza five. The setting of any poem that has an odd number of verses necessitates a compromise in the structural symmetry of the music. One technique would be to compose a contrasting central section. However, Moeran's simple but rather clumsy solution was to omit the fifth stanza. The problem is that this verse is the key to the emotional content of the poem and contains the most powerful symbolic element 'black spawn swimmin''.[8] Moeran's attempt to balance the musical requirements results in a severe textual weakening. This compositional decision reflects Moeran's inexperience as a song composer at the time. Although, in a musical sense, the word setting was quite appropriate, he had not appreciated the necessity to incorporate the meaning of the entire poem into his song. The most effective part of Moeran's setting is the last line, where he employed an ethereal, monotone for the vocal line, accompanied by *pianissimo* extreme bass notes. The impression of the dead lying in the depths of the sea is unmistakable. Overall, however, the song gives the impression of having been composed quickly. The completion date of 4 April 1915 written on the manuscript is less than two weeks after the *Punch*

---

[8]   The phrase 'black spawn' refers euphemistically to the German mines that posed an ever-present danger to the trawlers in the North Sea.

publication date, so clearly it was written in a few days at most. Alongside *Dance* and *Fields at Harvest*, *The North Sea Ground* represents Moeran during the earliest part of his compositional evolution, and it illustrates how some of the musical influences he had experienced were shaping that development.

On 22 May 1915, Roland Perceval Garrod was killed in action at Festubert in northern France. He was serving as a second lieutenant in the 6th Battalion of the City of London Rifles Regiment commanding a machine-gun battery. Vera Brittain wrote to her fiancé Roland Leighton after hearing the news: 'I have some sad news for you to-day ... R. P. Garrod, who was with you at Uppingham, is dead.'[9] Garrod's next-of-kin would have been informed of his death, probably by telegram, within a few days of the event, and Moeran would have heard the news either directly from the family, or by reading the report in the newspaper. Since the nature and depth of Moeran's relationship with Garrod may have extended beyond schoolboy friendship, it is necessary to consider the effect the news of Garrod's death would have had on the young composer and soldier. Moeran's immediate response seems to have been that within a few days of Garrod's death, Moeran had himself applied for and been awarded a commission as second lieutenant.

Garrod was not the first of Moeran's school or college friends and colleagues to have been killed. The previous December, Roger Assheton Young, a Lorne House contemporary between May 1909 and April 1912, had also died at Festubert while serving with the Royal Munster Fusiliers, and by late May 1915, the Uppingham School magazine had reported that at least fifty Old Uppinghamians had lost their lives, some of whom must have been known to Moeran. Young and Garrod were the first of the Lorne House boys included in the 1911 photograph to lose their lives, and the next three years would see many others suffer the same fate. With most casualties being diligently reported in both national and local newspapers, it is probable that Moeran knew about the deaths of and injuries to his friends and colleagues, and, like countless other young men, he had to absorb and process the emotional trauma that each of these would have aroused. It is at this point that the life experiences of a twenty-first century biographer are wholly inadequate to apprehend how a young man of twenty might even begin to do this. For the more distant friendships or acquaintances, it may have been possible for Moeran to shrug them off as of little concern to him, but it must be assumed that the death of Garrod would have had an almost life-changing impact. It is possible that Moeran had already been considering making an application for a commission, but the coincidence lends weight to the supposition that Garrod's death prompted a significant personal reaction.

As a former public schoolboy, Moeran's officer application had a distinct advantage over those of his fellow enlisted men who had not been to public school or university, and, with the benefit of Sir Hubert Parry's attestation to his good moral character, he was successful. On 4 June, Moeran was awarded a commission as second lieutenant in the Norfolk Regiment. There is no direct evidence to suggest what effect the receipt of a commission had on Moeran's daily life, but his regular

9   Alan Bishop & Mark Bostridge (eds), *Letters from a Lost Generation: First World War Letters of Vera Brittain and Four Friends: Roland Leighton, Edward Brittain, Victor Richardson, Geoffrey Thurlow*, (Abacus, London, 1999), 13.

duties would have changed. Now he would have been expected to give orders and be responsible for organising a platoon of men, rather than mostly doing as he was told. He may have travelled occasionally to London for meetings of the musical club, although there is no record in the surviving club programmes archive of his having participated in any of the Thursday evening recitals during 1915 or 1916. The only direct evidence for Moeran's musical activity during the summer of 1915 is a set of folksongs that he published in the *Journal of the Folk-Song Society* in December 1922.[10] Moeran included several that he cited as having been collected at Winterton, Norfolk, in July. At that time, there were two public houses in Winterton, and anecdotal evidence suggests that both played host to convivial evenings when songs were sung by the fishermen.[11] Among the songs that Moeran collected were: 'The Bold Richard', 'The Captain's Apprentice', 'The Royal Charter', 'The Pressgang' and 'The Farmer's Son'. The tunes of all these songs are in the Dorian mode and the words of each describes a nautical subject, as might be expected from songs sung principally by fishermen. It may also be supposed that Moeran made more than one collecting expedition. The mobility provided by a motorcycle would have enabled him to travel some distance either from his home or from his barracks for an evening's singing in public houses along the coast and inland across the Norfolk Broads landscape.

Further news of casualties amongst Moeran's friends and colleagues would have added to the sorrow occasioned by Garrod's death. Moeran's violin-playing friend Anthony Thornton Walker was killed at Hooge in Belgium on 30 July, and his Lorne House colleague Charles Henry Norman Scholey (also included in the 1911 photograph) was killed at Ypres on 25 September. There were also casualties amongst Moeran's Royal College of Music friends and contemporaries, with organist Philip Evershed Chapman losing his life on 5 September. Finally, a year of tragedy for Moeran ended with the news of the death of Roland Aubrey Leighton from wounds received after having been shot by a sniper while inspecting the wire at Hébuterne.

Four Songs from 'A Shropshire Lad'

Moeran's mental state as he paid his musical club subscription for 1916 can only be surmised. Regular news of the deaths of and injuries to his close musician and school friends and colleagues must have affected him, although his daily life and patrols as a Cyclist Battalion officer may have provided some reassurance that he was contributing to the national effort, and he would have absorbed himself in music whenever he was able. His earliest surviving set of songs, the *Four Songs from 'A Shropshire Lad'*, were completed in 'Midsummer 1916', and it is apparent that Moeran must have spent considerable time during the months beforehand working on its composition. In common with many composers during the first few decades of the twentieth century, Moeran set several poems from A. E. Housman's cycle

---

[10] E. J. Moeran, 'Songs Collected in Norfolk', *Journal of the Folk-Song Society*, Vol. 7, No. 26, (December 1922), 1–24.

[11] 'In Winterton fishing predominated as the main means of male employment ... [and] the fishermen did adjourn to the village's two pubs, *The Fisherman's Return* and *The Three Mariners*, for what ... were lengthy bouts of singing and step dancing.' www.mustrad.org.uk/articles/s_larner.htm; (accessed 31 October 2019).

A Shropshire Lad during his career. Much has been written about the attraction of Housman's verse for composers, but the factors that probably most influenced Moeran would have been the metrical simplicity and the folksong characteristics of the texts. Geoffrey Self, in *The Music of E.J. Moeran*, asserted that the composer's wartime experiences heavily informed his approach to composition,[12] and the obsession with death in its various forms that is evident in virtually all the poems of *A Shropshire Lad* might have resonated with Moeran in the context of the events that were taking place around him. Although Moeran's own war had thus far been spent just a few miles at most from his home, and he had no personal experience of battle, the news that numerous friends and colleagues from school and college had been involved in action, and that many of these had been killed or wounded on the battlefields of France and elsewhere, would have resulted in an ever-present sense of mortality. Moreover, given his possible ambivalent sexual identity, the homo-erotic sub-text of much of *A Shropshire Lad* may well have spoken strongly to Moeran, even if, as is probable, he did not realise it as such.

Whether or not Moeran selected the texts for *Four Songs from 'A Shropshire Lad'* through any emotional reason, or whether they were chosen at random is not known. He wrote no commentary about them, and they were not published in their original form during his lifetime. However, the nature of Housman's verse is a fertile bed for speculation. If it is assumed that the songs were composed during the period May to June 1916, which, given the manuscript completion date of 'Midsummer 1916' and a knowledge of Moeran's rate of working, would seem to be reasonable, then aspects of the texts and the timing of the composition could be regarded as significant: the set of songs may have been composed as a tribute to or memorial for Roland Perceval Garrod. In the year since Garrod's death, Moeran would have been in contact with the family through his musical club fellow member and Roland Perceval's brother, Geoffrey, who was a fine baritone singer and regular performer at the musical club. It is possible that Garrod requested the composition of a set of songs in memory of his brother.

Until John Talbot edited his four-volume *Collected Solo Songs* in the *E. J. Moeran Centenary Edition* in 1994, the *Four Songs*, with one exception detailed below, were not published, and they had remained in manuscript as part of the *E. J. Moeran Collection* at the Southbank Library of the University of Melbourne since they were deposited there on the death of Moeran's widow Peers Coetmore in 1977. Talbot included the *Four Songs* as an appendix to volume three of the *Collected Solo Songs*, with the following editorial comment:

> These four early Housman settings are published together here for the first time, primarily in the interests of scholarship. Although Moeran did allow the second song to be published early in his career, in an arts journal, his significant revision of the fourth some nine years after it was written indicates perhaps his ultimate dissatisfaction with the set.[13]

[12] Geoffrey Self, *The Music of E.J. Moeran*, (Toccata Press, London, 1986), 245–247.
[13] John Talbot, *E. J. Moeran, Centenary Edition, Collected Solo Songs, Vol. 3* (Thames Publishing, London 1994), 64.

Talbot's assertion that Moeran was dissatisfied with the songs was made on the basis that Moeran did not publish them in their original form, and that when the fourth song, 'Far in a Western Brookland', eventually appeared in print, it was in a revised version. However, the evidence from Moeran's later life attests that his being dissatisfied with his compositions almost invariably led to their destruction. For example, in a letter Moeran wrote to Elizabeth Wieniawska in November 1932, he mentioned:

> I have been getting out the MS of another string trio I wrote some time ago, but I came to the conclusion it is quite unsuitable for public performance and so I put it on the fire, together with a very long-winded pianoforte trio I wrote about the same period.[14]

Moreover, Moeran's peripatetic lifestyle as an adult ensured that manuscripts would regularly be either overlooked, left behind somewhere, or otherwise lost. Since the manuscripts of the *Four Songs* were part of Peers Coetmore's bequest to the Victorian College of the Arts in 1977, they must have remained in Moeran's possession until his death. This implies that he must have had a compelling reason for holding on to them and ensuring they were not misplaced. Having composed the songs in memory of Garrod would indeed be such a reason.

While Moeran was presumably seeking originality in his settings, a survey of the Housman songs that had been published up to 1916 and with which he would have been familiar reveals several possible models. Sets such as *On Wenlock Edge* by Ralph Vaughan Williams (1909), *Six Songs from 'A Shropshire Lad'* (1911) and *Bredon Hill* (1912), both by George Butterworth and the cycle *A Shropshire Lad* by Arthur Somervell (1904) were all popular items for performance at the musical club, and Moeran would have known them from accompanying the singing members in their practice and performances. The influence of these forerunners is plain in Moeran's songs. Except for 'When I Came Last to Ludlow', none of the settings follows closely the natural rhythm of the metre of the verse, and, at times, the strophic form is ignored. Moeran seems to have allowed the music to dominate the texts, and the appropriateness of the word-setting is sometimes questionable. For example, the vocal line of the first song, 'Westward on the High-Hilled Plains', is set in a dramatic, declamatory style, whereas the sense of the verse is surely more introspective, particularly the final couplet: 'And the youth at morning shine, | Makes the vow he will not keep', which suggests nostalgic regret. Even less suitably for the sense of the verse, Moeran provided a florid Brahmsian accompaniment that adds little to the melody apart from distraction (music example 2).

This pattern is maintained for the accompaniment for the first two stanzas and changes to a different motif for the third and fourth. Considered as an exercise in word-setting in the style of Brahms or Schumann, 'Westward on the High-Hilled Plains' is competent and the effect is quite pleasing, but as an original, twentieth-century setting of a Housman poem, it lacks real distinction of idea and fails to convince. A consideration of the songs that Geoffrey Garrod included in his musical club recitals suggests Moeran may have had his voice and singing style in mind. The vocal

---

[14] McNeill, 359.

Music example 2. *Four Songs from 'A Shropshire Lad'*,
'Westward on the High-Hilled Plains': bars 1–6

range is exactly that of those songs most favoured by Garrod, and the declamatory nature of the melody is also consistent with much of his repertoire.

The second song, 'When I Came Last to Ludlow', is by far the most musically competent setting of the cycle. After an introductory two bars comprising parallel chords, the sense of optimism and determination apparent in the first verse is well-symbolised in the quaver accompaniment (music example 3). The staccato broken chords depict the striding toward Ludlow of the protagonist and his two friends: 'Two honest lads and hale', with the mood seeming cheery and companionable. As with many of the poems in *A Shropshire Lad*, a sinister aspect appears in verse two: 'Now Dick lies long in the churchyard, | And Ned lies long in jail', and Moeran successfully rose to the challenge of providing an accompaniment that contrasts with the sense of the opening verse. The melody throughout is folksong-influenced, as is the prolongation on the words 'Two honest lads' at the end of the first verse. The effect achieved by adding one or more beats into an established rhythm was exploited by Moeran throughout his composing life, and this is one of the earliest examples. 'When I Came Last to Ludlow' demonstrates the economy of material that would become a characteristic of his mature compositional style and thus contrasts dramatically with the pianistic over-indulgence of 'Westward on the High-Hilled Plains'. As will be shown later, Moeran's studies with John Ireland impressed upon him the importance of achieving the intended effect in the most parsimonious way, to make every note and marking have a purpose and to eliminate padding. Nonetheless, the similarity of form and content of 'When I Came Last to Ludlow' to song IV ('Oh, when I was in love with you') of Vaughan Williams' cycle *On Wenlock*

Edge cannot be overlooked, and so the apparent originality must be tempered by the existence of this model. As with the first song, the vocal range and occasional declamatory effects suggest that the composer had Geoffrey Garrod's voice in mind. 'When last I came to Ludlow' was published, after a fashion, three years after its composition. A facsimile of the manuscript was included in the Autumn 1919 edition of the magazine *Arts and Letters*.

The third song, 'This time of year a twelvemonth past' also has an evident model in *On Wenlock Edge*, in this case it is song VI ('Clun'). Moeran's rather staid setting lacks the impetus that carries the Vaughan Williams song forward. The time signature is continually adjusted between 6/4, 5/4 and 4/4, and the recitative-like result is a rhythmic confusion that does not reflect the natural metre of the text. The underlying form of the setting is strophic, but this is not immediately apparent, either in the vocal line or in the accompaniment. Musically, the most interesting aspect of the song is in the variation of the melody of each of the four stanzas, and it is apparent that Moeran was imaginative in devising different rhythmic arrangements for what is essentially the same tune. His intention may have been to emphasise certain words that he judged to be carrying the dramatic force, but which fell naturally on an unstressed syllable, and he may also have contrived to weaken stressed syllables. The most significant aspect of the song regarding its possible composition as a memorial for Roland Perceval Garrod is the first line of the text and title of the song: 'This time of year a twelvemonth past.' While the remainder of the verse, concerned as it is with the narrator's memories of his struggle with a rival for the affections of his inamorata, seems to have only a passing relevance to the relationship between Moeran and Garrod, there is a definite poignancy in the sub-text that Moeran successfully captures in his varied setting. Moreover, the hymn-like Mixolydian mode accompaniment endows the song with an appropriately sombre quality. This is established from the outset in the introduction (music example 4).

The fourth song, 'Far in a Western Brookland', features a Dorian mode, folksong-like melody that matches well the sentiment expressed in the text (music example 5). Moeran chose to provide a high-register harp-like piano accompaniment with simple triad chords in the left hand, and it is possible that he intended this to represent the trickling sounds of the water in the brooks and pools referred to in the text. Unfortunately, it was a poor choice to complement the inventive and characterful tune, being both fussy and distracting. Moeran cast the song in AABA form, with a contrasting but derived melody for the third verse. The harp-like accompaniment was abandoned for the third and fourth stanzas and a more harmonically interesting chordal texture – similar to that employed in 'This time of year a twelvemonth past' – provides a better frame for the vocal line. Moeran was clearly dissatisfied with the overall effect, and he revised this song for publication in 1925. For the revision, he retained most of the tune but recast entirely the piano accompaniment. The result, from the older and much more experienced composer, was a far superior and atmospheric setting that skilfully reflected the nostalgic sentiment of the text.[15] The most significant aspect of

---

[15] The revised version of 'Far in a Western Brookland' was published in a loose grouping together with ''Tis Time, I Think, by Wenlock Town' (1925), 'Loveliest of Trees' (1931), and 'Oh Fair Enough Are Sky and Plain' (1931–1934), as *Four Housman Songs*, in John

Music example 3. *Four Songs from 'A Shropshire Lad'*,
'When I Came Last to Ludlow': verse 1

Music example 4. *Four Songs from 'A Shropshire Lad'*,
'This Time of Year a Twelve-Month Past': bars 1–7

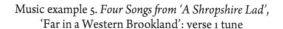

Music example 5. *Four Songs from 'A Shropshire Lad'*,
'Far in a Western Brookland': verse 1 tune

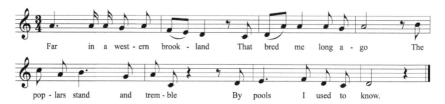

the text may be the third stanza line 'Here I lie down in London, | And turn to rest alone', and it may be that this particularly resonated with Moeran in the context of his life after Garrod's death.

Despite the criticisms levelled against some of songs, the set is competent and aesthetically consistent, but with internal contrast that maintains interest throughout. The manuscript dating of 'Midsummer 1916' means that Moeran was twenty-one when he composed these settings and therefore several years younger than were the composers of the songs that were clearly his inspiration. Leaving the emotional and subjective implications aside, the songs show a distinct advancement in structural and stylistic proficiency from the rather simple and four-square setting of *The North Sea Ground* composed some fifteen months earlier and so provide strong evidence that Moeran must have been exercising and practising his compositional technique during this period. Notwithstanding the fact that the set was not available in printed form until 1994, it was popular for a time. While the individual songs were probably first sung informally by Geoffrey Garrod with the composer as accompanist, the first presentation of the set at the Oxford & Cambridge Musical Club was given by Walter T. Ivimey (baritone), accompanied by H. V. Anson at the 417th Thursday recital on 14 February 1918. Although the audience would have been limited to club members and their guests, this was the first known performance of any composition by Moeran, and, thus, it represents a significant landmark in his career as a composer. It is unlikely that the composer himself was able to attend this recital, since his regiment was posted to Ireland early in 1918. Nonetheless, the reception of the songs was evidently a success, as Ivimey and Anson repeated their performance twice during the next few months.[16] A few years later, a professional recital of the songs was given by the baritone John Goss, accompanied by Harriet Cohen, at the 100th programme of Walter Willson Cobbett's *Sunday Evening Concert Society* at the London Working Men's College on 14 December 1925.[17] As far as can be ascertained,

---

Talbot, *E. J. Moeran, Centenary Edition, Collected Solo Songs*, Vol. 3 (Thames Publishing, London 1994).

[16] These performances took place at the Oxford & Cambridge Musical Club 423rd Programme on 9 May 1918 in London and at a repeat of this programme in Corpus Christi College, Cambridge on 11 May 1918.

[17] *A.L. Bacharach Collection Box 7 1923–26*, Oxford University Library Mus 317 c.7, fol. 45.

this performance was the last, and the set of songs was forgotten until its publication in John Talbot's *E. J. Moeran Centenary Edition, Collected Solo Songs* in 1994.

As casualties mounted in France during 1915 and 1916, the need for replacement fighting soldiers and officers increased, and the call went out to members of home-based Territorial units for volunteers for secondment to front-line regiments. It had been a founding principle of the Territorial Force that those who had enlisted could not be compelled to transfer to a Regular Army unit, or, indeed, to any other unit of the Territorial Force, and the government had stated categorically that even the so-called front-line Cyclist Battalions were so valuable as assets to allay public concern at home that there was little prospect of their being deployed overseas. Thus, the fact that Moeran had signed the Imperial Service Obligation rendering him liable for overseas service meant little in practice for any prospect of his seeing any action.

By the time of the completion of the *Four Songs from 'A Shropshire Lad'*, presumably towards the end of June 1916, Moeran would have known about the deaths of some half dozen of his closest friends and colleagues. While the set of songs may well have had their origin in his response to these tragedies, composition seems to have been insufficient extirpation for what may have become feelings of impotence and ineffectiveness, and he volunteered for transfer to a front-line unit. Perhaps he felt that remaining in the security of home-based duty – however important that was deemed to be – was betraying the memory of those friends who had laid down their lives. Perhaps he sought an opportunity to pursue those responsible for their deaths. It is even possible that he felt that his life now held little value in comparison with those that had already been lost and that dying for the same cause was all he could realistically hope to achieve. Whatever his reasons, on 20 July, Moeran reported for duty in the West Yorkshire Regiment at Somerlyton Park, near Lowestoft in Suffolk and was assigned to be second-in-command of a platoon in A company of the 2/8th battalion. The issue of the *London Gazette* dated 11 July 1916 had reported that Second Lieutenant E. J. S. Moeran had been given the rank of temporary lieutenant, as of 12 July, so it is possible that this promotion was an incentive or a reward for his volunteering for service in a front-line unit.[18] Several of Moeran's fellow 1/6th battalion officers were also transferred to the West Yorkshire Regiment at the same time, so he would not have been alone amongst strangers in his new unit.

The 2/8th Battalion West Yorkshire Regiment had been recruited for the purpose of acting as a Reserve Unit for the 1/8th (Overseas) Battalion that had existed as a fully manned unit before the outbreak of the war. Unlike Moeran's home battalion, the 8th Battalion of the West Yorkshire Regiment had been established from the outset as a fighting unit, and the 1/8th was deployed to France early in the war. On the formation of the 3/8th (Reserve) Battalion during 1915, the 2/8th was reassigned as a front-line unit, and any recruit who had not signed the Overseas Service Obligation, or who was medically unfit for foreign service was transferred to the 3/8th reserve unit. The 2/8th battalion war diary records that on 23 June:

> Six officers proceeded on final leave. Medical inspection for foreign service of A and B companies. Instruction received to prepare to close Battalion & Company

---

[18] *London Gazette*, (11 July 1916), issue 29660, 6861.

books. Order received from Brigade 'As a tactical exercise, prepare to march at once'. Battalion exercised accordingly.

The publication of the war diaries of many regiments that took part in front-line action has provided an insight into the operations of a great army at war, ranging from major strategic plans down to the minutiae of finding billets and rations. The detail of recording depended very much upon the battalion officers responsible for keeping the diaries, and since most of them were written by hand, the legibility also varies greatly. Moreover, some diaries have either been lost or remain embargoed. However, one and a half million pages of first-hand information about one of the most significant events of human history have provided researchers with a unique perspective. While the diaries of the 1/6th (Cyclist) Battalion of the Norfolk Regiment have not survived – if indeed they were kept in the first place – Moeran's transfer to the West Yorkshire Regiment, whose diaries were kept assiduously, enables a detailed account of his activities from July 1916 to early May 1917 to be reconstructed.

The order to decamp did not arrive, and when Moeran and his other Norfolk Regiment volunteer colleagues Lieutenants Davies, Fowler and Ridgway, joined the battalion a month later, they found it still in a state of preparation for imminent deployment to France. The new officers were sent on final leave, presumably expecting on their return to travel to France. In fact, they spent the next six months, first at Somerlyton Park near Lowestoft and then at Bedford, training in trench warfare and the use of the charger-loading Lee-Enfield rifles that had recently been issued to the unit. If Moeran had sustained any doubts about his decision to request a transfer, they would surely have been dispelled by the regular news of more casualties amongst his friends and colleagues. Early July saw the deaths both of two more of his Lorne housemates – Frances Joseph Hicking and Philip Clifford Knight – but perhaps more significantly, that of his Royal College of Music colleague Francis Purcell Warren, who was reported missing on 3 July and whose body was never found. Warren had been awarded the Royal College of Music Morley Scholarship the year Moeran entered the college. While the extent and depth of Warren's friendship with Moeran is not known, it seems likely that – being about the same age and both viola players – they had been, at the very least, acquaintances. Further tragic news came later that July as several more of Moeran's Lorne housemates were killed or injured, and in August there came the reports of the deaths of George Butterworth and Adolphe Goossens, both at the Battle of the Somme. A year of devastation for British music continued when composer Frederick Septimus Kelly was killed on 13 November.[19] It is unknown when and how Moeran would have received the news of the casualties of his friends and colleagues, but, given the regular newspaper reporting, it is hardly conceivable that he did not know that many of his fellow musicians had been killed.

---

[19] According to Therese Radic of the University of Melbourne, it seems probable that Moeran knew Kelly through his connections at the Oxford & Cambridge Musical Club and other chamber music performing activities in London (personal communication with the author, October-November 2015).

While the West Yorkshire Regiment war diary for July to December 1916 records the battalion's preparations for deployment to the front line, it seems that alongside his duties as second-in-command of his company, Moeran spent some of his time during these months in musical activities. Although the battalion was a front-line unit, preparing and being trained to engage the enemy in the trenches, some consideration was clearly given to the men's morale. The evidence for this comes from the following news item in the edition of the *Yarmouth Independent* dated 7 October 1916:

> Empire Concert – We are asked to state that on Thursday evening 'The Starboard Lights' Concert Party, 2/8th West Yorks. Leeds Rifles, will give a grand concert, by kind permission of Lieut.-Col. Hepworth V.O. and officers … the 2/8th have got together a very strong party of nine talented performers, many of them being artistes who in civil life hold prominent positions in the music hall and theatrical world … Each item will be accompanied by the Regimental Orchestra, under the direction of Lieut. Moeran, which will prove an attraction in itself.[20]

The concert took place on Thursday 12 October in the Empire Theatre, and the programme was repeated on Saturday 14 October at the Coliseum. No further detail of these concerts, or, indeed, any others given by either 'The Starboard Lights' concert party or the West Yorkshire Regimental Orchestra have been found, and all archives and records relating to the groups seem to have been lost. However, the fact that Moeran was the conductor of the Regimental Orchestra suggests that his contribution to the regiment was not confined to his role as second-in-command of a platoon.

[20] 'Empire Concert', *The Yarmouth Independent*, (7 October 1916), 3.

6

A Composer Goes to War
(1917)

Early in the New Year came the news for which Moeran and his fellow officers had been waiting, and on 8 January, two trainloads comprising thirty-three officers and nearly one thousand men of the battalion travelled to Southampton, where they embarked on the SS *Archangel* for Le Havre. On arriving in France shortly before midnight, they marched to a rest camp. Since Moeran did not keep a personal diary, or if he did, it has not survived, and since any letters that he may have written home have been lost, it is not possible to know how he spent what free time he may have had. Although front-line soldiering was a full-time occupation, there were periods away from the trenches, and there are countless stories of soldiers occupying themselves with creative activities, such as writing poetry, stories and diaries, playing and composing music, the creation of which has become known as trench art. Thus, while none of Moeran's surviving works can be dated to the period January to May 1917, there is no reason to suppose that he gave up composition entirely. Until the publication of the war diaries, the belief had been that soldiers spent weeks or even months in rain-sodden, freezing cold muddy trenches, contending with disease, rats and the continual bombardment from German artillery. The diaries have revealed that, in practice, a rotation system ensured that most units spent no more than eight days at a time in the trenches at the front line. They were then replaced by another unit and were moved back to reserve trenches for a few days and then moved further back to a rest camp for a further few days, before taking their turn again in the front-line trenches. While this knowledge in no way diminishes the appalling conditions often experienced by many solders, it reveals that some consideration was given to enable the men to rest and recuperate regularly in safety.

At the beginning of February, Moeran's company was sent to Beaussart as a working party to assist the 252nd Tunnelling Company creating dugouts. On their return, Moeran, together with three of his colleagues, was assigned to the 5th Army Group Divisional School of Instruction for trench mortar and other specialised weapons training. Such training was only given to those that displayed the skills and potential for the investment of time away from the front line to be worthwhile for the battalion, and Moeran remained at the school for two months. This extended deployment testifies to his aptitude and potential; the usual assignment for officers at the divisional schools was two to four weeks. Moeran was evidently regarded as an officer with promise, and his extended training would have provided him with advanced capabilities using the most modern military technology. Although undergoing this training made it necessary for him to miss the first extended period of action experienced by his battalion, it also meant that he was still alive and unscathed. During his two-month absence, front-line action involvement had resulted in the loss of several officers, including two commanders and numerous other ranks killed or wounded.

When Moeran returned from his training at the beginning of April, he found that his battalion had moved its headquarters forward into what he would previously have known as enemy territory.[1] The German withdrawal had taken the Allied forces by surprise, and, indeed, they had only become aware of its extent when regular nightly patrols found that German outposts were unoccupied. Since it was far from clear where the enemy forces had gone, patrols were intensified and extended, and on re-joining A-Company on 4 April, Moeran was immediately involved in front line action to relieve the 2nd Border Regiment forward of the ruined village of Mory. The march to the Allied front line established to the south and west of nearby Bullecourt would have begun shortly after sunset, but with the full moon due a few days later on 7 April there would have been sufficient light for the column of several hundred men to find their way. It is apparent that the battalion encountered no problems, as the war diary entry for 4 April records that the operation was a success and that the relief was complete by midnight. The next day, the battalion moved its forward advanced posts to within 500 yards of the new German lines. These new posts were relieved during the night of 5 April, during which operation Lieutenant Christopher George Fowler, who had transferred from the 1/6th battalion of the Norfolk Regiment at the same time as had Moeran the previous July, was killed. Moeran must have known Fowler since he enlisted, and they had clearly shared a great many experiences during the previous two and a half years. Moeran had no time to grieve; the operations being carried out each night by the battalion were part of the preparation for what would later become known as the Second Battle of Arras.

The participation of the 2/7th and 2/8th battalions of the West Yorkshire Regiment in the Second Battle of Arras was peripheral but essential. While the main attacks were planned to take place further north along the Hindenburg Line, flanking operations on either side were intended to tie down German resources that would otherwise have been available for counterattack. Further relief operations took place during the nights of 6 to 9 April, and on each occasion several officers and men were killed or wounded. The week-long local preparation for the main operation resulted in fourteen officers and men killed and several dozen wounded.

At dawn on 10 April, the attack on the Hindenburg Line began, and Moeran led one of the patrol groups, as the war diary recorded:

> At dawn three strong patrols under Lt. Alexander MC, Lt. Moeran and Lt. Burrows attacked the Hindenburg Line (Operation Order No. 13) but met with considerable resistance and had to retire.

The method of attack was simple: on receipt of the signal, usually a whistle, the patrols, each led by its officer, would climb up out of the defensive position (in the

---

[1] The so-called *Alberich Bewegung* during February and March had resulted in the German front line moving back twenty miles to the east of the former Allied positions.

case of Moeran's battalion this was a sunken road, rather than an excavated trench)
and advance towards the German line under the cover of Lewis gun fire. Between
the attacking patrols and the German lines was open ground of about a quarter of a
mile, obstructed by a tangle of barbed wire, many metres deep, which it was hoped
had been broken by an earlier artillery barrage. Opposing them was concentrated
machine-gun fire from embedded German positions. On being given the signal,
Moeran and his men tried to progress across the muddy field in a heavy snowstorm
and freezing temperatures, but it soon became apparent that the heavy artillery
barrage that had been intended to destroy the barbed wire and to force the German
infantry deeper and further back into their entrenched positions had been unsuc-
cessful. They ran into heavy opposition and were forced to withdraw to the sunken
road. The attack on Bullecourt was Moeran's first experience of going into battle.
Descriptions of him in his later life, most particularly those of Lionel Hill, present
him as a gentle and deeply sensitive man, commensurate with the popular notion of
a composer. While Hill's portrayal is somewhat rosy-tinted, it indeed jars violently
with the image of Moeran's younger self going into battle, surrounded by death
and destruction on all sides. Whether Moeran himself killed any enemy soldiers is
not known, but, like his fellow officers and men, he would have been determined
to do so, had the opportunity arisen. The notion that he would have shot and killed
another human being without compunction is an aspect of Moeran's character with
which the First World War endowed him, and without consideration of which the
assessment of his creative life would be incomplete.

After the failure of the attack, a new set of operations orders was hastily drawn
up for a resumption the following morning. The plan was that the 4th Australian
Division, supported by a brigade of tanks, would clear what was left of the village
of Bullecourt, and the 2/6th and 2/8th West Yorkshire Regiments would attack
the Hindenburg Line, which lay a few hundred yards to the north. However, there
had been too little time to modify the orders sufficiently in the light of the experience of the previous day, and the attack again failed dismally. According to military historian Paul Kendall, the battle at Bullecourt was a catastrophe for each of
the Allied units involved.[2] Numerous things had gone wrong. The capabilities of
the tanks had been over-estimated and misunderstood, tactical decisions by senior
command had been made on the basis of inadequate intelligence, the impact of
the weather had not been taken into account, there had been little, if any, con-
tingency planning, and the reliability of supplies of ammunition had not been
assured. The failure of the artillery to destroy the German wire and to degrade the
defensive positions ensured that the enemy had a significant strategic advantage
which resulted in a huge casualty imbalance. While the allied forces lost more
than 10,000 killed, wounded, or captured, the German casualties numbered just
1,000 men. After this failure to break the German lines and capture the village
of Bullecourt, more intelligence was required. The war diary entry for 12 April
records that Moeran participated in dangerous night operations:

---

[2]   See Paul Kendall, *Bullecourt 1917: Breaching the Hindenburg Line*, (The History Press,
    Stroud, 2010) Chapters 10 (*The Tanks' Day of Disaster*) and 11 (*The West Yorkshires Go In*).

Lt. Moeran went out on patrol to examine the enemy wire last night (11–12 April). Lt. Pothecary and 2nd Lt. A.R. Moore went out on a patrol to find out the strength with which the Hindenburg Line was being held. 2nd Lt. A.R. Moore was killed. Lt. Moeran, Lt. Alexander M.C. and Serg. Potts each patrolled a portion of the enemy wire on our front.

Patrolling the wire was an extremely dangerous undertaking, requiring close visual inspection of the barbed wire entanglements that were spread out forward of the German lines, sometimes as close as a few metres away from the enemy trenches. Officers would be asked to volunteer for the task in turn. Contemporary accounts suggest that during the night, No Man's Land was busy with men from both sides, each spying on and trying to avoid the other. The most dangerous aspect of the mission was frequently the return to friendly trenches as the officer ran the risk of being mistaken for an enemy operative, and sentries often fired at anything that moved. Even if he had no choice but to do it, Moeran displayed immense courage in going out on such patrols and was sufficiently skilled and competent to perform the task. Later that night, Moeran's unit was relieved, and the next three weeks were spent away from the front line at the town of Béhagnies.

As the end of April approached, the Allied High Command strategy required that another attack on the Hindenburg Line would be made. The German army had counter-attacked a few days after the action at Bullecourt, and although this had been repelled, it was realised that progress in pushing back the German army to the north and east depended upon taking the heavily defended and secured Bullecourt salient. A set of operations orders to cover this attack was issued in late April, and a briefing to all officers took place on 30 April informing them that the attack would begin at 3:45am on 3 May. The weather had improved considerably over the previous few weeks, with most of the lying snow having melted. There would also be a reasonable amount of moonlight during the short period before dawn broke. Moeran and his battalion marched the few kilometres from Béhagnies back to Ecoust-St-Mein, and they took up their positions on the forming-up line just outside the village in the early morning of 3 May. The line covered several kilometres to the north-west and south-east and comprised tens of thousands of British and Australian officers and men, most of whom, like Moeran, would have been veterans of the April 10–11 battle. The war diary report summarises the ultimately futile operation and its consequences:

> The attack began at 3:45 am. The 186th Brigade reached the first objective with considerable loss and was unable to establish itself in the enemy front line owing to enfilade machine gun fire. Being unable to get into the front line the remnants of the brigade took up their position in the sunken road some 400 yards from the enemy line, and there held on until dusk when they were ordered to retire on the original line of resistance ... Killed other ranks 5; Wounded Officers 3: Lieut. E. J. S. Moeran, 2nd Lt. R. D. Netherscot and 2nd Lt. B. W. Thornhill. Other ranks: 49. Missing Officers 2: Lieut. Tansley and 2nd Lt. Muirhead; Other ranks 37.

Other than what may be gleaned from the war diary entry, the exact circumstances of Moeran's injury are not known, although the course of the action around Bullecourt that day is well understood by military historians. His battalion would have attacked as ordered, with Moeran leading his platoon, encouraging them to carry on forward and trying not to be distracted by those falling on either side as they came under the *enfilade* machine-gun fire. As well as a hail of bullets from left and right, there would have been flying shrapnel from rounds that had struck obstacles and fragmented. The nature of Moeran's injury suggests that at some point during the advance he was hit by one or more of these fragments in the right rear side of his neck. The impact would probably have knocked him off his feet, and within a few seconds he would have begun to experience considerable pain. While he may have been somewhat surprised to discover that he was still alive, he would have been in a state of shock as he realised that he had been injured, perhaps fatally. Nevertheless, he would have had to assess his immediate situation and deal with it as far as he was able.

Moeran could not have expected any of the other advancing officers and men to stop and help him. Such assistance was strictly forbidden and would have resulted in court martial. Soldiers received some rudimentary instruction in what to do if they were wounded in action, and this is all that he could have relied on. His personal equipment would have included a field-dressing and morphine tablets, and he would have had to treat himself: at the very least to staunch his wound. What would have happened next would have been dependent upon how debilitating his injury was. If he had been able to patch himself up sufficiently with the field-dressing and could get back onto his feet, he would have been required to resume his advance towards the enemy. Under no circumstances could he have tried to make his way back towards his own trenches as this would have been regarded as desertion.[3] If he was unable to carry on, he would either have had to remain where he was, or to have found shelter in a shell-hole, and his hopes for survival would have rested on his being found by the medical orderlies or stretcher bearers that followed behind each attacking battalion. However, the field of battle was a large area and the stretcher bearers were just as likely to be shot at as were the attacking forces, and it could have taken some time before he was discovered and taken back to a front line first aid post for preliminary treatment and assessment.

All that is known for certain about Moeran's experiences on 3 May 1917 is that, by the evening, he was in the care of the medical officer of his battalion. Had he not yet been found, the report of the attack in the war diary would have listed him as missing, rather than wounded. The following day, he would probably have been transferred to a casualty clearing station where his condition would have been more thoroughly determined, and it seems that it was deemed sufficiently serious to warrant his repatriation and admittance to a hospital in England. A War Office Arrival Report in his army medical record attests that Lieut. E. J. Moeran of the 1/6th Cyclist Battalion of the Norfolk Regiment, attached overseas to the 2/8th Battalion of the West Yorkshire Regiment, embarked on *HMHS St Denis* at Boulogne on 7 May and arrived in Dover later the same day, the cause of his return being noted as a shrapnel wound in his neck. The report also records that he was admitted to and examined at the Cambridge Research Hospital on May 10th:

---

[3]   British combat casualty protocols recognized just two statuses: dead or incapacitated. If a man was neither of these, he was regarded as well enough to fight.

The Board having assembled pursuant to order ... proceed[ed] to examine [Lieut. E. J. Moeran] and find that he has a small gunshot wound on [right] side of neck just below the mastoid process of the temporal bone. The X-ray plate shows a piece of metal near the vertebra on the [right] side. There is a small discharging of wound, no nerve complications.

The cause of the injury was recorded as a bullet wound, and Moeran was ordered to remain in hospital for the time being. His attachment to the West Yorkshire Regiment was rescinded and he was re-attached for pay and rations to his former battalion of the Norfolk Regiment. By the time that his Arrival Report was written up a week or so later, it seems that the cause had been revised from bullet wound to shrapnel wound. A further Medical Board examination took place on 22 May, and it is apparent that Moeran had been relocated, as this Board was convened at the Prince of Wales' Officers' Hospital in Marylebone Road, London: 'the metallic fragment is still in situ. Wound has healed and leaves no disability. There is considerable thickening around wound. No operation is advised meantime.' Moeran was discharged from hospital and sent on three weeks' leave. It is evident that his condition was no longer considered to be serious and that the shrapnel or bullet fragment was small, although it remained in place. While the Medical Board Report is enough to verify the relatively minor nature of Moeran's injury, additional substantiation may be found by a consideration of some of his activities following his discharge from hospital. A report in the issue of the *Thetford & Watton Times* dated 2 June suggests both that Moeran had returned to being musically active and that his injury was not hindering him. The report is of a memorial service that took place in Bacton Parish Church to dedicate a granite cross that had been erected to the memory both of local landowner Lieutenant-Colonel Arthur Paston Mack and those that had lost their lives during the war. The report includes the information that 'Lieutenant Jack Moeran, Norfolks, presided at the organ'.[4] This is the first documented confirmation of Moeran's musical activities since his participation in the Great Yarmouth *Starboard Lights* concert the previous October.

Apart from practising the organ, Moeran also re-acquainted himself with the piano and the repertoire that he had assimilated during his later years at Uppingham and his time at the Royal College of Music. This is evidenced by his involvement in the 408th musical club programme in London on 2 August. Lieut. E. J. S. Moeran is recorded as having contributed the central, solo feature of the programme, performing the *Sonate Fantastique* Op.44 by the Ukrainian composer Théodore Akimenko. There are stylistic aspects of the technically demanding *Sonate Fantastique* that are found in Moeran's own piano music which suggests that Moeran knew the work well. The use by Akimenko of parallel octaves in the left hand as a means of emphasising tonal underpinning finds a parallel in Moeran's piano works *At a Horse Fair*, *Toccata* and *Elegy*, and the characteristic split arpeggiated chords that appear in the Akimenko *Sonate* were also extensively used by Moeran throughout his piano music. He also employed this pianistic device in many of his song accompaniments

4 'Bacton – Memorial Unveiled', *Thetford & Watton Times and People's Weekly Journal*, (2 June 1917), 5.

to lighten the sound texture without compromising the harmonic effect. A few days after the musical club programme, Moeran was examined again by the Army Medical Board at Smallburgh in Norfolk: 'his condition has improved. The discharging wound mentioned in [Medical Board Report] of 10/5/17 has now healed. Any excessive muscular exertion gives rise to pain on right side of neck, at other times, he is quite free from any inconvenience.'

While the Medical Board assessment suggests that it was believed that Moeran had recovered from the worst of his injury, the recommendation remained that he was still not fit for active or general service, and he was ordered to return to his unit for what was termed 'Light Duty at Home'. Moeran's unit was based at Worstead Camp, near Norwich, which was a short railway journey or motorcycle ride from his parents' house at Bacton, so it is likely that he was able to spend time at home. It is evident that even during his period of recovery he was still considered to be an asset to the Territorial Force. As has been shown, Moeran had been given a temporary promotion to lieutenant on 12 July the previous year, and it seems now to have been decided that this appointment should be made permanent. The following announcement appeared in the London Gazette: 'Norfolk Regiment: 2nd Lt. (temp. Lt.) E. J. S. Moeran to be Lt. with precedence as from 8th July 1917, 28th Aug. 1917.'[5] Moeran was still suffering from some discomfort, and he appeared before another Medical Board at Smallburgh on 21 September: 'he has improved, but there is still some pain on excessive movement of neck. A recent skiagraph shows a foreign body just below right mastoid process.'[6] Moeran was deemed to be fit for 'Home Service' but remained unable to rejoin any active service. Despite this, he was still able to pursue his musical activities. The 412th musical club programme on 15 November again featured Moeran as the central item soloist, performing Ravel's Sonatine. The influence of Ravel pervades much of the music that Moeran composed during the next ten or so years – a notable example being the String Quartet in A minor – and it is known that the composer was important to Moeran.[7]

By the beginning of December, Moeran had spent six months on leave or undertaking light duties, and he had been in a favourable position to pursue his musical activities. Thus, it may be asserted that, from both a personal and a musical perspective, his injury at Bullecourt turned out to have been to his considerable advantage. Compared with countless of his fellow officers and men, he was extremely fortunate, first that his injury was minor, and second that it led to his removal from the front line. Unfortunately, it was becoming clear that the injury was not healing thoroughly. A Medical Board Report at Wroxham on 21 December noted that

---

5   The London Gazette, Supplement 30254, (24 August 1917), p. 8884.

6   The word 'skiagraph' refers to X-ray photography.

7   Apart from Ravel and Debussy, the influence of late-nineteenth and early twentieth century French composers on Moeran has not yet received much attention in writing about the composer and his music. Moeran himself mentioned such figures as Vincent d'Indy and Ernest Chausson in his correspondence. Moreover, the testimony of Nina Hamnett suggests that Moeran may have had a friendship with Francis Poulenc during the 1920s: see Nina Hamnett, Is She a Lady? A Problem in Autobiography, (Wingate, London, 1955).

'any special exertion causes pain in the affected region' and that 'An operation will be necessary'. The conclusion was that Moeran was 30 per cent disabled. He was signed off active service for a further three months and remained assigned to home duties in Norfolk. A Medical Board examination at Wroxham on New Year's Day 1918 reported 'that the wounds in the right occipital region have healed. He complains of pain in the head at times especially if he moves it quickly – a skiagraph shows fine pieces of metal embedded.' Nonetheless, Moeran was described as 'fit for general service', his disability degree was rated as 'nil' and he was instructed to return to his unit.

7

Ireland, and Recovery
(1918)

Early in 1918, elements of the Norfolk Regiment, including Moeran's 1/6th battalion, were transferred to Ireland to support efforts to control escalating Nationalist disturbances. While the exact date of this deployment is not known, it was probably during the first two weeks of February. This is suggested by the fact that Moeran did not play the piano accompaniment in the first performance of his *Four Songs from 'A Shropshire Lad'* at the musical club on 14 February.[1] He was still in some discomfort from his injury, and, on his arrival in Ireland, he was again required to attend several Medical Boards. The first of these was dated 23 March, and it confirms that he was based at Boyle Barracks in County Roscommon. The Medical Board itself was held at the King George V Hospital in Dublin, to which it may be presumed that Moeran travelled from Boyle. No mention is made of the pain from which he had been suffering a few weeks earlier, and the conclusion of the Report was that 'He has considerably improved since [the] last board [and] [h]e is now fit for general service: instructed to rejoin [sic] his present unit.'

Moeran was still assigned to light duties, with dispatch riding being the most likely activity, particularly since this is how he chose to recall his wartime experiences in later life. He was evidently able to travel around the country to some extent, the main evidence for this deriving from a manuscript notebook in the possession of Trinity College Library in Dublin and catalogued as *Moeran's Last Notebook*. During the mid-1940s, Moeran transcribed musical examples and compositional notes into a notebook he had acquired for the purpose, and this notebook contains information that is useful both in examining his music and in tracing his locations.[2] However, when he compiled the notebook from his original manuscripts, it is probable that he mis-remembered or mis-transcribed dates that he had originally recorded, and so the evidence must be considered in the contexts of unreliable memories, poor

---

[1] See p. 66.

[2] The dating of the compilation of *Moeran's Last Notebook* (Trinity College Dublin Library reference number IE TCD MS 6451) is facilitated in large part by its contents. It bears a stamp indicating that it was purchased in Hereford, and it contains references to Cahirciveen, where Moeran spent considerable time from 1936 onwards, and to Peers Coetmore's cello, which Moeran could not have known about before 1943. According to its custodial history in Trinity College Dublin Library, the item was owned by Professor Brian Boydell until September 1974 when it came into the possession of Trinity College. It is presumed that it was labelled *E. J. Moeran's Last Notebook* after the composer's death.

handwriting and an agenda to reconstruct his own past. While some of the dates recorded are undeniably incorrect, it would be unrealistic to assume that they are all either wrong or misleading. Nonetheless, Moeran's imprecision has left the biographer with a conundrum, and a decision must be made as to which dates are to be regarded as dependable. The notebook includes transcribed material with the following dates and locations:

- 8 October 1917
- 19 April
- 23 May – on *RMS Scotia*
- 25 July
- August 1919 – Shannon
- 2 September
- 1919 – West Ireland
- 10 May 1921 – Glenmore

At first sight, the sequence of dates running from 19 April to 2 September and including the next date 1919 could be consistent with all of them being in the year 1919. However, as will be shown in the next chapter, Moeran could not have been in Ireland on 19 April in 1919, and the 23 May date on *RMS Scotia* was in 1936.[3] This leaves the dates 25 July, August 1919 (Shannon), 2 September and 1919 (West Ireland) as perhaps chronicling a period of a few weeks that Moeran spent in Ireland – and particularly the west and south-west of the country – between early July and mid-September 1919. Regarding the other dates, 8 October 1917 cannot be correct, since Moeran is known to have been in Norfolk at this time, and it will be shown later that it is unlikely that Moeran could have been in Ireland on 10 May 1921. Thus, it seems to be probable that the page with the 19 April date contains items that Moeran recorded during his posting to Boyle in 1918.

As an officer in what many of that local population would have regarded as an occupying army, and with a distinctively English public-school manner of speaking, it may be thought that visiting bars and local clubs where folksongs were sung could be fraught with danger.[4] However, Moeran did not lack courage, and his later life demonstrates that he was possessed of a personal *bonhomie* that was able to charm others easily. Moreover, there is strong evidence that his phenomenal memory for sound enabled him to mimic convincingly.[5] Lieutenant E. J. Moeran of the Norfolk Regiment would not have been welcome in the bars of West Ireland, but Mr Jack Moeran of County Cork may have had a different reception. It is even possible that, despite his military duties, Moeran became involved in the Nationalist cause and made the acquaintance of some of its participants. Incidents later in his life support

---

3   See p. 200.

4   Moeran's refined accent is evident in the Eamonn Andrews interview that he recorded for Irish Radio in 1947 (see pp. 24–5), and it is likely that thirty years before this – being that much closer to his public school and army officer antecedents – it would have been even more pronounced.

5   This ability is recorded by Lionel Hill: 'Jack's mimicry was superb'; Hill, 96.

the assertion that he had associations with the Nationalist or Republican movements at some time.[6]

Although evidence of any of Moeran's activities during his posting to Boyle
Barracks in 1918 is scant, the Membership Register of the Grand Lodge of Freemasons
of Ireland records that he was Entered Apprentice on 6 March at Lodge Number 76
at Longford, County Longford.[7] Moeran's grandfather and great-grandfather had
been Freemasons – as were most of his living male relatives – and it seems that he
made the decision join them at this time. His 'Vocation' was entered as lieutenant
in the Norfolk Regiment, and it is interesting to note that another lieutenant from
the regiment, Hilary P. Kaufman, is recorded as having joined the same Lodge just
a few weeks after Moeran did.

Moeran's progression from E. A. (Entered Apprentice) to G. L. Cert. (Grand
Lodge Certificate) in just four weeks indicates that he must have made numerous
visits to Longford to attend instruction in Masonic Rites.[8] It also suggests that he had
ample spare time, or that his Masonic training had the blessing of his commanding
officer. Since Kaufman's Grand Lodge Certificate is dated 21 June, it is likely that the
Norfolk Regiment remained in Boyle until at least that date.

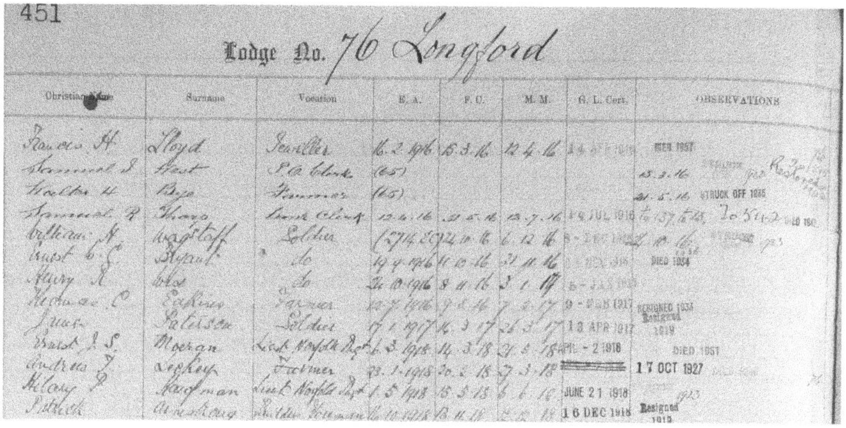

Figure 5. Freemasons of Ireland Membership Registers 1900–1923, Volume I: p.451

[6] See Chapters 8 and 14.

[7] Longford is situated some thirty miles to the south-east of Boyle, and in 1918, a regular
Midland Great Western railway service connected the two towns. Longford was probably
the most convenient Lodge for Moeran to join.

[8] According to the Grand Lodge Membership Register, there are/were four degrees of
membership: Entered Apprentice (E. A.), Fellow Craft (F. C.), Master Mason (M. M.),
and Grand Lodge Certificate (G. L. Cert). In comparison with other entrants at about the
same time, Moeran's progression from Entered Apprentice to Grand Lodge Certificate in
a period of less than one month seems to have been very rapid.

String Quartet in E flat

The String Quartet in E flat was published in 1956.[9] No date of composition was indicated, but the following note was included at the beginning: 'The autograph score of this quartet was found among the composer's MSS by his widow, Peers Coetmore. The MS bears no date, but it is clearly an early work.'[10] Since publication, there has been discussion by scholars and Moeran enthusiasts concerning the appropriateness of the statement 'it is clearly an early work', with some suggesting that the quartet was composed very early in Moeran's career and others asserting that it stands as one of his last compositions. A forensic examination of the manuscript, an examination of the music and scrutiny of Moeran's correspondence all lead to the conclusion that the two movements were most probably composed as much as thirty years apart, with the first having been completed in County Roscommon in April 1918 and the second having been written between the early 1930s and 1949. The manuscript of the second movement bears no specific dating information, and while a determined effort has evidently been made to obscure or remove all original such information from the manuscript of the first movement, sufficient remains to draw a reasoned conclusion. On the front page, handwritten notes below the composer's signature have been scratched out, and a similar piece of vandalism has been performed on the notes below the final bar on the last page. Nonetheless, it is possible to decipher the words 'Co. Roscommon' and 'finished' and 'April'. Since there is no evidence from Moeran's life that locates him in Roscommon in April in any year other than 1918, it is reasonable to conclude that he composed this quartet movement during his posting to Boyle between January and April 1918. The circumstances of the composition of the second movement, together with the presentation (or 'concoction') of the two movements as a single work, will be examined in Chapter 19.

The movement is cast in what may be regarded as a conventional sonata form, with a repeated two subject-group exposition, a development section, a recapitulation and a brief coda. This uncomplicated structure ensures that the movement is undemanding in reception, with aural cues providing reference points for the sections. As the earliest surviving example of Moeran's string quartet writing, the movement is an important marker on the path of the composer's stylistic evolution. While there is no possibility of comparison with the works that it is presumed that he composed for his school string quartet and during his two years at the Royal College of Music, the maturity and sophistication of the instrumental writing indicates that Moeran's compositional technique was becoming more refined. This is the first of several compositions that most probably date from Moeran's posting to Ireland in 1918, and each exhibits a significant improvement in musicality and consistency over the few surviving works from two years earlier. Although the string quartet movement is relatively uncomplicated in the context of Moeran's entire oeuvre, it represents the most intricate construction he had attempted up to the spring of 1918 and,

---

9   After its publication, the manuscript was accessioned by the Royal College of Music on permanent loan: *Moeran String Quartet in E flat*, Royal College of Music Library MS 4985.

10   E. J. Moeran, *String Quartet in E flat*, (Novello, Sevenoaks, 1956), Introductory Note.

as such, may be regarded as the link between his juvenile compositions and the more advanced works that appeared during the next two years. The first subject is a mostly pentatonic, folksong-inspired tune played by the first violin, tracing an undulating melodic contour (music example 6). The second subject enters at bar 28 in the cello line (music example 7), but is transferred to the next instrument every four bars. This device, although far from original, holds the attention through the resulting timbral changes and demonstrates that Moeran was thinking carefully about his effects. Similarly, the periodic juxtaposition of *pizzicato* chords in the lower two instruments against a flowing violin line which implies rather than backwashes the harmonic rhythm reveals a discernment that can only be acquired through practice and experience. However, the movement includes none of the more advanced formal and harmonic sophistication that increasingly informed Moeran's style from the early 1920s onwards. Had it been composed late in Moeran's life, as other writers have suggested, it is unlikely that he could have avoided such inclusion, even as an attempt to mimic his work of thirty years earlier. The movement may therefore be confidently dated to April 1918.

Moeran's folksong collecting jaunts and his frequent journeys to and from Longford for his Masonic instruction may have exacerbated his injury, and a Medical Board Report, dated 22 May from the Officers' Hospital, 33 Upper Fitzwilliam Street in Dublin, records that he had been admitted to hospital at the beginning of the month:

> About two weeks after Medical Board of 23.3.18, the piece of metal in back began to cause pain. He was admitted into above hospital on 4 May 1918 ... The foreign body is to be removed from his neck tomorrow. His general health is very good.

The report also concluded that he was presently 100 per cent disabled. Clearly the pain caused by the bullet fragment was debilitating, and it may be presumed that the operation to remove it finally took place on 23 May. Moeran would have spent the next few weeks recuperating, and he returned home to Norfolk to facilitate this.[11] It is likely that about this time, he would have received the news of the death of his Uppingham friend Edward Brittain in Italy on 15 June, the result of having been shot by a sniper.[12]

The Moeran biographer is continually faced with a frustrating shortage of surviving manuscript material from the composer's early life. That Moeran composed a great deal of juvenilia is not in question, since he later admitted to having disposed of it, so it is reasonable to assert that between 1912 and his first acknowledged works dating from the early 1920s, he composed much that has been lost. Thus, it is implausible to suggest that his mature music from the early 1920s was not preceded by many other works that gradually extended and improved his compositional technique

[11] A newspaper report recorded that 'Lieut. Moeran (West Yorks. Regt.) [is] now at home recruiting his health, after being severely wounded', 'St Nicholas Men's Service', *The Yarmouth Independent*, (6 July 1918), 5.

[12] Moeran's other Uppingham friend Victor Richardson – the third member of the 'Three Musketeers' group – had also died in early June 1917 from injuries received at the Battle of Arras.

Music example 6. String Quartet in E flat, first movement: first subject

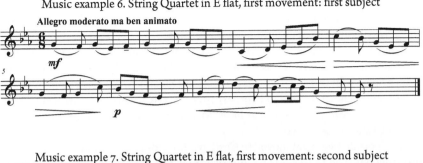

Music example 7. String Quartet in E flat, first movement: second subject

and facility. Another extant work for which the hitherto accepted dating may be incorrect is the symphonic impression *In the Mountain Country*. This composition was originally titled *Cushinsheeaun*, and while it was first performed in 1921, it was probably begun and possibly even completed in first draft during the period when Moeran's unit was based at Castlebar in County Mayo in July and August 1918. The main evidence for this suggestion is provided by Moeran himself in a letter he wrote to Aloys Fleischmann dated 10 February 1937: 'I wrote a work on an Irish landscape subject some years ago; it is called *In the Mountain Country* and was the direct outcome of a stay in Co. Mayo.'[13]

The Norfolk Regiment moved to Castlebar towards the end of June, and Moeran probably returned to Ireland at about that time. His army medical record suggests that the 'stay in Co. Mayo' would have been the six-week period between the end of June and early August 1918, since – as was the case with his three months in County Roscommon – there is no evidence that he ever visited again in later life. Moeran had recovered from his operation, and his ability to travel about the countryside surrounding the barracks on his motorcycle would have been limited only by whatever military duties he was required to perform.

Cushinsheeaun is a townland a few miles to the south-west of Castlebar and is served by the Castlebar to Westport railway.[14] Although the area is now studded with recently built houses, when Moeran visited, it would have been in an area of moorland landscape, punctuated by lakes and tarns, woodland, rocky hills and occasional cottages or crofts. Taken together with Moeran's own assertion in his letter to Fleischmann, the suggestion that he spent some of his time at Castlebar working on an orchestral symphonic impression of the surrounding landscape is certainly persuasive. *In the Mountain Country* will be examined in more detail in the next chapter.

The Lake Island and *At a Horse Fair*

The prevalence of lakes, islands and village horse fairs in County Mayo and indeed many other parts of Ireland, also provides a convincing narrative for the creation of two of Moeran's early piano works, *The Lake Island* and *At a Horse Fair*.[15] Throughout his working life, Moeran's use of environment and location both as inspiration for and representation in his music was pervasive, and it is probable that, where a title has a specific connection, he did intend the music to be evocative. For example, the shimmering nature of the almost continuous triplet-quavers that run through *The Lake Island* could suggest the rippling surface of a small body of water, and the 'clip-clippety-clop' beat that occurs throughout *At a Horse Fair* is very convincing musical onomatopoeia: the result, perhaps, of Moeran's having come across such a fair during his motorcycle meanderings. While the published editions of the works assert that they were composed in 1919, *At a Horse Fair* was given its first

[13] A transcript of this letter was provided to the author by Dr Ruth Fleischmann.

[14] In ancient times, Ireland was split for administrative purposes into provinces, which were divided into counties, which were subdivided into baronies, and baronies were split up into townlands.

[15] *The Lake Island* and *At a Horse Fair* were published in 1921, together with the later *Autumn Woods*, as a set entitled *Three Piano Pieces*.

performance by its dedicatee, Archy Rosenthal, in London on 24 May 1919, and thus it must have been composed some time before that date. As will be shown in the next chapter, Moeran did spend time in Ireland during 1919, but the earliest he could have travelled there was July. Thus, *At a Horse Fair* must have been composed during Moeran's posting to Ireland between January and September 1918.

Both *The Lake Island* and *At a Horse Fair* reveal structural features indicating that Moeran, even at this early date in his composing career, thought very carefully about every aspect of his music. The pieces are each based on an identifiable folksong style melody but one that in performance is difficult to distinguish. In *The Lake Island*, this is because it is played slowly and, in performance, is liable to be submerged by the other activity. Indeed, Moeran emphasised notes in the left hand by *tenuto* markings, possibly to further disguise the melody. The music of the entire piece seems to derive from the three-note motif of the first quaver triplet. This motif and its three variations – retrograde, inversion and retrograde inversion – appears frequently in Moeran's compositions, either as the basis for a melody or dictating the harmonic foundation. In *The Lake Island*, it can be found in one form or another in almost every one of the forty-eight bars, and the piece contains examples of structural techniques that characterise Moeran's individual style, techniques that pervade his entire oeuvre (music example 8).

In *At a Horse Fair*, the extremely fast tempo continually propels the listener onwards. The piece is in the form of an extended variation on an eight-bar pentatonic melody that, after an introductory twelve bar section, is stated twice (music example 9). This melody does not appear again in its entirety, although fragments form the basis of the continually evolving variations that make up the remainder

Music example 8. *The Lake Island*: bars 1–12

Music example 9. *At a Horse Fair*: folksong-style melody

of the piece. Rhythmically, while a time signature of 3/4 persists throughout the piece, the juxtaposition of off-beat chords in the left-hand conveys what Rhoderick McNeill called, 'the impression of a simultaneous presentation of 3/4 and 2/4'.[16] However, a strong first beat throughout underpins the momentum. Harmonically, the piece is diatonic but with some early examples of Moeran's use of chord substitution, a technique he employed increasingly throughout his career.

At the beginning of July, Moeran travelled from Castlebar to Dublin for his next Medical Board Report. It states simply that the 'Operation wound [is] healed', and he was assessed as 'Fit for Home Service'. A few weeks later, Moeran's unit moved to Shanes Park Camp, Randalstown in County Antrim, and his final Medical Board Report assembled at the barracks on 5 September. It summarised his medical condition: 'He has improved very much since last appearance, [and] [h]e has completely recovered. General health excellent.' Moeran was classed as fit for general service, and he was directed to resume duty with his unit at Randalstown, and no more Medical Boards were convened. Finally, some sixteen months after the injury he sustained while attacking the German lines at Bullecourt, Moeran was again in full health and capable of fully resuming his role in the battalion.

It is worth noting the degree of care that Moeran received for what was undoubtedly a relatively minor wound. In comparison with countless other much more serious injuries that were being suffered by his fellow officers and men, Moeran's seems to have been hardly worth an immediate repatriation and the number of Medical Boards that he attended. Nonetheless, reading the reports in their entirety does suggest that Moeran received particularly favoured attention. While officers always did take precedence over lower ranks, even as an officer Moeran had especially good connections, and certainly the combination of his being an Old Uppinghamian, a prize-winning student of the Royal College of Music and a long-standing and valued member of the Oxford & Cambridge Musical Club, would have been to his

---

[16] McNeill, 26.

considerable advantage. Moeran's developing Masonic association would also have been an influencing factor that facilitated preferential treatment. As was the case with his exceptional election to membership of the musical club, the response to and treatment of Moeran's injury indicates the distinct possibility that, even at such a young age, he was regarded as special.

The battalion returned from Ireland in September or early October. With the end of the war approaching, it was clear that Moeran would not return to active service abroad, and he seems to have decided to join the Royal Air Force. When he enlisted in 1914, he had signed up for four years or the duration of the war, whichever was the longer period, and he was now into his fifth year of service. His military record indicates that he joined the No.1 School of Military Aeronautics in Reading on 14 October, and the record also provides a possible hint to Moeran's plans for his future after his imminent demobilisation. Under the section 'Occupation in Civil Life', he wrote 'Undergraduate at Clare College, Cambridge'. While it may have been his intention to go to Clare College once his army service was over, claiming that he was an undergraduate would seem to have been presumptuous.[17] On 11 November 1918, the Armistice was announced and the war was over, but this meant little for Moeran, and he continued his training for the Royal Air Force. He had maintained his membership of the musical club during the year, and on 21 November, he was back in London playing at the 433rd programme, once again featuring as the central item soloist in performances of *Poème* and *Enigme* from *Three Pieces* Op.52 by Scriabin and *Sylphides* from *Crépuscules* Op.56 by Florent Schmitt. On 5 December, Moeran participated in the 434th programme, accompanying Walter Ivimey in three of his own songs: *Looking Back, A Cradle-Song* and *The North-West, Canada*. While *Looking Back* and *The North-West, Canada* are now lost, *A Cradle-Song* was eventually re-titled *Mantle of Blue* and is a setting of the Padraic Colum poem beginning 'O, men from the fields', which was published in 1907 as part of the cycle *Wild Earth*.[18] In his centenary edition of the *Collected Solo Songs of E. J. Moeran, Vol.2*, John Talbot speculated that the song was composed 'pre-1920?' and its appearance on the musical club programme in December 1918 confirms this. Talbot noted that the manuscript of *Mantle of Blue* was discovered amongst the papers of singer George Parker, to whom Moeran dedicated some of his song settings during the 1930s.[19] Although it is quite simple, Moeran's setting contains characteristic features of his later music and thus demonstrates his growing compositional facility and sophistication. An aspect

[17] The truth of Moeran's association or otherwise with Clare College, Cambridge remains unknown. Exhaustive examination of the college archives has failed to uncover any reference to or mention of Moeran during the years 1912 to 1920.

[18] *Looking Back* and *The North-West, Canada* are both poems from the set *Songs of the Glens of Antrim* by Moira O'Neill, published in a collection around 1909. The settings of these two poems were probably composed during Moeran's few months in Ireland earlier in the year, while *A Cradle-Song*, due to its Christmas subject, may well have been composed during November or early December. It is also noteworthy that Moeran had spent a few weeks in County Antrim during the summer, and he may have gained a familiarity with its distinctive landscape.

[19] John Talbot, *E. J. Moeran, Centenary Edition, Collected Solo Songs, Vol. 2*, (Thames Publishing, London 1994), 66.

of Moeran's compositional style that was apparent throughout his career was his willingness to re-use ideas. There is a section in the piano piece *Stalham River*, composed in 1921, that bears a striking aural resemblence to part of *Mantle of Blue*. There are numerous such examples to be found in Moeran's music where a basic familiarity with his oeuvre is sufficient to recognise apparent repetitions and material re-use, but where a closer examination generally reveals that, while the underlying ideas may be similar, the details can be quite different. However, the adaptation and re-cycling of musical ideas and features is part of what identifies a composer's individual style, and to suggest that this was exceptional for Moeran is surely unreasonable.

Moeran completed the initial four-week training period at the School of Aeronautics, and his military record shows that he was 'struck off the strength of the school' on 4 December, and that he was ordered to report to the 3rd Reserve Battalion of the Norfolk Regiment at Felixstowe to resume military duty. Moeran would probably have spent Christmas with his parents at home in Bacton, and he would have prepared to return to the Norfolk Regiment early in the New Year. In early January, the orders for him to rejoin his battalion were cancelled, and he was disembodied from the Territorial Force as of 8 January 1919. His Medical Category was given as A1, and his military service was over. The next part of his life was about to begin.

PART 3

RISE AND FALL

8

The Establishment of a Composer
(1919–1920)

There are no contemporary letters, diaries or personal recollections that could indicate Moeran's state of mind as he was faced with the task of re-adjusting to civilian life, and the biographer must again resort to reasonable speculation. Moeran had spent the previous four and a half years in the army, participating in the hitherto most significant and destructive event in human history. He had witnessed death and injury as a matter of course on a scale unimaginable to those fortunate enough to be living one hundred years later. Almost all his Uppingham friends and many of his Royal College of Music classmates and colleagues had been killed, and the obvious question is whether these experiences had led to some form of post traumatic stress disorder. It is tempting to assert that this must have been the case. Although Moeran's early war years were spent safely in Norfolk, they were punctuated by news of the deaths of his friends, and when he eventually went into action in France, he saw friends and colleagues being killed or injured alongside him, and he was himself shot at and wounded under the worst circumstances of a poorly planned and ineptly executed large-scale military operation.

Much of Moeran's life since September 1914 had been circumscribed by his military service, with his daily activities constrained within a rigid framework of army discipline, and this had been removed abruptly. In 1919, there was no training or counselling for ex-soldiers in how to adapt to civilian life: men were just expected to return home and get on with it. All that can be suggested in Moeran's case is that the finality of having been discharged from the army may have established a boundary behind which his wartime experiences could be confined, providing the possibility of disconnecting that life from whatever was to come. It is probable that he initially found himself with some sense of lacking in purpose, and it is apparent that music, as it would be on so many occasions throughout his life, was the familiar domain to which he resorted. A brief item in the *Musical Times* reported that a concert took place in London on 10 May: 'Two new Violin Sonatas, by E. J. Moeran and Miss Mary Barber, were performed at Wigmore Hall … by M. Edgardo Guerra, accompanied by the composer, on the occasion of a joint recital with M. José de Moraes (vocalist).'[1] Guerra had entered the Royal College of Music alongside Moeran in September 1912 and it is possible he was the dedicatee of the sonata. The recital was reviewed later in *The Musical Standard*: 'A first performance of a sonata for violin

---

[1]   'London Concerts', *The Musical Times*, Vol. 60. No. 916 (Jun. 1, 1919), 306.

and pianoforte in one movement by E. J. Moeran (with the composer at the piano) introduced one to a work of optimistic but fragmentary character.'[2] The reviewer's comment that the sonata movement had an 'optimistic but fragmentary character' conveys little, other than to support the assertion that Moeran was endeavouring to move on. However, the most significant aspect of this concert is that it was the first fully public performance of a work by Moeran. Although several of his songs had been presented at the musical club during the previous year, the audiences had been limited to club members and guests. The 10 May Wigmore Hall recital was Moeran's first exposure to the London musical public. Two weeks later, pianist and dedicatee Archy Rosenthal gave the second public performance of a work by Moeran, when he included *At a Horse Fair* in a recital at the Aeolian Hall.[3]

The 1919 Uppingham Old Boys' Day took place on 19 and 20 June, and Moeran, together with more than 250 other former pupils, travelled to the school for the two-day event.[4] This reunion was the first that had been arranged since 1914, and it was enormously symbolic in the post-war journey of a school that had more than 450 names in its memorial book. Of the 112 pupils who entered the school along-side Moeran in 1908, 30 had died on active service. There were between 110 and 120 new pupils each academic year, and this statistic of around 25 per cent killed in action seems to have been consistent across all entry years between 1903 and 1913, corresponding to an age range in service of between 18 and 32.[5] The list of attendees at the reunion included Moeran's violinist friend Christopher Whitehead, who was the only other survivor of the group of friends that had passed so many happy hours playing and studying music together. It was probably the first time they had met since Moeran left the school some seven years earlier, and their conversation must surely have touched on the missing members of their string quartet. The reunion would have given rise to bitter-sweet moments, not only for Moeran and Whitehead, but also for many of the former pupils, all of whom would have had friends whose absence was keenly felt. Whether it provided catharsis for Moeran, or, indeed, exacerbated his feeling of loss is not clear. It is likely that the most enduring legacy of Moeran's school experiences was the effect of the deaths of those who had become his closest friends. If it may be suggested that Moeran had been happy during his years at Uppingham, then it may also be asserted that part of the reason for that happiness was the development of friendships with boys who shared his love for music, with whose companionship he felt comfortable and whose approaches to life were compatible with his own. The loss of so many of these friends so soon after cannot have been anything but devastating for Moeran, and it may have left an emptiness in his life from which it is possible that he never fully recovered.

The evidence from *Moeran's Last Notebook* indicating that the composer visited Ireland between late July and early September 1919 was presented in the previous

2   *The Musical Standard*, (24 May 1919), 181.

3   The concert took place on 24 May 1919 and was reviewed in *The Athenæum*.

4   'Old Boys 1919', *Uppingham School Magazine*, Vol. 57, No. 450, (July 1919), 154–158.

5   See Timothy Halstead, 'The First World War and Public School Ethos: The Case of Uppingham School', *War & Society*, Vol. 34, No. 3 (2015).

chapter, and it may be wondered why he went and what he was doing there. The Irish War of Independence had been raging for some months, and parts of the country were dangerous territory, particularly for Englishmen – and especially so for former officers of the British Army – so casual travel for holiday or to visit relatives would seem to have been unlikely. It is also unlikely, given the dangers of travelling alone in rural parts of the country, that Moeran's visit was motivated solely by a desire to seek compositional inspiration in the countryside and the Irish folk music with which he had become familiar the previous year. He must have been aware of the political situation, and he would have realised that by visiting Ireland, he would be travelling to a dangerous region. Therefore, it must be supposed that he did this deliberately and after due consideration of the risks he would be taking and with the possible intention of participating in some way in what was taking place. If, as suggested in the previous chapter, Moeran had become involved with the Nationalist movement in 1918, then he must have had some sympathy with their aims, and amongst these was safeguarding of the identity of the country. He may have idealised and romanticised the movement into a force acting for the protection of Irish culture, thus prompting him to become involved. His passion for folksong collecting and preservation would have resonated with Nationalist aspirations, and it could have provided common ground that enabled other aspects of his life – his former army officer status for example – to have been overlooked. The undoubted propagandist and rebellion-inspiring power of Irish folk music was well understood, and the underpinning of the Nationalist struggle by what was regarded as indigenous song (and dance) was an essential part of the movement. Amongst the witness statements recorded by the Irish Bureau of Military History during the 1940s and 1950s there are numerous references to the deployment of music as a focusing force:

> Scarcely a Sunday passed through the Summer and Autumn of 1915 that there was not a muster of Volunteers for some parade, exercise, or to attend a football match or *aeriocht*. Generally, these were followed by a *ceili* in Swords, Lusk, St Margaret's or somewhere ... we sang and danced all night to the music of a lone violin ... The rebel songs of these gatherings had more than a little to do with the fostering of a rebel spirit in those who listened to them ... It has become a commonplace saying that 'poetry and music appeals to the Irish temperament' and no doubt that is so ... music and poetry is an attempt to express our dominant feelings.[6]

The effect of folksong and music on the local population would have been familiar to Moeran from his convivial experiences in the public houses of Norfolk and in the bars of Roscommon and Mayo the previous year. It is easy to imagine that the young composer – perhaps consumed with bitterness at the recent senseless loss of his musician friends – would find solace and purpose in the company of those that he believed shared his passion for the music of the people.

Thus, a theory may be advanced that in July 1919, Moeran travelled to the west of Ireland, perhaps ostensibly to visit relatives in Galway, but in reality to renew his contacts with those members of the Nationalist or Republican movements whom

---

[6]   Bureau of Military History (*Buro Staire Mileata*) 1913–1921, Witness Statement WS.1043 (Colonel Joseph V. Lawless) *National Activities, North Co. Dublin, 1911–1922,* 32–34.

he had met the previous summer and to contribute to what he may idealistically have seen as a fine cause, by collecting and recording the folksong from rural parts of the country. The evidence provided by the Trinity College notebook suggests that Moeran had some success with this endeavour. Nonetheless, after his return to England in mid-September 1919, it seems that he did not visit Ireland again for more than fifteen years, and this extended absence requires a convincing rationalisation. The records of the musical club confirm that Moeran paid his 1919 London resident subscription in person on 25 September. However, subscriptions were normally due by the end of the first quarter, and the fact that Moeran had not paid his on time suggests that he had not intended to remain a member during that year. Since membership had been a key feature of his life for the previous six years, only an expectation of his not being present in London would have been sufficient reason for him to allow this to lapse, and this would be consistent with his having planned to spend an extended period in Ireland during 1919. Thus, the paying of the Town subscription in September indicates that now he was back in London, he intended to remain there.[7]

Moeran's return to England after no more than a few weeks in Ireland seems to have been precipitous, and it may be speculated that this was occasioned by his having encountered difficulties. If he had been attempting to pass himself off as a local, his cover may have been blown – so to speak – or it may be that although he had been honest about his English connections, as conditions deteriorated these were no longer acceptable to his Nationalist friends and acquaintances. It is also possible that he eventually realised for himself that violence had become an integral pillar of the Nationalist cause, and he decided – or was persuaded by his family – that he should no longer be a part of it. While other conjectures that would both explain Moeran's 1919 visit to Ireland and account for his subsequent absence from the country for the next fifteen years are possible, the author has been unable to devise an alternative that adequately accommodates all the evidence. In particular, it is hardly conceivable that Moeran was not fully cognisant of the political and military situation in Ireland in the summer of 1919 and of the consequent risks that going there and travelling about would pose for someone in his position. When his undeniable Irish Republican Army associations are also taken into account,[8] the probability that Moeran had some involvement with the Nationalist movement becomes very high, and the fact that he stayed away from Ireland for the next fifteen years adds credibility to the notion that he ultimately had to extricate himself – or to be extricated – from a difficult or dangerous set of circumstances. Had he simply travelled to Ireland for a two-month holiday or expedition purely to collect folksongs, there

---

7   When the Oxford & Cambridge Musical Club was established in 1899, two categories or memberships were defined: Town and Country. A Town member was defined as one whose permanent residence was within twelve miles of Charing Cross or who had his place of business or regular occupation within four miles of Charing Cross. Originally, Country members were everybody else, although additional membership categories were introduced over the years to cater for those living in Scotland or abroad.

8   See Chapter 14.

is no reason why such visits would not have been repeated periodically during the years that followed.

By mid-September, Moeran's romantic Irish adventure – if such it had been – was over, and he was forced to reassess his immediate future. Perhaps as an incentive and with the condition of his remaining in London indefinitely, his mother established a regular maintenance allowance for her son that liberated him from the constraints of having to earn a living.[9] As far as can be determined, the conditions of this private income were simply that he was to spend his time composing, with no restriction on the style or quantity of music that might be expected, and it is reasonable to assume that additional sums were available where required for the promotion of his music. Moeran made use of his financial independence to establish himself centrally in the musical life of London and gain an advantage over his fellow young composers whose time was more restricted. He was a member of a generation of artistic talent, born around the turn of the century, who embraced a cultural freedom that was per-haps due in part to the changes brought about by the social upheaval consequent upon the four-year global conflagration. Moeran became part of the creative and artistic milieu that formed during the years immediately following the end of the First World War, and he joined a social tumult of parties, concerts, recitals, read-ings and gatherings, employing what would now be called networking. He knew people – from his time at Uppingham, the Royal College of Music and particularly from his membership of the musical club – and the people that he knew, themselves knew people. In a short space of time, Moeran's circle encompassed many of the prominent people in the artistic and creative world of 1920s London, names that are now redolent of the period, such as Augustus John, D. H. Lawrence, Lady Ottoline Morrell, Herbert Hughes, Arnold Bax, Jack Lindsay and the Sitwells.

On his return to London, Moeran had temporarily taken rooms at 10 Victoria Grove, W8, a terraced mansion in Kensington, but after a few weeks, he moved to a flat in the house of novelist and biographer Catherine Carswell at 110 Heath Street, Hampstead.[10] That Moeran knew Catherine Carswell is significant for an apprecia-tion of how he conducted his life in London. A common thread that emerges from biographical writing about the composer – both during his life and since his death – is that he exuded a personal magnetism that many people found irresistible. This is particularly evident in Lionel Hill's account of his friendship with Moeran, in the ease with which he gained membership of the Oxford & Cambridge Musical Club and in Sir Arnold Bax's account of him as being 'as charming and as good-look-ing a young officer as one could hope to meet'.[11] Whether Moeran was aware of

---

9 According to Maurice Walter Knott in his article *The Moeran-Coetmore-Knott Connection* (Talbot (2009), 16), the value of this allowance was £10 per week, which would certainly have been sufficient to maintain the lifestyle evinced by Moeran during the 1920s and 1930s.

10 This flat was occupied a few years later by D. H. Lawrence and his wife Frieda. 110 Heath Street, Hampstead features in several biographies of creative and artistic personalities of 1920s London including painter Benjamin Nicholson. In 2020, the address is still an artistic studio.

11 Sir Arnold Bax, 'E. J. Moeran: 1894–1950', *Music & Letters*, Vol. 32, No. 2 (April 1951), 125.

and made deliberate use of his attraction is unknown, but its effect was to his considerable advantage. The social life of the Carswells would have provided Moeran with opportunities to charm any number of important and influential members of London literary, musical and artistic circles, and his rapid progression as an increasingly acclaimed composer was undoubtedly facilitated by these connections.

Autumn Woods

It is probable that several compositions were in progress by the time of Moeran's move to Hampstead. While the piano piece *Autumn Woods* was published in 1921 as the central item in the set *Three Piano Pieces*, its distinctiveness strongly indicates that it was not composed contemporaneously with the other two pieces: *The Lake Island* and *At a Horse Fair*, both of which date from the late spring/early summer of 1918. Moreover, the more advanced harmonic complexity of *Autumn Woods* indicates a progression of musical imagination from each of the works that preceded it. Nevertheless, the style of the piece owes a considerable debt to the piano music of John Ireland, to the extent that *Autumn Woods* could easily be mistaken for a work by the older composer. Although at the end of 1919, much of Ireland's piano music was still to be composed, enough had been published to have enabled Moeran to absorb the older composer's harmonic and rhythmic ingenuity. The evidence for a composition date for *Autumn Woods* is the title itself, and Moeran's address in Hampstead during the autumn of 1919 would have provided him with ample opportunity to be inspired through afternoon walks in the ancient woodlands on Hampstead Heath.

Ludlow Town

Moeran also returned to Housman's *A Shropshire Lad* and selected four more poems from the collection to set in a cycle that he called *Ludlow Town*. Although it had been more than three years since his previous venture into the emotionally perilous territory of Housman's imagination and Moeran may still have been mourning Roland Perceval Garrod, the passage of time and his Irish adventure would inevitably have tempered the rawness of his loss – or even replaced it with more recent loss – and the selection of texts is worth some consideration. 'When Smoke Stood Up from Ludlow' and 'Farewell to barn and stack and tree' each have murderous violence as their premise, and in neither is a motive explicitly stated. Could this have resonated with Moeran in the sense of his desire to inflict revenge on those responsible for his loss? The text of 'Say, Lad, Have You Things to Do?' suggests that the time for action is now; if it is delayed it will be too late. Again, Moeran may have found that this struck a personal chord. He had spent some of the previous year in an ultimately purposeless adventure, and it was time to break from the past and apply himself to his own destiny. 'The Lads in their Hundreds' could easily be interpreted as a metaphor for the hundreds of 'lads' who had been with Moeran at Uppingham, many of whom would 'never be old'.

The word-painting in 'When Smoke Stood Up from Ludlow' is particularly striking. The focus of the text is an observation by Fate – in the form of a blackbird – on the pointlessness of the protagonist's existence. The British Library manuscript of this song bears the title 'The Blackbird', indicating Moeran's appreciation of the importance of the character. His strophic setting of the six-stanza poem takes the form AABCAB with a contrasting tune for the critical fourth stanza. The opening verse presents an early morning rural landscape with the smoke from the town rising and combining with the mist from the river as the ploughman works his team of horses. It is set to an undulating folksong-like melody, accompanied by a principally semi-breve and minim chordal texture that emphasises the slowness of the scene. In the second stanza, the ploughman sees a blackbird in the coppice. While the text is set to the same melody as the first stanza – with slight rhythmic variations as demanded by the text – the rhythm of the accompaniment becomes more agitated (music example 10).

In the third stanza, the blackbird replies to the whistling of the ploughman and seemingly points out the futility of his existence: 'Lie down, lie down young yeoman; | What use to rise and rise?' The setting of the fourth stanza presents the plough-man's annoyance with the blackbird as he picks up a stone and throws it, killing the bird outright. The rhythm of the accompaniment doubles to quavers, accelerating to a *sforzando* flourish as the stone is thrown. A mournful second inversion E flat minor seventh chord underpins 'Then the bird was still'. In the final two verses, the plough-man muses on the blackbird's message but remains uncertain of his purpose. This is reflected in the accompaniment as the tonality fluctuates and ends on an ambigu-ous A sixth or F♯ minor seventh chord. 'When Smoke Stood Up from Ludlow' also features the first inclusion of a stylistic device of which Moeran made extensive use throughout his later song-composing career. At key moments in the text – such as the final word of a verse, or of the entire song – the vocal line is set against a rest in

Music example 10. *Three Songs from Ludlow Town*,
'When Smoke Stood Up from Ludlow': bars 14–21

Music example 11. *Three Songs from Ludlow Town,*
'When Smoke Stood Up from Ludlow': bars 62–66

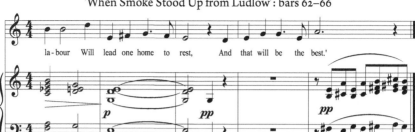

the piano. The same device is used at the end of each of the other three songs in the set (music example 11).

'Farewell to barn and stack and tree' is a dramatic setting of one of the most violent of the poems in the *Shropshire Lad* collection. The manuscript in the Royal College of Music bears the original title 'A Farewell'. The protagonist bids farewell to his friend Terence as he leaves his familiar environment for ever, having brutally murdered his brother: 'And Maurice amongst the hay lies still | And my knife is in his side.' The poet provided no reason for the deed. Could this text have resonated with Moeran's Irish adventure the previous year? As with the murderer in the poem, he suddenly had to leave what had become a familiar location. Since it is unlikely that the truth about Moeran's months in Ireland in 1919 will ever be known, it is fertile ground for speculation. Could he even have participated in Nationalist violence? As a recent soldier from the First World War who charged the German lines more than once, his ability and determination to kill fellow human beings in pursuit of a cause in which he believed is not in any doubt. Moreover, his extended advanced weapons training suggests that he was highly capable and may even have been regarded as an asset by his Nationalist friends. Thus, while there is no direct evidence for Moeran having been involved practically in violent actions, the possibility cannot be dismissed.

Moeran omitted the fourth and fifth stanzas of the poem. His textual sensitivity was questioned earlier when he left out a key verse in his setting of *The North Sea Ground* to balance the musical requirements. However, in 'Farewell to barn and stack and tree', the poem reads consistently without these verses, which are additional commentary on the protagonist's intention to leave the area. The form of the song is AABA. The violence and its consequences are aptly illustrated by the aggressive arpeggiated accompaniment. The declamation of the murder is underpinned by an C minor seventh chord with an added F flat that provides a suitable jarring effect. The third stanza is a contrasting, more lyrical, musing on the protagonist's mother, unaware of the dreadful events and that by 'Tonight she'll be alone'. The accompaniment changes to sequences of first and second inversion crotchet chords, moving through keys increasingly remote from the underlying C minor. While the violence returns briefly for the final verse, a sequence of minim added note chords highlights the protagonist departing: 'And long will stand the empty plate, | And dinner will be cold.'

'Say, lad, have you things to do' is a three-verse through-composed setting of poem 24 in the Housman set. The text is a reflection on the necessity to seize the day. The protagonist is offering his help now because by tomorrow, it may be too late. The words are set in a declamatory style, reminiscent of 'Westward on the High-Hilled Plains' from *Four Songs from 'A Shropshire Lad'*. It is in this setting that the harmonic influences of John Ireland and, to a lesser extent Roger Quilter, are most apparent. Moeran's familiarity with Ireland's piano music has already been mentioned, but Quilter's songs featured regularly on the recital programmes of the musical club, and Moeran later developed a friendship with Quilter. The accompaniment of the fourth line of verses 1 and 3 feature a stylistic device that clearly derives from the styles of Ireland and Quilter and which recurs in Moeran's oeuvre (music example 12).

'The Lads in their Hundreds', originally titled 'Ludlow Fair', is a strophic, jig-like setting featuring a melody in folksong idiom, with lines one and two being pentatonic and lines three and four in Mixolydian mode. The effect is a convincing song that appropriately reflects the traditional nature of the text. A town fair is attended by the 'lads' from the surrounding villages and farms, and they come in all types: 'And many to count are the stalwart, and many the brave, | And many the handsome of face and the handsome of heart,' and for all reasons: 'The lads for the girls and the lads for the liquor are there.' What they have in common is that many will die before their time. As the setting is strophic, the contrast in the sense of the verses is provided by the varying accompaniment. The most powerful trope is the last line, and Moeran provided a solemn chordal passage, leading to an ambivalent *pianissimo* ending that reflects the seemingly prophetic nature of the text (music example 13).[12]

The harmonic vocabulary and rhythmic complexities of *Ludlow Town* confirm that Moeran had advanced significantly since the composition of the *Four Songs*

Music example 12. *Three Songs from Ludlow Town,*
'Say, Lad, Have You Things to Do?': bars 6–8

---

[12] While *A Shropshire Lad* was written and published during the 1890s at a time when young British 'lads' were dying regularly in wars and conflicts all over the Empire, the mass casualties of the Second Boer War (1899–1902) and the First World War lend an even greater impact to the regret for wasted lives apparent in many of the poems.

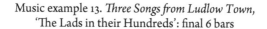

Music example 13. *Three Songs from Ludlow Town*,
'The Lads in their Hundreds': final 6 bars

from 'A Shropshire Lad'. The earlier cycle betrayed the composer's origins as a pianist in that the vocal lines generally give the impression of being afterthoughts, whereas in *Ludlow Town* the piano part is a genuine accompaniment. The compositional effort has incorporated both aspects with equal but focused importance. The set is more assured structurally and bears repeated listening more readily than does *Four Songs from 'A Shropshire Lad'*. Critical response was very favourable. *The Musical Times* review of the published edition asserted that the songs stood 'well even beside *On Wenlock Edge*' and that the set 'places Mr Moeran at once among the pick of our song-writers'.[13] The music critic of the *Sheffield Daily Telegraph*, also reviewing the published edition, singled out 'Farewell to barn and stack and tree' in which it was suggested that 'Mr Moeran touches real greatness.'[14] Writing in *The Music Bulletin*, Dennis Arundell heaped enthusiastic praise on the songs:

> E. J. Moeran's setting of four poems from *A Shropshire Lad* called *Ludlow Town*, show that these poems have not yet had their musical possibilities exhausted ... These new settings are excellent, original without being extraordinary, admirable with regard to verbal accentuation and interpretation of the poems, and most pleasing to sing ... *When smoke stood up from Ludlow* is perfect, *Farewell to barn and stack and tree* is uncannily dramatic, *Say lad, have you things to do?* is impres-

---

[13] 'New Music – Oxford University Press', *The Musical Times*, Vol. 66, No. 983, (January 1925), 46.

[14] 'Musical Topics – Oxford Press Songs', *Sheffield Daily Telegraph*, (9 March 1925), 6.

sively direct, and the jolly *The lads in their hundreds* is splendid. I do not apologise for being so fulsome; it is so seldom that the chance occurs that it is a great joy to find an opportunity.[15]

The songs of *Ludlow Town* were first performed informally at the musical club in 1920, although the first public performance of the complete cycle did not take place until a few years later. It is possible to criticise *Ludlow Town* as failing to stand as a coherent cycle. Trevor Hold, for example, asserted that 'there is no attempt to unify the poems into a true song-cycle, either by thematic cross-reference, or by tonal connections',[16] and some of the journal reviews also suggested that the songs were better as individual items. While agreeing that the set does not necessarily link well as a cycle, the author concurs with Arundell in his assessment of the quality of the songs. They indicate an advance in their composer's ability to create appropriate word settings – in appreciation of the sense of the text – and sympathetic piano accompaniments. *Ludlow Town* marks the beginning of Moeran's significant career as a composer of songs.

1920

Moeran paid his three guineas subscription for the musical club on 9 January, and his regular participation in the fortnightly *soirées* resumed on 1 April. This recital followed the established format by beginning and ending with a chamber music work, enclosing a central solo item and two sets of songs. The first item of the programme was the Pianoforte Trio in A minor by Tchaikovsky, in which Moeran took the piano part, with the violin part being played by Walter Wilson Cobbett and the cello part played by Harold Thomas Triggs. Moeran also acted as accompanist for the two vocal sets, the first comprising songs by Debussy and Reynaldo Hahn and the second featuring songs by Purcell, A.F. Jones, Roger Quilter and Arthur Somervell. Moeran and Triggs completed the evening by playing the Grieg Cello Sonata. Although most of the performing members of the musical club were amateur musicians, many professionals also regularly played, and the standard was high indeed; the participation of Walter Willson Cobbett in the programme being indicative of this. Cobbett was a talented violinist and had studied with Joseph Dando.[17] His enthusiasm for and dedication to chamber music would have ensured that the performances were as professional as possible. Moeran was again at the club on Saturday, 10 April attending a social event with his guests Lionel Jellinek and J. E. Norbury.[18]

[15] *The Music Bulletin*, Vol. VII, No.1, (January 1925), 23.

[16] Trevor Hold, *Parry to Finzi: Twenty English Song Composers*, (The Boydell Press, Woodbridge, 2002), 376.

[17] Joseph Dando (1806–1894) was a violinist and viola player who, during the 1830s, inaugurated the first series of public chamber music concerts to be held in England. Walter Willson Cobbett (1847–1937) studied under Dando in the 1850s and absorbed his teacher's passionate enthusiasm for chamber music.

[18] Lionel Jellinek had been a contemporary of Moeran's at Uppingham and later became a judge. Moeran supported Jellinek's election to membership of the Oxford & Cambridge

Theme and Variations in F minor

Moeran performed Ravel's *Le Tombeau de Couperin* at a musical club recital on 15 April. While the *première* of this suite had been given in Paris the previous year by Marguerite Long, the first British performance was given by Emile Bosquet in a concert of music by Ravel at the Wigmore Hall on 29 October 1919, at which Moeran would almost certainly have been present. The technical difficulty presented by the suite – most especially the dramatic *Toccata* – indicates the level of Moeran's pianistic ability. The very fact of his selecting it for performance in an environment where only the highest standards were acceptable speaks volumes for his self-confidence. On 27 May, Moeran gave the first performance at the musical club of his recently composed Theme and Variations in F minor. This was his most extended work to date, lasting some fifteen minutes in performance, and it demonstrates the advances that he had made during the six months or so since he returned from Ireland. It comprises a 24-bar Dorian mode theme that bears a strong resemblance to the tune he had composed for his setting of 'When I Came Last to Ludlow' as part of the *Four Songs from 'A Shropshire Lad'* from 1916. Again Moeran, whether consciously or unconsciously, re-used and adapted material for a new purpose. There is also a quotation from John Ireland's *The Holy Boy* in the fifth variation: *Vivace*. The first public performance was given by Dorothea Vincent at a Wigmore Hall recital in October 1921, and it received a distinctly oblique review by the music correspondent of *The Times*:

> We did not make out Mr Moeran's music. It seemed as if it demanded the orchestra; for when the seven diatonic notes are sounded together it is obvious that some of them are substantive and intended, therefore, to be louder than others which are passing notes, and this distinction is easy for the orchestra, but difficult for fingers to make. Still, that the effect was a little 'muddy' did not seem to be any fault of the player; on the contrary, one was surprised that it came out as clearly as it did.[19]

Moeran's music was again included in a musical club recital on 24 June, when he accompanied W. T. Ivimey singing *A Cradle Song* and *A Dream of Death* – a setting of a poem by Yeats – and the first performances of the Norfolk folksong arrangements 'The Bold Richard', 'The Captain's Apprentice' and 'The Pressgang'. While 'The Bold Richard' and 'The Pressgang' arrangements were included in the *Six Norfolk Folksongs* collection published in 1924, 'The Captain's Apprentice' is no longer extant.

In July, Moeran's Royal College of Music enrolment was officially terminated. His studies had been suspended for the duration of the war in the summer of 1914, and it is probable that there was a time limit for returning. He may eventually have

---

Musical Club on 7 April 1921, the record of which indicates that he had attended Lincoln College, Oxford and was a viola player. During the 1920s, Jellinek became a close friend of Philip Heseltine, and in later life he was a noted collector of violins. The address provided by Jellinek was near to Moeran's home address of 110 Heath Street, Hampstead.

[19] 'Miss Dorothea Vincent's Recital', *The Times*, issue 42852, (15 October 1921), 8.

informed the college that he would not be resuming his enrolment, and his leaving Testamur was issued dated 30 July 1920. This was a certificate summarising his examination results for the period October 1912 to July 1914. Moeran achieved Grade III, Class 1 for pianoforte, Grade IV, Class 3* for composition, Grade V for harmony and Grade V for counterpoint.[20] While he may have been disappointed with his piano and composition grades – notwithstanding that these related to his studies in 1912 to 1914 – his achievements in harmony and counterpoint placed him in the top 10 per cent of students and underlined his technical competence.

In the summer, Moeran travelled with artist Robert Gibbings on a motorcycle tour of France and Spain. Gibbings wrote about the trip in his book *Coming Down the Wye*:

> Once upon a time I travelled to the Pyrenees with E. J. Moeran, in the sidecar of his motor bike. He had recently composed his symphonic impression, *In the Mountain Country*, and no doubt crystallisations of this work were appearing constantly before his eyes … carrying him in harmonies from peak to peak, from waterfall to waterfall, and from sunlit mist to vaporous shadow.[21]

In 1946, Moeran recollected his and Gibbings' journey in a conversation with the society correspondent of the *Irish Independent*:

> Hearing from Gibbings, I am reminded of a story which composer Moeran told me last week in Kenmare. The two of them were travelling together to the Pyrenees, Gibbings in the sidecar of Moeran's motor bicycle. One very hot day, having traversed the Landes, Moeran was most anxious to reach Bordeaux in time for a good dinner. When racing over the cobblestoned country road his passenger suddenly began to splutter. Moeran at first tried to take no notice of possible delays until agonised screams made him realise that Gibbings' eighteen stones had sunk through the bottom of the sidecar and were being bumped over the cobblestones in no uncertain manner. Observed Moeran drily: 'We stayed in Bordeaux for several dinners until repairs had been effected – and healed.'[22]

Moeran and Gibbings each had ancestors that lived in Cork, and their fathers and grandfathers were Irish-Anglican clergymen. Moreover, they had similar experiences during the First World War. Gibbings had also received a bullet wound in the neck, which had led to his being invalided home. It is likely that once they had met – possibly at some artistic event in Hampstead – their shared experiences would have established a bond that led to friendship. The motorcycle tour with Gibbings must have taken place during August or September, since after his appearance at

---

[20] Students were graded from V (highest achievement) down to I, Grade III being regarded as the minimum professional standard. In practice, few students were awarded grades II or I. Within each grade, there were classes, designated 1 (highest) to 3, which could themselves be inflected by the addition of one or more stars. See David C. H. Wright, *The Royal College of Music and its Contexts – An Artistic and Social History*, (Cambridge University Press, Cambridge, 2019).

[21] Robert Gibbings, *Coming Down the Wye*, (Dent, London, 1947), 1–2.

[22] 'Laws of Gravity', *Irish Independent*, (21 January 1946), 4.

the musical club recital on 24 June, Moeran did not participate in another musical evening until late October.

In the Mountain Country

By his own admission, Moeran was profoundly affected by natural landscapes. Indeed, he asserted that his very ability to compose to his own satisfaction was dependent upon the appropriateness of his surroundings. Thus, environment was an essential factor, both in the sense of providing inspiration for his musical imagination and in ensuring a congenial ambience to facilitate concentration. While the second of those was to become more significant later in his composing career, the stimulus of landscapes was key to Moeran's creativity from his earliest years. While for most of his extant compositions, the titles were dictated either by the words being set or by the genre, for a small number of pieces the title has an environmental association and is possibly an indication of where the work was either composed or conceived.[23] However, in the case of the symphonic impression *In the Mountain Country* mentioned in the Gibbings quotation above, this consideration has been compromised. As shown in the previous chapter, the work was originally called *Cushinsheeaun*, and the post-completion re-titling to *In the Mountain Country* embodies a grandeur that the music perhaps fails to deliver when compared with other acknowledged mountain music, such as Richard Strauss's *An Alpine Symphony*, Delius' *Song of the High Hills*, or even Hamish MacCunn's *Land of the Mountain and the Flood*. While none of these works can literally describe mountainous vistas, the process of listener consent has established certain common musical characteristics that may conjure visions of cloudy, snow-covered Munro summits or alpine crests in all their magnificence. Although the topography of County Mayo does include mountains in the north and west of the county, the area to the south and west of Castlebar – which includes the Cushinsheeaun townland – is conspicuously lacking in anything more than rolling moorland.

The question as to what extent – or even whether – music can communicate anything objectively has challenged musicologists, philosophers and even theologians for centuries and is beyond the scope of this book to discuss in detail. While, as stated in the Introduction, the author generally inclines to the view attributed to Igor Stravinsky that if music appears to express anything beyond itself, this can only ever be an illusion, he nonetheless accepts that some music or musical devices have, by mutual agreement, come to represent aspects of human experience. It is evident that Moeran believed in the communicative power of his music – more than once he referred to certain works as being 'about' something – and his occasional descriptions of what he intended it to convey are helpful in clarifying the envisioned reception. In the case of *In the Mountain Country*, the listener experience intended by the composer could only be fulfilled with knowledge of its former title, and it is likely that few if any members of his 1920s audiences in London would

---

[23] The complete list of Moeran's works that bear a descriptive title is: *Fields at Harvest*, *The Lake Island*, *At a Horse Fair*, *Autumn Woods*, *In the Mountain Country*, *On a May Morning*, *Stalham River*, *Windmills*, *Lonely Waters*, *Bank Holiday*, *The White Mountain* and *Summer Valley*.

have either heard of Cushinsheeaun or had any idea where it was and what the surrounding landscape resembled. Moeran probably changed the title shortly before its first performance at the Royal College of Music Patrons' Fund Concert, having considered *Cushinsheeaun* to be too obscure for a London audience.[24] It is also possible that having made the decision to abandon Ireland the previous year, he wanted to remove the specific Irish association. Nevertheless, and irrespective of the retitling, the music remains that which Moeran composed in the rural landscape of Cushinsheeaun in Co. Mayo, and bearing this in mind when listening, it perhaps better achieves its composer's objective.

Although as an orchestral work *In the Mountain Country* is superseded both technically and musically by his rhapsodies and the Symphony in G minor, as Moeran's earliest surviving large-scale composition it warrants a detailed examination. One of the first observations that may be made about *In the Mountain Country* is that it is very competent to be the first orchestral composition by a composer whose mature works up to that point had apparently been some solo piano pieces, a few songs and a string quartet movement. In the list of Moeran's surviving compositions, *In the Mountain Country* stands out as an exception to such an extent that one is inevitably led to suppose that he must have worked on other orchestral or large ensemble compositions. Geoffrey Self observed that 'as a student work, its orchestral assurance is astonishing, showing itself in an adventurousness, a willingness to use open, spare textures, with little fail-safe doubling'.[25] While there is no doubt that the orchestration does owe a debt to both Sibelius and Ravel, its accomplishment is unmistakable, and as an early orchestral work by a young composer that had apparently little experience in the technique, it is remarkable. The instrumental contrast and combinations and the juxtaposition of various ensembles within and across orchestral families reveal a capacity for fine textural judgement: again, something that comes with practice, rather than appearing spontaneously or serendipitously. The work is in a ternary 'slow/fast/slow' form but one in which the conventional elements of sonata form – exposition, development and recapitulation – may be identified. As with many of Moeran's works, the underlying structure reveals much thought and careful attention to detail. The result is a generally satisfying 'impression' that was enthusiastically received by audiences at numerous performances both during the 1920s and 1930s and more recently in recordings made since the revival of the piece in the early 1990s.

The work opens with a timpani roll, which, if well-performed, emerges imperceptibly from silence to a moderate climax and then fades away. This is followed by a pentatonic, birdsong-like flourish by a solo clarinet, reminiscent of the more extended violin solo introduction in Vaughan Williams' *The Lark Ascending*. The composition date of *The Lark Ascending* is not known, but its first performance pre-dates that of *In the Mountain Country*. Although the two composers knew of each other's music through recitals at the musical club, and the club archives have

---

[24] There is evidence on the manuscript score that Moeran also considered using the title *Prelude for Orchestra*.

[25] Self, 33.

revealed that several of Vaughan William's compositions were first performed there before the recorded first public performances, there is no conclusive evidence to demonstrate an influence in either direction.

The first theme is stated *andante sostenuto* on low woodwind, with a clarinet and horn chordal accompaniment that hints at a D minor/A minor tonal disjointedness that is a feature of the entire work (music example 14). Moeran's use of unison bass clarinet and bassoon for the first part of his theme is inspired. Conventionally, tunes are played by higher register instruments, with an accompaniment spread across the lower register instruments. The darker texture of the two low reed instruments imparts here a sensation of emergence from shadow, which is enhanced when the clarinet takes over from the bassoon for the second half of the theme. During the next dozen or so bars, more instrumental layers are added – each stating a part of the theme and building up the orchestral texture – until the first full orchestral tension/release point is reached at bars 29–30. A short bridge passage played by muted brass leads into a contrasting middle section. This quadruples the tempo to a frantic *presto* with high woodwind and string flourishes entering *fugato* over a cross-rhythmic theme stated in the brass and low woodwind. The orchestration here is strongly reminiscent of Ravel, particularly the high woodwind and string oscillating triplet runs. At bar 99, the running triplet accompaniment transforms into a broad statement of the middle section theme, which builds to the main tension/release point at almost exactly two-thirds of the way though the work (both by bar count and running time).[26]

After a pause, the opening theme returns in variation and builds to a secondary tension/release point a few bars later. Occasional half-hearted instrumental flourishes provide brief recollections of the dynamism of the middle section as the piece tails off into silence with another almost imperceptible timpani roll. Thus, the symmetry of the work is realised. Although in performance *In the Mountain Country*

Music example 14. *In the Mountain Country*: bassoon/bass clarinet theme

---

[26] Moeran's use of proportions in his musical forms was a structural characteristic that can be observed throughout his oeuvre.

lasts just over seven minutes, it encompasses a wide range of orchestral textures produced through clever compositional techniques. In particular, the tossing to and fro of accompanying runs, off-beat timpani and cymbal punctuation and a breadth of dynamic markings, from *pppp* to *fff*. Sadly, no notes or sketches that Moeran may have made for *In the Mountain Country* have survived, so it is not possible to determine to what extent he experimented and revised. Given that he would have had no opportunity to listen to his composition being played before the rehearsals leading up to its first performance, the fact that it works so successfully as a short orchestral piece is a clear statement of technical refinement and creative flair. The impression conjured by *In the Mountain Country* could be that of a spring day in the moorlands of Cushinsheeaun, beginning with a sunrise and a gradual awakening of nature, continuing through a brisk morning as the wind picks up and occasional showers fall, through the middle of the afternoon as the sun breaks through the clouds to bathe the landscape in a warm glow, with sunset and twilight as the day ends. Moeran left no hint that such was his intention, but his music allows for and inspires such imagery, and since it was imagery that prompted him to create this music, such interpretation is surely as valid as any other.

Moeran was back at the musical club on Thursday 28 October, again taking a major role. He accompanied D. J. Wardley in a set of songs by Roger Quilter; he undertook the central, solo spot, performing the piano pieces *The Holy Boy* and *Fire of Spring* by John Ireland, followed by his own *At a Horse Fair*, and he again accompanied D. J. Wardley in songs by John Ireland and H. Walford Davies. Finally, he and Harold Triggs played the Delius Cello Sonata. This was Moeran's last performance at the club in 1920, and it rounded off a particularly fruitful year for the composer. In addition to the other works mentioned in this chapter, he had composed the songs *Spring Goeth All In White*, a setting of a poem by Robert Bridges and *Twilight*, a setting of a poem by John Masefield. However, it is probable that the known works represent only a part of his output for the year.

9

London
(1921–1922)

As 1920 ended, Moeran's journey from invalided war veteran and romantic Irish nationalist to established composer and artistic man-about-town was complete. While there was little possibility that he could forget his wartime experiences and the loss of so many of his friends and colleagues, he had undergone a renewal that had provided him with the possibility of looking forward. Although the previous few years may have left him unable to re-forge the kind of close friendships that characterised his time at Uppingham and the Royal College of Music, his natural charm and personal magnetism led to the construction of new and important relationships, most particularly through his Oxford & Cambridge Musical Club membership which was fundamental to his developing career as musician and composer and which facilitated his rise to prominence. The musical club was a unique institution in which the playing and enjoyment of music was of an importance equal to social interaction, whose membership comprised intelligent, educated and musically talented men, many of whom were in the professions and occupied senior positions in government, the law, academia and the colonial service.[1] Moeran's talent ensured that he was in constant demand as performer and accompanist, and he played and heard an extensive repertoire of solo performances, songs and chamber music, an experience that would have been difficult for him to gain elsewhere and which informed and shaped significantly his own compositional style. On 10 January, Moeran paid the Town rate subscription of four guineas for his continued membership of the club, establishing that he regarded London as his principal place of work and residence and that he intended to make full use of the club facilities.

Moeran's stylistic debt to other composers is a common theme of writings about him hitherto, and it cannot be doubted that he was influenced by the music that he heard and which resonated with his own tastes. However, there was one composer whose influence on Moeran was probably stronger than any other, and this was John Ireland. Exemplars for many of Moeran's stylistic characteristics abound in Ireland's work, most particularly in the piano music, which was the genre of Ireland's oeuvre with which Moeran would have been most familiar during his compositional

---

[1]   Amongst the members that Moeran would have known and with whom he would have associated were: Adrian Boult, Edward J. Dent, Lytton Strachey, Arthur Bliss, E. M. Forster, Arthur Eaglefield-Hull, Percy Scholes, Donald Tovey, Walter Willson Cobbett, Ralph Vaughan Williams, H. Selwyn Lloyd, William Henry Hadow, Thomas Dunhill and M. Compton Mackenzie.

adolescence. Moeran's discovery of Ireland was probably a performance of the unison voice and piano work *In Praise of Neptune* at the July 1912 Uppingham School Speech Day concert, in which Moeran played the accompaniment. Some stylistic aspects of this work, particularly the repeated dominant in the vocal line, the use of dominant pedal in the accompaniment and sparing use of secondary harmony, are apparent in Moeran's own early compositions, such as *The North Sea Ground* and the *Four Songs from 'A Shropshire Lad'*. The chiefly English Hymnal harmonic idiom of *In Praise of Neptune* owes a discernible debt to Ireland's teacher Stanford, and Moeran's acquisition and adaptation of this idiom parallels his own studies at the Royal College of Music during 1913 and 1914.

Ireland published more than a dozen piano works before 1920, and it is reasonable to suggest that Moeran would have played and been familiar with most of them. Five of Moeran's pre-1920 piano compositions are extant, and it is useful to compare these with contemporaneous Ireland piano works. What is evident is a tracking by Moeran of the older composer's evolving style, most especially in the development of harmonic variety. The increase in complexity from Ireland's early piano music – such as *Pastoral* and *A Sea Idyll* – to later works, for example, *London Pieces* (1917) and the Piano Sonata of 1919, finds a reflection in a similar harmonic intensification between Moeran's pre-1914 *Dance* and *Fields at Harvest* and his 1918 works *The Lake Island* and *At a Horse Fair*. However, in works composed from 1919 onwards, the range of Moeran's vocabulary clearly supersedes that of Ireland in the use of secondary, chromatic and added note harmony. This is particularly apparent in *Autumn Woods* (1919) and Theme and Variations (1920), when compared with Ireland's *Summer Evening* (1919) and *The Darkened Valley* (1920). Interestingly, a richer harmonic vocabulary – similar to that employed by Moeran – is apparent in works Ireland composed after 1920, such as *For Remembrance* and *Amberley Wild Brooks*. While for Moeran the music evidences a continuous evolution of the harmonic language of his earlier music, in the case of Ireland the change in harmonic vocabulary seems to be more abrupt, suggesting the possibility that he adopted some of Moeran's harmonic innovations. Since Moeran had, by the end of 1920, not yet published any music and there had been few performances, the mechanism for this can only have been a close personal relationship between the two composers that began in late 1920.

Moeran had first met John Ireland at the musical club. Although the older composer spent little time there, he attended recitals if any of his own music was on the programme, and he occasionally performed himself. Moeran admired Ireland sufficiently to approach him with a view to his receiving private lessons in composition. When the one-year lease on the flat at the Carswells' house in Hampstead expired towards the end of 1920, Moeran rented a mews apartment at 20 Glebe Place – just off the King's Road in Chelsea – a short walk from Ireland's studio in Gunter Grove. Since Moeran could have afforded any of a plethora of flats or lodgings anywhere in the west of London, the proximity to Ireland's studio was probably the reason behind choosing the address in Glebe Place. Although it is not known exactly when Moeran began his composition studies with Ireland, his relocation probably coincided with this, and thus it may reasonably be asserted that from late 1920 or early 1921, he was attending regular lessons. It is, perhaps, also significant that Moeran's opus list shows a substantial reduction in completed works during 1921 and early 1922. While there are fifteen surviving individual compositions that date from 1920, just five can be dated to the period January 1921 to June 1922. The discipline imposed by Ireland's teaching methods probably restricted Moeran's output.

The significantly higher profile enjoyed by Ireland in British music and the fifteen-year age gap between the composers has ensured that, hitherto, it has been assumed that Moeran was always the recipient of influential effect. However, the evidence provided by the dates of composition and harmonic characteristics of the piano works mentioned above, together with the knowledge of Ireland's concentrated exposure to Moeran's creative imagination enable this assumption to be challenged. While Ireland never acknowledged a stylistic debt to Moeran, he did admit to a close similarity: 'Moeran ... was one of my early pupils ... He developed an idiom very much like my own.'[2] In works composed from 1922 onwards, it becomes much more difficult to trace influential direction – at least in the piano music – such that by the mid-1930s, the two composers' styles were so similar that, for example, Moeran's *Berceuse* (from *Two Pieces*, 1933) could have been composed by Ireland, and Ireland's *The Cherry Tree* (from *Green Ways*, 1937) could be mistaken for a work composed by Moeran.

On 21 February, Moeran re-enrolled as a composition student at the Royal College of Music, having perhaps decided that formal instruction at the college would complement his private tuition with Ireland.[3] Nevertheless and perhaps preferring Ireland's individual teaching to that available at the college, he cancelled his registration after just five weeks. In an interview in 1950, Moeran spoke about his time studying with Ireland, and he gave an impression of how the tutoring process worked in practice:

> Ireland was a marvellous teacher and a good friend. It wasn't just a question of going to his studio for a few hours of lessons – he took a personal interest, and often I would go to him for tea and then continue with a lesson for the rest of the evening. He would even go to the extent of sending me home while an idea was still fresh in my mind, to rewrite and correct, and then, later in the same evening, I would go back to him.[4]

The most profound influence Ireland exerted on Moeran was the imbuing of a sense of the importance of detail. Throughout his later composing life, Moeran was intensely self-critical, and the creation of music eventually became a lengthy and laborious process. Each note or score marking had to be necessary and precisely notated. In 1931, Moeran wrote an appreciation of Ireland which clarifies this:

> [Ireland] has no use for padding in any form, and he does not consider a piece of work done with until the minutest detail has been scrutinised again, down to the

[2] John Longmire, *John Ireland – Portrait of a Friend*, (John Baker Ltd, London, 1969), 52.

[3] The composition teachers on the college staff in 1921 included Ralph Vaughan Williams, Thomas Dunhill and Cecil Armstrong Gibbs, but it is not known with whom Moeran studied.

[4] Quotation included in Senior (1950), 31.

last semiquaver rest and the smallest mark of phrasing and dynamics. 'What about that sforzando?' he will ask. 'Have you thought carefully about it?'[5]

Moeran's and Ireland's idioms nourished each other from the early 1920s to the point where their individualities can sometimes be difficult to differentiate. The principal distinction between the composers was the quantity of output. Ireland evidently composed and published far more than did Moeran, although Moeran's intense self-criticism (seemingly bestowed by Ireland) led to his rejecting much of his own work.

Ireland's sexual orientation is now understood, despite efforts that were made after his death to conceal his homosexuality. Thus, the inevitable question arises as to whether Moeran was more than just a student. Fiona Richards has asserted that despite his attraction to younger men, there is 'no direct evidence that Ireland ever had a close sexual relationship with a man or boy'.[6] However, given the illegality of such activities at the time, it is doubtful that such evidence could ever be found. Therefore, the exact nature of Moeran's friendship with Ireland can only be surmised. No correspondence between Moeran and Ireland has survived, and Moeran's name rarely appears in Ireland's letters or other writings. Richards has argued compellingly that Ireland's expression of his sexuality was largely confined to his music,[7] and it must therefore be presumed that, despite their lengthy periods alone together and the ambiguity that may be read into the recollections quoted above, there was little, if any, physical expression of intimacy between Moeran and Ireland. After their teacher-student relationship ended, there may have been some form of estrangement that led to the distancing evident from the apparent subsequent lack of communication, and this may argue for a former closeness beyond that of the student and teacher or of professional colleagues.[8] In September 1929, Ireland wrote somewhat slightingly about a performance of Moeran's revised Second Rhapsody for Orchestra in a letter to Alan Bush:

> Last night I went to the Prom to hear Moeran's piece ... From many points of view it was regrettable (the work & its performance, I mean). Moeran (very unwisely) conducted himself – & any alterations he may have made in the music or scoring are to the bad. It was most distressing.[9]

It is by no means impossible that Moeran heard about this and perhaps took umbrage. While Ireland wrote a couple of years later in July 1931 in a more amicable tone: 'I met Moeran a few weeks ago, he can get about well on crutches, he looks as

---

5   E. J. Moeran, 'John Ireland as a Teacher', *Monthly Musical Record*, (March 1931).

6   See Fiona Richards, *An Anthology of a Friendship – The Letters from John Ireland to Father Kenneth Thompson*, in Sophie Fuller & Lloyd Whitesell, *Queer Episodes in Music and Modern Identity*, (University of Illinois Press, Urbana IL, 2002), 245–268.

7   See Richards in Fuller & Whitesell (2002), also Fiona Richards, *The Music of John Ireland*, (Ashgate, Aldershot, 2000), especially 143–174.

8   As will be shown later in this book, a similar apparent disaffection took place between Moeran and Benjamin Britten.

9   Letter transcribed in Rachel O'Higgins (ed.), *The Correspondence of Alan Bush and John Ireland 1927–1961*, (Ashgate Publishing, Aldershot, 2006), 20.

florid as ever, & seems to be writing quite a lot of music,'[10] the memoirs of Dora Foss suggest that all was not well between the two men. She wrote:

> One day Jack [Moeran] came over from Ling[wood Lodge] and brought John Ireland with him … Jack and John were in melancholy mood (not, I think, entirely due to the disastrous luncheon, as they arrived in this condition, but to the effect each had on the other).[11]

Regardless of their later relationship, however, both composers gained from their time together. For Ireland, the legacy of Moeran's harmonic and formal ingenuity enhanced his own musical imagination, while for Moeran, the music he composed from 1921 onwards benefitted from tidier and more economic structures, and the reduction of superfluous decoration and fussiness that is evident in some of his pre-1920s work (the *Four Songs* for example). Alongside the piano works and a string quartet that emerged during the second half of 1921, the influence of Ireland's teaching is apparent in a rhapsody for orchestra that Moeran began working on during the summer and which he dedicated to his teacher.

On a May Morning, Stalham River, Toccata

In early May, Moeran's paternal grandmother Frances died at her home in Bacton at the age of eighty-four. Moeran contributed to a fund in her memory and that of his grandfather, for the erection of an inscribed tablet mounted on the north wall of Bacton Church. It is, perhaps, only coincidental that his first extant composition from 1921 is a short piano piece entitled *On a May Morning*. However, there is no intimation of mourning in this work. McNeill described it as a 'pastoral miniature' and suggested that it 'belongs more to the drawing room than to the concert hall'.[12] Two other piano works date from 1921 – *Stalham River* and *Toccata* – both of which were composed at Bacton during the autumn. Each is a much larger-scale conception than *On a May Morning*, and each has a formal structure based on Moeran's favourite ternary-sonata form, which was earlier observed in *In the Mountain Country*. The ability to combine two distinct musical forms convincingly provides an insight into Moeran's structural ingenuity. Although far from unique in employing this composite form, Moeran's application stands out in reception as providing a satisfying aural experience. *Stalham River* was originally titled *Ballade for Pianoforte*, with the change of name being made for the published edition of 1924. *Toccata* is heavily indebted stylistically to John Ireland and harmonically to Delius, and it contains at least three distinct folksong-style tunes, each of which appears to be original. The tunes are disguised within the overall arrangement and stand out only if emphasised as such in performance. They contribute to a more traditional impression than that evoked by *Stalham River*. After *In the Mountain Country*, *Toccata* was the most advanced work Moeran had composed (of those that have survived) up to

---

[10] Letter transcribed in O'Higgins (2006), 39.

[11] Stephen Lloyd, Diana Sparkes, Brian Sparkes (eds), *Music in Their Time: The Memoirs and Letters of Dora and Hubert Foss*, (Boydell & Brewer, Woodbridge, 2019), 76.

[12] McNeill, 58.

the end of 1921. It has a fast/slow/fast ternary form with a short coda based on the opening few bars. It is the *andante con moto* central section that is the most impressive, and, while the influences of Ireland and Delius cannot be doubted, a distinctive individual sound was beginning to emerge. In his 1924 *Music Bulletin* article, Philip Heseltine wrote, 'in the *Toccata* ... we have as brilliant – and in its middle section, as sensitive – a piece of piano writing as any British composer has given us.'[13]

String Quartet in A minor

The most extended work that Moeran composed during the year was his String Quartet in A minor. As shown in Part I, he had considerable experience composing and playing string quartets, and so it is unsurprising that the work is a mature example of the composer's early output. It was composed during the summer – most probably in July and August – which he spent at his parents' home in Bacton. Moeran's familiarity with the string quartet genre was extensive, both creatively and from the point of view of knowing the repertoire. Nonetheless, the informed listener will discern similarities to the String Quartet in F major by Maurice Ravel, a favourite amongst the string quartets that were played at the musical club. Moeran clearly knew Ravel's work intimately, with stylistic aspects of it having fixed themselves in his musical memory. In particular, Ravel's extensive use of secondary harmony would have immediately attracted Moeran's attention, and the quasi-orchestral texture of the first movement would have impressed him by its sensation of fullness. For example, at the opening of the first movement, the two violins are cast in an accompanying role with shimmering tremolos that carry the harmonic duty for the first dozen or so bars, while the first subject is presented both in the cello and the viola (music example 15).

While Moeran's debt to Ravel is palpable throughout all three movements, this did not seem to have worried the critics, whose praise of the work at its first few performances was high. For example, the reviewer of the first performance writing in the *Pall Mall Gazette* noted:

> The [String Quartet] ... gains in interest as it proceeds, the opening section being ground upon material such as young composers favour sometimes because it 'works well'. The slow movement is more personal, but it is the Finale that makes one realise how rich in promise this music is.[14]

Perhaps most significantly Moeran himself maintained his regard for the quartet throughout his life. In January 1950, talking about his music to Peers Coetmore he wrote: 'I ... would gladly scrap a lot that is in print ... barring a few of the songs & the string quartet.'[15] The String Quartet in A minor was dedicated to Désiré Defauw, a Belgian violinist with whom he had become friends at the Oxford & Cambridge Musical Club. His admiration of Defauw, and perhaps his gratitude to him, is clearly shown by the dedication not only of the quartet but also of the Sonata in E minor

---

[13] Heseltine (June 1924), 173.

[14] 'New Composer', *Pall Mall Gazette*, (16 January 1923), 4.

[15] McNeill, 644.

Music example 15. String Quartet in A minor, first movement: bars 1–16

for Violin and Piano, which Moeran composed in 1922. It is probable that Moeran became acquainted with Defauw as early as 1915 when the latter first began performing at the club. Defauw, along with several other Belgian musicians, had been stranded in London at the time of the German invasion of Belgium in August 1914 and the club had provided a musical refuge.

Moeran's extended stay in Bacton enabled him to go on folksong-collecting expeditions to nearby Norfolk village pubs in Catfield, Hickling, Sutton and Potter Heigham, where at the Falgate Inn he made the acquaintance of one Harry Cox, who would, over the next few decades, be acknowledged as one of the most important figures in the preservation of English folksong during the twentieth century.[16] Moeran also made at least one trip further afield – to East Stonham in Suffolk – collecting, amongst other songs, 'The Mare and the Foal' from the singing of George Hill. In 1931, Moeran arranged this song as *Parson and Clerk*, and it has since become one of his more popular Suffolk folksong arrangements. He was back in London by early October and resumed his sessions with John Ireland. He participated in the 500th anniversary programme of the musical club on 27 October, at which he performed his own *Toccata*, and on 23 November, the club marked its 21st anniversary with a celebration dinner at Oddenino's Imperial Restaurant in Regent Street. Moeran took part in the after-dinner musical programme, accompanying W. T. Ivimey who sang some of the Norfolk folksong arrangements – including 'The Bold Richard', 'The Captain's Apprentice' and 'The Pressgang'. Moeran must also have composed a piano trio, since, on 12 November, the Harmonic Trio (comprising Dorothea Walenn (violin), Edith Vance (cello) and Olive Byrne (piano)) performed the work at the Wigmore Hall. There was a somewhat unforgiving review in the press:

> [the work] proved to be rather too dependent on rhythmical considerations, so that the lengthy slow movement loses interest, and the whole trio, which is in modern vein, and couched in the language with which John Ireland's chamber music has made us familiar, does not grip very well. But the composer has ideas not without originality, and if he can develop them into more closely-knit movements, with a power in them other than that of rhythm alone, he will produce some strong work one day.[17]

Moeran evidently took the reviewer's criticisms on board. Over the next three years, he revised the trio substantially, and he destroyed the manuscript of the 1921 version. Just over a week later, on 22 November, Moeran conducted the first performance of *In the Mountain Country* at a Royal College of Music Patrons' Fund Concert, and on 1 December, *On a May Morning* was played by Evlyn Howard-Jones at another Wigmore Hall recital. A few days later, according to a report in *The Times*, Moeran relinquished his army commission, thus detaching himself finally from his First World War years. 1921 had been a good year for Moeran. His music had received several public performances – alongside continued exposure to his friends and colleagues at the musical club – and he had completed several new compositions. He was also able to celebrate his first publications, the three piano pieces *The Lake Island*, *At a Horse Fair* and *Autumn Woods*.

---

[16] Moeran (1922). Harry Cox (1885–1971) was a singer and fiddler, and he has been the subject of numerous articles and papers on English folksong in folk music journals. See particularly Christopher Heppa, 'Harry Cox and his Friends – Song Transmission in an East Norfolk Singing Community c.1896–1960', *Folk Music Journal*, Vol. 8, No.5 (2005), 569–593.

[17] 'The Harmonic Trio', *The Observer*, (13 November 1921), 16.

Moeran would have spent his birthday and the New Year holiday in Bacton, and he took the opportunity to revisit the Falgate Inn at Potter Heigham, where he noted down more songs, mostly from the singing of Harry Cox. Amongst the songs Moeran collected during these visits included 'The Man of Burnham' (Birmingham?), 'Town' and 'Down by the Riverside (The Bold Fisherman)'. He paid his musical club subscription on 8 February, and he gave his parents' Bacton house as his home address, thus entitling him to the lower Country member rate. One of the recurring issues of Moeran's composing life was that peace and quiet was essential for him to work, and with his increasing output of music, perhaps he felt that he would be more successful in completing work away from London more of the time. However, since he maintained the tenancy and indeed occupation of his Glebe Place apartment, the provision of his parents' Bacton address can most readily be explained as Moeran taking the opportunity to save a bit of money. Nevertheless, his close involvement with the musical club continued throughout the year. He performed at several Thursday evening programmes, and at the end of March, he was co-opted onto the House Music Sub-Committee, which advised on and managed the musical activities of the club, including the coordination of the recitals repertoire and the maintenance of the music library. Moeran served on this committee unofficially until the end of the year. Away from music, his enthusiasm for motorcycles continued with his entry in the Motor-Cycling Club London to Land's End trial, which took place over the Easter weekend. Moeran successfully completed the trial and was awarded a Gold Medal. Shortly after this, his parents moved from Bacton to The Old Rectory in Laverton, near Bath. The extensive East Anglian coastal erosion that had occurred since the Moerans had built their house perhaps convinced them to realise the value of their property before its endangered location reduced its life expectancy much further.[18] Moeran had to adjust himself to a new home location and a different railway route to London.

Rhapsody for Orchestra

In the meanwhile, Moeran's music was being heard abroad. Evlyn Howard-Jones was engaged to give piano recitals of music by living British composers in several European capital cities – including Amsterdam and Paris – and on his programme were Moeran's *On a May Morning* and Theme and Variations. More significantly was a Royal College of Music Patrons' Fund Rehearsal Concert on 22 June, at which Moeran conducted his Rhapsody for Orchestra as the last item on the programme. Stylistically, the work appears to follow on quite naturally from *In the Mountain Country*, and while it was clearly inspired as a work based on folksong by the earlier *Norfolk Rhapsody* of Vaughan Williams, Moeran dedicated it to John Ireland. It continued a series of similar orchestral rhapsody-type works composed during

---

[18] The coastal erosion did continue over the years but the Moerans' house actually survived long enough to benefit from the protection of the defences that were constructed in the 1950s and 1960s. As of January 2020, the house remains and is the residence of the owner-managers of a holiday park.

the first two decades of the twentieth century, such as Holst's *Somerset Rhapsody* and Butterworth's *A Shropshire Lad*. The Rhapsody is on a larger scale than *In the Mountain Country*, and it further demonstrates that Moeran was confident working with orchestral forces in an almost symphonic genre. It is an 'English Phantasy', a form that had originally been developed by Walter Willson Cobbett for use as a suitable framework for new English chamber music.[19] It comprises five distinct and contrasting but thematically related sections, and Moeran's idiosyncratic formal imagination is apparent from the beginning. After a 10-bar opening *lento* in which fragments of the thematic material are presented, the listener is confronted with what appears to be the main theme in *animato* 7/8 time by horns and lower wood-wind and strings. However, this is quickly abandoned, and the tempo reverts to *lento* for a further fragment. The introduction ends a few bars later with a paused rest. With this, Moeran both set out his thematic palette and stated an intention to challenge listener expectation. Pizzicato chords in the lower strings then introduce the subject I folksong-like theme – now in a more conventional 6/8 time – played first by the bassoon. This is taken over by the oboe with the full strings providing a counter-melody (music example 16).

Development of subject I continues, gathering both pace and intensity, up to a climactic *fortissimo allargando* presentation of one of the opening thematic fragments. The third section (*andante*) is introduced by a flute statement of another introductory fragment and continues with a lyrical and pentatonic subject II theme played by the horn with oscillating clarinets and sustained lower strings accompaniment. This is developed and interspersed with further occurrences of the opening

Music example 16. First Rhapsody for Orchestra: bars 37–44

[19] See 'British Chamber Music', *The Musical Times*, Vol. 52, No. 818 (April 1911), 242.

Music example 17. First Rhapsody for Orchestra: multiple time signatures

section fragment, leading into the lively 5/8 time fourth section. This is the most musically complex part of the rhapsody due to the juxtaposition of a 3/4 time theme in upper woodwind against the 5/8 cello, bass and bassoon ostinato (music example 17).

Development of the 5/8 ostinato continues across all sections of the orchestra, building up to the second and principal climax with the ostinato theme presented by the full orchestra *molto maestoso* mutated into a stately 3/2 time signature. This is followed by a rapidly accelerating 5/4 *presto* in which Moeran again misdirects the listener, this time to the expectation of a triumphant ending. Instead, the music abruptly stops, and an *andante molto tranquillo* coda based on subject I and scored for reduced orchestra draws the work to a *pianissimo* close.

The Rhapsody for Orchestra is a technically complex but nonetheless assured work. It builds on the experience gained in the composition of *In the Mountain Country*, and it reveals Moeran's continuing development as an orchestral composer. It occupies a prominent position in Moeran's stylistic evolution as it extends the folksong-inspired harmonic and rhythmic ideas that he had begun to explore in the String Quartet in A minor and the piano works *Toccata* and *Stalham River*. Several themes that are reminiscent of folksong are used, and all, as far as can be ascertained, are original. By early 1922, folksong had become one of the principal influences underpinning Moeran's maturing musical style. Of the two dozen or so surviving original works composed between 1912 and 1922, three quarters contain melodies in a folksong idiom. While this high proportion was not maintained throughout Moeran's composing career, of the approximately 150 catalogued original works in his oeuvre, folksong-inspired melodies are used as principal themes in about half of these, and all are original.[20] This represents an impressive feat of invention that sets Moeran's melodic imagination apart from many of his contemporaries. When Vernon Lee Yenne asserted that Moeran was principally a composer of songs, he was missing the obvious: that Moeran was a composer of melody.[21] Indeed, on the few occasions where Moeran said or wrote anything about how or why he composed, he asserted that inventing the tunes was the first task. For example, when asked by Eamonn Andrews in the 1947 Radio Éireann interview mentioned earlier what his musical plans for the future were, Moeran replied (referring to his intended second symphony):

> I'm planning a new symphony that I've been commissioned to write by John Barbirolli and the Hallé Orchestra. I want to write this symphony about the mountains of Kerry and I'm planning to get back there and walk the mountains and think out the themes and try to get on with the work.[22]

This comment is significant for revealing two elements of Moeran's working practice. Firstly, the necessity to begin the composition by thinking out the themes, and secondly, the notion that Moeran intended his music to be 'about' something, in this case the mountains of Kerry. However, Moeran was not merely a tune-writer; rather his tunes provided the raw material for a sophisticated composing style that, while it drew on many influencing resources, may be considered original in the results it produced. This melodic creativity may have had its origin in the hours and days that the young Moeran spent at the piano with *Ships, Sea-songs & Shanties* and the *National Song Book*. Inevitably, the quality of some of his themes is better than others, but his ability to create numerous original melodies and to capture a folksong idiom in many of them was prodigious.

The Rhapsody enjoyed moderate success for a couple of years following its first presentation at the Patrons' Fund concert, although critical appraisal was varied. There was a brief report of the first performance in *The Times*:

---

[20] This statistic does not include the forty or so works that are arrangements – in one form or another – of existing folksongs and traditional melodies.

[21] Vernon Lee Yenne, *Three Twentieth Century English Songs Composers: Peter Warlock, E. J. Moeran and John Ireland*, (University of Illinois DMA. Thesis, 1969), 3.

[22] A recording of the interview was formerly at http://www.moeran.net/Writing/Radio-Interview.html (accessed 1 January 2013 – website now defunct) and the transcription was made by the author.

The new music brought forward at the Patrons' Fund public rehearsal at the Royal College of Music yesterday was hardly so interesting as usual. There was decided promise in a Rhapsody by E. J. Moeran though more of a technical than inventive nature. Certainly, the music was well-made and well-orchestrated, but the actual thematic material seemed to reflect the folk-song influence in a too conscious and artificial manner to sound convincing.[23]

Although the remarks of the critic seem a bit precious when considered in isolation from their contemporary context, it must be borne in mind that by June 1922 very little of Moeran's music had been heard outside the confines of the musical club, and his position as a composer was far from established. Perhaps reflecting the changing approaches to what was deemed acceptable in art music, the critic may well have been seeking a more abstract approach to melody and its treatment from an emerging composer. William Robert Anderson of the *Musical Times* reviewed a Promenade Concert performance in 1924 in a similar vein:

E. J. Moeran's *Rhapsody* is the kind of music that, in itself arousing no great enthusiasm, makes one hope to hear more from the composer. His use of folk-song-like themes does not quite give us the best chance of estimating his talent. I hope the good things I feel sure he has to say will not be spoiled by his insistence on this folk-song idiom ... His command of colour is already great, but we want to be sure of his constructive power.[24]

Anderson's remarks – like those of *The Times* critic quoted above – are understandable in their contemporary context. In mid-1920s London, new composers were supposed to be saying something new, eschewing traditional melody and harmony in the process. However, Moeran had no interest in following new trends. While the use of folksong as thematic material was not in itself original, Moeran's ability to conceive new but familiar-sounding melodies and to weave them into complex musical forms that exhibit both creativity and originality set him apart from some of his older colleagues. It is this, the author contends, that argues for precisely the constructive power of which Anderson was uncertain. There were repeat performances of the Rhapsody during 1922 and 1923 conducted by Moeran in London and Bournemouth, and in January 1924, Hamilton Harty and the Hallé Orchestra gave a performance in Manchester. Moeran attended the concert, and he wrote to Harty on 28 January to express his gratitude:

I feel I must write you just a few lines to express my thanks & appreciation of the splendid performance you gave of my Rhapsody ... I was immensely impressed by the good-feeling & keenness of the orchestra ... my new work [the Second Rhapsody] will be done at Norwich, as originally arranged[25]

The critical response to this performance was favourable:

[23] 'New British Music', *The Times*, issue 43065, (23 June 1922), 7.
[24] 'Promenade Concerts', *The Musical Times*, Vol. 65, No. 980 (October 1924), 938.
[25] McNeill, 347.

One might venture to call [the work] a *Celtic Rhapsody* from the lilt of its melody ... The composer had brought into the Celtic scale something of the old contrapuntal manner and showed much ingenuity in snatches of imitation and interlocked melody at the half-octave in the way of the old fugal writers ... One subject on the solo flute had even something of Delius in its softness ... and though ... there was no attempt at greatness of style, there was a vitality in the music which will make us look eagerly for something more from the same hand.[26]

The reviewer had astutely identified three key aspects of Moeran's compositional style that would be sustained throughout his oeuvre:

- prominence of melody and melodic development
- use of classical structures – albeit imaginatively modified – providing internal consistency
- absorbing rather than regurgitating of influencing factors, such as Delius and folksong

Three Fancies

In August, Moeran took a holiday in Norfolk with John Ireland and Ireland's seventeen-year-old friend Arthur Miller. Miller had been a choirboy at St Luke's church in Chelsea, where Ireland was organist and choirmaster. Ireland was evidently besotted with the boy, although, according to Richards, the exact nature of their relationship is unclear.[27] Apart from a series of photographs, now in the archive of the John Ireland Trust, which show Ireland, Moeran and Miller apparently enjoying time together in various locations on the Norfolk Broads, there is no evidence that sheds any light on how this odd *ménage à trois* spent their time together, or, indeed, where they stayed. Although Moeran's parents had moved to Somerset in April – thus depriving him of a Norfolk residence – it is possible that there were family friends in the area, and there were numerous inns and public houses that provided basic accommodation. Moeran possessed a Matchless Model H motorcycle and sidecar combination, which may have provided transport for the three as they meandered around the Norfolk landscape. Their days were probably spent boating, picnicking and visiting the many churches that are scattered across the Broads, and the evenings perhaps provided an opportunity for composition. A very tenuous connection through the title of the first of the set of piano pieces *Three Fancies* could suggest that they were composed during and after the holiday spent with Ireland and Miller. It is entitled *Windmills*, and the landscape of the Norfolk Broads is peppered with numerous windmills, many of which would still have been operational in 1922. While more imagination is required to tie the composition of the other two pieces *Elegy* and *Burlesque* to the holiday, Moeran's ad hoc collection of the three pieces as fancies suggests an impromptu and perhaps less formal

---

[26] 'The Hallé Concerts', *The Guardian*, (25 January 1924), 9. In mentioning the 'Celtic scale', the reviewer was perhaps referring to the Mixolydian Mode since the use of the flattened leading note is very apparent throughout the Rhapsody.

[27] Richards (2000), 152.

compositional effort, such as might have been possible during the quieter moments of a summer vacation. Moeran also found time to compose a madrigal-like setting of Robert Herrick's poem 'Gather Ye Rosebuds'. Soon after returning from the Norfolk holiday, Moeran moved from Glebe Place to Ireland's former flat at 54 Elm Park Mansions, where the older composer had lived between 1904 and 1915.

Sonata in E minor for Violin and Pianoforte

The principal work that Moeran was working on during the summer of 1922 was his Sonata in E minor for Violin and Pianoforte, but this was neither the first nor the only work for this instrumental combination that he composed. In the 1924 *Music Bulletin* essay, Heseltine had referred to 'three or four predecessors of the form lying in manuscript',[28] and, as was shown in the previous chapter, a violin sonata was performed at the Wigmore Hall on 10 May 1919. Moeran's membership of the musical club had provided him with ample opportunity to hear and play countless pieces of chamber music, and violin sonatas – especially those by Scandinavian composers – were popular items. Thus, by 1922, his repertoire of instrumental sonatas would have been extensive. Moeran's Sonata exhibits a fast-slow-fast three movement structure common to many such works. In the first two movements, the violin and piano parts generally show little relationship to each other. The violin part is the structural line which bears responsibility for establishing the formal components, while in the third movement, there is more thematic inter-relationship between the solo and accompanying parts. Formal analysis of the first movement reveals a modified sonata form, with an exposition of thematic material, a developmental section that exploits this material, incorporating some new thematic ideas and a final section that restates aspects of both exposition and development. Moeran had many antecedent models available to him where modifications to the so-called classic sonata form had been successfully accomplished. The violin sonata was a popular genre during the nineteenth century, and the numerous virtuoso violinists playing in Europe led to many new and imaginative works being composed.

As one of the purposes of sonata form is to provide a consistent framework, within and upon which the music is arranged, modifying the basic form requires the ability to maintain consistency whilst also achieving structural originality. One of the most effective techniques for achieving this is to conceive a strong motif, to state it unequivocally at or near the outset and then to use it as the basis for subsequent thematic ideas. Moeran's Sonata does precisely this. After the first two bars of slight harmonic ambiguity in the piano introduction, there is a bold statement with the first four notes of the solo line (music example 18). This motif is immediately memorable – due not the least to its low register timbre – and it is fundamental as the main structural component, not only of the first movement but of the entire Sonata. This motif appears throughout the work variously in its original form and in inverted and retrograde variations. In isolation, the phrase is suggestive of four tonal centres: E minor, A minor, C major and G major, and Moeran fully exploited this tonal ambiguity. Indeed, this was another persisting characteristic of Moeran's composing

---

[28] Heseltine (June 1924), 173.

style. The main intervals embedded in the phrase, together with their inversions – minor 3rd/major 6th and major 2nd/minor 7th – are the defining intervals of the pentatonic scale, of which Moeran made extensive use during this period of his stylistic evolution. The intricate structure and harmonic aggression of the violin sonata sets it apart from most of the music that Moeran had previously composed, and this style was not repeated for some considerable time. He returned to a more pastoral, folksong-based style for his music during the next two or three years.

Music example 18. Sonata in E minor for Violin and Piano: 2-bar motif

10

Meteoric Rise
(1923–1924)

Much of Moeran's time during the last two months of 1922 was occupied with the arrangements for a chamber music recital – featuring principally his own music – that was planned to take place at the Wigmore Hall early in the New Year. The promotion of a concert of Moeran's music was facilitated by his mother's financial support. Not many young composers in 1920s Britain could hire a prestigious central London venue for a recital showcasing their music and Moeran was taking an artistic risk. Only half a dozen of his compositions – all piano pieces – had been published during the previous two years, and there had been few public performances outside the limited audiences of the musical club Thursday evening recitals. Moeran was very new on the scene, and there was no guarantee that concert goers would be attracted to a recital of mostly unknown music. Nonetheless, the fact that the project was being underwritten financially by his mother enabled Moeran to devise a programme that combined his own music with a well-known and popular work for which there would always be an audience. He could have relied on some of his musical club friends and colleagues to attend, and his personal network would have enabled him to engage performers who may well have provided their services for a reduced fee or even free of charge. The recital took place on 15 January, and it began with the Allied String Quartet giving the first public performance of Moeran's String Quartet in A minor. This was followed by the first performance of his Sonata in E minor for Violin and Pianoforte, played by dedicatee Désiré Defauw, accompanied by Harriet Cohen. Cohen then played the *Three Fancies* that Moeran had composed during his Norfolk summer holiday the previous August. The recital ended with the Allied Quartet playing Ravel's Quartet in F major. The coupling of his quartet with that of Ravel was a risky strategy for Moeran – given the unmistakable influence of the Ravel work on his own – but as a means of attracting an audience to a recital of new music, it was apparently successful. The beginnings of Moeran's rapid rise in the esteem both of his peers and the music-loving public may be found at this Wigmore Hall recital.

However, critical reception was mixed, with Edwin Evans of the *Musical Times* giving his impressions of the Moeran works succinctly encapsulated in the phrase 'we cannot entirely overlook the circumstance that with the pentatonic scale it is next to impossible to go wrong.'[1] Percy Scholes, writing in *The Observer*, said:

> [E. J. Moeran] is a name to note, for it is likely to be met with again before long. It has been seen once or twice during the past year on piano recital programmes as that of the composer of some small pieces, but only came into prominence last Monday, when … to a surprisingly large audience for such an occasion, its owner submitted to public judgement his qualities as a composer.[2]

Interesting is the remark that the audience was 'surprisingly large'. While it is problematic to quantify this exactly, the capacity of the Wigmore Hall in 1923 was about 600, so it may reasonably be supposed that the audience comprised perhaps 200 to 300 people. As the reviewer noted, this was exceptional for a concert of mostly new music by an unknown composer. The *Pall Mall Gazette* enthusiastically appreciated 'music that is rich in promise',[3] while the music critic of the *Daily Telegraph* was particularly perceptive:

> In the slow movement of the quartet and in the two concluding movements of the sonata, Mr Moeran appears able to free himself from all foreign influence and to express characteristic ideas in a characteristic way. He has mastered the technique of his art, and all that he needs to do now is to forget the guides, friends and philosophers who have helped him so far … The sonata abounds in good strokes, a clear sign that there is no lack of imaginative resource. The most convincing pages were by far, also, those which were most free in technique and invention from the taint of imitation – and this is high praise. Mr Moeran's present achievements are considerable for so young a musician, and of unquestionable promise.[4]

In early April, Moeran was in Bournemouth for a performance of his Rhapsody for Orchestra conducted by Dan Godfrey at the Bournemouth Festival. He also continued with his non-musical interests, again entering the Motor-Cycling Club London to Land's End Easter trial. Riding his Matchless sidecar combination, he achieved a Gold Medal in the event. However, early 1923 was most significant for Moeran in his meeting with Philip Heseltine, probably in late February or early March. According to Ian Copley, 'Moeran … first met Warlock when the latter had called on him to say how much he had liked one of Moeran's songs.'[5] Copley provided no evidence for this assertion, but if it is assumed to be authoritative, then the only song that Heseltine could have come across at that time would have been the facsimile publication of 'When I Came Last to Ludlow' that appeared in the Autumn 1919 issue of the magazine *Arts & Letters*. Since this publication was generally available and was the kind of periodical that Heseltine would have read, there is no reason to

---

1   'E. E.' (Edwin Evans) 'E. J. Moeran', *The Musical Times*, Vol. 64, No. 960, (1 February 1923), 131.

2   'P.A.S.', 'Music of the Week: E. J. Moeran', *The Observer*, (21 January 1923), 8.

3   'New Composer', *The Pall Mall Gazette*, (16 January 1923), 4.

4   'Concerts', *The Daily Telegraph*, (17 January 1923), 8.

5   Ian A. Copley, *The Music of Peter Warlock: A Critical Survey*, (Dennis Dobson, London, 1979), 45.

disbelieve Copley's claim. The addresses from which he wrote his many letters suggest that Heseltine was in London from about the middle of February, and he could easily have discovered where Moeran lived. For example, members addresses were published in the *Journal of the Folk-Song Society*, which, again, Heseltine was likely to have read. Indeed, in the December 1922 edition, Moeran had published a collection of folksongs from Norfolk.[6] Heseltine himself, in his 1924 *Music Bulletin* article, suggested that he had first encountered Moeran as a name in the *Daily Telegraph*. Regardless of how Moeran and Heseltine met, it is apparent that they quickly discovered many shared musical and other interests. There was a mutual appreciation of the music of Delius, they were both keen motorcyclists, and they were both fascinated by trains and railway timetables. Moeran and Heseltine would have played their music to each other, very probably including sketches and ideas and uncompleted works, and it is likely that aspects of the other's musical imagination would have appealed to each composer. It is also apparent that they quickly developed an enthusiasm for each other's musical interests, although it was more often the case that Moeran adopted those of Heseltine, such as renaissance music and madrigals.

The relationship soon became close, and it is possible that a sexual element developed. A few years before his death, the art critic Brian Sewell, who was Heseltine's son, asserted that his father was 'sexually voracious, happiest with three in his bed – men or women'.[7] Sewell, who was born several months after Heseltine's suicide in 1930, only discovered quite late in life who his real father had been, so his opinion can only be regarded as anecdotal. However, there is evidence, documented elsewhere, that supports his assessment of Heseltine's character.[8] There is no doubt that Heseltine's life and personality were complex, and it is inevitable that his relationship with Moeran would have been pervaded by this complexity. Moreover, the well-documented shenanigans that were commonplace during Heseltine's tenancy of a cottage in Eynsford some years later lend credence to the notion that their friendship may have included a homo-erotic component.

Hitherto, Heseltine/Warlock has been cited as a major influence on Moeran's musical style, but, as has been shown to have been the case with John Ireland, Moeran's originality and creative individuality was such that it is entirely possible that some of the identifying features of Warlock's music that have been previously assumed to have comprised this influence ultimately derive from Moeran. Thus, the influence may have worked in both directions, and this will be examined below in more detail.

When June Is Come, The Bean Flower, Impromptu in March

Moeran's meandering lifestyle and increasing levels of self-criticism, both of which became more extreme as the years progressed, led to many of his manuscripts being

---

[6]   Moeran, (1922).

[7]   'Brian Sewell: My Family Values', *The Guardian*, (24 November 2012).

[8]   For a comprehensive study of Heseltine's personality and behavioural characteristics, see Judy O. Marchman, *Peter Warlock (1894–1930): A Contextual Analysis of his Art Songs Related to Symptoms of Mental Illness*, (Unpublished DMA Thesis, University of Miami, 2013).

either lost or deliberately destroyed. Original manuscripts for less than half of his output have survived and, of these, only a dozen or so bear reliable dating evidence, such as a date of completion. Although most of Moeran's music was published during his lifetime, many works did not appear in print until several years after their composition, and it is, therefore, problematic to date anything more precisely than between several years and a few months before publication.[9] Thus, when a manuscript with a completion date exists, it is significant for the tracing of Moeran's stylistic evolution. One such work is the song *When June Is Come*, a setting of a poem by Robert Bridges, the manuscript of which bears the signature 'Laverton, Somerset, Apr.16th, 1923'. The composition of other works may be dated by performances, an example being *Impromptu in March*, which is a setting of a poem by Doreen Wallace (1897–1989). This song was performed by its dedicatee Philip Wilson at a recital at the Steinway Hall in London on 5 May. This was the first public performance of a song by Moeran, outside the confines of the musical club. The concert was programmed jointly by Philip Wilson and Philip Heseltine to mark the tercentenary of the death of lutenist and composer Philip Rosseter. It included several of Rosseter's works that had been transcribed by Wilson and Heseltine as well as *Lovelocks*, a song by Arthur Bliss. Since Philip Wilson was a close friend of Heseltine, it is probable that he became a friend of Moeran through Heseltine. This evidence dates the composition of *Impromptu in March* to between his meeting with Heseltine – probably in late January – and its performance date in early May. While the title may be coincidence, it may be taken as fortuitous and thus it is quite possible that the song was composed in March. Stylistically, both *When June Is Come* and *Impromptu in March* appear to betray an influence from Peter Warlock in that the accompaniments act as foils to the vocal line, rather than reinforcing the implied harmony.[10] While each song has a defined tonality, the prevalence of secondary and added note harmony

9   An opus list of Moeran's works, prefixed with the letter 'R' – deriving from the name of the compiler of the list Andrew Rose – has been circulating for some years. The list includes dates of composition and seems to have originated in the comprehensive *Catalogue Raisonée* that Rhoderick McNeill included in his University of Melbourne 1982 PhD thesis *A Critical Study of the Life and Works of E. J. Moeran*. The research for this book has shown that many of these dates are incorrect. Thus, unless a manuscript date exists, none of the 'R' list dates may be regarded as reliable. The author has examined all available evidence for every work that Moeran is known to have composed and has created a list of works that is as chronologically consistent as possible. This 'M' list is presented in Appendix II.

10   The piano accompaniments to many of Warlock's songs are notoriously difficult, and some require an exceptional technique. The inevitable question is whether the composer himself was able to play them convincingly. Although Heseltine had studied the piano at school and at the Cologne Conservatory of Music, there is sufficient evidence to suggest that his technique was never developed to an advanced level. In a letter to Frederick Delius dated 15 December 1911, the young Heseltine wrote: 'I told my piano-teacher … that I would have no more piano lessons.' He confirmed this to his friend Colin Taylor in a letter written a few weeks later: 'I have definitely abandoned piano lessons in Germany … it is impossible for me to work hard at a subject without enthusiasm for it,' Barry Smith, *Frederick Delius and Peter Warlock: A Friendship Revealed*, (Oxford University Press, Oxford, 2000), 15. In 1923, Jelka Delius wrote to Percy Grainger: 'We had a very nice visit of Heseltine and Cecil Gray … H's friend – but unfortunately neither of the two

misleads the ear. Moeran's growing penchant for secondary seventh, ninth and above chords is heavily indulged, but in neither of the songs does this harmonic richness become oversweet. A criticism that may be directed at Moeran's song settings is that he sometimes overblew the accompaniments, to the detriment of the overall effect. After all, Moeran was a pianist and by no means a singer. However, the excesses evident in some of his earlier songs – particularly the *Four Songs from 'A Shropshire Lad'* – became less apparent as his song writing technique improved, and it is quite possible that this was also due to the influence of Warlock's more balanced songs.[11]

Impromptu in March was published in 1924, together with *The Bean Flower*, as *Two Songs*. *The Bean Flower* is a setting of a poem by Dorothy L. Sayers (1893–1957) and, judging by its slightly more conservative idiom, was probably composed earlier than *Impromptu in March* and *When June Is Come*. It features a distinctly folksong-like vocal line that is principally pentatonic. Stylistically, the song tends more towards Moeran's works of 1921 and 1922, and there is no apparent influence from Warlock.

By May, Moeran and Heseltine had been friends for some time. In a letter to Frederick Delius dated 14 May, Heseltine wrote:

> A great friend of mine E. J. Moeran ... has gone to Norway for the wedding of a friend of his, and if his money lasts out, he wants to stay there a bit and take a trip up to the North Cape. He is a very good composer and a great admirer of your work and would very much like to come and see you if you are in Norway and have no objection. According to his plans when he left, his trip would finish up at Bergen about the 28th of this month.[12]

In addition to verifying the depth of his and Moeran's friendship, Heseltine's letter provides evidence that Moeran spent much of May in Norway. He probably departed at the end of the first week of the month, having attended both the Philip Wilson Steinway Hall recital mentioned above and a musical club Thursday evening recital on 3 May, at which his piano pieces *On A May Morning* and *Burlesque* (from the *Three Fancies*) were played by Harold Rutland. It is not known whether the visit to Delius in Norway materialised. Indeed, it is uncertain whether Delius was in Norway at the time, and Heseltine had sent copies of the letter to the composer's Norwegian and German addresses. Moeran was back in London in time for a musical club recital on 31 May, which featured songs by Warlock and by Dowland edited by Warlock. It is interesting to note that this was the first club recital at which anything by Peter Warlock had been included. By October, Moeran's friendship with Heseltine had progressed to the point where they had been spending considerable time in each other's company, and Heseltine joined Moeran on a folksong collecting trip to Sutton, a Norfolk village lying between Hickling and Stalham. At

---

can play the piano', Barry Smith, *The Collected Letters of Peter Warlock, Vol.4 1922–1930*, (Boydell & Brewer, Woodbridge, 2005), 86n3.

[11] While some of Warlock's song accompaniments are over-indulgent, this is rarely as gratuitous as those of Moeran occasionally are. A judicious approach to dynamics in performance can generally improve the overall effect.

[12] Transcribed in Smith (2005), 73.

that time, the village had a motorcycle and bicycle shop, the proprietor of which was one Cecil Walsingham. According to Walsingham's son William, Moeran was friendly with his father – probably due to the motorcycle connections – and he would visit their Sutton home during his folksong collecting expeditions.[13] Thus, Moeran and Heseltine probably stayed with the Walsinghams in Sutton on this trip. According to Fred Thomlinson, Heseltine possessed a recording phonograph which he brought on the trip.[14]

Back in London, Moeran's music was being performed more frequently, and, after its first performance at the chamber music concert in January, the String Quartet in A minor continued to be successful. The British Music Society promoted a concert of new music on 24 October which included the quartet. The reviewer for *The Times* was quite impressed: 'We liked Mr Moeran's quartet much; there is a warmth and large-heartedness in it that lend conviction to a melodic flow which is far from being trite.'[15] It is apparent from the increasing number of performances of his music that Moeran was beginning to achieve success as a composer. While he was still reliant on the allowance he received from his mother, he augmented this with occasional freelance work. This included a brief stint as music critic of the *Weekly Westminster Gazette*,[16] and an engagement to play the 'scoring-board' in a performance of Richard Strauss's *An Alpine Symphony* at the Queen's Hall on 13 November. The review of the concert explained:

> The *Alpine* Symphony took us up hill and down again, with an appropriate waterfall, tempest, and evening hymn. There was no lack, either, of yodels and cow-bells. At the back of the stage Mr Moeran diligently exhibited numbers corresponding to the explanations in the programme, so that no one should mistake the glacier for the thermos flask.[17]

In addition to the works mentioned above, during the year Moeran had also composed two more piano pieces: *A Folk Story* and *Rune* (published together in 1924 as *Two Legends*), a setting of *The Monk's Fancy* (a poem by Henry J. Hope), an arrangement of the folksong *High Germany* and a setting of Munday and Chettle's *Robin Hood Borne on his Bier*. This last is a technically difficult unaccompanied choral work which, in performance, demands precise intonation from the singers if a muddy and incoherent effect is to be avoided. While the harmonic complexity recalls aspects of both Delius and Warlock, the overall sound is not unduly derivative. Nevertheless, the tonal drifting inherent in the use of such extreme chromatic harmony leads to

---

[13] See Heppa (2005).

[14] Unpublished letter dated 6 January 1986 from Fred Thomlinson to Barry Marsh, the original of which is in the Barry Marsh Collection.

[15] 'Concerts – British Music Society', *The Times*, issue 43483, (27 October 1923), 8. Evidently, this was a different critic from the one that had written the less enthusiastic review of the first performance.

[16] The regular music critic Aldous Huxley vacated the post of music critic in June 1923, and Moeran and Heseltine shared the job for the next four months.

[17] 'The *Alpine* Symphony', *The Musical Times*, Vol. 64, No. 970 (Dec. 1, 1923), 865.

a foundational vagueness that seems to be unsatisfactorily resolved in the final few chords: but that may have been Moeran's intention.

1924

The year began auspiciously for Moeran with the performance of the Rhapsody for Orchestra given by Harty and the Hallé Orchestra in Manchester on 24 January. As mentioned in Chapter 9, the work was positively reviewed in *The Guardian* with the critic concluding, 'Mr Harty was in a good mood throughout.' In this way Moeran's lifelong relationship with Manchester and the Hallé orchestra began. The Rhapsody had another outing at the Bournemouth Festival in April, conducted by Moeran, and he also conducted a performance of *In the Mountain Country* at the same festival. The first few months of 1924 also saw performances of Moeran's smaller works, including the String Quartet in A minor by the Philharmonic String Quartet on 8 February, the Sonata in E minor for Violin and Piano at the Wigmore Hall on 1 March, and, on 28 March, the recently-published *Six Norfolk Folksongs* received their first public performance when they were sung by John Goss at the Wigmore Hall. There were smaller recitals and concerts featuring his piano music and songs. Further underlining his permanent place on the London musical scene, the *Chesterian* published in their *Newcomers* section a short appreciation of Moeran written by Heseltine.[18] With the advantage of an improved understanding of the circumstances of Moeran's childhood, education and early adulthood, it is now apparent that much of the content of the short article, which must have derived from Moeran himself, was either over-generalised, exaggerated or invented. Nonetheless, it was the first biographical writing on Moeran to be published, and it has since been taken as an authoritative account of the details of his early life. Consequently, it was the basis for many of the misconceptions that have, over the years, inhibited the formation of an accurate and consistent portrait of the composer. The most interesting aspect of the *Chesterian* article is a list of immature string quartets and violin sonatas that Moeran claimed to have composed from the age of about seventeen. Since there is no reason to doubt the former existence of these compositions, this supports the repeated assertions made in this book that the extant works form just a proportion of Moeran's total musical output.

At the Folk-Song Society Annual General Meeting held at the end of 1923, Moeran had been elected to the committee, and he added to his official roles when, at the Oxford & Cambridge Musical Club Annual General Meeting on 12 March, he was appointed to a position on the club House Music Sub-Committee. He had spent a few months on this committee in a co-opted capacity in 1922, but was now a full member, and he remained so for the next few years, for a time serving as sub-committee chairman. Moeran again subscribed as a Country member, and he found the time for just one appearance during the year in a musical club Thursday recital. This took place on 17 April and the programme featured a set of songs sung by Mr B. E.

---

[18] Philip Heseltine, 'Newcomers: E. J. Moeran', *The Chesterian*, No. 36, (January 1924), 124.

C. Davis accompanied by Moeran, which included *To Gratiana dancing and singing* and *Diaphenia* by William Denis Browne.[19]

Six Norfolk Folksongs

Moeran spent part of the summer in Norfolk on more folksong collecting expeditions, again probably staying with his friend Cecil Walsingham in Sutton. Heseltine and others, such as John Goss and Augustus John, accompanied Moeran on some of these trips. Heseltine also published an extended appreciation of Moeran in the June 1924 edition of *The Music Bulletin*.[20] As had been the case with the *Chesterian* article in January, the biographical content originated with Moeran, and, again, much of it is now known to be unreliable. Nonetheless, in this piece, Heseltine wrote more about Moeran's music and this is meticulous. In particular, he drew attention to what he called Moeran's 'classical predilections' and how these ensured that his work is 'always distinguished by clear melodic outlines and firm rhythmic structure'. Referring to the arrangement of *Lonely Waters* in the *Six Norfolk Folksongs* collection, Heseltine also wrote that Moeran had treated it 'in a more extended manner in a very attractive little piece for small orchestra'.[21] While this reference suggests that the work for small orchestra, *Lonely Waters*, was completed, there is no record of its having been performed or published. Heseltine concluded his piece with the comment: 'there is no British composer from whom we may more confidently expect work of sound and enduring quality in the next ten years than from Jack Moeran; there is certainly no one of his years who has as yet achieved so much.'

Moeran had been working periodically on arrangements of some of the folksongs he had collected over the years, and in 1924 he offered a set of six to Augener for publication. These were accepted and appeared as *Six Norfolk Folksongs*. Although the date of the collection was 1924, the composition date of each arrangement is not known. However, the stylistic features included in the accompaniments suggest they are either contemporary with or later than the songs of *Ludlow Town*. Most particularly, Moeran made extensive use of the stylistic device in which the first vocal note of a line or the final bar is sounded alone, with the accompaniment delayed for one or more beats. This was first seen in the first song in the *Ludlow Town* set, 'When Smoke Stood Up from Ludlow'. The six songs Moeran selected for the set were: 'Down by the Riverside' (collected Potter Heigham January 1922), 'The Bold Richard' (collected Winterton July 1915), 'Lonely Waters' (collection

---

19 William Denis Browne was a promising young English composer whose life was cut short at Gallipoli in 1915 at the age of twenty-eight. Alongside George Butterworth, he was one of the greatest losses to English music occasioned by the First World War. Just a handful of his manuscripts survive after most were destroyed on his posthumous instruction. *To Gratiana dancing and singing* is a setting of a text by the seventeenth century English poet Richard Lovelace. The fifteen extant manuscripts are held in the archives of Clare College, Cambridge: *Denis Browne Music Manuscripts*, Cambridge University Archives Repository Reference CLARE/CCPP/BRO.

20 Heseltine, (June 1924), 170–174.

21 The issue of the *Journal of the Folk-Song Society* dated December 1925 also reported that 'Mr. E. T. [sic] Moeran's composition *Lonely Waters* – Idyll for small orchestra, is based on a tune from Norfolk'.

date and location not known), 'The Pressgang' (collected Winterton July 1915), 'The Shooting of his Dear', (collected Sutton October 1912) and 'The Oxford Sporting Blade' (collection date and location not known). While arrangements of 'The Bold Richard' and 'The Pressgang' had been presented at a musical club recital on 24 June 1920, it is not known if these were revised for publication. A persistent characteristic of Moeran's folksong arrangements was his faithfulness to the song as sung by the singer from whom he recorded it. This differentiated Moeran's arrangements from those of others who felt it necessary to make them more conventionally 'song-like'. Writing in *The Bookman*, C. Henry Warren appreciated this aspect of Moeran's technique:

> By his work of collecting folksongs, Mr E. J. Moeran is carrying on the work of the late Cecil Sharp; but his trophies never suffer the mutilation they too often did in the hands of Mr Sharp … In *Six Folk Songs from Norfolk* he gives us some completely new finds … Mr Moeran has not trimmed the songs into a definite rhythm but is wisely content to leave them in their native disorderliness; and his accompaniments (often very spare and never too heavy) are modern and right. A very fine collection indeed, and one that makes us hope Mr Moeran will continue in East Anglia the collection he has begun.[22]

A debate had been raging in the folksong revival community for decades concerning the appropriateness of 'arrangements'. There were those that denounced any meddling with the purity of the unadulterated song, while others believed that sensitive arrangements – while not replacing the original song – could add to their appeal, thus contributing to their preservation. However, even those in favour of arrangements were divided on how far a composer should go. C. Henry Warren decried Cecil Sharp's rhythmic modifications as 'mutilation', while Ralph Vaughan Williams, in his review of Moeran's *Six Suffolk Folksongs* in 1934, justified sympathetic arrangement with: 'the form and content of a folk-song may be simple, but its emotional implications may be complicated and elaborate.'[23] During his life, Moeran collected more than seventy folk songs in Britain and Ireland, and he produced arrangements of more than thirty of these, mostly for solo voice and piano but some arranged as part-songs. While he was not the most prolific collector, the songs that he recorded – together with their arrangements – represent a significant contribution to the preservation of British and Irish traditional culture.

Bank Holiday

During 1924, Moeran made the acquaintance of the pianist Gordon Bryan, who soon became a champion of Moeran's piano music. Moeran was evidently impressed with Bryan's technique, and he composed *Bank Holiday* for him. Although the exact date of composition is not known, Bryan gave its first performance at a South Place Sunday Concert on 8 March 1925. If the title of the piece is significant, then it is likely

---

[22] 'Some Music of Yesterday, Today and Tomorrow', *The Bookman*, Vol. 67, No.397, (October 1924), 63.

[23] 'Reviews: Six Suffolk Folksongs', *Journal of the English Folk Dance and Song Society*, Vol. 1, No. 3 (December 1934), 173.

to have been composed, or at least begun, on or around one of the public holidays of the previous year. Since the late summer bank holiday in 1924 was 25 August, in the absence of any more convincing evidence it may be assumed that the piece dates from late August/early September. The piece is one of Moeran's more exuberant creations, fully exploiting the percussive characteristics of the piano in the opening and closing sections. Of note is the frequency of left-hand tenth stretches, at certain points including three in sequence. Such chords require a large hand and exceptional technical skill to play convincingly. Gordon Bryan had been a pupil of Percy Grainger who also composed piano works with chords requiring wide stretches, so it is entirely possible that Moeran had Bryan's hands in mind when he composed *Bank Holiday*.[24] The most difficult of these left-hand chords occurs at the very end. Bryan would have recognised the note cluster emphasising effect that was also employed by Grainger in works such as *Mock Morris*. Moeran had performed some of Grainger's music at the musical club, and the stylistic similarity between *Bank Holiday* and Grainger's *Mock Morris* may be thus explained. The *Musical Times* reviewer also noted this: 'E. J. Moeran's *Bank Holiday* is in a mood reminiscent of Grainger: there is a swinging diatonic tune and an ostinato middle section that provides effective contrast – the whole thing being very high-spirited and game.'[25]

Second Rhapsody for Orchestra

Moeran fulfilled the Norwich Festival commission (mentioned in his letter to Harty quoted above), completing the Second Rhapsody for Orchestra just in time for rehearsals and its first performance at the St Andrew's Hall, Norwich on the morning of Friday 31 October.[26] The concert was attended by the Queen, accompanied by the Duchess of York, and Moeran was amongst those presented to the royal party after the event. There were numerous newspaper and periodical reviews of the festival, including the performance of the Rhapsody, conducted, as was now regularly the case, by Moeran himself. The reviewer for *The Times*, although admiring the work, bemoaned the fact that the Rhapsody followed immediately after a performance of Vaughan Williams' *Sea Symphony* and felt that the enduring impact of the symphony had overshadowed the new work. He suggested that on another occasion, with the Rhapsody given prominence, the reception would be enhanced. Percy Scholes, writing in *The Observer*, noted that neither Vaughan Williams nor Moeran could be regarded as the best conductors for their own music. However, it was the reviewer for *The Guardian* who seemed to be most informed about the music itself:

> Considered ... as a work of art the rhapsody certainly has its merits. Mr Moeran limits its appeal deliberately by the very drastic application of local colour. It is a piece of painting whose interest lies chiefly in its subject and associations. The

[24] While this may well be correct, many of Moeran's other piano compositions include wide stretches, particularly in the left hand, and it may reasonably be supposed that Moeran himself had large hands.

[25] 'Occasional Notes', *The Musical Times*, Vol. 69, No. 1023 (1 May 1929), 426.

[26] The manuscript is dated 'October 20th'.

thematic ideas are loosely strung together, and one has the feeling that the orchestral tints result here and there from an experimental blending of the colours, but
within the bounds the composer has set himself he has achieved a fresh, healthy,
and pleasant work.[27]

The Second Rhapsody for Orchestra continued the development of a sophisticated orchestral technique that Moeran had begun with *In the Mountain Country* and
then extended in the Rhapsody for Orchestra. While much may be said about the
technical aspects of the music, the most obvious feature that emerges on repeated
listening is that it embodies Moeran's musical philosophy of melody, harmony
and structure. It is full of memorable tunes and luscious harmony, and the form
– that of an English Phantasy – keeps the listener engaged throughout. A feature
of the harmonic vocabulary is the contrasting use of added sixth and added seventh chords. The greater astringency bestowed by the major seventh requires more
careful deployment across instrumental groups, whereas an added sixth chord has
a less abrupt harmonic impact. Moeran had used the effect of added sixth chords
from his earliest works, but more prevalent inclusion of sevenths and ninths was a
stylistic feature that is apparent in works dating from 1922 onwards. While the piece
is undoubtedly a patchwork – 'loosely strung together' (as the *Guardian* reviewer
put it) – rather than a homogeneous construction, this surely reflects the East
Anglian landscape that provided the inspirational motivation for the composition
of the work. There are brief moments when one could be forgiven for mistaking
it for a work by Delius, or Elgar, and, indeed, Moeran also quotes from himself.
The listener familiar with Moeran's folksong arrangements will recognise melodic
fragments from 'The Bold Richard' and 'The Pressgang'. Nonetheless, the stylistic amalgam into which these disparate elements blend is uniquely Moeran. Two
musical examples illustrate his melodic and harmonic invention. First, the stirring
– indeed almost Elgarian – extract shown in music example 19 exemplifies Moeran's
ability to command the most expansive of orchestral resources. The central section
is one of Moeran's most lyrical inventions, although its debt to Delius is evident, as
shown in music example 20.

Moeran's musical administration work was extended further when he was
approached by the East Anglian Association of Musical Societies to assist in their
initiative to preserve the folksongs of Norfolk and Suffolk. Moeran's folksong collecting activities had attracted the attention of the secretary of the Diss Musical
Society – Mr W. H. Aldrich – who had noted that while a large number of folksongs
had been collected from Norfolk, just a handful of Suffolk songs had been recorded.
Since Diss lies on the border between Norfolk to the north and Suffolk to the south,
perhaps the secretary felt a responsibility in both directions. It was reported that
Moeran had agreed to help redress this balance in any way that he could.[28]

---

[27] 'The Norwich Musical Festival', *The Guardian*, (1 November 1924), 14.

[28] Although perhaps his family connections with Norfolk eventually proved too strong.
While Moeran continued his folksong collecting in that county, it was several years
before he published his *Suffolk Folksong Arrangements*.

Music example 19. Second Rhapsody for Orchestra: 'Elgar' theme

Music example 20. Second Rhapsody for Orchestra: 'Delius' theme

While Moeran's main work for the year was the Second Rhapsody for Orchestra, he had also been composing an overture, the partial manuscript of which now resides in the E. J. Moeran Collection at the Southbank Library of the University of Melbourne.[29] While Moeran never finished the overture, he made use of some of the ideas in the *Overture for a Masque* composed some twenty years later. During the year, Moeran's music also featured over the still relatively new radio waves. The retitled First Rhapsody for Orchestra, conducted by the composer, was broadcast in studio performances from 2LO[30] on 27 March and 17 July, and *In the Mountain*

---

[29] *E. J. Moeran Collection*, MS number VCA 16, Southbank Library, University of Melbourne; catalogue made by Stephanie Brown in 2009.

[30] One of the broadcasting stations that eventually merged to form the British Broadcasting Company (later Corporation).

Country was broadcast on 27 August, as part of the sixteenth Promenade Concert of the 1924 season from the Queen's Hall. Piano works were heard in London, Oxford and Manchester, and, in October, the recently completed part-song *Weep You No More, Sad Fountains* was selected as one of the test pieces for the Blackpool Music Festival. Moeran also created some imaginative folksong arrangements for John Goss, who, together with his Cathedral Male Voice Quartet, performed them enthusiastically. These included: *Can't You Dance the Polka, Mrs Dyer the Baby Farmer,*[31] *The Sailor and Young Nancy* and *Gaol Song*. At the end of December, the song-cycle *Ludlow Town* received its first public performance in a recital by John Goss, accompanied by G. O'Connor Morris, at the Wigmore Hall. The review in *The Times* was positive, remarking on 'the right earthy flavour' of the musical settings and, while noting some similarities with Vaughan Williams' *On Wenlock Edge*, excused this as the result of the two composers talking with the same Norfolk dialect.[32] As described in Chapter 8, *Ludlow Town* had originally been composed in 1920, and it is possible that the renaming of three of the songs was the result of revision.

Moeran also completed the song *Commendation of Music*, arrangements of the folksongs *Under the Broom, Sheep-Shearing Song* (a Dorset folksong), *The Jolly Carter* and a Norwegian folksong with text by Robert Burns *O Sweet Fa's the Eve*. In November, he made an ebullient arrangement of the traditional *Christmas Day in the Morning*, which he dedicated to Robert Sterndale Bennett and was clearly intended for the boys' choir at Uppingham. Set for unison treble choir, Moeran probably obtained the text and tune from Heseltine, who had collected several folk carols. The text is a variant of the well-known *I Saw Three Ships*, but the tune is different from that now usually associated with the carol. Musically, the arrangement is simple: four verses with primarily chordal accompaniment and an *allargando* final line of the fourth verse. The different accompaniments in each verse provide musical interest, with the first two lines of the third verse exhibiting the most imaginative variant. A descending bass is cleverly harmonised to exploit the diverting effect of implying a modulation to the subdominant. This was a device also used frequently by Warlock in such songs as *Mr Belloc's Fancy, Captain Stratton's Fancy* and in the accompaniment to the Moeran-collected tune that ended up as the song *Yarmouth Fair*.

As the year drew to a close, Moeran would have celebrated his thirtieth birthday at home with his parents in Somerset, and he could have reflected on a year that saw the completion of about a dozen new works, nearly two dozen publications and regular performances in two of the major musical centres of England: London and Manchester. Moreover, his music was being reviewed in the influential music and artistic periodicals, such as *The Musical Times* and *The Bookman*. Moeran's sound appealed to performers, audience and reviewers in equal measure, and negative criticism was by now almost non-existent. The financial support

[31] *Mrs Dyer the Baby Farmer* is a Victorian Crime Ballad that had been taken down by Heseltine from the singing of one William Bushnell of Begbroke in Oxfordshire. The lyrics tell the story of the notorious Amelia Elizabeth Dyer who, between 1880 and 1896, murdered as many as several hundred babies that had been placed in her care.

[32] 'Recitals of the Week – Miss Ursula Nettleship', *The Times*, issue 43838, (19 December 1924), 12.

provided by his mother enabled him to compose whatever he wanted, and while his works were frequently directed towards specific musicians – thus ensuring at least one performance – he was not reliant on commissions. This meant that he was free to pursue his own path of stylistic evolution, unencumbered by commercial considerations or the need to follow innovative trends. While modernism was rapidly establishing itself elsewhere in Europe and being enthusiastically embraced by some of his younger colleagues in Britain, Moeran was content to create the attractive, melodic and tonal harmony-based, folksong-inspired music that the post-war 1920s British audiences clearly appreciated.

11

The Composer Ruined
(1925–1927)

Moeran was on the cusp of greatness. He was an established composer, with the patronage of Hamilton Harty: one of the great musical personalities of the time. Numerous performances of his works were programmed for the first few months of 1925, and new music was flooding from his creative imagination. Plans were in train for a series of recitals at the Wigmore Hall featuring his chamber music and that of his friends and contemporaries. Moeran's rise to prominence during the previous two years had indeed been meteoric, and his was the name in town. The musical world lay at the feet of the thirty-year-old composer. On 2 January, he paid the one and a half guineas Country subscription for the musical club, again providing his parents' house in Laverton as his home address. However, he continued to reside mostly in London, although towards the end of the previous year he had chosen not to renew his lease on John Ireland's former flat in Elm Park Mansions and had taken rooms at 162 Haverstock Hill, NW3, in Belsize Park. Meanwhile, Philip Heseltine had decided to move out of the city, and in mid-January he took a sub-lease on a cottage in Eynsford in Kent that was rented by pianist, composer and music publisher Hubert Foss from the local grocer Stanley Munn, whose shop was next door.[1] Foss had lived in this cottage with his wife for some years, but their separation had caused him to seek other accommodation. During the years of the Foss residence, their home had been the centre of musical gatherings, where composers in whom he took an interest were invited to talk about and play their works. In leasing the cottage, Heseltine's intention was not only to continue Foss's tradition but also to establish a creative commune where 'open house' was kept, and writers, painters, sculptors and other artistic members of 1920s London society, together with composers and musicians, were welcome to visit and remain as long as they liked.[2] Regular visitors included Constant Lambert, Arnold Bax, Cecil

---

[1] Heseltine wrote to Gwen Shephard on 19 January: 'I've left London for good and live in a pleasant village 20 miles out', Smith (2005), 114.

[2] Hubert Foss described the cottage life after Heseltine had taken the lease: 'It was not an orderly house, the habits were in no sense regular. On the other hand, it was acutely, sometimes insanely, alive; each day it blossomed into a new unpredictable, semi-exotic flower. It was not exemplary, but it contained genius. The inmates and many visitors were joined in a pursuit of art. The underlying interest was a quest for beauty ... They just were brilliant, eccentric, passionately alive'; from Hubert Foss, 'The Warlock Gang', *The London Symphony Orchestra Observer*, (November 1951), 99–100.

Gray, Augustus John, Patrick Hadley, William Walton, Bernard van Dieren, Jack Lindsay, Nina Hamnett, John Goss and, for the first few months of Heseltine's tenancy, Moeran himself. However, this initially well-intentioned objective was rapidly overwhelmed by the increasingly hedonistic lifestyle indulged in by the cottage inhabitants both long- and short-term. Tales of the Eynsford cottage have entered the folklore of 1920s English music, and while a detailed excursus on what did or did not happen during its four-year duration would be too extended to include in this book, it is sufficient to record that Heseltine thrived in the environment, spending his time composing, writing, researching, drinking and debauching.[3] It has hitherto been believed that Moeran joined Heseltine at the start of the tenancy and that he remained until Heseltine moved out in October 1928, but it is more probable that he lived in the cottage only for a limited period, making shorter visits during the remainder of the tenancy. Moeran had other addresses continuously through the entire Eynsford period. He maintained his Haverstock Hill address until at least early 1928, and his parents' home was always available to him. Moreover, none of the extant letters written by Moeran during this period were addressed from Eynsford, and none of the letters Heseltine wrote from Eynsford mentions Moeran as a resident.

'Tis Time, I Think, by Wenlock Town and *Far in a Western Brookland*

Moeran continued the steady output of new music that had characterised his life for the previous three years, and he returned to Housman's *A Shropshire Lad*, completing settings of *'Tis Time, I Think, by Wenlock Town* and *Far in a Western Brookland*. While the first of these was a new song, *Far in a Western Brookland* was a reworking of the elaborate 1916 setting of the text as part of the *Four Songs from 'A Shropshire Lad'* that Moeran had probably composed in memory of his friend Roland Perceval Garrod. While the structure of the 1916 song was retained, the florid piano accompaniment of the original was discarded, and a more austere, primarily chordal piano part relying extensively on parallel fifths and sixths was substituted. The vocal line was slightly modified to provide a contrast at the emotional pivot point in the third verse of the poem: 'Here I lie down in London | And turn to rest alone.' The result is a greatly improved song that more appropriately frames the poignant impact of the text. *'Tis Time, I Think, by Wenlock Town* is constructed in an ABB form, with a tonally ambiguous vocal melody oscillating between F major and D minor. The chromatic chordal accompaniment continually veers into unrelated keys, resulting in a series of abrupt resolutions. Indeed, there are at least two points in the published edition at which an incorrect transcription may be suspected, but in the absence of a manuscript source, this cannot be verified. Although the final vocal line clearly implies D minor, the accompaniment fails to support this, and the brief four-bar

---

3 Having claimed that the cottage was exactly what Heseltine was searching for: 'It is very peaceful and congenial for work, and one can easily get to town if one wants to', he soon discovered that it also had disadvantages: 'The only drawback is when one goes to sleep in the last train down and finds oneself penniless in the small hours of the morning at Maidstone whence I had to walk a few nights ago. I have also visited Whitstable under similar circumstances'; Smith (2005), 117 and 133.

coda that ends the song further reinforces the ambiguity. The opinion of the author is that *'Tis Time, I Think, by Wenlock Town* is one of Moeran's least successful song settings, and its overall effect is that of an experiment. However, it may be that, like the choral work *Robin Hood Borne on his Bier*, the seemingly unsatisfactory harmonic leading may have been Moeran's intention.

Moeran had evidently come to be regarded as an authority on modern music or, at least, the modern music that he and the others of the post-war pastoral school composed. Accordingly, when the Royal Musical Association planned to hold a discussion at their council meeting on 10 February on 'Modern Harmony from the Standpoint (*a*) of the Composer and (*b*) of the Teacher', with a view to 'breaking new ground' as the *Musical Times* put it,[4] they invited Moeran to speak from the composer's perspective. Professor C. H. Kitson of Trinity College, Dublin was asked to provide the teacher's point of view. Unfortunately, neither participant appeared, both citing illness as the reason. While Professor Kitson sent a transcript of his presentation, which was read to the assembled members, Moeran did not send anything, and so the composer's perspective was omitted from the discussion. He had clearly recovered from his illness the following week because he participated in the musical club recital on the evening of Thursday 19 February. This programme was Moeran's final appearance at a club musical evening, and it is perhaps fitting to note that his contribution to the concert was comprehensive as soloist, accompanist and composer. In addition to playing a Bach suite as the central, solo item, he accompanied his own Norfolk folksong arrangements *The Shooting of his Dear* and *The Sailor and Young Nancy*, and he played the piano part in Mozart's Trio in E flat for Piano, Violin and Viola. The evening concluded with the *Rhapsodie Gaelic for Piano Duet* by Paul Ladmirault, in which Moeran was joined by fellow pianist H. V. Anson. The inclusion of the *Rhapsodie Gaelic* would undoubtedly have been the suggestion of Philip Heseltine. Ladmirault, along with Béla Bartók and Bernard van Dieren, was a composer for whom Heseltine had developed a strong affinity during his early twenties and whose cause he strongly espoused.[5] He had begun a correspondence with Ladmirault a few weeks earlier and had specifically discussed the *Rhapsodie Gaelic*, suggesting that a transcription for orchestra might result in its receiving greater attention in England.[6]

At the end of March, Moeran was in Manchester, conducting the 2ZY Augmented Orchestra[7] in a broadcast performance of the First Rhapsody for Orchestra, but he returned to London for a series of concerts at the beginning of April in the city featuring the violin sonata, some folksong arrangements and several of the short piano pieces. Moeran also attended the studios of HMV for a recording by John Goss and the Cathedral Male Voice Quartet of his arrangements of *O Sweet Fa's the Eve* and *Can't You Dance the Polka*. Moeran would have been present when the Second

4   'Modern Harmony', *The Musical Times*, Vol. 66, No. 986 (1 April 1925), 351–352.

5   Ladmirault was the dedicatee of Warlock's *Capriol Suite* (1926).

6   Smith (2005), 115.

7   The forerunner of the BBC Philharmonic Orchestra.

Rhapsody for Orchestra was broadcast by the 2LO orchestra conducted by Dan Godfrey on 5 May.[8]

Piano Trio in D major

It was probably in May that Moeran finished the revised version of his 1921 Piano Trio. Since the original manuscript was destroyed, it cannot be known how much of the original material survived. According to the programme note Moeran wrote for its first performance in June, 'The work … has recently been entirely re-cast both as to form and material.' The result was Moeran's most extended work to date and the most extended work of chamber music that he composed. It comprises four movements: a sonata form *allegro* opening movement, a *lento molto* slow second movement, a ternary form *allegro vivace* scherzo and trio and a modified sonata form *allegro* finale. Most of the themes of each of the movements are in a folksong idiom, most especially the third subject of the first movement (music example 21) and the main theme of the second movement (music example 22).

Music example 21. Piano Trio in D major, first movement: third subject

Music example 22. Piano Trio in D major, second movement: main theme

---

8   Later the Wireless Symphony Orchestra, which was the forerunner of the BBC Symphony Orchestra.

Critical reception of the work was mixed. The reviewer for *The Times* was non-committal:

> The third of Mr Moeran's chamber concerts took place at the Wigmore Hall on Saturday. It included a Pianoforte Trio of his which was sound enough music but contained little that was arresting. The final two allegros were, as usual with him, the best of it.[9]

The music critic of the *Musical Times* averred that the trio was 'not good trio-writing'.[10] 'B.V.', reviewing the published music in the *Musical Times*, wrote:

> The Moeran trio ... is extensive (four movements), and not always 'neat' in execution. The composer seems to have excellent ideas which, however, do not easily bear extended treatment ... Mr Moeran has worked for himself a technique which serves him well, but he should look more closely into the difficult problems of length and construction to discover how much the effect can be heightened by what is left unsaid. This, if not the only one, is at least one of the secrets of successful composition.[11]

Jack Westrup, writing in *British Music of our Time*, asserted that the third movement 'irresistibly recalls *Brigg Fair*'.[12] While there are undoubtedly influences from Delius in some of the harmony in the Trio, the author does not share Westrup's conclusion and perceives much more originality in the work than the comment might suggest. However, at about twenty-three minutes in performance, the trio is overlong and might have benefitted from some pruning, of both the extended development sections in the first and fourth movements and the somewhat rambling slow movement.

The Merry Month of May

Throughout May and into June and perhaps inspired by Heseltine's own song-setting activity, Moeran continued to turn out new songs at the rate of about one per week. The songs that date from this period are: *The Merry Month of May*, *In Youth is Pleasure*, *Troll the Bowl* and *Come Away, Death*. With a text by Thomas Dekker – also probably introduced to Moeran by Heseltine – *The Merry Month of May* is one of Moeran's most satisfying and successful vocal compositions. Again, Moeran made use of the pentatonic scale for the vocal line, only deviating from its constraints for a contrasting third verse which sees the appearance of an evil and unwelcome cuckoo. The jovial nature of the piano accompaniment to verses one, two and four matches the frolicsome and happy atmosphere invoked by the protagonist as he indulges in the carefree enjoyment of the company of his love (music example 23). These arpeggiated flourishes are replaced by a block chordal sequence for the end of the second verse as a transition into the more sinister minor mode third verse: 'But O,

---

9 'Week-end Concerts', *The Times*, issue 43988, (15 June 1925), 12.

10 'London Concerts', *The Musical Times*, Vol. 66, No. 989, (July 1925), 640.

11 'New Music', *The Musical Times*, Vol. 68, No. 1010, (April 1927), 334.

12 Jack A. Westrup, 'E. J. Moeran', in A. L. Bacharach (ed.), *British Music of our Time*, (Penguin, Harmondsworth, 1951).

I spy the cuckoo'. The structure includes a characteristic descending progression of open sixths and sevenths in the left hand (music example 24).

Having dispatched the cuckoo and its astringent major and minor seventh block chords, the ebullience returns for the fourth verse, which is a repeat of the text of the first. The vocal line is almost the same as in the first verse, but the accompanying piano flourishes become even more elaborate. After a final chordal triumph: 'Thou shalt be my summer's Queen', another flourish leads to the ending major sixth chord spread across almost the entire piano keyboard. Much of Moeran's compositional wizardry is displayed in this song, most particularly the exploitation of the pentatonic scale, the result of which belies its underlying simplicity. In performance, the song requires considerable technical expertise by both singer and accompanist to deliver adequately the intricacies of the setting.

Music example 23. *The Merry Month of May*: bars 4–7

Music example 24. *The Merry Month of May*: bars 19–21

In Youth is Pleasure

Moeran's choice of text for this song was undoubtedly influenced by Warlock, who, by 1925 had already produced two settings of this extract from Robert Wever's *Lusty Juventus*. However, in contrast to Warlock's more boisterous songs *In an Arbour Green* and *Lusty Juventus*, which each emphasise the youthful joy expressed in the text, Moeran's restrained and reflective setting underlines the protagonist's sorrow at being separated from his love, although his use of the Scotch snap on the word 'pleasure' achieves a very subtle but more carefree tinge. Perhaps recalling Edwin Evans' assessment of the works presented in his 1923 chamber music recital, Moeran devised an almost entirely pentatonic tune for the vocal line. This is presented in a quadruple rise-and-fall wave structure with the top note of the phrase being raised each time for waves one, two and three, falling back again for wave four (music example 25). This simple but effective tension-release melodic form was frequently exploited by Moeran throughout his oeuvre and is one of his most characteristic stylistic features. While the vocal line is definitively and unambiguously F major, the piano accompaniment meanders through a variety of tonal anchors, seemingly without committing to any. Moeran again makes use of the major sixth chord to underline uncertainty between the major key and the relative minor, while the coda ends the song with an echo of the 'pleasure' motif underpinned by a very uncertain tonal resolution (music example 26). In this song, unlike in *'Tis Time, I Think, by Wenlock Town*, Moeran's intention to leave the listener wondering is clear. Does the protagonist seek out his love, or does he indulge his longing for personal pleasure? We cannot know.

Alongside his composing activity, Moeran had been deeply involved in the organisation and programming of the Wigmore Hall chamber music recitals, which, again, were financed by his mother. The series of three concerts was announced in the April issue of *The Music Bulletin*, the monthly journal of the British Music Society.[13] The programme of three recitals was on a much larger scale than had been Moeran's January 1923 chamber music concert, and there was less emphasis on Moeran's own music. Just two larger scale works were included: the popular String Quartet in A minor and the reworked Pianoforte Trio. While the purpose of the series of recitals was to showcase both Moeran's music and that of composers he admired, it might be more accurate to state that they were composers that Heseltine admired. Indeed, it is reasonable to suggest that the title of the series, 'Mr Moeran's Concerts', was

Music example 25. *In Youth is Pleasure*: verse 1

In an ar-bour green, a-sleep where-as I   lay, The birds sang   sweet in the mid-des of the

day; I   dream-ed   fast of mirth and   play: In youth is pleas-ure,__ in youth is pleas-ure.__

[13] 'Mr. Moeran's Concerts', *The Music Bulletin*, Vol. VII, No. 4, (April 1925), 122.

Music example 26. *In Youth is Pleasure*: final 3 bars

due to his having financed the enterprise, with the programming having been mostly Heseltine's work. Nonetheless, the series achieved its objective, and Moeran's music was brought to further public attention, although press reviews were mixed. 'E.B.' in *The Guardian* wrote:

> Moeran's work reminds one of Grieg's quartets, not because of any idiomatic resemblance, but because it is national in colour, and the composer is so absorbed in uttering the music he has in him that he cares comparatively little if he does not always write ideal quartet music. The texture of the finale, for instance, is orchestral, but the violation of the medium is justified by results that are agreeable in their own way.[14]

Despite this lukewarm appraisal, the concerts were well-attended, but more importantly for Moeran, they established further his reputation amongst both his musical friends and admirers and the London concert-going public. Of his admirers, none had greater significance for Moeran than Hamilton Harty, and during the late spring of 1925, Harty commissioned Moeran to compose a symphony for the Hallé Orchestra. Although no documentary evidence for the actual commission has been found, the symphony was included in the prospectus for the 1925–1926 season of the Hallé Concerts Society that was announced in *The Guardian* on 26 September, and it may safely be assumed that Moeran had accepted the commission with alacrity. His motivation would have been twofold. Firstly, in Harty, Moeran had a very influential champion, and by agreeing to compose his First Symphony for him and his

[14] 'London's Week-end Music', *The Guardian*, (25 May 1925), 10.

orchestra, he could reasonably have imagined that a successful *première* would lead to multiple repeat performances and almost certainly further commissions. Secondly, although Moeran lived in the south of England and regarded London as his musical base, cementing his reputation and becoming equally accepted in Manchester, with its proximity to other northern musical centres – such as Liverpool, Leeds and Huddersfield – was a sound career move.

Summer Valley

In early July, Moeran and Heseltine travelled together to Grez-sur-Loing to visit Fred and Jelka Delius. Heseltine mentioned this expedition in a letter he wrote to his friend Colin Taylor in January 1929: '[Moeran's] last composition – a fantasy for small orchestra on a theme by Whythorne – was unfortunately not picked up by the kindly Brussels gendarme who found its composer in a state of beatific coma in the gutter some years ago.'[15] Since its publication, this colourful anecdote has provided writers on Moeran with ample opportunity for speculation as to the circumstances of the incident. While Brussels is not on a direct route from Dover/Folkestone to Grez, there is no reason to suppose that their itinerary did not include a visit to the Belgian capital. The sixteenth-century composer Thomas Whythorne had been a favourite of Philip Heseltine, who had published an essay on him, and it is entirely possible that Moeran would have absorbed his friend's enthusiasm to the extent of composing a fantasy for small orchestra based on one of Whythorne's songs, and it is quite likely that Moeran had brought the manuscript with him in the hope of showing it to Delius. It is also credible that Heseltine and Moeran, finding themselves spending an evening in Brussels, indulged in an extended carousal that ended as Heseltine so vividly described.

Heseltine wrote that on their eventual arrival in Grez, they found the composer 'in a very sad state – completely blind and so paralyzed that he [could not] stand or walk even with assistance, or hold anything in his hands',[16] but according to Eric Fenby, Heseltine and Moeran did not reach the Delius house together. In *Delius As I Knew Him*, Fenby wrote:

> One morning, on going down to lunch, I discovered that Heseltine and several other people had arrived unexpectedly. They were not at their full strength, they told us, for they had missed 'Old Raspberry' on the way; he would probably be coming along later in the day … Our rowdy friends had not been gone more than a few minutes when 'Old Raspberry' drove up in a taxi; but we pushed him in again and directed the driver to Marlotte. Delius had had enough for one day.[17]

Fenby also wrote that Heseltine visited again a couple of weeks after the above incident, whereas Heseltine himself wrote to Jelka Delius on his return to Eynsford to apologise that he and Moeran ('Old Raspberry') had not returned to Grez because their funds had run short and the visit to France had been curtailed. On

[15] Smith (2005), 218.

[16] Smith (2005), 138.

[17] Eric Fenby, *Delius As I Knew Him*, (G. Bell & Sons Ltd, London 1937), 59–63.

his return home, Moeran would have had little time to reflect on Delius' condition: the Whythorne fantasy manuscript had been lost and the symphony had to be composed. However, he seems to have been sufficiently inspired by the visit to France to compose a short piano piece as a tribute to Delius. It was later reviewed in the *Musical Times*: 'Moeran's *Summer Valley* is an essay in the manner of Delius, dedicated to that composer. The piece might easily have been called *After hearing Brigg Fair*. It has many beautiful moments, even if the voice is not the voice of E. J. Moeran.'[18] While the harmonic style of *Summer Valley* does indeed recall not only Delius but also John Ireland and Peter Warlock, there are sufficient distinguishing elements to enable one to disagree with the assertion that its voice is not that of Moeran. The piece is an extended series of variations on the opening 4+4+2 bar folksong-like siciliano theme that, while it does bear similarities to *Brigg Fair*, is an original Moeran melody. The initial harmonisation derives from sequences of cycles of fifths with tritone substitution on occasional third and sixth quaver beats. This has the effect of creating a lower register countermelody that mostly mirrors the theme. Moeran's harmonic vocabulary is utilised to its limits and, while individual chords may immediately remind the listener of Delius, Ireland or Warlock, the progressions are uniquely Moeran.

Nonetheless, the question as to the extent to which Moeran's style bears an indebtedness to both Delius and Warlock has exercised the minds of writers on Moeran over the years. However, as was shown to be the case with Moeran's stylistic relationship with John Ireland, the conventional belief that the influence must have originated in the music of Delius and Warlock does not stand up to thorough scrutiny. It is chiefly on the basis of the songs and piano music that Moeran composed during the mid-1920s and early 1930s that an assertion of his heavy debt to Delius and Warlock has hitherto been predicated, and there is no doubt that Moeran does sometimes sound like these two composers. Nevertheless, the suggestion that Moeran's music is excessively derivative may be successfully challenged by considering the seemingly Warlockian or Delius-like elements in the music that Moeran composed before he would have heard anything by Warlock and long before his friendship with Heseltine and ensuing enthusiasm for Delius began. Works such as *The North Sea Ground* (1915), *At a Horse Fair* from *Three Piano Pieces* (1919), *Twilight*, *Spring Goeth All in White* and the song-cycle *Ludlow Town* (all 1920) all contain stylistic elements that may be regarded as similar to some of those employed by Warlock in such of his earlier songs as *As Ever I Saw* (1918), *There is a Lady* (1919), *Mr Belloc's Fancy* (1921) and *Good Ale* (1922), all of which were all composed either contemporaneously with, or later than, the Moeran works mentioned. The assumption that Moeran was heavily influenced by Warlock (and by extension, Delius) probably derives from a conflation of three factors: a) that Warlockian elements exist in Moeran's style, b) the fact that they were close friends and, c) the superior prominence of Warlock as a song composer. However, it is mistaken to attribute the apparently Warlockian stylistic features in Moeran's music solely to the influence of Warlock. Both composers were harmonic innovators using the same original

[18] 'Occasional Notes', *The Musical Times*, Vol. 69, No. 1023 (1 May 1929), 426.

material and with similar motivating inspiration, and their close association from early 1923 onwards ensured that a mutual sharing of ideas would inevitably lead to similarities in their own, individual compositions. The subsequent establishment of Warlock as the dominant figure is probably the result of his more extrovert personality and his much more public and sensational later life and death.

After completing *Summer Valley*, Moeran evidently suspended or postponed any other composition projects during the second half of 1925. Perhaps the visit to Grez had given him an impetus to make the effort to get his symphony completed while Delius was still alive. However, the freedom that Moeran had enjoyed during the preceding few years to compose what he liked and when he liked had ill-prepared him for the task of composing to tight deadlines. Accepting the commission of a major orchestral work – far more extended than anything he had previously attempted and with an actual performance date a matter of a few months hence already decided – suggests that Moeran's confidence in his ability to deliver was optimistic. From correspondence published in *The Guardian* towards the end of the year, it seems that the Manchester concert-going public had a more realistic appreciation of the problems such a commission might encounter. In a letter to the editor published in the edition dated 7 December, 'Musicus' wrote, after having complained about the habit of substituting programmed works at the last minute, 'Can we be blamed if we speculate on the eventual fate of Elgar's Second Symphony, or of the new works by [Benjamin] Dale or Moeran which have been announced?'[19] Harty replied in the edition published the following day:

> A letter from 'Musicus' in today's *Manchester Guardian* makes some complaints regarding the Hallé programmes. It is very difficult to carry out a series of 21 concerts without making some alterations; but I should like to assure 'Musicus' that such alterations are not merely the result of caprice. The Elgar Symphony will be given as announced, as well as the Symphony of Moeran and other new works.[20]

Thus, a mere three months before its scheduled performance, Harty was providing a public pledge that Moeran's symphony would be performed according to the published programme. It is probable that this was not simply Harty's own initiative and that he had himself received an assurance from the composer that the work was on track. This is supported circumstantially by a line in a letter Philip Heseltine wrote to Jelka Delius in September, even before the announcement of the symphony in *The Guardian*: 'Moeran has just finished a Symphony, commissioned by the Hallé orchestra. It will be produced in Manchester next March.'[21] Given that the earliest date by which the commission can have been confirmed was April or May, it is very unlikely that Moeran had actually completed the score of the symphony by 21 September, and it is interesting to reflect on why Heseltine would have thought it so. Clearly this can only have come from Moeran himself, who was still spending

[19] 'Manchester Letters', *The Guardian*, (7 December 1925), 11. Elgar's Symphony No. 2 in E flat had not been performed by the Hallé since 1911. Its having been programmed again for the 1925–26 season seems to have been not without some controversy.

[20] 'Manchester Letters', *The Guardian*, (8 December 1925), 13.

[21] Smith (2005), 146.

most of his time either at his parents' house in Somerset or at his London lodgings. Moeran may well have thought that he was making excellent progress with the composition of the work in his head and that the task of producing the full orchestral score would be relatively trivial.[22] Heseltine's (or rather Peter Warlock's) musical fecundity enabled him to turn out finished works – albeit mostly songs and miniatures – at a phenomenal rate, and this, together with his supposition that other composers were similarly gifted, may have forced Moeran into trying to emulate his friend's facility. Such a compulsion to be what he believed Heseltine wanted him to be (or perhaps even what Heseltine thought he was) provides a possible explanation for much of Moeran's behaviour during the years of his friendship with the other composer.

Unfortunately, Moeran's need for perfection, nurtured by his tuition sessions with John Ireland, superseded any attempt to compose to order. While he may well have cleared his desk of other composition projects, the technical and time requirements of composing a symphony overwhelmed him. The terms of the only previous commission that Moeran had accepted, the rhapsody for the 1924 Norwich Festival, had given him at least nine months to compose a single movement work of much shorter duration, and he had only just achieved this ahead of the rehearsal deadline. This experience was of little help to Moeran, and he probably spent much of the remainder of the year trying to adjust his working practice to accommodate the immense task that he had set himself.

On 26 August, a chamber music recital was broadcast by 5WA Cardiff.[23] The talented nineteen-year-old cellist Peers Coetmore Jones, together with her duo partner Kathleen Jacobs, made their debut performance on the radio, playing works for two cellos and piano by Handel, Bach and Mozart.[24] Wherever Moeran was in the south of England on that summer evening, it is unlikely that he could have received the broadcast intended, as it was, for 'listeners-in' in Wales and the west of England. The broadcast has a retrospective significance in as much as it was an early step in a sequence of events that culminated in Coetmore's meeting with Moeran nearly twenty years later.

1926

It is problematic to date exactly when Moeran made the decision to take up residence in Heseltine's Eynsford cottage, or to determine even that he made such a conscious decision. Nevertheless, it is apparent from the abrupt decrease in his musical output from late 1925 onwards that a substantial change in his circumstances took place, and that the new state resulting from this change persisted for several years. While

---

22 In later life, Moeran frequently referred to the task of creating a full score of a work as congenial or pleasant. Clearly, he regarded this aspect of the process of composition as relaxing, the main creative work having already been done.

23 One of the broadcasting stations that eventually merged to form the British Broadcasting Company (later Corporation).

24 Jacobs and Coetmore Jones performed together regularly as a cello duet, including making several broadcasts, during the late 1920s and the 1930s.

the reduction in compositional activity is partially explained by Moeran's concentrating on the Harty symphony commission, another factor must be introduced to show why, having either completed or abandoned the symphony, he did not return to his previous productivity. It is probable that Moeran was spending more and more time at the cottage, staying longer and longer on each occasion. Possibly this started with Heseltine's having suggested that living in Eynsford was exactly what Moeran needed to get his symphony finished. The environment would be an escape from the pressures and distractions of London and closer to the artistic inspiration provided by the various cottage guests than was the creative loneliness of Moeran's parents' house in Somerset. It is easy to understand how Moeran could have been seduced into believing that the atmosphere of the cottage would kick-start work on the symphony, with a superior result than would be possible elsewhere.

However, Moeran had composed most of his music in locations that provided quiet and a guarantee that he would not be disturbed. While at his parents' home, or whatever flat or lodgings he took in London, he could generally rely on these circumstances most of the time, at the cottage sustained work was impossible. Even if Moeran had the symphony more or less complete in his head, he still had to write the orchestral score, and the conditions that were indispensable to Moeran for such a task – despite Heseltine's opinion that the cottage was 'peaceful and congenial for work' – simply did not exist.[25] It must soon have become apparent that, contrary to his and Heseltine's expectations, he could not work on the symphony in the cottage. An obvious question that may be posed here, is why did he not go somewhere else to ensure the completion of the most important composition of his life thus far? The probable answer is that he soon became accustomed to the easy cottage lifestyle, replete with non-musical distractions which resulted in an alcohol-fuelled procrastination. While there is no evidence that Moeran had indulged in excessive drinking before he moved to the cottage, the availability of free-flowing beer and spirits that resulted from Heseltine's enthusiasm for drink and the fact that the cottage was situated near the Five Bells public house may have proved too tempting. William Walton was a visitor to the cottage and astutely observed the effect that the excessive drinking was having on the inhabitants: 'It was the drinking that was the undoing of a number who were drawn into the Heseltine circle … Walton wisely steered a clear course away from such influences: "I knew [Heseltine] well but well enough to avoid his somewhat baleful influence".'[26] Heseltine's capacity to drink seemingly without deleterious impact, probably rendered him oblivious to the consequences

---

[25] Evidence for this may be found in Moeran's own recollections. In Gerald Cockshott, 'E. J. Moeran's Recollections of Peter Warlock', *The Musical Times*, Vol. 96, No. 1345 (1 March 1955), 128–130, the author paraphrases Moeran: '[Warlock] went to the piano and began fumbling about with chords, and whistling … quite undisturbed by conversation from the next room. All his work was written in this way – quickly, at the piano, and often in an atmosphere that was far from quiet'.

[26] Stephen Lloyd, *William Walton: Muse of Fire*, (Boydell Press, Woodbridge, 2001), 81. Other first-hand accounts of Moeran's drinking, and life in the cottage generally, have been made by several writers, including: Jack Lindsay, *Fanfrolico and After*, (The Bodley Head, London, 1962), Nina Hamnett, *Is She A Lady? A Problem in Autobiography*, (Wingate, London 1955), and by Heseltine himself in numerous letters.

for those that tried to keep up with him. It is unlikely that Heseltine had any malicious intent in drawing his friends into his personal alcohol enjoyment. He probably just assumed that they enjoyed it too, and that the creative inspiration he apparently experienced when alcohol had so severely dulled his other senses was also experienced by others. Heseltine had years of drinking experience that had acclimatised his body to the resulting effects, whereas Moeran had not and was ill-equipped to deal with the consequences of living up to what he believed his friend expected.

Sex was another ever-present reality and distraction in the cottage. The possibility that the Heseltine/Moeran relationship included a homo-erotic element was introduced in Chapter 10, but regardless of whether this was true, there is evidence that Moeran was a willing participant in at least some of the sexual activities for which the cottage has since become notorious. Augustus John's biographer asserted that John and Moeran both had sex with Eileen Hawthorne, which on more than one occasion resulted in a pregnancy: 'It was John who, after some grumbling, paid for the abortions.'[27] Another frequent visitor to the cottage, Jack Lindsay, observed that Moeran seemed to be in a relationship with Nina Hamnett: 'On my second visit, Nina was there, living with Jack Moeran.'[28] While it is apparent from this scant evidence that Moeran's sexual experiences with women did not lead to any long term relationship, it is problematic to ascertain whether this was due to his sexuality, or to the cottage milieu, or, indeed, to some aspect of his character.

Even if he was unable to compose much, Moeran did continue other musical activities sporadically. His parents moved from Laverton to a townhouse at 11 Constitution Hill in Ipswich, which was convenient for Moeran as it provided him again with a base in East Anglia. He made at least one folksong expedition during the year, collecting songs at the Pleasure Boat Inn at Hickling in Norfolk.[29] Moeran was also the subject of occasional items in various newspapers and periodicals, and these were not confined to Britain. In February, *Billboard Magazine* of New York featured a brief article on the singer John Goss, in the course of which was written, 'E. J. Moeran is another collector and editor of folk songs whose work would seem well worth the serious consideration of theater men on the lookout for original and attractive material.'[30] On 8 February, Moeran was invited to give a talk to the Birmingham University Music Society and he chose the subject 'The Influence of Spohr on Contemporary Music'. What Moeran said about Spohr has not survived, but the *Midland Musician* issue of 3 March 1926 reported that the talk by 'Mr Ernest Moeran, the well-known Norfolk composer' had been 'interesting'.[31] The notion that Spohr had such an influence on contemporary music that it was worth writing a paper about it is so curious that one is forced to wonder whether it was a spoof,

---

[27] Michael Holroyd, *Augustus John, Vol.2 The Years of Experience*, (William Heinemann Ltd, London, 1975), 90.

[28] Lindsay, (1962), 84.

[29] Moeran was probably accompanied again by Heseltine on this trip, and the pair would have stayed with Cecil Walsingham at Sutton.

[30] *Billboard Magazine*, 38.6 (26 February 1926), 29.

[31] *Midland Musician*, (March 1926), 118.

possibly instigated by Heseltine. On the other hand, when Moeran's Norwegian folksong arrangement, *Oh, Sweet Fa's the Eve* was originally published as 'Sæterjentens Søndag', the reviewer for *The Musical Times* observed that 'One or two touches of harmony at the end are distinctly Spohrish.'[32]

Regular performances of works by Moeran also continued, including several outings for the popular String Quartet in A minor. However, it is evident from newspaper and periodical announcements and reviews that the number of performances and the range of works included declined steadily from early 1926. In comparison with the preceding five years Moeran seems to have made much less effort to promote himself, and it is probable that the musical establishment gradually forgot about him. While visitors to the cottage would have been reminded that Moeran was still alive, his failure to produce any new music and the decline in performances of the works he had previously composed may have reinforced the impression that he was no longer a central figure.

In early February, it had been necessary for Moeran to communicate to Hamilton Harty that the symphony would not be ready in time. He claimed that he was not satisfied with the form and that the consequent re-structuring would take some time. The change of programme was announced in the edition of *The Guardian* published on 27 February, just five days before the concert:

> Plans for the Hallé concert on Thursday have been broken up, first by Mr Moeran's resolution to remodel his promised symphony, which will consequently not be ready; and next by the inability of Miss Yolando Mero to reach England in time for the concert.[33]

It seems that the entire programme was changed, thus realising the earlier-expressed worst fears of 'Musicus', and Moeran's Second Rhapsody for Orchestra was announced as the substitute for the symphony. Even then, things did not go well, and at the very last minute, Moeran's Rhapsody was itself replaced on the programme by Stanford's *Irish Rhapsody No. 1*. Thus, the concert that Moeran had perhaps anticipated just a few months earlier as the beginning of a long and fruitful relationship between him and the Hallé orchestra, probably marked the confirmation of his disintegration as a successful composer of the 1920s. While Harty evidently accepted and even sympathised with Moeran's reasons for withdrawing the symphony at such short notice, it can be seen in retrospect that the proposed remodelling may have been a ruse to conceal the fact that it was not ready, perhaps even nowhere near ready. The issue of *Musical Opinion* of April 1926 published a letter from Moeran purporting to explain the non-appearance of the symphony: 'The work was practically in a state of completion when I came to the conclusion that I was (and still am) discontented about its structure. I have decided to rewrite a large portion of it.'[34] Those of a generous disposition may believe Moeran's artistic concern, while the more cynical might well read this as covering up failure. Harty

---

[32] 'Male-Voice', *The Musical Times*, Vol. 66, No. 993 (1 November 1925), 994.

[33] 'Music and Drama', *The Guardian*, (27 February 1926), 9.

[34] *Musical Opinion*, (April 1926), 701.

continued to support Moeran resolutely even though every indication must have been that the symphony was a hopeless case. Even ten years later, when Moeran started work again, Harty wrote to him:

> [Robert Nichols] spoke of your symphony as being partly completed. This was good news, and I am looking forward so greatly to seeing the work finally completed, with the orch: [sic] parts ready – and the score lying between us as we discuss various points of interpretation. Good luck to your pen, and may this summer bring you the necessary inspiration and lucky moods for work so that the Symphony may be finished. All your friends, like myself, are steadfast in their trust in your gifts.[35]

Whatever the truth, by the spring, Moeran had effectively abandoned composition, not just of the symphony, but of anything at all, and this abandoning remained in place for the next three years. Moeran himself wrote about it in a letter to Peers Coetmore in February 1948: 'I lost faith in myself once round about 1926 & composed nothing for several years. I even nearly became a garage proprietor in partnership with Cockerill, the ex air ace'.[36] The letter continued, 'I had an awfully lazy period in Eynsford. If you knock off for a long time it is frightfully hard to get going.' Moeran's admission to laziness supports the idea that he gave way to the multitude of distractions present in the cottage, and that having finally decided to go there, he just did not want to leave. The *laissez-faire*, hedonistic way of life had perhaps liberated Moeran from a lifetime of reserve and abstemiousness that was probably a legacy of his strict Anglican childhood. In Heseltine, he also had, possibly for the first time since Roland Perceval Garrod, a close friend with whom he could relax, and he would have made every effort to ensure that the friendship was not threatened. Thus, it is probable that Heseltine himself was the primary inhibiting factor for Moeran's ability to compose. The drinking, society, sex and free-living of the Eynsford cottage milieu seems to have been exactly the stimulation and nourishment that Heseltine's intellect and imagination craved, and it resulted in a free flow of creativity. It is possible that observing his friend's ability to consume quantities of alcohol throughout the day and evening and then work all night on an article or a song that was completed by the morning may have driven Moeran to despair and triggered a paralysing self-doubt, the only resolution for which was even more drinking. Observing the work of visitors to the cottage – Arnold Bax and William Walton, for example – could only have exacerbated his predicament.

The barren period lasted from early 1926 until 1929, but it was punctuated by a few high points where Moeran found the inspiration or motivation to produce

---

35 McNeill, 681. This keeping of the faith by Harty over a period of more than a decade, considered objectively, is quite extraordinary and warrants some investigation. Research by Jeremy Dibble following the publication of his book *Hamilton Harty: Musical Polymath* (Boydell & Brewer, Woodbridge, 2013) has uncovered evidence that raises the intriguing possibility of a familial connection between Harty and Moeran. A further link is suggested by the common interest in Spiritism that was shared by Harty and Moeran's father.

36 McNeill, 563.

something. The collaboration with Heseltine on *Maltworms* is well-known,[37] and he made piano arrangements of two Irish folksongs: the *Irish Love Song* and *The White Mountain*. He also composed an odd little song called *The Blossom*, a setting of a poem by William Blake, for a book of songs for children.[38] His name remained before the public in concerts in London, Liverpool and Manchester, in broadcasts of the ever popular works *In the Mountain Country* and the String Quartet in A minor, and several pre-1926 works were published between 1926 and 1929. While it is possible that he composed other works that have not survived, given his own testimony that he had succumbed to laziness, this seems unlikely. However, Heseltine continued with his mission to increase public awareness of his friend's compositional genius, and he wrote a miniature essay on Moeran, which was published in June 1926.[39] As was the case with Heseltine's writings of two years earlier, the biographical content of the essay derived from Moeran's recollections of his life, and it is apparent that he again adjusted these to accommodate a desire to preserve Heseltine's impressions of him, particularly those that pertained to his wartime experiences. There is no evidence that Moeran ever spoke about his active involvement at Bullecourt in 1917. His account was that he had been wounded accidentally while performing duties as a motorcycle dispatch rider. Heseltine's personality engendered an influence that Moeran may have found difficult to resist even if he had been inclined to do so, and Heseltine's attitude to the war, which he would hardly have concealed from his friend, was entirely negative and critical, and this may have been expressed so forcefully as to compel Moeran to reconsider his own participation less favourably. His deep sense of personal insecurity, possibly exacerbated by or even the result of his sexual identity issues, and his desire – perhaps even need – for a close friend would probably have driven him into confrontation-avoiding compliance. Thus, he may have believed that explaining his wartime injury as effectively being in the wrong place at the wrong time and being wounded accidentally would resonate better with Heseltine than the truth. While much of the essay repeated what had been said in the 1924 writings, Heseltine highlighted some of Moeran's more recent compositions, and he closed his piece with: 'one is amply justified in expecting that [Moeran's] talent will expand during the next ten years no less certainly than did that of his illustrious predecessors.'

In December, Moeran drove to the south of France to visit Augustus John in Martigues, apparently to collect French folksongs. John later recalled the occasion in his autobiography *Chiaroscuro*:

> The composer E. J. Moeran, spent some time with us, whether profitably or not I cannot say. He came to collect folk songs but, as far as I could see, only succeeded

---

[37] Cockshott (1955), 129.

[38] Cyril Winn (ed.), *The Roundabout Song Book*, (Thomas Nelson, London, 1929).

[39] Heseltine, (1926). Moeran wrote a similar essay on his friend: E. J. Moeran, *Miniature Essay: Peter Warlock*, (J & W Chester, London, 1926).

in getting hold of a defective piano on which to record them. We made, at any
rate, some memorable jaunts together, for he had brought his car with him.[40]

John's autobiography contains several references to Moeran's visits to various locations in the south of France but the dating is problematic as John did not write
chronologically, preferring to sprinkle the book with anecdotes – 'fragments' as he
called them – from various episodes of his life. Moeran visited Delius again on his
way back from Martigues, a letter from Heseltine to Jelka Delius making a passing
reference: 'I was so glad to hear from Moeran the other day that Fred seemed better
than he was when we were last in Grez.'[41]

1927

The year began for Moeran with the first performance in Belfast of *In the Mountain
Country*, which was broadcast on the local network 2BE.[42] This was followed by two
performances of the violin sonata at the Wigmore Hall by Florence Lockwood,
accompanied by Alan Bush. A performance of the String Quartet in A minor also
took place in January in Frankfurt, according to a letter Moeran wrote to Kenneth
Wright of the BBC in July. While no confirmation of this has been found, if it is
true, then it was an important milestone for Moeran. Although some of his piano
music had previously been performed abroad, Moeran's name was not known
outside Britain, and it is unlikely that the Quartet – with its intensely English
sound – was regarded as anything more than a curiosity to the modernist German
audience. There is no evidence that Moeran travelled to Frankfurt to hear the
performances.

Moeran's surviving correspondence suggests several addresses and locations
for him during the year, but he probably spent the first few months at Eynsford,
continuing his 'awfully lazy' time. The chronicles of the cottage mention numerous
anecdotes about the activities of the inhabitants, but few can be dated precisely.
However, it is reasonable to suppose that Moeran's mother was becoming increasingly anxious about not only her son's failure to continue the success that he had
so recently achieved, but also his apparent descent into a dissolute lifestyle. Ada
Esther Moeran's financial support had been predicated on his using his time to
compose, and, while he had spent more than five years amply fulfilling her hopes
and ambitions, the most recent three years could only have led her to increasing
despair. Since Moeran had no regular source of income other than the allowance
from his mother, he was dependent on her continuing generosity. It may be that,
as had been the case in 1920, she presented him with an ultimatum: that he must
come home (to Ipswich) and get on with composition again.

---

[40] Augustus John, *Chiaroscuro; Fragments of Autobiography*, (Jonathan Cape, London,
1954), 114–115.

[41] Smith (2005), 166.

[42] One of the broadcasting stations that eventually merged to form the British Broadcasting
Company (later Corporation).

While Moeran probably did endeavour to comply with his mother's demand – if such it had been – his ability to compose had been severely compromised. Moreover, his abstemious parents would not have been able to understand the unrelenting drinking of the previous eighteen months. However, a mother's love is unconditional, and Ada Esther probably saw it as her duty to get her son back to where he had been before coming under the unfortunate influence of Heseltine. Moeran's correspondence during the second half of 1927 and into 1928 provides confirmation that he was resident at 11 Constitution Hill, Ipswich. Several of his works are recorded as having been performed during 1927, but the frequency was lower than it had been in 1926. Again, it was his chamber music that accounted for most of the performances. Moeran also journeyed from Ipswich to stay with his friend Cecil Walsingham in Sutton as a base for folksong collecting both in the village and in nearby Potter Heigham.

Towards the end of the year, the BBC were apparently making plans to broadcast a performance of the Second Rhapsody for Orchestra, and on 9 November, Moeran wrote to Edward Clark to ask when they needed the instrumental parts by. Clearly nothing happened during the next three weeks, and at the end of the month, Moeran seems to have decided to travel again to Norway, hitching a lift on a tramp steamer – the *SS Rensfjell* – to Oslo. He wrote to Edward Clark, explaining that it was a short-notice trip, having been invited on board by the captain of the ship who was apparently Moeran's friend,[43] and again enquired about when the parts were required. If Moeran was still not capable of composing, at least he was regaining interest in the performance of his music.

---

[43] Possibly the friend whose wedding Moeran had attended several years earlier. How he developed a friendship with the captain of a Norwegian tramp steamer is not known.

Part 4

Reconstruction

12

Starting Again
(1928–1931)

Moeran wrote to Edward Clark in January, inviting him to lunch in London for a discussion about the Second Rhapsody for Orchestra. Moeran was planning to make some amendments to the score but wanted to hear the present version before doing so. It is not known whether the lunch invitation was accepted, but in any event, the broadcast of the Second Rhapsody did not materialise until some eighteen months later. There is little other evidence to account for Moeran's movements and activities during most of the year. There were a few performances of his music around the country, including *In the Mountain Country* played by the Hallé orchestra in Manchester and Leeds in March. Apart from occasional travels and visits to Eynsford, Moeran probably spent much of 1928 at his parents' home in Ipswich. There is also no evidence that Moeran had yet resumed any composing. Earlier in the year, he had submitted some of his pre-1926 compositions to publishing houses, and the piano pieces *Bank Holiday* and *Summer Valley* and the choral piece *Christmas Day in the Morning* soon appeared in print. However, no new works can be dated to 1928, although there is no means of knowing if he composed material that he later destroyed. As he later admitted, once he had let the impetus go, it was difficult to recover it. While he was living with his parents, he was able to restrict his drinking. Moeran's father was a strict abstainer, and so there would have been little opportunity for alcohol consumption. Nonetheless, drinking elsewhere was possible, and even if he was not spending extended periods in Eynsford, Moeran visited the cottage, and he ventured on folksong collecting expeditions across East Anglia.

In October, the Eynsford *ménage* finally came to an end, largely because the perpetually impecunious Heseltine was no longer able to pay the rent.[1] The lease on the cottage was terminated, Heseltine had returned to his mother's home in Wales, and Moeran had apparently been left to sort out the disarray. Heseltine wrote, displaying a somewhat casual attitude:

> I have been gathering up the energy to clear out of Eynsford and have got so far as to clear myself out, never to return, though Colly [Hal Collins], cats and

---

[1] By September, the rent arrears had accumulated to £100, according to a letter Heseltine wrote on the 12th of that month. Smith (2005), 205.

Raspberry [Moeran] are remaining until the quite preposterous financial situation is eased a little.[2]

Since the cottage sub-landlord, Hubert Foss, was a friend of both Moeran and Heseltine, it is difficult to conceive precisely what was the nature of the 'preposterous financial situation', unless Foss was dissatisfied with the state in which the cottage had been left and was demanding some sort of recompense. It has been suggested that the sub-tenants left a large quantity of rubbish lying around and that when the owner Munn came to clean up the cottage, much valuable work was also thrown away.[3] It is quite conceivable that Moeran had to appeal to his mother for funds to resolve the situation. In any case, the Eynsford artistic experiment was over. For Heseltine, it had been (mostly) a great achievement, compounding the successes – albeit erratic – of the previous ten years, and he was (again mostly) unaffected by the unremitting hedonistic lifestyle in the cottage. Moeran, in contrast, having entered the cottage as a successful composer pursuing an increasingly glittering career, had emerged mostly forgotten having composed practically nothing for several years and with an uncontrollable taste for alcohol. In a letter dated 23 October, Heseltine wrote:

> I can easily postpone my departure [from his mother's house] until the first few days of November if necessary. Raspberry, who has been pronounced 'not guilty', leaving the court without a beer stain on his waistcoat, so to speak, wishes to come here at the end of this week, to recuperate from the strain, and attendant insomnia, of his period of suspense.[4]

Heseltine's dismissal of the tribulations of his friend is again evident. 'Raspberry' (or sometimes 'Monsieur Framboise') was Heseltine's nickname for Moeran, bestowed after the excessive alcohol consumption had left Moeran with a ruddy complexion. Moeran had evidently been up before the magistrate on a drink-related charge, and such events – together with an apparent accident-proneness – were from that time onwards common in Moeran's life.[5] According to Heseltine's correspondence, Moeran did indeed travel to Wales to stay with Heseltine at his mother's house for a few days, after which they both visited poet Bruce Blunt in Hampshire.

1929

With the possibility of returning to the cottage and its associated distractions eliminated and probably under pressure from his mother, Moeran continued with the task of reconstructing his life and career. In the more stable and peaceful environ-

---

2   *Ibid.*, 200.
3   Unpublished letter dated 6 January 1986 from Fred Thomlinson to Barry Marsh, the original of which is in the Barry Marsh Collection.
4   Smith (2005), 205.
5   Moeran spent the next twenty years of his life apparently lurching from one illness or accident to another. His letters frequently mention recovering or convalescing from ailments or injuries.

ment of his parents' house at 11 Constitution Hill, Ipswich, Moeran's ability and urge to compose seems slowly to have returned.

Seven Poems of James Joyce

Moeran read James Joyce's *Chamber Music* collection, a set of thirty-six poems mostly concerning love in its various forms with many containing barely concealed sexual connotations, originally published in 1907. Moeran set seven poems from the collection as a cycle, simply called *Seven Poems of James Joyce*. The poems that he selected are all concerned in some way with the meetings of the poet and his lover and their unspoken consequences. Each of the settings is interesting, but the fifth, 'Donnycarney', has a special significance in the context of Moeran's oeuvre. It is the thirty-first poem in the Joyce set and recounts a tryst by the poet and his lover in the rural idyll of Donnycarney (*Domhnach Cearnach*) on a balmy summer's evening. Although Donnycarney is now a residential suburb east of the centre of Dublin, at the time of the poem's composition it was a wooded area with dells and thickets. While the main purpose of the line of the poem – 'When the bat flew from tree to tree' – is to signify an evening stroll taken by the poet together with his love, it also inserts an undercurrent of the macabre into the otherwise romantic image. The apparent perfection of the scene is therefore disturbed, and the lovers' meeting is imbued with uncertainty. However, the sub-text is clearly sexual, and it is likely that the force of this did not escape Moeran. He was aware of the power of music to evoke mental imagery, and an appreciation of this is essential for an understanding of his ability to manipulate the listener's emotional responses. As has already been mentioned, Moeran's use of nature as an inspirational tool was an intrinsic and vital characteristic of his compositional technique.[6] His setting of the first verse of 'Donnycarney' evokes a pleasant pastoral scene as the location for the lovers' walk together. Although the setting of the second verse generates a contrast to the initial effect leading more to an impression of *sehnsucht* on the part of the listener, Moeran was clearly concentrating on a romantic interpretation of the text. There is ambiguity as to the outcome of the lovers' walk. Was this long in the past and the poet is remembering a lost love, or is he recalling a happy and recent time spent with his love? This uncertainty is communicated by the ambivalence of the final chord of the song, which may be spelled either as the second inversion sub-dominant major 9th or as a bitonal combination of the sub-dominant and tonic triads. Perhaps the lover was still recalling the kiss (music example 27)?

Of the other six settings in *Seven Poems*, four ('Strings in the Earth and Air', 'The Merry Green Wood', 'Bright Cap' and 'The Pleasant Valley') have folksong-style melodies, which suggests that Moeran had been able to recover his melodic inventiveness. 'Strings in the Earth and Air' has the tempo marking 'Slow and liltingly' and is cast in a siciliano-like form with a 6/8 time signature that is occasionally extended to 9/8 to accommodate the extended second line of each verse of the poem. The song is through composed, although the final two bars of the vocal line recall the

---

[6] Huss has examined this aspect of Moeran's music. See Fabian Gregor Huss, 'The Construction of Nature in the Music of E. J. Moeran', *Tempo* Vol. 63, No. 248, (1 April 2009), 35–44.

Music example 27. *Seven Poems of James Joyce*, 'Donnycarney': ending

opening two bars. In common with other Moeran song settings, the piano accompaniment is primarily diatonic for the first verse, with increasingly dissonant added-note chords through the second and third verses. A four-bar coda recalls the three-bar introduction.

'The Merry Green Wood' is a strophic setting with a lively Mixolydian mode tune that was inspired perhaps by the use of the word 'merry' in Moeran's song title, which actually forms the end of the third line of the poem 'Who Goes Amid the Green Wood'. While it is possible to read the poem as a contemplative expression of the poet's love, Moeran's interpretation is more joyful, and his setting emphasises delight and gaiety in the duple time melody that bounces along as if carefree. The piano accompaniment varies for each of the verses, culminating with Moeran's characteristic chromatic block chord sequences for the final verse. The key moment of the text: 'O it is for my own true love | That is so young and fair' is accompanied with an appropriately dramatic sequence, leading into a short playout. While Moeran's tempo marking is 'Fast' throughout the song, an interpretative *rallentando* into 'young and fair', followed by an accelerating tempo through the five-bar postlude provides a more satisfying effect (music example 28).

In 'Bright Cap', the personification of love instructs the protagonists to follow him and not waste time in contemplation: 'Leave dreams to the dreamers'. Moeran's setting is marked 'Fast and gay' and rushes headlong through a two-verse strophic form that seems to end as soon as it has begun. Within the forty-five-second duration of the song, several characteristic Moeran stylistic features may be observed, from the opening dominant to tonic pedal in the left-hand – first observed as early as 1915 at the opening of *The North Sea Ground* – to the initially unaccompanied final note of the song, a technique also employed in 'The Merry Green Wood', 'The Pleasant Valley', 'Donnycarney' and 'Rain Has Fallen' in the Joyce cycle and in many other Moeran song settings.

Moeran chose a hymn-like context for 'The Pleasant Valley', perhaps in response to the line 'For many a choir is singing'. This, together with the strict tempo instruction, results in a fittingly solemn framework for the poet's exhortation to his love to come with him to the valley where it is cool and pleasant. While the melody is

Music example 28. *Seven Poems of James Joyce*, 'The Merry Green Wood': final 8 bars

Music example 29. *Seven Poems of James Joyce*, 'The Pleasant Valley': bars 17–23

cast steadfastly in F major, deviating to F minor for one bar: 'Calling us away', the accompaniment implies modulations to and through several keys. As in the previous two songs in the cycle, the tonal meanderings in the final verse are resolved in the last chords. The use of the unresolved dominant thirteenth on 'we', followed by a prolonged resolution over the final three bars was inspired, aptly highlighting the final word 'stay' (music example 29).

The sixth song, 'Rain Has Fallen', is the most complex of the cycle harmonically; McNeill asserted that it recalls Warlock's *The Curlew* in its idiom.[7] The setting invokes a doleful atmosphere, which suitably frames the melancholy implicit in the text: 'The leaves lie thick upon the way | Of memories' (music example 30). The chord on the first beat of bar eight is particularly interesting, evoking the dark and smoky atmosphere of a 1930s jazz club. Its symbol is C7b9#9, although Moeran's enharmonic notation with a C sharp instead of a D flat was probably for readability. Moeran was not an admirer of jazz, but the more harmonically advanced jazz that would have included such six-note chords as that employed in 'Rain Has Fallen' did not develop into general use until some years after the composition of this song.[8] The song ends with a similarly advanced jazz chord, GmM7#11 (music example 31).

There are few conventional harmonic progressions in the piano accompaniment, which – in a similar manner to the songs *When June Is Come* and *Impromptu in March* that were examined earlier – underlies rather than supports the vocal line. The dynamic markings range from *p* at the outset, reducing to *ppp* at the end, with a brief crescendo to *mf* at the climactic point 'Come, my beloved'. 'Rain Has Fallen' is, perhaps, the most extraordinary song that Moeran composed. While the influence of Warlock is clear and the spectral figure of Bernard van Dieren may be detected hovering over the more exotic note combinations. the harmonic inventiveness is characteristically Moeran, as is the formal symmetry, with the climax occurring at the golden section point in the song.

The final song in the cycle, 'Now, O now, in this Brown Land', is a sombre setting of one of the last poems in Joyce's set. The text is a contrast to the happiness encountered earlier in 'The Merry Green Wood', and Moeran's choice of lugubriously fluid tonality aptly frames the hopeless longing embedded in the first two verses. As in 'Rain Has Fallen', the harmony recalls Warlock, and the breath of van Dieren is again felt in the chromatic chord progressions, which flow smoothly and without jarring (music example 32).

In the third and final verse, the accompaniment shifts to rich tonal harmony: 'Now, O now, we hear no more | The villanelle and roundelay', with Moeran revisiting the style of his early 1920s piano pieces *Stalham River* and *Toccata*. The song ends with a return to the siciliano-like rhythm of the introduction to 'Strings in the Earth and Air', bringing the cycle to a close. In the *Seven Poems of James Joyce*, Moeran achieved a synthesis of influences with his own individuality, which produced a set of seven songs that stand out from the others in his oeuvre. While the *Seven Poems of James Joyce* was the third set of songs produced by Moeran, it was the first that exhibits the characteristics of a song-cycle.

Despite his gradual musical rehabilitation, Moeran seems to have made no effort to re-establish himself at the Oxford & Cambridge Musical Club. Apart from recording his annual subscription payments, Moeran is not mentioned in any club archives during 1928 and 1929, and it seems to be likely that he took no part in activities, or,

---

7   McNeill, 111.

8   Amongst others, the guitar-playing of Django Reinhardt of the Quintette du Hot Club de France beginning in the mid-1930s was highly influential in the development of complex jazz harmony.

Music example 30. *Seven Poems of James Joyce*, 'Rain Has Fallen': bars 6–8

Music example 31. *Seven Poems of James Joyce*, 'Rain Has Fallen': bars 12–16

Music example 32. *Seven Poems of James Joyce*,
'Now, O Now, in this Brown Land': bars 4–9

indeed, made any use of the club facilities. The fact that he was expelled at the beginning of 1930 for non-payment suggests that a more serious rift had occurred between him and the committee, and it is not too much of a leap of imagination to attribute this to his probable failure to attend the music sub-committee meetings. Moeran had served conscientiously on this committee since 1922 – including a period as its chairman – and his increasing lack of diligence, together with his failure to attend any of the club events, was probably met with dissatisfaction. Thus, it is reasonable to assert that Moeran had probably burned his boats during his sojourn in Eynsford and that, two years later, he found the club doors closed to him.

Moeran's break with the musical club is significant in that it had been central to his life in London since his arrival as a student, and it had been on the foundations created by membership that Moeran's impressive rise to prominence had been constructed. While it could be argued that his mother's financial support and his innate talent would have ensured his eventual success, the performing opportunities and social networking facilitated by the club assisted the achievement of that success more rapidly than might otherwise have been possible. Thus, his abandonment of it requires an explanation. Although Moeran maintained his membership until the end of 1929, his last recorded participation at a recital evening was on 19 February 1925. The minutes of the 1925 Annual General Meeting record that he was still a member of the House Music Sub-Committee and it is also recorded that he donated some scores. His decline in interest in the club began at around that time, and this was probably due to his developing relationship with Heseltine. Having failed to graduate from Oxford, Heseltine was not eligible for standard membership of the club, and his notorious reputation and unconventional lifestyle possibly disqualified him from selection under the other available entry routes. Despite his music having been included by Moeran in one of the programmes, it may be that Heseltine considered the club to be elitist and anachronistic.

Thus, Moeran would have faced a dilemma; continuing his membership and participation in the activities of the club would have meant going against the undoubtedly strongly-expressed views of his friend, while forsaking it altogether meant that he would lose the important and useful contacts he had established and, perhaps, even his own reputation. While there is nothing recorded, it is likely that Moeran's decision was one of prevarication in that he continued to pay his subscription, but no longer participated actively. This assertion is supported by the club archive record that confirms that, from 1926, Moeran ceased paying 'programme money'. This was a subscription supplement to cover the costs of producing the printed programmes for each of the fortnightly Thursday evening musical recitals. While it was not compulsory, any member not paying the supplement was not entitled to keep copies of the printed programmes. That Moeran stopped paying this is a strong indication that he did not attend any musical evenings after 1925. Although the minutes of the 1926 Annual General Meeting record Moeran as still a member of the House Music Sub-Committee, there is no other mention of him in club records after that date except for the note recording his ejection in January 1930. It is likely, therefore, that he did not participate actively as a committee member after 1926 and that he was removed from this position a few months later.

In the summer, Moeran took rooms at 22 Priory Road, London, NW6. Although he did not remain there for long, it was the address from which he wrote several letters to the BBC between July and September concerning performances of his Second Rhapsody for Orchestra. The work had been performed in a concert on 3 June given by the Wireless Symphony Orchestra conducted by Ernest Ansermet and broadcast by 2LO. The programme was a concert of works by British composers and included music by William Walton, Lennox Berkeley, Constant Lambert and Peter Warlock. Victor Hely-Hutchinson played the solo piano part in his own concertino work *The Young Idea*. The *Radio Times* featured the broadcast as a 'special concert by the younger generation of British composers' and provided brief programme notes on each work. Regarding the Second Rhapsody, the *Radio Times* said: 'This Second Rhapsody has a fine wholesome English flavour and is throughout fresh, breezy music ... the main body of the piece is founded on two tunes of folk song character, one merry and mischievous and the other bigger and more smoothly flowing.'[9] A further performance was arranged for the 1929 Promenade Concerts at the Queen's Hall, and on 18 July, Moeran wrote to the Director of Programmes at the BBC accepting an invitation to conduct the work at the concert on 12 September. As he mentioned in a postscript, this was the first concert performance in London.[10] Moeran's presence on the wireless after an almost complete absence during the previous two years had been resumed towards the end of 1928 with broadcasts of the piano pieces *Windmills* and *At a Horse Fair*, and from mid-1929, Moeran's music was again broadcast regularly, including the String Quartet in A minor by 5GB Daventry[11] on 7 July as part of a chamber music recital given by the Charles Woodhouse Quartet. A programme note in the *Radio Times* mentioned the composer's enthusiasm for 'native folk music'. Away from music, Moeran's legal problems continued. In August, he was fined £10 by Watford magistrates for having been drunk in charge of a car.

1930

The January 1930 edition of *The Musical Times* published an article by Hubert Foss, intended to revive interest in Moeran's work by the music-appreciating public, and perhaps to stimulate the composer himself into pulling himself together and start producing music again.[12] Foss pulled no punches in lamenting the 'over-long silence' into which Moeran had fallen. He suggested that the fault lay equally with the composer, with performers and with his audiences. He made a compelling case that those who failed to see beyond Moeran's undoubted use of folksong as an inspirational tool were missing the essence of his creative genius. Foss used examples from the String Quartet in A minor and the Sonata in E minor for Violin and Piano, which he described as Moeran's 'best achievements in the longer form', to illustrate

---

9   'The Evening's Symphony Concert', *Radio Times*, Vol. 23, No. 296, (31 May 1929), 465.

10   The earlier performance on 5 May 1925 had been a broadcast performance from the BBC studios.

11   The Midlands-based Daventry transmitter could reach much of the UK and was the first truly national radio service in the country. 5GB was one of the stations that eventually merged to form the British Broadcasting Company (later Corporation).

12   'E. J. Moeran: A Critical Appreciation', *The Musical Times*, Vol. 71, No. 1043, (1 Jan 1930), 26–29.

some of his most characteristic features: sonic colouration through secondary and added note harmony, descending bass lines, primarily pentatonic melodic invention and the use of the added sixth chord to produce 'fullness without any harsh clash of sound'. Foss also highlighted Moeran's folksong arrangements, in particular *The Little Milkmaid*, as exemplifying how the melody line is 'lit up' by the use of 'subtle suspensions and harmonies changing from one concordant discord to another', thus raising the mere folksong more to the level of a work of art. Foss's assessment of Moeran's compositional style was precise and insightful, but it was informed by a full appreciation of the composer's career during the previous ten years. As has been mentioned, Foss was a champion of the younger British composers of the early twentieth century, having an almost infallible ability to discern real talent.

Moeran could reasonably assert, however, that he was no longer silent. He had completed his *Seven Poems of James Joyce* the previous year – although they had not yet been published or performed – and he was working on a song, *The Sweet o' the Year*, for the tenor John Armstrong. This is a jaunty and exuberant setting of Autolycus's song 'When daffodils begin to peer'.[13] It is in a three-verse strophic form but with melodic modification in the second and third verses using prolongation to highlight certain words and provide a contrast across the verses. Many of the composer's stylistic features are apparent, and the song ends with a typical Moeran flourish (music example 33).

Moeran seldom travelled beyond the British Isles. Until 1930, the only exceptions to this had been his motorcycle tour of western France and the Pyrenees in 1920 with Robert Gibbings, his short visit with Heseltine to Delius's house in Grez-sur-Loing in 1925, his drive to the south of France for a winter holiday in Martigues in late 1926 and two trips to Norway. It is, therefore, interesting to discover a letter written by Moeran dated 5 April on board the *SS General Buonaparte*, voyaging to Calvi in Corsica. His reasons for visiting Corsica are not known, but it may be guessed that he was again in search of indigenous folksong. The letter was addressed to Alan (H) of the BBC, and it concerned a programme for the *Children's Hour* that Moeran had

Music example 33. *The Sweet O' the Year*: final 6 bars

---

13 William Shakespeare, *A Winter's Tale*, Act IV, Scene III.

been engaged to broadcast on 12 May. The National Programme schedule for that day as printed in the *Radio Times* stated that, 'E. J. Moeran will play some of his own compositions, including *An April Evening*, which has been specially written for the Children's Hour.'[14] However, on 18 June, Heseltine wrote to Arnold Dowbiggin, explaining that Moeran had suffered another accident on board the ship returning him from Corsica:

> Please forgive this long delay in replying to your letter of a month ago. It lay for some while at 22 Priory Road which is now untenanted owing to Moeran having fallen down (drunk again?) on the boat crossing from Corsica to France and given himself water-on-the-knee which had kept him in a nursing home since his return to England.[15]

The interjection 'drunk again?' again speaks volumes regarding Heseltine's casual attitude to Moeran's misfortunes. On his return to England, Moeran spent much of the remainder of the year in a nursing home. Another letter from Heseltine explained this:

> I am sorry to say that [Moeran] will be laid up for some considerable time. What was originally diagnosed as water-on-the-knee has now been proved, by blood tests and X-rays, to be a form of localised tuberculosis from which recovery is bound to be a slow and tedious process.[16]

Moeran had probably spent much of April touring Corsica, and he would have made the return voyage to France towards the end of the month. Since, according to Heseltine, his injury happened on this crossing, it is probable that he travelled back to England by train and was immediately admitted to hospital. It may therefore be supposed that Moeran's participation in the *Children's Hour* broadcast was cancelled. It is not known what happened to *An April Evening*, or even whether it was ever composed.

Anglican Church Music

The surviving correspondence between Moeran and Heseltine confirms that Moeran was an invalid and bed-bound after his discharge from hospital until mid-November 1930 and that he was not fully mobile for a further few weeks. Nevertheless, during these few months, he had worked on several compositions, the most significant of which were a sonata for two violins, a string trio and some Anglican church music. He had also, almost certainly at Heseltine's behest, entered into a legal action against Eric Thiman for copyright infringement.[17] In early October, Heseltine had written to Moeran to thank him for the loan of his piano – which his being confined to bed had rendered temporarily useless to him – and had suggested in a postscript

---

14 'The Children's Hour', *Radio Times*, Vol. 27, No. 345, (9 May 1930), 321.

15 Smith (2005), 272.

16 *Ibid.*, 274.

17 Eric Thiman (1900–1975) was an eminent conductor, organist, and teacher. He was also a prolific composer, and he spent many years as Professor of Harmony at the Royal Academy of Music.

that a piano piece by Thiman published in the *Monthly Musical Record* infringed Moeran's copyright. While the work by Thiman – called *In a Hammock* – bore a resemblance to Moeran's piano piece *Bank Holiday*, it was questionable whether this really amounted to copyright infringement. Moreover, given that Thiman's piece had been copyrighted by Augener in 1926 some two years before Moeran's piece was published by Oxford University Press, there was plenty of opportunity for legal argument on both sides. Moeran referred to his ongoing case in a letter that he wrote to Heseltine on 5 November:

> I am afraid that my chancery affair will become a case of Jarndyce & Jarndyce and that I shall be hard up for some time to come. That is why I am writing this bilge for the Church. It is very easy to do, and it is financially a waste of time to write songs or piano pieces.[18]

It is not known how the legal case ended, but Moeran's reference to 'bilge for the Church' is interesting. Despite having been brought up in the confines of a series of Anglican vicarages with a father whose faith was extreme, there is no evidence that Moeran himself was at all religiously inclined. None of his music up to 1930 could be thought of as sacred in any sense, so it is curious that he should have chosen this moment to enter the realm of Anglican church music. However, his childhood experiences in church would have given him a thorough grounding in hymnody, the various service settings and anthems. Consequently, the characteristics of mid to late Victorian sacred music would have been an innate aspect of his musical identity. The 'bilge' comprised an Evening Canticles in D (*Moeran in D*), a Te Deum and Jubilate (*Moeran in E flat*) and an anthem *Praise the Lord, O Jerusalem*. Moeran's 5 November letter provides an interesting insight, not only into the composition of the church music, but also how he was able to work under trying circumstances:

> I have a fairly easy Te Deum all ready & copied out & am well on with an evening service into which I cannot resist inserting some luscious Stainerisms. I spend a good deal of time writing music, but lack of privacy prevents me from doing any-thing on a larger scale, as I am still too helpless to be free of constant attendance.[19]

The letter continued in a frank and detailed manner about the practical consider-ations of being bed-bound and its consequent indignities. Moeran had evidently sought refuge in composition, by necessity entirely in his head, and the resulting music is a testament to his ability to overcome adversity. Despite his extended illness, his musical recovery was progressing. However, while the 'bilge for the Church' was dismissed by its composer, *Moeran in D* has subsequently become one of the most popular twentieth-century settings of the canticles in the reper-toires of many cathedral choirs. Together with the Te Deum and Jubilate, it appears regularly on the service sheets of cathedrals and larger churches throughout the

---

[18] Smith (2005), 286. The mention of Jarndyce & Jarndyce refers to a seemingly never-ending civil court case that is the central plot device of Charles Dickens' novel *Bleak House*. The implication is that any financial settlement that either side would be awarded would be more than consumed by the eventual legal costs.

[19] *Ibid.*

country. Although relatively minor when considered in the context of Moeran's entire oeuvre, the church music well represents his ability to appreciate and satisfy genre through the use of distinctive stylistic devices. While Moeran undoubtedly composed the first versions of these works when confined to bed in Ipswich, it may be reasonably supposed that, once he had regained the possibility of playing the piano, he was able to verify and correct to ensure the final result was exactly what he had imagined.

Sonata for Two Violins, String Trio in G major

It is probable that this was also the case with the other significant music that he began to compose during his enforced convalescence: the Sonata for Two Violins and the String Trio in G major. The exact dates of completion of these two works are problematic to determine since Moeran – as is frequently the case – has left contradictory evidence. The first reference to the sonata comes from a letter Hubert Foss wrote to his wife Dora on 21 October while he was staying with the Moerans in Ipswich:

> I haven't time to tell you much as I have to go out and get petrol and also take Moeran out for his drive. He's doing splendidly and the nurse is excellent. You'd like him so much; he's quietened down a lot and is very nice indeed. His new work is very interesting – rather dry but beautifully written. It's a Sonata for Two Violins alone.[20]

Moeran first mentioned working on the sonata and the trio in a letter to Heseltine dated 23 November: 'I … have occupied my unlimited leisure through being laid up by finishing a sonata for two violins and a trio for strings.'[21] Taken literally, this would suggest that both works were complete by the date of the letter. However, later in the same letter, he wrote, 'I have started a String Trio and if I can keep it up I hope the purgative effect of this kind of writing may prove permanently salutary.' Further evidence that the sonata at least was fully composed exists in a letter that the violinist Anne Macnaghton wrote to Geoffrey Self in June 1983. Macnaghton recalled that she and André Mangeot visited Moeran in Ipswich in November 1930 and played the sonata to him. She also asserted that Moeran had paid Heseltine two guineas to make a fair copy, since his manuscript was more legible than was Moeran's.[22] The work was admired by Heseltine, who wrote to Lionel Jellinek on 10 December:

> Are you proposing to visit Raspberry in the near future? He has written a very good sonata for two violins (unaccompanied) which I am putting forward next

---

[20] Letter transcribed in Stephen Lloyd, Diana Sparkes, Brian Sparkes (eds), *Music in Their Time: The Memoirs and Letters of Dora and Hubert Foss*, (Boydell & Brewer, Woodbridge, 2019), 75.

[21] Letter quoted in Self, 74. Self does not state where this letter is archived, and the author has not been able to locate it.

[22] *Ibid.*

week to the committee of the International Festival. It is by far the best thing he has ever written.[23]

Together, this evidence strongly suggests that the Sonata was complete by early December. However, the date of completion of the Trio is clearly in some doubt. To complicate matters further, the manuscript of the Sonata for Two Violins in the Royal College of Music library bears the signature 'Lingwood Lodge', as does the manuscript of the String Trio in G major in the British Library. It will be shown below that Lingwood Lodge (near Norwich) became Moeran's parents' address in April 1931, and thus it is unlikely that the extant versions of each work are those that Moeran composed while confined to bed in Ipswich during October and November 1930. Moeran's normal practice of composing at the piano dated back to his earliest works and probably to his childhood. As a talented pianist – as indicated by the piano music that he performed during his youth and early adulthood – it would have been natural for him to think pianistically when composing his own music. However, evidence of Moeran's ability to hear his music clearly in his head abounds, and his usual composing process – like that of many other composers – was probably a combination of imagination and piano verification.

Writers on Moeran hitherto have seized upon Moeran's apparent hope of a 'purgative effect' of being compelled to compose for restricted instrumental forces as suggesting a general desire to rid himself of certain characteristics of his musical style up to that point and to have engaged in an extensive technical re-education or stylistic re-evaluation.[24] Much has also been made of his apparent claim to have been obsessed with Delius's harmony and an indication of an apparent resolve to reduce this in his music. In his 23 November letter to Heseltine, Moeran also wrote:

> It is an excellent discipline in trying to break away from the mush of Delius-like chords, which I have been obsessed with on every occasion I have attempted to compose during the last two years. Perhaps some good has come of being abed and unable to keep running to the keyboard for every bar.

On first consideration, the suggestions of stylistic re-evaluation seem cogent, since the evidence clearly comes from Moeran himself. However, the 23 November letter to Heseltine is the only place where Moeran mentions the subject, and the Sonata

---

[23] Smith (2005), 293. Heseltine's intention to submit the work to the jury of the International Society for Contemporary Music was with a view to its being considered for inclusion in one of the concerts that would form the 1931 ISCM Annual Festival, which was to take place in Oxford between 24 and 28 June. Unfortunately, Heseltine's death just a week after he wrote the letter to Jellinek forestalled the plan, and it is likely that Moeran's Sonata was never put before the judging panel.

[24] See Self, 73–74, McNeill, 114, Vernon Lee Yenne (1969), 147, and Fabian Huss, 'Technical focus and 'stylistic cleansing' in E.J. Moeran's Sonata for Two Violins and String Trio', in Gareth Cox, Julian Horton (eds), *Irish Musical Analysis 11*, (Four Courts Press, Dublin, 2014). The suggestion that Moeran retired to the Cotswolds for a period of study and re-evaluation is incorrect. It results from a confusion originating with Peers Coetmore in the early 1950s about the location of Moeran's parents' house. They lived for a time in Laverton near Bath in Somerset, rather than Laverton near Tewkesbury in Gloucestershire.

for Two Violins and the String Trio in G major are the only extant works in his entire oeuvre to which the suggested stylistic re-evaluation could apply. Moreover, while it cannot be doubted that Moeran revelled in a 'mush of Delius-like chords' in some of his pre-1930 compositions, there can also be no doubt that he continued to do so in much of the music he composed after 1930. Any stylistic re-appraisal – if it really was a deliberate process – should be apparent throughout the music Moeran composed from 1931 onwards, and even more particularly, it should not be apparent in music that he composed before that date. However, much of Moeran's post-1931 work is as rich and luxuriant in chordal textures as is his pre-1926 music, and while it may be agreed that the Sonata for Two Violins and the String Trio abound in contrapuntal writing, these works are also unique in Moeran's oeuvre. Thus, there is nothing with which they may be compared. Furthermore, as suggested above, the extant versions of these two works are those that were completed after April 1931, after Moeran's confinement to bed had ended and long after he had regained access to a piano. It may reasonably be presumed therefore that the original November 1930 manuscripts were destroyed and that the extant works benefitted from revision after Moeran was once again able to compose with the help of his piano. There is no way of knowing how much of the existing Sonata for Two Violins and String Trio in G major were composed in Moeran's head during the time he was unable to get to his piano.

Nonetheless, given the circumstances of their composition and notwithstanding the fact that the extant versions date from after Moeran had regained access to his piano, the Sonata and the Trio are significant works. Alongside the church music, they display Moeran's technical facility and the precision of his aural imagination. However, regardless of the sparseness of the instrumental textures available to him, he did not abandon his guiding composing principle: first create some good tunes. Moeran invented several folksong-style themes to provide a melodic interest in the Sonata for Two Violins. The first movement opens with a beguiling melody (music example 34). In the String Quartet in A minor, Moeran demonstrated that he was familiar with the techniques for creating the impression of fuller textures on individual and combinations of stringed instruments, and he again employed these extensively in the Sonata (music example 35).

While Heseltine's endorsement of the work would have given Moeran undoubted pleasure and satisfaction, asserting that it was 'by far the best thing he has ever written' is perhaps tending towards over-egging. Much has also been claimed for the String Trio in G major. Self called it 'a masterpiece of [Moeran's] mature style' and 'a work of consummate technical mastery',[25] while McNeill asserted it was 'an even more impressive achievement than the Sonata for Two Violins'.[26] The first performance in October 1931 was positively reviewed in *The Times*:

> The string trio by E. J. Moeran ... is an attractive work of definitely English flavour, avoiding in its workmanship the extremes of bareness and fussiness, into either of which writing for three melodic instruments may easily fall. It also avoids prolix-

[25] Self, 94–97.
[26] McNeill, 146.

Music example 34. Sonata for Two Violins, first movement: bars 1–4

Music example 35. Sonata for Two Violins, second movement: bars 61–72
(2nd violin slurs omitted for clarity)

ity, and the slow movement is striking for its terse combination of lyrical feeling and astringent quality. Many of the epithets applicable to English folk-melody are applicable to this trio, but the thematic material is neither 'folk' nor 'folky', being instrumentally conceived.[27]

Moeran was again faced with self-imposed limited resources, and he used similar technical devices to thicken the texture: *arco* broken chords, *pizzicato* and *arco* double and triple-stopped chords and tremolos. The work has many points of interest that make it compelling listening, and many hours may be spent in enjoyable study of the score in the hunt for variations on the several themes that are stated across the four movements. While acknowledging Moeran's technical skill in creating from extremely limited instrumental resources two such attractive works, the author does not share the encomiastic assessments presented by other writers. Had Moeran genuinely determined to change his style and eschew forthwith the textural indulgences of the past, he would surely have composed more works in these limited genres and his former characteristic melody and harmony-based musical style would be less apparent in his other works, and this is manifestly not the case.

[27] 'Recitals of the Week', *The Times*, issue 45961, (23 October 1931), 10.

However, it may reasonably be wondered why Moeran decided to compose both the Sonata for Two Violins and the String Trio. While there were several motivations during his career that drove his choice of works for composition, by 1930 one of the most frequent of these was that someone asked him for a piece. André Mangeot had known Moeran for some years and had performed his violin sonata several times. He visited Moeran during his convalescence in Ipswich and, thus, it is possible that he had asked Moeran to compose something for him. Indeed, both the Sonata and Trio may have their origins in conversations with Mangeot.

The *Seven Poems of James Joyce* were given their first performance in a broadcast on the London Regional wavelength on 9 December. The singer was the tenor John Armstrong, and the song-cycle formed the central item in a recital of chamber music. The *Radio Times* had printed the titles of two of the songs incorrectly, and Moeran wrote to the BBC the day before the broadcast in the hope that the 'announcer be informed of these errata'. The songs had been published by Oxford University Press just a few weeks before the scheduled broadcast, and the final proofs had included the same mistakes. On the same day, Augustus John wrote to Moeran to express his thanks for a copy of the published songs. John also mentioned that he had spoken to Philip Heseltine who had told John that Moeran had now recovered from the extended illness that had kept him bed-ridden for several months. John said nothing about Heseltine to indicate that anything might be amiss, but just one week later, on 17 December in his flat at Tite Street, Chelsea, Heseltine took his own life. Why he did this has been the subject of much speculation and sensational reporting during the subsequent ninety years.[28]

Heseltine's death had a profound effect on Moeran. In a letter to Heseltine's mother he wrote, 'I have very few really close friends, [and] Philip was one of the closest ... His loss will mean a terrible gap to me when I get back again to normal life [and] find he is no longer there.'[29] Whether or not their relationship had had a physical element and whether or not they had temporarily fallen out, the underlying friendship of two musically very like-minded individuals cannot be doubted, and when Moeran wrote that he would miss Heseltine, this was undeniably true. Nevertheless, Heseltine's death may be regarded in retrospect as having been a liberation for Moeran.

1931

Two Pieces for Small Orchestra: Whythorne's Shadow, Lonely Waters

The year began with Moeran still unable to walk unaided. On 18 February, he wrote to Arnold Dowbiggin: 'I am now back here [Ipswich] embarking on the next stage

---

28 See particularly Barry Smith, *Peter Warlock: The Life of Philip Heseltine*, (Oxford University Press, Oxford, 1994), 279–290.

29 Letter from Moeran to Edith Buckley Jones dated 27 December 1930; part of *Heseltine Papers*, Add.MS 964, British Library, London.

of my recovery – that of walking on my two legs. Up to now, I have been on one leg and two crutches.' He was re-elected as a committee member of the Folk-Song Society, and, as he became more mobile, he continued his folksong collecting expeditions. Although walking was difficult, Moeran could certainly work, and the first three months of the year were spent mostly in his composing studio in his parents' Ipswich house. Perhaps as a means of reconciling himself to Heseltine's death, he decided to revise or reconstitute the two small orchestral works *Lonely Waters* and *Whythorne's Shadow* that had previously been discarded or lost, but each of which had associations with his friend. However, Moeran's plan to negotiate the final stages of recovery from his long period of illness by working undisturbed in his studio in Ipswich was thwarted in late March when his parents, having once again grown dissatisfied with their home, decided to relocate. At the beginning of April, they bought Lingwood Lodge in the village of Lingwood, a few miles east of Norwich. This house was the largest and most luxurious of those that the Moerans occupied after leaving Bacton a decade or so earlier and was close to the Norfolk Broads district where they had spent so many years. The disruption of the move seems to have been too much for Moeran, and he decided to go and stay for a few weeks with his friend Robert Nichols in Winchelsea.

The poet Robert Nichols had lived with his wife in Yew Tree House in Winchelsea since their return from California in 1926, and the couple hosted regular artistic house parties.[30] Moeran had met Nichols through Heseltine and had previously visited Yew Tree House several times. Although the principle resembled that of the Eynsford cottage, with artistic and cultural personalities mingling together in a nourishing creative environment, the hedonism was largely absent. Moeran found his visits to Winchelsea stimulating, and, despite his continuing reliance on crutches to help him move about, he was able to work in a peaceful environment, free from the distractions that had plagued his time in Eynsford. As Moeran himself wrote, 'I had the use of a fine music room at Yew Tree House with a first rate Bösendorfer grand [piano].' According to the manuscript of *Whythorne's Shadow*, the score was completed at Winchelsea in May, and he finished *Lonely Waters* shortly after his return to Lingwood Lodge in June. The two works are now collectively titled the *Two Pieces for Small Orchestra*. Since neither of the original scores exists, it is impossible to determine to what extent the 1931 versions resemble the former works. Nevertheless, they comprise a satisfactory pair of complementary orchestral works that were evidently intended by Moeran to be played one after the other. The fair copy manuscript places *Whythorne's Shadow* first, and it was played first when the *Two Pieces for Small Orchestra* were performed by the BBC Orchestra (Section C) under Harold Brooke in a concert broadcast on 14 July 1935. Since Moeran had been consulted about the programming of this concert, the order may be regarded as definitive. The

---

[30] 'Yew Tree House [was] a rambling abode with plenty of rooms and a pleasant garden', Anne & William Charlton, *Putting Poetry First: A Life of Robert Nichols 1893–1944*, (Michael Russell Publishing, Norwich, 2003). Nichols' wife Norah Denny was Roger Quilter's niece. In addition to Moeran and Quilter, regular guests over the years included Philip Heseltine, Eric Fenby, Arnold Bennett, Aldous Huxley, Arthur Bliss, and Augustus John.

dynamic markings at the end of *Lonely Waters* suggest that it should fade away to nothing, so following it with the sprightly opening to *Whythorne's Shadow* perhaps spoils the intended effect.

Moeran spent several productive weeks at Yew Tree House. In addition to the work on the *Two Pieces for Small Orchestra*, he composed two songs, both inspired by the late spring. He returned to Housman and produced a lush setting of *Loveliest of trees*, replete with an accompaniment that is reminiscent of the piano music of John Ireland. Indeed, the opening few bars foreshadow Ireland's solo piano piece *The Cherry Tree* composed a few years later. In honour of his host, Moeran created a madcap setting of Nichols' poem *Blue-Eyed Spring*, initially as a solo song with piano accompaniment, but he also re-arranged it for tenor or soprano solo with unaccompanied double chorus. The tempo marking for both versions is 'As fast as conveniently possible', and the tongue-twisting nature of some of the text renders the songs difficult to negotiate convincingly. However, the Winchelsea house party probably included several fine singers, and their efforts to enunciate 'The lithe cloud shadows chase | Over the whole earth's face, | And where winds ruffling veer | O'er wooded streams' dark ways' in triplet quavers as fast as possible against Moeran's energetic piano accompaniment probably led to much merriment in the music room at Yew Tree House.[31]

After returning from Yew Tree House, Moeran paid a visit to the Fosses at Nightingale Corner in Rickmansworth. Hubert Foss and his second wife Dora had bought this house in 1930, and it had quickly become a congenial meeting place for musicians and literary and artistic personalities, similar to the philosophy Foss had espoused at Eynsford during the early 1920s. According to the memoirs of Dora Foss, Moeran arrived late 'a little the worse for wear' and with his leg 'in some form of iron splint'.[32] Another guest was composer Herbert Murrill, who had brought some piano compositions to play through to Hubert Foss, and Dora Foss related an anecdote in which Moeran became entranced by one of Murrill's works and excitedly demanded to hear it repeatedly, to the embarrassment of both Murrill and the Fosses.[33] It is not known how long Moeran remained in Rickmansworth, but on his return to his new home in Norfolk later in June, he would perhaps have felt revitalised and determined to build on his recovered compositional facility. However, he arrived to discover that he had been given a job. The Moerans were sociable people and it was not long after their move to Lingwood Lodge before they became part of the local community. A significant social connection developed when Ada Esther Moeran made the acquaintance of Edith Rhoda Britten. How the two women first met is not known but it was probably through the Women's Institute or some similar organisation. It has been asserted that Edith Britten had endeavoured to raise the

---

[31] While the manuscripts of the scores of both versions of *Blue-Eyed Spring* that are held in the E. J. Moeran Collection at the Southbank Library of the University of Melbourne each bear the signature 'Lingwood Lodge, nr Norwich' on the front cover page, the author's opinion is that these are later additions and refer to the corrections and score modifications that are evident on each manuscript.

[32] See Lloyd, Sparkes, Sparkes (2019), especially 75–79. It is apparent that Moeran's leg never healed completely and he was reliant on a walking stick for the rest of his life.

[33] *Ibid.*

social status of the Britten family by arranging *soirées* at their house in Lowestoft,[34] and it is probable that Moeran's mother was invited to one of these events. On discovering that they each had a musical son, the two women evidently became friends. Through Edith Britten, Ada Esther also became acquainted with Audrey Alston, a prominent musician in the Norwich and Lowestoft areas. Alston was the viola player of the Norwich String Quartet, the leader of which was Moeran's friend André Mangeot, and she had been Benjamin Britten's viola teacher during his early years.[35] Although ostensibly good friends, Edith Britten and Audrey Alston were also competitive when it came to the musical talents of their respective sons. Benjamin Britten and John Alston were about the same age and both were exceptionally talented pianists. According to the recollections of Beth Britten, each mother thought their own son to be the more able.[36] It is, therefore, not too much of a leap of imagination to suggest that Edith Britten, on discovering that her new friend Mrs Moeran had a son who was already well-regarded in music circles, prevailed upon her to persuade Moeran to take on some form of mentoring role for her son Benjamin, and that seems to be what transpired.

Determining the exact nature of the relationship between Moeran and Britten is problematic, because few tangible traces remain, comprising some letters, odd entries in Britten's diaries and a small number of newspaper articles. While it is inevitable that what is now known about Britten's personality and sexuality and the assertions about Moeran's sexuality that have been presented in this book raise the question of a possible physical relationship between the two composers, the evidence for such a supposition is flimsy and circumstantial. There are occasional references in Britten's diaries to sea-bathing with Moeran and an entry stating that Moeran visited Britten's London flat late one evening. While the possibility cannot be dismissed, it is more probable that Moeran mentored Britten musically – in as much as the ambitious younger composer made possible – and that he did so mainly because his mother had asked him. Moeran and Britten had a former music teacher in common, Walter Greatorex, and the discovery of this fact had perhaps facilitated the initial stages of their friendship.[37] The phenomenon of 'Britten's corpses' – former friends and colleagues whom Britten no longer regarded as useful to him – is well-known, and it was probably inevitable that Moeran would eventually join the list. The last surviving communication between the two men is a letter from Moeran to Britten dated 16 September 1938, and in 1945, Moeran was confiding to his friend Lionel Hill that the opera *Peter Grimes* contained the 'music of a shit'.[38]

---

[34] Neil Powell, *Benjamin Britten: A Life for Music*, (Hutchinson, London, 2013), 7.

[35] Alston was also a friend of fellow viola player Frank Bridge, and it was through Alston that the fourteen-year-old Britten began his composition lessons with Bridge in 1927.

[36] See Beth Britten, *My Brother Benjamin*, (Faber & Faber, London, 2013).

[37] The composer and teacher Walter Greatorex taught at Uppingham between 1900 and 1911, when he moved to the post of Director of Music at Gresham's School in Holt, Norfolk, where Britten was a pupil between 1928 and 1930. Greatorex is probably best known for his popular hymn tune *Woodlands* ('Lift up your hearts').

[38] Hill, 70. It is not known when or how Moeran and Britten's relationship broke down, but it was probably after October 1941, if only for the fact that it was then that Moeran wrote

Tilly

Despite his initial misgivings and the disruption of the house move, Lingwood Lodge turned out to be ideal for Moeran the composer. He established his studio in a ground floor garden room, overlooking the croquet lawn with trees behind, and during the next few years he produced several successful compositions there. One of the first works that he completed was a setting of a James Joyce poem *Tilly*. On the initiative of Herbert Hughes and Arthur Bliss, thirteen contemporary composers had each been asked to compose a setting of the poems from the Joyce's collection *Pomes Penyeach*, the result being a limited edition bound in silk with an introduction by Hughes, an essay on Joyce by Padraic Colum, an epilogue by Arthur Symons and including a frontispiece portrait of Joyce by Augustus John. The volume, called *The Joyce Book*, was published in a limited edition of 500 copies in 1933 for Joyce's benefit, and none of the contributors was paid a fee. Moeran had previously asked Joyce for permission to set *Tilly*, so his choice of poem had already been decided.[39] Moeran's setting is one of the most challenging of all his songs, for performer and listener alike. The poem had been written by Joyce in 1904 in the aftermath of the death of his mother, and it is tempting to attribute Moeran's choice of the verse to his own efforts to resolve the emotional crisis precipitated by Heseltine's death, which may itself have resurrected deeper memories of Roland Perceval Garrod. The setting is certainly bleak and unforgiving, with the text being presented by the vocal line in a recitative-like form. The melody for the first two stanzas (like many of Moeran's tunes) has a pentatonic base, although the tonic note changes from phrase to phrase (music example 36).

The parallel first inversion minor sixth chord accompaniment serves to dispel any suggestion of a tonal anchor and perhaps represents the meandering of the cattle on the road. The broken-chord accompaniment style of the second stanza appears in many songs throughout Moeran's oeuvre, the earliest use being in 'Westward on the High-Hilled Plains' from his *Four Songs from 'A Shropshire Lad'* of 1915. The third stanza, which commentators on the poem have suggested represents the raw emotion felt by Joyce, is treated musically in a manner which brilliantly emphasises the dramatic impact (music example 37).

The *sforzando* chord in bar 20 is a bitonal aural assault. It is a root position C minor triad juxtaposed with a second inversion C flat major triad. Moeran's placing of the chord one beat ahead of the vocal line cry of anguish 'I bleed by the black stream' establishes the utter agony conveyed through the top G flat of 'bleed', followed by

---

to the *Musical Times* defending Britten against the attacks that had been made on him and Peter Pears for not returning to Britain to do their patriotic duty. It is possible that Edward Sackville-West may have been involved in whatever caused the rift (See Chapter 15).

39 The other composers were Arnold Bax: *Watching the Needleboats at San Sabba*, Albert Roussel: *A Flower Given to My Daughter*, Herbert Hughes: *She Weeps Over Rahoon*, John Ireland: *Tutto è Sciolto*, Roger Sessions: *On the Beach at Fontana*, Arthur Bliss: *Simples*, Herbert Howells: *Flood*, George Antheil: *Nightpiece*, Edgardo Carducci: *Alone*, Eugene Goossens: *A Memory of the Players in a Mirror at Midnight*, C.W. Orr: *Bahnhofstrasse* and Bernard van Dieren: *A Prayer*.

Music example 36. *Tilly*: bars 1–6

Music example 37. *Tilly*: bars 17–21

the unremitting desperation of the downward E flat octave leap 'black stream'. *Tilly* is one of Moeran's most extraordinary creations, but, considered in the context of it being a response to the loss of his closest friend(s?), it reveals a heartfelt sorrow that the knowledge of its composer's circumstances makes clear. The three songs that Moeran composed during the space of two or three months in 1931, *Loveliest of Trees*, *Blue-Eyed Spring* and *Tilly*, could hardly be more contrasting, but they each provide an insight into aspects of Moeran's complex personality.

Living locally and with his London connections, Moeran soon became a key member of the Norwich-Lowestoft musical axis, and later in the year, he was asked to join the organising committee for the Norwich Festival. He probably spent most of the remainder of the year composing in his studio, although he travelled frequently to London, including a visit to hear the first performance of his String Trio in G major at a Music Society concert. Alongside some Suffolk folksong arrangements, he began work on a suite for orchestra which he called *Farrago*.[40] He also made occasional collecting expeditions in the East Anglian villages, in August travelling as far afield as Coddenham in Suffolk. He recorded several songs from the singing of local singer Oliver Waspe, including 'Harriet and Young William', the melody and words of which were published in an issue of the *Journal of the Folk-Song Society* in December. This month also saw what was probably the first performance of Moeran's music in Ireland, when the International String Quartet, led by André Mangeot, performed the String Quartet in A minor in a recital for the Royal Dublin Society at Ballsbridge. The recital was reviewed in the *Irish Times*, and while the reviewer was very enthusiastic about the work, he regretted the fact that Moeran himself was prevented from attending the concert in person by the onset of a sudden and severe illness. Some light may be shed on the sudden illness by the contents of a letter Moeran wrote to Arnold Dowbiggin on 30 December: 'the day after I got back here I sprained my right hand & am only now able to write just a little'. No other information is available, so it must be supposed that Moeran had planned to go to Ireland for the recital and that the hand sprain prevented him.

---

[40] There is no direct evidence for this date but the copies of the manuscript in the E. J. Moeran Collection at the Southbank Library of the University of Melbourne bear the date 1932, so it is reasonable to suppose that Moeran began the composition of *Farrago* in mid to late 1931.

13

Rebuilding a Reputation
(1932–1935)

Six Suffolk Folksongs

In February, Moeran was checking the final proofs of his *Six Suffolk Folksongs*, and he wrote to Roger Quilter about the set:

> I was wondering if you would have any objection to a dedication to yourself of it [the book of songs]. I think in some ways it is the best thing I have done in the way of songs. I assure you it would give me great pleasure if you would allow me to do this.[1]

Moeran had long been an admirer of Quilter's songs, having accompanied many of them at the musical club, and the older composer's music had been a significant influence during Moeran's early compositional development. The set of folksong arrangements was published in late April, and he wrote again to Quilter on 8 May, enclosing a copy of the printed volume. Coming some ten years after the publication of Moeran's earlier *Six Norfolk Folksongs* and with his having composed music of much formal and harmonic originality during the intervening years, Quilter may have expected more complex arrangements than those delivered. The accompaniment harmonies are mostly simple, with few accidentals evident, and most of the songs have a straightforward strophic form with accompaniment for the first verse or pair of verses repeated. However, Quilter would probably have enjoyed Moeran's characteristic stacked fourth chords, particularly in the first song of the set 'Nutting Time' and in the last song 'A Seaman's Life'. Moeran's assessment that the set was 'the best thing I have done in the way of songs' seems very curious, given their general lack of sophistication and overall musical simplicity. However, that is perhaps what he meant.

The Day of Palms

While establishing precisely when many of Moeran's works were composed can be problematic, creative interpretation of other evidence can suggest a possible date, and the song *The Day of Palms* is a case in point. The song is a setting of a poem by Arthur Symons, 'Palm Sunday: Naples', which articulates the poet's world-

---

[1] Letter from Moeran to Roger Quilter dated 23 February 1932; part of *Roger Quilter Papers*, Add MS 70604: 1924–1933, f168, British Library, London.

weary response to the elaborate annual Palm Sunday celebrations at Santa Chiara. Moeran's setting was published in 1932, and the style of the piano accompaniment resembles that of *Tilly*. This information, together with the subject matter of the poem, suggests that *The Day of Palms* was composed on or near Palm Sunday in either 1931 or 1932. The author favours the 1932 date (10 March), as the 1931 date (29 March) seems too close to the time when Moeran's working routine was disrupted by his parents' house move.

In his 8 May letter to Quilter, Moeran also mentioned that he was planning again to visit Winchelsea: 'Are you going to Winchelsea this next month or two? I hope to be going down in about 10 days time & shall probably stay there some 3 weeks.'[2] Moeran spent a few weeks in May and June in the creatively stimulating environment of Yew Tree House – working mainly on the *Farrago Suite* – but by the beginning of July, he was back at Lingwood Lodge. He wrote to the director of the Wireless Chorus,[3] Stanford Robinson, enclosing a copy of the recently published choral version of *Blue-Eyed Spring* and suggesting that it 'may be of some use to you & your excellent body of singers'. This was unashamed self-promotion, but Robinson seems to have liked the piece and relished the challenge the difficult vocal music presented. In early November, the Wireless Singers[4] performed *Blue-Eyed Spring* in a programme of madrigals and part-songs on the National Programme, and Moeran wrote to Stanford Robinson the following day: 'I was delighted with your performance … It seemed to come off very well over the radio & your tempo was just right. Thank you indeed for the care you must have given to the preparation of it.'[5] On 5 November, Moeran conducted the Norwich Municipal Orchestra in the second performance of the *Two Pieces for Small Orchestra*, and in December the tenor George Parker broadcast performances of *Loveliest of Trees* and *'Tis Time, I Think, by Wenlock Town*. Moeran ended the year by producing arrangements of two seasonal folksongs, which he called *Ivy and Holly* and *Alsatian Carol*. *Ivy and Holly* was an arrangement for tenor solo and four-part male voice choir of the Irish traditional 'O'Carolan's Lament' (*'Uaill-Cuma ui Cearballain'*) with the text adapted from a poem by John Keegan (1809–1849): 'Come Buy My Nice Fresh Ivy'. *Alsatian Carol* was an arrangement for mezzo-soprano or baritone solo, four-part male voice choir and piano of a French traditional tune from the book *Cantiques de Strasbourg* of 1697, with the text from Watts' *Cradle Song*.[6]

---

2 Letter from Moeran to Roger Quilter dated 8 May 1932; part of *Roger Quilter Papers*, Add MS 70604: 1924–1933, f169, British Library, London.

3 The forerunner of the BBC Singers.

4 An SSAATTBB octet drawn from the larger Wireless Chorus.

5 McNeill, 358.

6 'Hush my dear, lie still and slumber …' Isaac Watts (1715).

1933

Much of Moeran's life between mid-November 1932 and the end of 1933 is untraceable. No correspondence from this period has survived, nor was he mentioned in newspaper articles, apart from some notifications of works being performed around the country. However, a letter to the conductor Heathcote Statham dated 21 April 1935 suggests that Moeran travelled to Vienna in January 1933. The letter to Statham concerned possible works for a forthcoming concert: 'The ideal choice would be that glorious Adagio which is all that exists of Mahler's last & unfinished symphony. I heard it when Scherchen gave it's [sic] 1st performance when I was in Vienna in 1933.' Although Moeran did not mention precisely when in 1933 he was in Vienna, it is known that the first performance of the *Adagio* from Mahler's Tenth Symphony took place on 31 January as part of a concert given by the Vienna Studio Orchestra conducted by Hermann Scherchen at the Vienna Concert Hall. The issue of *Der Wiener Tag* dated 29 January 1933 reported that Scherchen had overseen extensive improvements to the acoustics of the hall and that this concert was the first to benefit from this. The *Adagio* was again on the programme of the next Scherchen concert a few days later. Further evidence for Moeran's presence in Vienna is provided by documents in the archive of the Czech composer and teacher Arthur Willner.[7] Willner wrote about having met Moeran, and while the exact date is unclear, this must have been in Vienna because there is no evidence that Willner visited Britain until after he left Austria permanently in 1938. From 1933 onwards, there is occasional mention of Willner in Moeran's correspondence, and Moeran made efforts to promote Willner's music in Britain.

Farrago Suite

Moeran probably returned to Britain in early February. His *Farrago Suite* had its first performance arranged for a radio broadcast of British music by the BBC Orchestra (Section C) conducted by Julian Clifford on 21 April. The concert began with Warlock's *Capriol Suite* and, in addition to *Farrago*, included music by Herbert Howells and William Walton. There was a brief description in the *Radio Times*:

> The composer calls his work *Farrago*, which the Pocket Oxford tells us means medley or hotch-potch – harsh words for what is really a sequence of four short movements, *Prelude*, *Minuet*, *Rondino* and *Rigadoon* joined together by association, but by no particular spirit of affinity one with another; in short, a suite in the orthodox tradition. It was composed last summer.[8]

The *Farrago Suite* had been assembled as a medley of movements, some of which had been composed for separate purposes. However, the four-movement suite was seemingly successful for a time, and there were performances during 1933 and the next two or three years. Each of the movements of *Farrago* was included in the orig-

---

7   *Arthur Willner Collection 1849–1960*, AR 10707 / MF 911, Leo Baeck Institute Archives, New York, United States of America.

8   'Orchestral Concert', *Radio Times*, Vol. 39, No. 498, (14 April 1933), 114.

inal eight-movement Serenade in G for Orchestra of 1948.[9] *Farrago* was dedicated to journalist and author Dominic Bevan Wyndham Lewis, although it is not known what Moeran's relationship with him was or how the two men became acquainted.

Songs of Springtime

Moeran probably spent most of the year at Lingwood Lodge, and he seems to have concentrated on vocal music, the principal work being a set of seven madrigal-like songs for unaccompanied SATB chorus, the *Songs of Springtime*. Stylistically, the work is indebted to Elizabethan music, Moeran's discovery of which had been a result of his friendship with Philip Heseltine. While Moeran had composed an earlier work for unaccompanied four-part chorus, the 1924 version of *Weep You No More, Sad Fountains*, his first work in madrigal form was *Gather Ye Rosebuds* from later the same year. The composition of madrigals eventually became quite important to Moeran, and this may have been as a tribute to his friend, although the claim he made in a letter written in 1949 to Coetmore perhaps exaggerated his devotion to the form: 'I think I am the only person in England if, being run in by the police, had to give my profession could describe myself as "Madrigalist."'[10] In the *Songs of Springtime*, Moeran aspired to the rich and intricate choral writing techniques of Campion, Weelkes, Dowland and others of the English Madrigal School. That he succeeded is amply shown by the review written by Ernest Newman in the *Sunday Times* of the first broadcast performance by the Wireless Singers under Leslie Woodgate on 5 December:

> Here is finely imaginative music, turned out, in addition, with exquisite craftsmanship. If these things had been broadcast under the names of Marenzio, Morley, and any five composers of the madrigalian epoch, the general verdicts would probably have been that these ancient gentlemen were writing at the top of their form, if not, indeed, a bit above it.[11]

While the formal style of the songs is that of the Elizabethan English Madrigal, the music is undoubtedly that of Moeran. He combined adroitly the melodic lines and harmonic progressions that would not have been unfamiliar to those composers who were his models together with the rich chromatic harmony that is Moeran's most characteristic stylistic feature. The result was a sound that may be situated equally comfortably in the company of either sixteenth or twentieth century vocal music. The eminent choral director and founder of the Oriana Madrigal Society, Charles Kennedy Scott, wrote an extended article about the *Songs of Springtime* in the *Musical Times*: 'we must give thanks to Mr Moeran for some exceedingly beautiful and distin-

---

9 Although the *Farrago Suite* was completed and performed several times, after he had cannibalized the work for movements for his 1948 Serenade in G for Orchestra, Moeran refused to acknowledge it. He reportedly said to Gerald Cockshott 'It doesn't exist'; letter from Cockshott to Stephen Wild, quoted in McNeill, 160.

10 McNeill, 625.

11 'The Week's Music', *The Sunday Times*, issue 5774, (10 December 1933), 7.

guished music.'[12] Scott subjected each of the seven songs to a detailed and penetrating examination. Regarding the sequence included in the extract from 'Love is a sickness' (music example 38), he wrote, 'This shows how Moeran can deal with advanced harmonic colouring, and yet give it an antique appearance – much as could Peter Warlock.' Scott ended his piece: 'The best service that one can render to a composer's work … is to perform it … I shall therefore hope to try to make my appreciation of these songs more clear by performing them at the first opportunity.'

Scott was as good as his word, and his Oriana Madrigal Society gave the first public performance of the *Songs of Springtime* at the Aeolian Hall in London on 13 March 1934. The work was dedicated to Robert and Norah Nichols, probably in gratitude for the hospitality they provided on the several occasions during the 1930s when Moeran spent extended time at Yew Tree House. Indeed, it is probable that Moeran spent a few weeks in Winchelsea during April and May and may well have composed some of the *Songs of Springtime* during this visit. He wrote to Leslie Woodgate after the first broadcast performance: 'thank you and your singers for a performance, the splendid quality of which, I find agreed upon by everyone I have come across who heard it. I was immensely pleased with your reading of *Songs of Springtime*.'[13] Several other works probably date from 1933, composed either in Winchelsea or Lingwood Lodge, although their exact dating is problematic and, again, the year of composition for each has been deduced solely from the known dates of publication. After a break of several years, Moeran returned to composition for solo piano and produced a set of two pieces, *Prelude* and *Berceuse*, which he dedicated to pianist and composer Freda Swain. It is not known how and when Moeran met Freda Swain, but it is possible that she spent time at Winchelsea and that she asked him to compose something for her.

As the end of the year approached, Moeran could reasonably consider that he had essentially recovered the position of prominence in British music that had ebbed away during the Eynsford years. On 11 December, the BBC broadcast a recital of his chamber music on the National Programme. The concert included the String Quartet in A minor, the Sonata in E minor for Violin and Piano and the Piano Trio in D major. The *Radio Times* included an extended article by Hubert Foss on Moeran and his music, which began: 'The apparent neglect of E. J. Moeran's chamber music this last few years has been very surprising to the writer, for this is music of primary

Music example 38. *Songs of Springtime*, 'Love is a Sickness': bars 6–11

---

[12] 'E. J. Moeran's Songs of Springtime', *The Musical Times*, Vol. 74, No. 1089 (November 1933), 982–984.

[13] McNeill, 360.

pleasure.' After introducing each of the works to be played in the recital, Foss ended: 'One has great hope that this concert of Moeran's works will bring to many a realisation of a simple and skilful, poetic and inventive composer, one whose music needs no knowledge to understand, whose appeal is English, whose first or last word is ever musical.'[14]

1934

Nocturne

On 10 January, Moeran sent a telegram to W. W. Thompson at the BBC confirming his intention to attend rehearsals for a broadcast performance of the Second Rhapsody for Orchestra, which took place a couple of days later. Later in the month, he travelled down to Winchelsea for his annual few weeks at Yew Tree House. It was during this visit that he read and became fascinated with Robert Nichols' verse play *Don Juan Tenorio, the Great*. While Nichols had been working for years on this play, revising and rewriting, there was one extract that '[came] closest to fulfilling his mature poetic aspirations',[15] and this was Don Juan's 'Address to the Sunset'. Moeran had recently agreed a commission from the Norwich Philharmonic Society for a work for baritone solo, large chorus and orchestra, and it seems that a setting of Nichols' text was what he had in mind for the work to be called *Nocturne*. The inspiring environment of Yew Tree House and the presence of the poet appears to have aroused a creative magic in Moeran, and he composed much of the work during his visit.[16]

Nocturne is one of Moeran's most harmonically lush creations, and, of his post-Eynsford works, it belies the assertions of a stylistic re-appraisal most comprehensively. While unmistakably indebted to the musical style of Delius, Moeran's individuality is apparent throughout: in the descending bass lines, sequences of parallel fourths, extensive use of major and minor seventh and ninth harmonies and the oscillating first and second inversion chords. The orchestral prelude begins in E minor but includes so many added notes that the tonality is obscured, with the predominant sonority being the minor ninth (music example 39). The orchestra meanders through several key bases in an opulent representation of the sunset that is the focus of the text, with a brief passage in D flat major adding the most vibrant colour (music example 40) until the unaccompanied solo voice unobtrusively begins Don Juan's declamation: 'Exquisite stillness! What serenities | Of earth and air!' The text

[14] 'Moeran's Chamber Music', *Radio Times*, Vol. 41, No. 532, (8 December 1933), 724.

[15] Anne & William Charlton, *Putting Poetry First: A Life of Robert Nichols 1893–1944*, (Michael Russell Publishing, Norwich, 2003), 251.

[16] In a letter written in 1984 to Barry Marsh, Stephen Lloyd quoted from a programme note for *Nocturne* written by Moeran himself which began: 'The *Nocturne* was composed during the late summer and autumn of 1934', letter from Stephen Lloyd to Barry Marsh dated 23 October 1984, the original of which is in the Barry Marsh Collection. However, this should be regarded in the knowledge of Moeran's tendency to inexactness in the dating of his work. *Nocturne* was probably completed in the autumn of 1934, but it was certainly begun in Winchelsea in the spring of that year.

Music example 39. *Nocturne*: bars 1–4

Music example 40. *Nocturne*: bars 18–24

setting remains restrained through much of the poem, but builds through an allegorical description of a white crane flying over the landscape of 'cloud-like mountains' and 'mountainous cloud' to a tremendous climax at the end of the phrase: 'Now, spirit, find out wings and mount to him, | Wheel where he wheels, where he is soaring soar', culminating in a *sforzando* E flat major seventh chord. The final line of the poem 'happiness is here' provides the text for a quiet G major coda, juxtaposing C major seventh and G major sixth harmonies. This highlights the restful ending of the sunset as the last rays dip below the horizon.

The *Nocturne* is an impressive creation. There is no awkwardness in the vocal lines and the orchestral textures flow and intermingle smoothly. The modified sonata form structure provides an appropriate frame for the text, as Heathcote Statham wrote in his extended analysis of the work in the *Musical Times*: '*Nocturne* is a sincere and moving setting of a fine poem.'[17] Comparison with Delius is inevitable, especially since the published vocal score bears the inscription 'To the memory of Frederick

[17] 'E. J. Moeran's New Work', *The Musical Times*, Vol. 76, No. 1106 (April 1935), 312–315.

Delius', and the *Songs of Sunset* immediately spring to mind.[18] There are indeed similarities, not only with *Songs of Sunset*, but also with other Delius works, and it is the acknowledgement of an influential debt, inherent in the dedication, that rescues the work from the perception of its simply being a Delius pastiche. The press responses to the work were positive, but all mentioned its tribute.

During his stay in Winchelsea, Moeran attended a performance of his *Farrago* suite by the Hastings Municipal Orchestra conducted by Julius Harrison at the White Rock Pavilion on 8 February. According to the report in the *Hastings & St Leonards Observer*, one of the largest audiences of the season thus far attended the concert. The music correspondent, Allan Biggs, commented:

> A new work from the pen of E. Moeran, a suite called *Farrago*, was produced at this concert. If the composer intends the title to be accepted literally he has chosen a very apt one for this music, which (save for the *Rigadoon*, which has a lilt not to be resisted) contains long stretches that could hardly be taken seriously. The composer himself was there and was given a very cordial reception.[19]

Indeed, the *Rigadoon* was sufficiently successful for Harrison to have included it in another concert a month or so later. Moeran returned to Norfolk with the score of the *Nocturne* essentially complete, but his time was immediately taken up with preparations for a concert at the Stuart Hall in Norwich. Moeran had organised this concert, together with Audrey Alston, principally to present Britten's *Simple Symphony*. Britten wrote in his diary:

> At 2:45 show starts at Stuart Hall. Mangeot (cond. Moeran) plays two concerti (Vivaldi & Haydn) with orch. – v. badly. I conduct my *Simple Symphony* which doesn't go too badly – except for a 'swim' in the *Saraband*. A Scratch Quartet scrambles through 2 movs. of Mozart G maj.[20]

The arranging of the Stuart Hall concert seems to have been the first practical result of Moeran's agreement to help the young Britten, and from this date, Moeran's name appears occasionally in Britten's letters and diaries. On 16 March, Britten recorded that he had a '[l]ong telephone talk with Moeran about various musical matters'.[21]

Moeran's *Farrago Suite* had interested the BBC, and they arranged a broadcast performance in a concert given by the BBC Orchestra (Section E) conducted by Julian Clifford on 24 May. Moeran wrote to Julian Herbage in advance of this to say that he would be in London to attend the performance. According to Britten's diary, he met Moeran at the publishers (Hawkes) during the morning of 24 May to play over the piano duet arrangement of *Farrago*. Moeran evidently wished to capitalise on the publicity surrounding the BBC broadcast by providing a popular version of the suite. The BBC also broadcast a Promenade Concert performance of *Farrago* a

---

[18] Delius had died on 10 June 1934, as Moeran was completing the final score of *Nocturne*.

[19] 'Thursday Symphony Concert', *Hastings & St Leonards Observer*, (10 February 1934), 13.

[20] Extract from Benjamin Britten's diary, quoted in John Evans, (ed.), *Journeying Boy: The Diaries of the young Benjamin Britten 1928–1938*, (Faber & Faber, London, 2009), 201.

[21] *Ibid.*, 202.

STUART HALL, NORWICH.

Programme of Concert

TO BE GIVEN AT THE ABOVE HALL ON

Tuesday, March 6th, at 2-45 p.m.

Violinist: ANDRE MANGEOT

Conductors { E. J. MOERAN
            { B. BRITTEN

Leader : HARRINGTON KIDD

1. Concerto for Violin with Strings *Haydn*

   Solo—ANDRE MANGEOT

   Allegro moderato—Adagio—Finale

2. A simple Symphony for Strings *E. B. Britten*

   1st Performance (*arr. B. B.*)

   Boisterous Bouree—Playful Pizzicato
   Sentimental Saraband—Frolicsome Finale

3. Quartet for Strings

4. Concerto for Violin with Strings *Vivaldi*

   ANDRE MANGEOT

   Allegro—Largo—Presto

A Second Concert will be given on Thursday,
April 5th, at 2-45 and 8 o'clock

WITH

JOHN ALSTON, HARRINGTON KIDD AND
AUDREY ALSTON.

Figure 6. Stuart Hall, Norwich, Concert Programme: 6 March 1934

few months later. The suite accumulated at least half a dozen performances in 1933 and 1934 before disappearing from the BBC repertoire. A performance in Cork in 1937 was the only other hearing of the work before it was absorbed into the Serenade in G for Orchestra, Moeran's last major composition.

Britten's diary records several occasions when he and his mother visited Lingwood Lodge, either for lunch or for tea. The house had a full-size, well-maintained croquet lawn, and games were played throughout the summer. These afternoon parties often moved back to Lowestoft in the late afternoon, where Britten and Moeran (and occasionally others) would go sea-bathing. Britten recorded that he had conversations with Moeran about music, and he mentioned Moeran driving him to concerts and rehearsals. These diary entries provide glimpses into a relationship the true extent of which is difficult to extrapolate from the limited information. As suggested earlier, while knowledge of Britten's and Moeran's probable sexual identities makes speculation inevitable, there is not enough in phrases such as 'Mrs. & Jack Moeran come over for tea. J & I bathe before tea' to form a definitive assessment of their personal bond.[22] Moeran undoubtedly assisted the development of Britten's career – at least for a while – although it could be argued that his career would have developed without the older composer's help. Moeran's motivation was probably more to do with accommodating his mother's wishes than any real interest in Britten as a musician. Indeed, as their friendship progressed – if such it was – Britten's diary entries refer more to actions that he took to help Moeran.

It has been shown that the extant corpus of works by Moeran represents just a proportion of the music that he composed during his career. His propensity to discard or destroy manuscripts that he felt were not up to the high standards that he set himself has resulted in gaps in his oeuvre that can be filled only by speculation. Another phenomenon that may be observed through examining Moeran's output in overview is that he tended to concentrate his efforts in specific genres at different periods of his life. For example, most of his piano music was composed during the 1920s, and his chamber music is mainly clustered into ten-year periods at the beginning and end of his composing career. During the mid-1930s, he seems to have favoured the composition of part-songs above other forms. As a composer, Moeran was an opportunist. Where there was a good possibility of a performance (ideally repeated performances), he would compose for that possibility. Thus, during the period of his membership of the Oxford & Cambridge Musical Club, he produced much that could be performed at the Thursday evening recitals, and when he developed friendships with other musicians, he composed works for them. During 1934 Moeran composed a set of songs that he grouped together under the title *Four English Lyrics* for the Welsh tenor Parry Jones. It is possible that Moeran met Parry Jones at Winchelsea and conceived the set of songs while staying there. The set was evidently composed quickly because it was published later in the year. Herbert Hughes, critiquing the songs for the *Saturday Review* wrote:

> If [Moeran] has been influenced by Warlock, no one will blame him; they were intimate friends and shared a love for fine English lyrics. Here are Campion's

[22] *Ibid.*, 215.

Cherry Ripe, Fletcher's *Willow Song*, *The Constant Lover* of William Browne and *The Passionate Shepherd* of Christopher Marlowe, each of which must have been set to music many times. This would have required either vanity or courage, and Moeran is without any sort of vanity, one must put this achievement down to plain courage.[23]

Moreover, works such as the 1924 version of *Weep You No More, Sad Fountains* and *Blue-Eyed Spring* were occasionally being selected as test pieces for competitive music festivals, and it seems that Moeran identified this as another opportunity. During 1933 and 1934, he composed several part-songs for female voices, which, according to a letter he wrote to Leslie Woodgate in September, were for 'competition festival purposes'. These works included three works for two soprano parts and piano: *The Echoing [Ecchoing] Green*, a setting of a poem from the *Songs of Innocence and Experience* by William Blake; the delightful *Green Fire*, a setting of an anonymous text; and *The Lover and his Lass*, setting a text from William Shakespeare's *As You Like It*. Moeran also produced another setting of *Weep You No More, Sad Fountains* for soprano and alto voices and piano, and he composed a setting for unaccompanied female voices of a poem by Robert Herrick *To Blossoms*. He also added an alto part to *Cherry Ripe*, from the *Four English Lyrics*, to create an arrangement for soprano and alto voices and piano.

From mid-1934, Julian Herbage of the BBC music department became a regular correspondent, establishing a friendship that lasted until Moeran's death. Herbage facilitated many performances and broadcasts of Moeran's music by the BBC, and his organisational capability expedited situations that the composer's propensity for misconstruing communications sometimes precipitated. In August, the BBC and Sir Richard Runciman Terry were working on a series of radio programmes entitled *From Plainsong to Purcell: The Foundations of English Music*, and Terry wanted to include an authentic folk singer in one of the programmes. Moeran, having heard about this, volunteered the services of Harry Cox of Catfield, Norfolk, seemingly without having first cleared this with Mr Cox. Moeran had known Cox since his folksong collecting days in 1922 and perhaps felt he had a proprietorial interest in Cox's singing. There followed a series of misunderstandings largely caused by Moeran having made certain arrangements and then failing to notify those involved. Harry Cox himself was fully aware of his abilities and clearly believed that he might have been better treated. Nonetheless, through the good offices of Herbage, Cox attended the BBC studios as agreed and Terry's programme – including Cox singing such Norfolk folksongs as 'The Captain's Apprentice' and 'The Shooting of his Dear' – was broadcast as scheduled.

A notable characteristic of Moeran's letter-writing was that after such occasions, he never referred to them again. There were no apologies or acknowledgement of blame or guilt. While it is possible that letters of apology were written by Moeran and that they have not survived, the frequency of embarrassing situations – particularly during the 1940s – is such that at least one such letter might have been expected

---

[23] 'Some New English Songs', *The Saturday Review of Politics, Literature, Science & Art*, Vol. 158, No. 4127 (December 1934), 476.

to have been retained by its recipient. It is, perhaps, of some significance therefore that the next letter to Herbage written by Moeran that has survived was dated 14 December 1936, some two years later. While the blame for the misunderstandings of the Harry Cox programme can mostly be laid at Moeran's door, he could claim that he was distracted by the preparation of a BBC programme of his own music. Since the programme of chamber music arranged by Hubert Foss that had been transmitted in December the previous year, there had only been sporadic broadcasts of Moeran's music: the Second Rhapsody for Orchestra in January, several broadcasts of the *Farrago Suite* and a few songs included in various singers' recitals. Therefore, when the deputy director of music at the BBC, Kenneth Wright, had asked him to assemble a concert programme of piano music and songs to be given by baritone singer George Parker and pianist Kendall Taylor, Moeran devoted much time and effort to thinking out a suitable combination. The programme of music that Moeran eventually settled on and which he communicated in a letter to Wright on 18 September was broadcast on the National Programme a fortnight or so later.

Moeran's music administration work in Norfolk continued in October when he chaired a meeting of the joint committees of the Norfolk Musical Competition Festivals, the Norfolk Federation of Women's Institutes and the Music Teachers' Association to consider the work of the rural schools of music. In a brief address, Moeran explained that the meeting was intended to discuss how to 'give people who lived in the country and who were fond of music a chance to be taught and meet together to play and sing'. Since no other reference to Moeran's work on this joint committee has been found, it is not known whether the laudable aims of the project were realised. On a more personal note, Moeran's excessive drinking continued to result in serious consequences. At the end of October, Moeran found himself summoned to Aylesbury Magistrates' Court, where he was found guilty of having been drunk in charge of a car. According to an article which was printed in several national and regional newspapers, including *The Times* and the *Belfast Newsletter*, he was disqualified from driving for five years and ordered to be confined in a nursing home for nine months. Thus, Moeran spent the last few weeks of the year at the Devonshire Nursing Home in Cambridge.

1935

The old year having ended badly for Moeran, the new year began even worse. He was discharged from the nursing home into his parents' care over Christmas and New Year but had chosen not to return to serve the remainder of his effective sentence. Indeed, he believed himself to be fully recovered. Letters written to Moeran by Jelka Delius dated 3 January and 11 January suggest that he had told her he was better. Unfortunately, his recovery did not last long. On 21 January, he was arrested in Market Hill, Cambridge, again for being drunk in charge of a motor vehicle.

The catalogue of Moeran's alleged offences when read today seems rather alarming. In addition to the accusation of driving while under the influence of alcohol, he was also accused of driving while disqualified and had previously absconded from bail. The penalties now would have been very much more severe than confinement

Belfast Newsletter 1738-1938, 22.01.1935, page 11

FELL ACROSS STEERING WHEEL

Composer Drunk in Charge of Motor Car

Ernest John Moeran (40), described as a music composer, was bound over for two years at Cambridge yesterday and ordered to enter a nursing home, after he had been found guilty of having been drunk in charge of a motor car.

Detective-Constable Cummings said that he saw Moeran staggering about Market Hill. He afterwards entered a motor car, sat down in the driving seat, and fell forward over the wheel. He said: "It is my car, and I am going to drive home."

Dr. Ralph Noble, of Cambridge, a specialist in nervous diseases, said that Moeran was referred to him last November through a professor of medicine at Cambridge, and it was agreed that Moeran should go into a nursing home until he was well enough to live in rooms. Since coming out Moeran had not taken any alcohol until last week-end, when he had been upset by the news that one of his best friends had died.

Inspector Sharman said that in August, 1929, Moeran was fined £10 at Watford for having been drunk in charge of a car, and in October, 1934, at Aylesbury, for a similar offence, he was disqualified from driving for five years and ordered to enter a home for nine months.

The Bench ordered Moeran to remain in a nursing home as long as his medical adviser, Dr. Noble, thought fit, and he was ordered to pay the costs.

Figure 7. Belfast Newsletter, 22 January 1935, 'Fell Across Steering Wheel'

in a nursing home. Moeran told his side of the story in a letter he wrote to the singer George Parker:

Nearly a month ago, having been a total abstainer for months, I met some old army companions and broke out. It was only one evening, not a question of a pro-longed bout, but I made myself very ill in addition to coming up against the local police force. I was wrongly accused of being drunk in charge of a car. As a matter of fact, I had no car but was looking for a taxi; it seems that in my fuddled state I have inadvertently got into a strange private car standing on the rank. I was not convicted or fined, but the matter was left entirely in the hands of my doctor, who decided I must have a complete rest; hence my being here in a nursing home.[24]

---

[24] From a letter to George Parker, dated 10 February 1935; transcribed in Geoffrey Self, 'E. J. Moeran – Unpublished Letters and Songs', *British Music*, Vol. 16, 1994, (British Music Society, London, 1994), 33–44.

Moeran's claim to have been wrongfully accused is interesting, as is his explanation for the drinking bout, which differs from the one he had given a fortnight or so earlier. His claim to have been a total abstainer for months also does not accord with his having been found drunk in charge in October. He went on: 'I hope soon to get back to work, if I could do that, it would be easier to forget about this affair, but at present I am prevented from working by the [doctor]. I had just finished the 1st movement of my symphony.' The suggestion that Moeran had completed the first movement of the symphony is the first indication in ten years that he was working again on this long-abandoned project. In other letters that he wrote to George Parker about this time, Moeran asserted that he had been working on the symphony since the previous summer. The fact that he was not fined or even imprisoned, either for the Cambridge incident or for the absconding from bail, suggests that the magistrate gave him the benefit of the doubt, probably on the strength of the fact that he was not actually driving the car. Nevertheless, he had given Moeran something of a dressing-down: '[The magistrate] had the impertinence in a public court to tell me he hoped I would one day make good, as if I were an idler and wastrel!' Nevertheless, Moeran did as he was told and returned to the Devonshire Nursing Home for a few weeks. On his discharge, rather than returning to live with his parents at Lingwood Lodge, he took lodgings in Adams Road, Cambridge.

Moeran's decision to remain in Cambridge instead of going home to Lingwood Lodge seems strange. The Lodge had been his home since his parents had moved there in April 1931, and it had been a conducive environment for work, to the extent that his compositional productivity between 1931 and 1934 had almost reached the peak that he had previously achieved in the mid-1920s. That he deliberately deprived himself of this creative advantage is, therefore, unlikely. One explanation – and perhaps the most reasonable – is that at least temporarily he was no longer welcome at home. Moeran's parents regarded his problems with alcohol through reductive euphemisms such as 'a tendency to drink' or 'his little problem', and they may have accepted it as such, provided he did nothing to embarrass them. However, during the previous few months, he had twice been arrested, twice appeared before a Magistrates' Court, been disqualified from driving, fined and sentenced to confinement in a nursing home. Moreover, the account of his shame was published in newspapers throughout the land. All this was probably more than they could bear, and they refused to have him in the house for a while. Indeed, early in the year, they shut up Lingwood Lodge, laid off their domestic staff and went to stay with relatives for several months.

Thus, when Moeran went to Norfolk for the first performance in early April of his *Nocturne* by the Norwich Philharmonic Society at the St Andrew's Hall, he stayed with the conductor Heathcote Statham. Moeran had written to Benjamin Britten on 1 April enclosing tickets for the concert for Britten and his mother, and he had made a tentative date to meet Britten during the late afternoon of the day of the concert. Britten's diary entry for the day (4 April) is interesting:

> I meet Mrs Nora Back, Gwenneth B[ack], Jack Moeran, & Robert Nicholls [sic] (a very nice man) at St Andrew's Hall, at a rehearsal of the evening concert. Go back to the Back's at 6.0. Play over with J. the 1st mov. of his new Symphony on

the piano ... go on to the Phil. Concert at 7.45. They do J's new *Nocturne* to a poem of R. Nichols, chorus well, & orch. Better than expected. It is rather lovely – tho' v. influenced by Delius, yet somehow stronger ... go back to a party at the Stathams.[25]

The following week, Moeran was back in Cambridge and anxious to capitalise on the successes of the Norwich performance of *Nocturne* and that of the baritone soloist Roy Henderson. He wrote to Kenneth Wright on 10 April:

> The *Nocturne* performance will be [the] first in London, as it was produced last week by the Norwich Philharmonic Society with Roy Henderson as soloist. I would strongly urge you to secure Henderson, if possible. He sang the work beautifully last week & is only too anxious for further opportunity of doing it.[26]

Moeran's publishers Novello had been in contact with the BBC about a concert devoted to his music and had suggested including *Nocturne* and the *Two Pieces for Small Orchestra*. The concert was duly broadcast on 14 July.[27] Other works performed during 1935 were the Second Rhapsody at a Promenade Concert on 29 August, the *Songs of Springtime* by the BBC Singers[28] under Leslie Woodgate on 30 August and the String Trio in G major performed by May Mukle's English Ensemble at a recital for the Royal Dublin Society at Ballsbridge. This was the second performance of a work by Moeran in Ireland.

Moeran's main concern was his symphony. In his 1 April letter to Britten, Moeran had mentioned the symphony as 'infinitely better' than the *Nocturne*, and when he wrote again to Britten a few weeks later, he went into much more detail:

> Have you anywhere the last four pages of my miniature score of Sibelius No. 5? They are missing. Do have a look amongst your scores. I may have lost them myself since you had it. I wanted to crib his scoring of those final chords. I have finished scoring my first movement (54 pages), & now I must copy it out in ink. I have done away with violins *divisi* in 8ves in the 1st noise in the coda, but the 2nd time it seems to me it will give the sort of sound I want leading to the string climax after the brass leaves off, which otherwise won't be a climax. The 2nd time I don't require that brilliant 'curtain' on the strings while the brass are working their way up from below.[29]

The wording of the letter suggests that it is a part of an extended conversation that Moeran and Britten were having about detailed technical and musical aspects of the symphony. Moeran ended the letter: 'What is the difficulty you objected to? You are more of a string player than I am, so please let me know. When are you coming to Cambridge?' This letter contains much of great interest, but it particularly high-

---

[25] Extract from Benjamin Britten's diary, quoted in Evans, (2009), 255.

[26] McNeill, 366.

[27] The *Radio Times* included an appreciation of Moeran written by Robert Hull; 'Norfolk Composer', *Radio Times*, Vol. 48, No. 615, (12 July 1935), 13.

[28] The Wireless Singers were renamed the BBC Singers in 1934.

[29] *Correspondence between Benjamin Britten and Jack Moeran*, BBA/MOERAN, Britten Pears Arts Archive.

lights that Moeran had come to regard Britten as much as somebody to consult as he was somebody that Moeran was supposed to be helping with his career. The letter has the tenor of being part of a conversation between friends. The question about when Britten is coming to Cambridge raises the possibility that he occasionally went to visit Moeran in his Cambridge lodgings. It is also interesting that Moeran mentioned 'cribbing' the scoring of the six chords that end Sibelius' Symphony No. 5. Although the evidence from Moeran's letters suggests that he was working sequentially, movement by movement, through the symphony, he had clearly already decided on how it was going to end.

Moeran spent the summer and autumn working on the symphony in Cambridge and corresponding with his friends and colleagues. There is no record of his having worked on any other music, and there are no completed compositions known to date from 1935. The two piano pieces for Freda Swain and the *Two Pieces for Small Orchestra* were published towards the end of the year. Moeran travelled to London for the Promenade Concert performance of his Second Rhapsody for Orchestra in August at which he met Britten, and he visited Freda Swain in response to a dinner invitation at the end of October. At the end of September, he wrote to Harriet Cohen from his new Cambridge lodgings at 2 Brookside about the possibility of composing something for her:

> I feel most honoured that you should want me to write something for you to play with orchestra … However, I ought to tell you frankly that I can't embark on it immediately, as I am in the throes of a symphony. 2 movements of this are completed & scored, but I have several months work ahead before I can think about anything else. The idea of a work for pfte & orchestra is certainly attractive to me, especially if you play it. The trouble about piano music as a rule is that there are such a lot of damned fools who set out to be pianists; they play one's works occasionally & completely misinterpret them & pull them about. However, most of my piano music is complete tripe & I wish it were not published. One of the exceptions is *The Lake Island* for which I still have a great affection.[30]

The content of the letter enables the progress of the symphony to be tracked. In April, Moeran had asserted that the first movement was completed and scored, and this letter shows that by the end of September, the second movement was also finished. His assessment of his piano music as 'tripe' and wishing it were not published seems to have been transient. He revised this opinion a few years later in conversation with Lionel Hill. Moreover, along with his published songs, the piano music generated good royalty payments from the Performing Right Society that he had recently joined. Moeran added a postscript to his letter: 'This is my address for the next 2 or 3 months, after which I go to Ireland (Co. Kerry).' This is the first mention in Moeran's correspondence about visiting Ireland.

Moeran had spent most of 1935 in Cambridge living under the restrictions imposed by his prosecution in January. There is no record that he returned to Lingwood Lodge during the year until the beginning of November, when he wrote

[30]   Letter from Moeran to Harriet Cohen, dated 2 Bankside, Cambridge, 27 September 1934, *Harriet Cohen Papers*, MS. Mus. 1641, f. 61, British Library, London.

from there to Harriet Cohen that he was laid up with influenza and what he called 'a touch of pleurisy'. While all may not have been forgiven and forgotten, Moeran's compliance with the requirements of the court and his Cambridge doctors and the fact that he had evidently refrained from excessive drinking had probably enabled Moeran's parents to welcome him home. He also had plans to travel, as he wrote to Cohen: 'I am … at the parental home for a few days, where it is warmer and more comfortable than in my bleak rooms in Cambridge. These I shall give up shortly & probably go to the South of Spain.'[31] During the year, Moeran had spoken with various friends about being ill; he had stoutly defended himself in the letters he wrote to George Parker, and there are few references in his correspondence about his movements being inhibited.

Had Moeran learned his lesson? He had spent a most unpleasant year away from the homely and beneficial environment of Lingwood Lodge and had undergone psychiatric and other treatment by his doctors in Cambridge. His freedom to travel where he pleased had been severely constrained, and he had caused his parents much anguish and embarrassment. On the asset side of his personal ledger, he had made significant progress on the composition of the symphony – something that had eluded him for nearly a decade – and having joined the Performing Right Society he was now making a more significant income from his music. As the year ended with him back at Lingwood Lodge recovering from influenza in the care of his mother, he might have reflected on an experience that he would not wish to repeat.

[31] Letter from Moeran to Harriet Cohen, dated Lingwood Lodge, Nr Norwich, 4 November 1934, *Harriet Cohen Papers*, MS. Mus. 1641, f. 62, British Library, London. Moeran had also mentioned going abroad imminently in a letter written to Adrian Boult in July: 'During the past six months I have scarcely been in London except for the past fortnight. I shan't be there before late Sept as I am on the point of going abroad', McNeill, 369.

14

Return to Ireland
(1936–1942)

Since September 1919, Moeran had not set foot on the island of Ireland. The abrupt termination of that visit had probably been due either to his having found himself in difficulties with some faction of the Republican or Nationalist movements or to his having become disillusioned with the increasing violence. Remaining away from Ireland may well have been a condition imposed by his mother in exchange for her supporting him in London. However, sixteen years later, the influence of his mother on his behaviour and actions was much less, and the passage of time since the establishment of the Irish Free State may perhaps have lessened any residual risk. Moeran travelled to Ireland for a visit in early January 1936, and by mid-month he was staying in The Lodge at the Lansdowne Arms Hotel in Kenmare. The letter that he had written to Harriet Cohen on 27 September confirms that his visit to Ireland had been planned some time in advance. It is, therefore, reasonable to ask why he decided after all these years to visit Ireland and with whom, if anybody, he travelled. Largely through his own fault, the previous year had been very trying for Moeran, but the possible rejection by his family may well have affected him emotionally. While a reconciliation was made later in the year, he had already made his plans to undertake an extended visit to Ireland.

According to Cunningham and Fleischmann, Moeran visited Ireland with Arnold Bax: 'In 1936, Arnold Bax brought another English composer to the Fleischmanns who, like himself, felt very much at home in Ireland: E. J. Moeran.'[1] While Bax had originally met Moeran in 1918, and they had also associated with each other during the Eynsford cottage years, it is not clear how close their friendship had become during that time. In writings on Moeran hitherto, much has been made of his friendship with Bax, but this has largely been predicated on Bax's unreliable memories as recorded in his writings. Nonetheless, it may be significant that Moeran addressed Harriet Cohen in his letters as Tania, which was Bax's private name for Cohen and was shared only with close friends. It is possible to identify at least five visits that Moeran made to Ireland in 1936, and Cunningham and Fleischmann do not specify when in that year Bax introduced Moeran to the Fleischmanns. Cunningham and Fleischmann asserted that Moeran, Bax and Aloys Fleischmann went together to

---

[1]   Joseph Cunningham & Ruth Fleischmann, Aloys Fleischmann (1880–1964): *An Immigrant Musician in Ireland*, (Cork University Press, Cork, 2010), 217.

Kenmare, and it is apparent that Moeran immediately fell in love with the town and its surrounding countryside.

His first visit to Ireland since 1919 lasted about three weeks, and on 8 February, he was back in London for a performance of his *Nocturne*. A week later he returned to Kenmare from where he wrote to Benjamin Britten about the work that Britten had composed in fulfilment of a commission for the Norwich and Norfolk Triennial Music Festival. Britten's piece was an orchestral song-cycle with text assembled and partly written by W. H. Auden, while the festival committee had requested a purely orchestral work. Moeran's creative idea was for Britten to revise the description of the work to include the soprano voice effectively as an instrument of the orchestra.

Moeran travelled several times between Britain and Ireland during the year. In early March, his parents sold Lingwood Lodge and moved to a temporary home at Lyndhurst in the New Forest. This was convenient for Moeran as his *Two Pieces for Small Orchestra* had been included on the programme of a Bournemouth Festival concert on 24 March. Moeran had been continuing his correspondence with Benjamin Britten, and they had arranged by telegram to meet in the town a few days later. Britten recorded in his diary on 27 March 'Jack Moeran meets me at B[ournemouth] ... Go for a long walk in afternoon with him to Poole'.[2] Moeran returned to Kenmare in early April and spent the next six weeks at the Lodge working on the third movement of the symphony. He travelled back to Britain on 23 May, sailing on *RMS Scotia* from Kingstown (Dún Laoghaire) to Holyhead, but stayed for just three weeks, during which he attended a meeting of the Royal Philharmonic Society of which he had recently been elected a member. On his return to Kenmare, he wrote to Keith Douglas (secretary of the Royal Philharmonic Society):

> I very much appreciate the compliment I have been paid by becoming a member of the Royal Philharmonic Society. I returned here [Kenmare] last week, but I do not anticipate remaining much longer in the South of Ireland as, this time of year, the climate becomes unpleasantly enervating. I shall have another address before long; as soon as I know what it is, I will let you know.[3]

Moeran spent his time in Kenmare working on the symphony, and by the time his commitments in Britain demanded his return in mid-July, he had completed the music of the third movement. On 31 July, the gossip columnist 'Big Ben' wrote in his regular item 'Talk of London', which was published in several regional newspapers:

> I ran into Mr. E. J. Moeran, the Norfolk composer, this afternoon. He told me he was just back from Ireland, where he lives and where he has been working on his first symphony, three movements of which are now finished. When I asked him about the other, he smiled, as composers do when you ask them such questions.

While Moeran's assertion that he was living in Ireland underlines the change in his circumstances that his January visit to Kenmare had apparently precipitated, it does not entirely accord with his having said to Keith Douglas just a few weeks earlier

---

[2]   Extract from Benjamin Britten's diary, quoted in Evans, (2009), 343.

[3]   *Royal Philharmonic Society Archive*, RPS MS 369, f. 206, British Library, London.

that he would probably not remain in Ireland for much longer due to the climate. Despite the inconvenience of travelling between Kenmare and the south of England several times during the past six months – each journey taking the best part of two days – Moeran had been able to make very good progress with the symphony, and it seems that The Lodge in Kenmare had become a replacement for his studio at Lingwood Lodge. However, several performances of his music had been scheduled for the summer and it was necessary for Moeran to remain in Britain for a few months. The *Two Pieces for Small Orchestra* were included on the programme of a Promenade Concert on 28 August, and *Nocturne* was performed at the Norwich and Norfolk Triennial Music Festival on 24 September. Britten's festival commission *Our Hunting Fathers*, which had eventually been accepted by the committee, was on the programme for the following day. Moeran himself had a small performing role in a concert at the festival, his duty being to perform 'one note on an anvil ... on an instrument borrowed from a smithy' in a performance of Patrick Hadley's *La Belle Dame Sans Merci*.[4]

After the festival, Moeran stayed in London for a few days for discussions with Novello & Co. about the publication of the symphony and with the BBC about the planned first performance.[5] Although the original commission had been made by Hamilton Harty through the Hallé orchestra, this had long since lapsed. Moeran had kept Harty appraised of the progress of the symphony since restarting work on it in 1934, and it was agreed between them that Harty would conduct the first performance, whenever that might be. The immediate problem was that Hamilton Harty had been taken ill earlier in the year, and there was some doubt about his being in a sufficiently recovered condition in time for rehearsals and the first performance.[6]

Moeran also met Britten in London for lunch or tea several times, most significantly on 13 October, after which Britten wrote in his diary: 'After dinner Jack Moeran comes with his new Symphony – it has some excellent things in it, but terribly under the Sibelius influence – mood, ideas & technique. This is going to be almost as bad as the Brahms influence on English music I fear.'[7] Leaving aside Britten's comment on the Sibelius influence, this suggests that the music of the symphony was complete by mid-October. Moeran's orchestral composing procedure was to think out the musical ideas and commit them to manuscript in short score or piano reduction, only creating the full score when he was satisfied that the music was exactly as he wanted.[8] Since the full score manuscript of the symphony bears the

---

4 'The Norwich Festival', *The Musical Times*, Vol. 77, No. 1124 (1 October 1936), 941.

5 Moeran's music was published by several publishing houses, but during the mid-1930s he seemed to favour Novello & Co.

6 Harty had been diagnosed with a brain tumour, the treatment for which had included the removal of his right eye. See Jeremy Dibble, *Hamilton Harty: Musical Polymath*, (Boydell & Brewer, Woodbridge, 2013), 260–265.

7 Extract from Benjamin Britten's diary, quoted in Evans (2009), 379.

8 Perhaps curiously, Moeran seemed to enjoy this final process of scoring his music. In a letter to Lionel Hill in April 1943, he wrote, 'I am struggling to finish a Rhapsody for piano and orchestra in time for the Proms. The piano part is written, thank Heaven, and I am now on the congenial task of making a full score'; Hill, 11.

signature 'Valencia Island, Co. Kerry. Jan. 22nd. 1937' and Moeran had completed and scored the first three movements of the symphony by the summer of 1936, it may be deduced that the composition and scoring of the final movement – including the 'cribbed' Sibelius chords – took him a further six months.

Moeran wrote to Aloys Fleischmann from his parents' house at Lyndhurst to inform him that he would probably be in Cork on the morning of 14 October, having taken the overnight ferry from Fishguard. Moeran's friendship with Aloys Fleischmann and his wife Tilly had developed very quickly during the short time that they had known each other, and for the remainder of Moeran's life he visited their home in Cork frequently. They also maintained a regular and extensive correspondence. After staying for a few days with the Fleischmanns, he travelled on to Kenmare, where he settled down again at the Lodge of the Lansdowne Arms Hotel and resumed work on the full score of the final movement of the symphony.

Unfortunately, Moeran received news in mid-November that his father had been taken ill, and he arranged to return at once to Lyndhurst, briefly pausing in Dublin to attend a recital at the Royal Dublin Society given by the Pasquier Trio at which his String Trio in G major was performed.[9] On arriving in Lyndhurst, he found his father mostly recovered, despite having been given what he described as 'increasingly alarming accounts of his condition'.[10] Moeran returned to Ireland a few days later but found that he would be unable to occupy what had become his usual rooms in Kenmare. He was recommended (probably by his friend Herbert Hughes) to try a hotel at Knightstown on Valentia Island, from where, after staying a few days over Christmas and New Year, he found lodgings which he took for a three-month period. On 14 December, he had written to Julian Herbage:

> The Symphony is almost finished; the composition is, in fact, done. I finished to-day. It only remains to translate & copy out into full score the finale, or part of it. This will take me another three weeks easy going, including a break-off for Christmas festivities. It plays 40 minutes … as to the projected performance on Mar 14th; if Harty is still on the sick list we shall have to postpone it. A long time ago I promised him, & he promised me, to do the first performance, & if he is temporarily out of action it would be rather callous on my part to make other arrangements … Harty has been helping me over this symphony by advising me over points of orchestration etc: I had a most encouraging letter from his secretary quite lately, giving a very optimistic view about his state of health, so I hope everything will turn out alright.[11]

9   The Pasquier Trio was a French violin, viola and cello ensemble comprising the brothers Pierre, Jean and Etienne Pasquier. As a result of this performance, Moeran dedicated the published edition of the String Trio in G major to the Pasquier Trio.

10 McNeill, 371.

11 McNeill, 372.

1937

In early January, while he was out for a walk in the hills, Moeran slipped and broke his ankle. He was 'laid up' – as he later described his condition in a letter to Herbert Hughes – for several weeks. Nonetheless, he soldiered on with the orchestration, and on 22 January (the date of completion according to the manuscript full score of the symphony) he wrote to Julian Herbage: 'The score of the last movement is en route for Novello's for copying purposes.' However, the previous day, Moeran had received a letter from Harty and another from Harty's secretary stating categorically that Harty was 'forbidden by doctor's orders to undertake any heavy work this spring'. The letters informed Moeran that conducting the première of the symphony would have to be postponed until the next concert season. While Moeran was probably greatly disappointed by this development, he seems to have been philosophical about it, and he chatted in his letter to Herbage about the state of his injured ankle and the local folksong collecting he had been doing.

With the first performance of the symphony postponed and the full score completed, Moeran could turn his mind to other things. He had already mentioned folksong collecting in his letter to Julian Herbage, and in the letter to Herbert Hughes, he wrote about his Republican connections:

> I am happy to say that I have succeeded in falling out with that impossible crowd of British Imperialists at the cable station here. First of all they threatened to be a nuisance with their invitations to frightful evenings of bridge, etc. But they have come to the conclusion that I am rather an outsider ... so now I am left in peace. I gather they do not approve of my IRA acquaintances & friends & look upon me as a sort of blackleg.[12]

The casual reference to 'IRA acquaintances' in the letter to Hughes could have several interpretations, the most likely being that it was entirely genuine. However, it is possible that Moeran was also endeavouring to establish a Republican-oriented identity that would enhance his standing with the ardently Nationalist Hughes.[13] Moeran's occasional tendency to say what he thought people wanted him to say is indicative of a personal insecurity that he exhibited throughout his life. When, in his obituary for Moeran, Arnold Bax wrote that Moeran was not even 'dimly aware that such matters [Irish politics] for violent debate existed',[14] he evidently had no

---

[12] Letter to Herbert Hughes, dated 11 February 1937; quoted in Angela Hughes, *Chelsea Footprints: A Thirties Chronicle*, (Quartet Books, London, 2008), 161–2. Hughes had written to Moeran in early February asking for news about the inhabitants of Cahirciveen (the town nearest the ferry to Valentia Island) as he and his wife planned to visit over the Easter holidays. Valentia Island was the eastern terminus of the transatlantic telegraph cable laid between Ireland and Newfoundland in 1858, and the cable station was in operation until 1966.

[13] A more detailed examination of the circumstances and activities of Hughes and others involvement in the predominantly Nationalist Gaelic revival movement can be found in Eamon Phoenix, *et al.* (eds), *Feis na nGleann A Century of Gaelic Culture in the Antrim Glens*, (Ulster Historical Foundation, Belfast, 2005).

[14] Bax, (1951), 127.

inkling of his friend's Nationalist inclination. If the testimony implied in the letter to Hughes is to be believed, then Moeran had friendships and acquaintanceships amongst members of the Irish Republican Army that he must have acquired during an earlier visit. Membership of the IRA was much smaller and its activities more limited in the mid-1930s than had been the case twenty years earlier, and so it is probable – as suggested in Chapter 7 – that Moeran made his IRA acquaintances and friends during his 1918 stay in Ireland.[15]

By the middle of March, Moeran had recovered his ability to walk with the aid of crutches, and he returned to his parents' house in Lyndhurst with time on his hands. He spent it attending concerts and social events in London, and it is probable that during these few weeks in Britain he discussed the composition of a violin concerto with the violinist May Harrison. He may also have spoken further with Harriet Cohen about the proposed piano concerto, which he had promised to work on after the symphony had been completed. Whatever form the various conversations took, by the time Moeran travelled again to Ireland in April he had promised to compose concertos for both May Harrison and Harriet Cohen. He again visited the Fleischmanns and attended a performance of the *Farrago Suite* played by the University Orchestra conducted by Fleischmann's son – also Aloys – at the Aula Maxima of University College Cork on 14 April. The day after the concert, Moeran journeyed via Mallow and Killarney back to Valentia Island, where he hoped that he would find the inspiration to begin work on the two concertos. The doctor had pronounced his ankle fully restored, and this enabled Moeran to spend time walking, both on the island and in the Kerry mountains. Rambles in the countryside were essential to Moeran's creative process. Unfortunately, he had presented himself with a significant problem. While in his younger (pre-Eynsford cottage) days he could work quickly and efficiently on several works in parallel, his mature (post-recovery) compositional process demanded that he concentrate on the music of one major work at a time. His decision seems to have been to put the Harriet Cohen piano concerto to one side and to devote his efforts for the next few months on developing ideas and themes for the violin concerto.

Moeran remained based on Valentia Island for four months working on the violin concerto, but he did occasionally travel to both Kenmare and Cork. He eventually crossed to England on 23 August and returned to the lodgings in Adams Road that he had temporarily occupied two years earlier. On 8 September, he spent much of the day composing a letter to Hamilton Harty to try to explain the complicated situation that had developed regarding the first performance of his symphony. He also asked the conductor if he would accept the dedication of the symphony. While Moeran may have been clear in his mind what it was that he wanted to say to Harty, he did not express it very well, and Harty evidently took umbrage at what he perceived to be a slight. Moeran had mentioned that he was working on a violin concerto, and Harty misunderstood this to mean that Moeran was offering him the opportunity to conduct the concerto instead of the symphony. Moeran immediately wrote back endeavouring to clarify his meaning, but the damage had been done and

---

[15]   See Brian Hanley, *The IRA: 1926–36*, (Four Courts Press, Dublin, 2002) for an in-depth history of the Irish Republican Army during the late 1920s and early 1930s.

Harty indignantly refused the dedication of the symphony. Moeran poured his heart out over the 'intrigues which take place under the auspices under which [music] is run in this country [Great Britain]' and blamed 'a certain individual' for letting him and Harty down. He said that he looked forward to '[getting] back to Kerry soon, where the inhabitants may be less intellectual, but at any rate possess directness and honesty'. Moeran compounded his unintentional gaffe by confiding to a gossip columnist that while he was happy that Sir Hamilton Harty was on the road to recovery from his recent illness, he was also pleased that the 'brilliant young conductor, Mr Leslie Heward' would shortly be giving the first performance of the symphony. Moeran had previously claimed that this could only be undertaken by Harty and that under no circumstances would he allow any other conductor to do it. Amongst other regional newspapers, the piece was printed in the *Belfast Newsletter*.[16] Sadly, the rift between Harty and Moeran, formerly such good friends, had not been resolved by the time of Harty's death a few years later, although when the symphony was finally published the year after Harty's death, Moeran included the inscription: 'To Hamilton Harty.'[17]

Moeran spent a month in Cambridge during which he probably started work on the piano concerto for Harriet Cohen. Although his creative process required that he concentrate his efforts on a single work, he also tended to associate compositions with specific places. Thus, the violin concerto was now linked in his mind with Ireland, and he had convinced himself that when he was elsewhere, he could not work on it. He explained this in the 8 September letter to Hamilton Harty as having started the concerto in County Kerry, he wanted to 'finish it in the same surroundings'. In Cambridge, therefore, he was able to do something else. Perhaps working on the assumption that he would have time in each location, Moeran informed the BBC that he was composing a violin concerto for May Harrison and a piano concerto for Harriet Cohen and that both would be ready for inclusion in the 1938 season of Promenade Concerts with each instrumentalist having agreed to perform. However, Moeran's ability to work to a pre-arranged schedule had rarely been tested successfuly, and he must surely have been aware of his inability to compose to order. Nonetheless, he travelled to Valentia Island at the end of September to resume work on the violin concerto, with the first ideas for the piano concerto having been committed to manuscript in Cambridge.

---

[16] Harty was recuperating in Northern Ireland and would undoubtedly have read the local Belfast newspapers.

[17] In November-December the following year, Aloys Fleischmann approached Harty about directing a festival in Cork. While Harty was very interested in the project, when he heard that Moeran might be involved, he wrote to Fleischmann, 'if you don't mind I think I would prefer not to include Mr Moeran at this preliminary meeting'. Letter from Bax to Fleischmann, quoted in Jeremy Dibble, *Hamilton Harty: Musical Polymath*, (Boydell & Brewer, Woodbridge, 2013), 282.

1938

Symphony in G minor

Previously arranged appointments required Moeran's return to Britain at the end of November, and he spent the Christmas and New Year holiday with his parents in their new house in Kington in Herefordshire.[18] On 13 January, the first performance of the symphony in G minor finally took place at a Royal Philharmonic Society concert that was broadcast on the BBC regional programme. The London Philharmonic Orchestra was conducted by Leslie Heward. In an extended introduction to the work published in the *Radio Times*, Robert Hull provided a detailed context to the creation and circumstances of the symphony.[19] While much of this must have derived from an interview with the composer himself, some of Hull's remarks were particularly insightful, although Moeran was not pleased with the article. As he wrote to Aloys Fleischmann: 'I should not have authorised Hull to write as he has done, had he given me any idea he was going to do so.'[20] Hull began by asserting that 'as regards the writing of symphonies, the present-day school of British composers is second to none throughout the world', referencing Walton, Rubbra and Vaughan Williams as examples of composers with 'strength of imagination and excellence of craftsmanship'. Concerning the symphony itself, Hull suggested that its 'highly individual style [resembled] some creation hewn out of granite', but that the music itself 'is for the most part tragic but nowhere gloomy in a negative style'. He averred that it sprang from 'a mind with ... a keen grip upon the realities of life'. Despite its having been programmed as the final work in a long programme – which included Rimsky-Korsakov's overture *Ivan the Terrible*, two tone poems by Ernest Bloch and a performance of the Piano Concerto in D minor by Brahms – the symphony was received enthusiastically by the audience. Press review was mixed, with the music critic of *The Observer* claiming that the symphony was 'a sequence of patches'.[21] He went on: 'It is becoming a fashion to name a key in which the piece is, in order, perhaps, to have something to contradict at the first possible moment'.[22] The music correspondent of the *Cork Evening Echo* wrote a piece emphasising the local connections of the composer. Titling his piece 'Cork Composer's Work', the correspondent had clearly prepared himself by reading Hull's *Radio Times* article, and he ended with 'Mr Moeran, who is of Cork parentage, is one of the most distinguished of contemporary composers.'[23] Generally, the symphony was well-received, and conductors were interested in programming it for their orchestras. The

---

[18] The Moerans had bought the house on Gravel Hill, Kington in the autumn of 1937. This was to be their home, and Moeran's base in England, for the next seven years.

[19] 'A Symphony of Granite', *Radio Times*, Vol. 58, No. 745, (7 January 1938), 14.

[20] Letter from Moeran to Aloys Fleischmann, dated Gravel Hill, Kington, 7 January 1938; a transcript of this letter was provided to the author by Dr Ruth Fleischmann.

[21] 'E. J. Moeran's Symphony', *The Observer*, (16 January 1938), 12.

[22] *Ibid.*

[23] 'Cork Composer's Work', *Cork Evening Echo*, (14 January 1938), 7.

honour of the second performance went to Richard Austin and the Bournemouth Municipal Orchestra, who included the symphony in their opening concert of the 1938 Bournemouth Festival in March at which Moeran made an appearance. A brief item in the *Daily Herald* boasted that Bournemouth possessed 'the only permanent seaside municipal orchestra which does not have to be augmented by London players'.[24] Moeran wrote to Kenneth Wright at the BBC that he had spoken to Sir Henry Wood at the festival and that the conductor had requested a copy of the score of the symphony. Moeran was hoping that the second London performance would take place at the 1939 season of Promenade Concerts. In the meanwhile, Eugene Goossens, Moeran's fellow Royal College of Music student to whom he had sent a score of the symphony, conducted two performances by the Cincinnati Symphony Orchestra at the end of March.

As Moeran's largest and most prominent composition, the Symphony in G minor justifiably occupies pride of place in his oeuvre. The composition of one or more symphonies has long been considered – rightly or wrongly – to establish a composer's maturity, and compared with some of his contemporaries, it may be suggested that Moeran was a bit late to the table, even though the symphony may be said to have been originally conceived some fourteen years earlier. Moreover, his achievement must be tempered by a consideration of the undoubted strong influences present in the music, most especially that of Sibelius. Moeran's own admission to having cribbed the final chords' scoring from the Finnish composer eliminates the possibility of coincidence. G minor might be thought to have been an unusual choice of key for Moeran. However, of the better-known classical symphonists, Mozart's symphonies numbers 25 and 40 and Haydn's symphonies numbers 39 and 83 were composed in that key. Several nineteenth-century symphonists also composed works in G minor, including Tchaikovsky with his *Winter Dreams* Symphony No. 1 and Joachim Raff with his Symphony No. 4. Most interesting is the number of Scandinavian composers that produced works in G minor. These include Franz Berwald (Symphony No. 1), Niels Gade (Symphony No. 6), Carl Nielsen (Symphony No. 1), Wilhelm Stenhammar (Symphony No. 2) and Kurt Atterberg (Symphony No. 4). While is it not known with which, if any, of these symphonies Moeran was familiar, the existence of the models and Moeran's acknowledged 'sponge-like' tendency to absorb music suggests that some inspiration from these and other works led to the composition of the symphony. The Symphony in G minor does sound 'Scandinavian' and perhaps much more so than do the symphonies of those of his contemporaries working in the same musical style at the time.

Understandably, given its status as Moeran's most extensive work, much has been claimed for the Symphony in G minor. Geoffrey Self devoted more than thirty pages of his book to the work and concluded that the work was a Requiem for those who perished during the First World War.[25] Edwin Evans wrote an extended piece in *The Musical Times* presenting the structure of the work as he saw it with several musical examples to illustrate his points. He summed up Moeran's achievement by

[24] 'Orchestra Needs No London Help', *The Daily Herald*, (21 March 1938), 9.
[25] Self, 102–133.

describing the première as a great occasion for English music.[26] Moeran wrote the sleeve notes himself for the HMV recording of the symphony that was released early in 1943. He explained the structure of each movement in some detail and provided an interesting insight into the composition process. Overall, he described the symphony as owing:

> its inspiration to the natural surroundings in which it was planned and written. The greater part of the work was carried out among the mountains and seaboard of Co. Kerry, but the material of the second movement was conceived around the sand-dunes and marshes of East Norfolk. It is not 'programme music' – i.e. there is no story or sequence of events attached to it and, moreover, it adheres strictly to its form.

The only subjectivity that Moeran allowed himself was to describe the opening of the third movement, in which 'the sunlight is let in, and there is a spring-like contrast to the wintry proceedings of the slow movement'. Moeran wrote these notes at the end of 1942 and, as will be seen, had made much effort during the previous few years to establish Irish credentials for his music. His claim that the 'greater part of the work was carried out among the mountains and seaboard of Co. Kerry' was clearly exaggeration: he simply was not in Ireland for long enough during the period of composition of the symphony for this to be true. While the attribution of the influence of the sand-dunes and marshes of east Norfolk stands up to scrutiny rather better, it is nonetheless a highly romanticised image. It is interesting to ponder how much, if any, of the original 1925 symphony had survived and was incorporated into the 1937 work. Hitherto, writers on Moeran have described him resuming work in 1934 on the previously abandoned symphony. These assertions have been predicated on the assumption that Moeran had completed much of the work in 1925. However, this author inclines toward the conjecture that Moeran's withdrawal of the symphony from performance in 1926 was due to its remaining mostly uncomposed, rather than his claim to want to remodel it. If this conjecture is true, then there would have been little original material on which to resume work. While Self averred that 'the slow movement is the one which irrefutably dates from 1924', he provided no evidence to support this.[27] Indeed, in a presentation given to the Midland Branch of the Delius Society in 1995, Stephen Lloyd convincingly demonstrated that Self's assertion was incorrect, since the strong Sibelian influence in the symphony was unlikely to have been possible during the 1920s.[28] The author's belief is that the Symphony in G minor was composed in its entirety between 1934 and 1937, and any similarity with whatever Moeran really did compose in 1925 is due to his having recalled his earlier ideas.

Other performances of Moeran's works had taken place during the first few months of 1938, and Moeran attended some of these. However, the constant round

---

[26] 'Moeran's Symphony in G minor', *The Musical Times*, Vol. 79, No. 1140 (1 February 1938), 94–99.

[27] Self, 117.

[28] 'E. J. Moeran – A Centenary Talk', *The Delius Society Journal*, No. 118, (Winter/Spring 1996), 48–49.

of concert-going, interviews with newspapers, visiting publishers and the other minutiae of promoting one's own music had diverted Moeran from the main task that he had set himself for the first half of the year – to complete the two concertos that he had promised to the BBC – and the solution necessitated a return to Kerry where he could work on the violin concerto. He arrived at his parent's house during the early evening of 29 March, en route for Ireland, to find a telegram from Kenneth Wright (Director of Programming at the BBC), requesting an assurance that the violin and piano concertos would both be ready in time for rehearsals for and performance at the Promenade Concerts in August. It must suddenly have dawned on Moeran that he had no chance of meeting the deadline that he himself had set just a few months earlier, and he dispatched a telegram back to Wright: 'Regret neither concerto completed in time Proms.'

Moeran left Kington the following morning and travelled via Fishguard and Cork back to his lodgings on Valentia Island. On 5 April, he wrote an explanatory letter to Wright:

> I was obliged to reply in the negative to your wire last week, as neither my piano rhapsody nor violin concerto are sufficiently advanced for performance at this year's proms. I am sorry about it, but it really isn't safe to fix a date & then perhaps not come up to scratch.[29]

And that was that. Having promised two new works for the 1938 Promenade Concerts to their respective performers and to the BBC, Moeran was withdrawing them both. Nonetheless, Wright and the BBC do not appear to have been particularly discomfited by the news. There were many other works available to programme for the Proms season, and, given the composer's history of late delivery, they may even have been relieved that Moeran was withdrawing the works himself at that stage. It is also interesting to note that within a period of a week, the planned piano concerto had been downgraded to a 'piano rhapsody'.

Having divested himself of the stress of composing two concertos within a few months, Moeran spent the next two months travelling around Ireland, visiting friends and attending performances of his music. Early in 1937, Professor Aloys Fleischmann had mentioned to Moeran that he was planning a concert of music by Irish composers at the Gaiety Theatre, Dublin, as part of a series of celebrity concerts by the Radio Symphony Orchestra to be promoted by Radio Éireann. Moeran wrote back to Fleischmann, expressing some doubt as to whether he himself was Irish: 'I doubt if I should be considered sufficiently Irish to be included in that programme. My father is an Irishman, but I was born in England. However, the fact that I now live more or less permanently in Kerry might help.'[30] By the date of this letter, Moeran had spent about half his time since the beginning of 1936 in Ireland. Thus, like his claim to columnist 'Big Ben' the previous summer, the statement that he lived permanently in Kerry – albeit 'more or less' – seems to be more one of desire

---

[29] McNeill, 384.

[30] Letter from Moeran to Aloys Fleischmann, dated Wellington House, Valencia Island, Co. Kerry, 10 February 1937; a transcript of this letter was provided to the author by Dr Ruth Fleischmann.

than reality. When considered in the context of his letter to Herbert Hughes – in which he blatantly identified with a Nationalist political slant – it seems as if Moeran was endeavouring to adopt Irishness by assertion. The problem of Moeran's Irish identity will be returned to later. In his letter to Fleischmann, Moeran also made some helpful suggestions about which Irish composers might be performed, including a suggestion about who should not be:

> I don't see how you can bring in Bax. It is true that much of his best work invokes the spirit of this country far more truly than that of any other composer, but the fact remains he is purely English in birth and blood. It would be like playing Debussy's *Iberia*, Ravel's *Rhapsodie Espagnole* ... in a concert of Spanish music in Madrid.[31]

The concert was arranged for 24 April, and it included Moeran's Second Rhapsody for Orchestra and a set of his songs to be sung by William Heddle Nash. There had been three other concerts in the series, and Moeran had asked Constant Lambert – the conductor of the previous event – about the orchestra. Lambert had told him that the orchestra in Dublin was 'fairly efficient as to playing notes and picking up tempi, but [made] a horrible noise in the wind and brass departments'.[32] It was with this somewhat alarming endorsement that Moeran, perhaps in some trepidation, travelled to Dublin from Valentia Island on 22 April.

The concert was widely reviewed in the Irish press, and Moeran's rhapsody was generally regarded as the most mature and musical of the works presented. The music correspondent of the *Irish Independent* ('R. Peggio') mentioned its 'individuality and power', noting that there was 'a certain dignity, amounting almost to grandeur' in Moeran's treatment of the themes of the work.[33] 'R. Peggio' also remarked on the 'delightful set of songs by Moeran' which closed the second part of the concert. However, 'P. T.', writing in the *Irish Press*, had—perhaps understandably—misunderstood the origins of the Rhapsody:

> I had some difficulty in deciding my proper mental approach to Mr Moeran's Second Rhapsody. This composition shows a thorough grasp of orchestral technique and resources, but in spite of its kinship idiomatically to Irish music, does it reveal the 'Hidden Ireland'. Listening to the composition as 'atmospheric' music, I certainly recognised pictures of wind-swept, sea-washed coasts, authentically Irish, but I found that this mental approach did not cover the full content of the work. Was Mr Moeran's complete heart in the work? I can vouch for his head.[34]

It is reasonable to suppose that the specific imagery and the reference to 'Hidden Ireland' had been mentioned in the concert programme note and that it had been intended to emphasise the 'Irishness' of the piece. Given that the work had been composed in Norfolk by a composer whose experience of Ireland at the time was

---

31 *Ibid.*

32 McNeill, 385.

33 *Irish Independent*, (25 April 1938), 9.

34 'Irish Composers Broadcast', *Irish Press*, (25 April 1938), 9.

limited and that until earlier in the year there had been no hint that the piece had any Irish connections whatsoever, the reviewer's perplexity is understandable.

A month or so after this concert, Moeran heard from the BBC that his symphony had been included in the programme for the coming season of Promenade Concerts and that it would be performed at the Queen's Hall on 11 August by the BBC Symphony Orchestra conducted by Sir Henry Wood. Moeran had been planning to remain in Ireland throughout August including a visit to the annual Puck's Fair at Killorglin, but he travelled to England at the end of July and settled back at his parents' home in Kington for the next few months. Henry Wood wrote to Moeran on 30 July to enquire about some tempo alterations that he felt were necessary. Moeran had specified an abrupt tempo change in the first movement that Wood thought should have a preparatory *ritenuto*. While Moeran's reply has not survived, the published score of the symphony did include Sir Henry's suggestion. After the concert, Moeran wrote to Heathcote Statham to report that the symphony had been 'splendidly played' and greatly appreciating Sir Henry Wood's care and preparation: 'Wood is very keen on the work & threw every ounce of himself into it.'

Diaphenia, Rosaline, Rahoon

During the summer, Moeran spent a few weeks at his parents' house in Kington, working in his newly established composing studio in a room with large windows overlooking the garden. He composed three new songs, the siciliano-like *Diaphenia*, a setting of a text by the renaissance poet Henry Chettle, *Rosaline*, a setting of a poem by Thomas Lodge and *Rahoon*, a setting of a poem by James Joyce. Apart from the Symphony in G minor, these songs were the first works that Moeran had composed since December 1934. He mentioned the songs in a letter to Benjamin Britten:

> I had a rather inexplicable letter from Ralph Hawkes [the publisher] about the songs, suggesting that one [*Rosaline*] ... should not be in 5/4 time, but 3/4. (a) If this were so, I should not have written it in 5/4. (b) One has only to read the poem over to realise that 5/4 is inevitable. I think Ralph thinks singers might be frightened at 5/4; God knows why they should be, especially as such unsophisticated people as Harry Cox of Potter Heigham sing normally in 5/4. Ralph says he is not keen on the Joyce song [*Rahoon*]; I am sorry, as I thought it the best song I have written in some ways & as it is not in a readily popular vein I rather regarded the other as something thrown in as a foil ... Meanwhile, I have perpetrated one for Heddle Nash [*Diaphenia*] (with a real tenor high A!), the MS of which has gone off to Hawkes. I am sorry if he turns down the Joyce song as if he does I must take them all elsewhere.[35]

Although none of the songs was mentioned by name, the information in the letter is sufficient to identify them with a high degree of certainty. As explained in the letter,

35 Letter from Moeran to Benjamin Britten dated Gravel Hill, Kington, 16 September 1938; transcript in the Barry Marsh Collection, which was made available to the author by Rachel Marsh. Since none of the songs was published by Hawkes, it may be assumed that Ralph Hawkes did turn down the 'Joyce song'.

Rosaline is a declamatory setting in 5/4 time throughout, mostly strophic but with a modified melody for the shorter final verse. Thomas Lodge's original text comprises four ten-line verses and a six-line final verse. Moeran, perhaps somewhat prudishly, decided to omit the third verse of the poem, which mentions 'paps' and 'breasts'.[36] While the accompaniment to the first two verses is mostly diatonic, an increasingly chromatic piano part diverges from the tonal melody through the second half of the song, culminating in a wildly disconcerting final few bars (music example 41). The harmonic palette of Warlock is detectable, although, as has been suggested, many of Warlock's harmonic characteristics may have derived from Moeran. In particular, the phenomenon of retrospective concord, where, provided that a harmonic sequence ends with a concordant progression that leads consistently from the harmony at the beginning of the sequence, the note combinations that come in between are largely irrelevant. Many of Warlock's songs – *Mr Belloc's Fancy* for example – exploit this effect, and Moeran also made use of it.

Rahoon was described by Moeran in his letter as 'the best song I have written in some ways'. It is a setting of a poem by James Joyce written in 1913 and which expresses the poignant sadness felt by the protagonist as she weeps by the grave of her dead lover.[37] The poem conveys bleakness and tragedy by the repeated use of words invoking negative emotions, such as 'dark', 'sad' and 'black'. The poem

Music example 41. *Rosaline*: final 9 bars

---

[36] It could be asserted that including every verse would have made the song unacceptably long. However, it is interesting to note that C. H. H. Parry's setting of the same text also omits the same verse.

[37] The lady in the poem was Joyce's wife Nora Barnacle, and the grave was that of her former lover Michael Bodkin who had died tragically from tuberculosis at the age of

comprises three verses, each of which juxtaposes short and long lines but in a different sequence. This form renders setting them to music problematic. Moeran's solution was to through-compose the song with little to connect or even distinguish the verses. The introduction is symbolic of the rain introduced in the first line of the text (music example 42).

The parallel descending minor major seventh chords in the left hand provide an establishing astringency that sets the tragic tone for the song. Idiomatically, the setting of *Rahoon* strongly recalls that of Moeran's 1931 Joyce setting *Tilly*. As in the earlier song, an intensely dissonant texture is punctuated by moments of consonant relief, including the use of one of Moeran's favourite sonic devices, a second inversion major sixth chord resolving to the sub-dominant (music example 43). Other characteristic Moeran devices, such as sequences of parallel fourths and bitonal triad juxtaposition are employed to underpin the tonal wandering apparent in both the vocal part and the accompaniment. Composed some twenty-three years after his first song *The North Sea Ground*, *Rahoon* perhaps represents the culmination of Moeran's song-writing art. In particular, the chromatic vocal line aptly and strongly reflects the sense of loss that emanates from the text.

Conversely, the delightful *Diaphenia* has an instantly memorable tune that catches the spirit of Chettle's text exactly. The song is constructed in an ABA three-verse form, although the B verse melody is mostly the same as the A verses: the difference being evident in the last line of the melody. This variation demonstrates

Music example 42. *Rahoon*: bars 1–8

nineteen. Despite its textual difficulties, the poem has attracted several twentieth-century composers, including Herbert Hughes, Brian Boydell and Muriel Emily Herbert.

Music example 43. *Rahoon*: bars 13–15

Moeran's highly developed sensitivity to the meaning of the text he was setting. A less perceptive composer might simply have kept the melody the same for each verse, but Moeran's lowering of the tonal level of the tune reflects the slightly darker reference to death in the text. Harmonically, Moeran's accompaniment hints at rather than emphasises the tonal modulations implied by the melody. Although it had been more than two years since his last work as a song composer, *Diaphenia* shows that Moeran's ability to absorb a text and invent an appropriate and compelling tune, together with an interesting and suitable accompaniment, had not diminished. Moeran dedicated his setting to the tenor Heddle Nash.

Phyllida and Corydon

Moeran stayed in Britain for the rest of the year, spending most of his time in Kington. Since he was not in Ireland, it must be supposed that he felt unable to work on the violin concerto, and he probably composed the short anthem *Blessed Are Those Servants* at this time, possibly for his brother William Graham Moeran's church in Leominster. However, as he later confessed in a letter to May Harrison, his mind went 'off at a tangent', and he decided to compose another set of madrigals. The result was the choral suite *Phyllida and Corydon*, a group of nine madrigal-type songs for conventional SATB choir. Moeran provided some idea of his reasons for composing the suite in a letter he wrote to Kenneth Wright in April 1939: 'I was perverse enough to temporarily abandon orchestral composition when I got bitten with the idea of an unaccompanied choral suite on the Phyllida & Corydon poems. I may now push on with the piano & orchestra work, but God alone knows when it will be finished.'[38]

Perhaps Moeran wanted to build on the success of his 1933 madrigal set *Songs of Springtime*, which was being sung by amateur choirs around the country and which received regular professional performances. The remarks made earlier about the *Songs of Springtime* are equally applicable to *Phyllida and Corydon*, with the exception that Moeran took the juxtaposition of the Elizabethan madrigal style with

---

[38] McNeill, 386–387.

thoroughly modern harmonic ideas to a greater extreme. This technique divided critical opinion and certainly leaves the suite open to the accusation of inconsistency. The suite was published in mid-1939 and was extensively reviewed in the press. In an extended piece for the Bristol-based *Western Daily Press*, the critic wrote:

> In this Suite the distinguished Norfolk composer has here and there combined the characteristics of Elizabethan madrigal writing with a modern idiom, but so naturally have the two styles become merged that nothing strained or artificial can be observed. In these respects it is a valuable specimen of modernised antique art and recalls Vaughan Williams's *Fantasia on a Theme of Thomas Tallis* and Peter Warlock's *Capriol Suite* ... Mr Moeran has been content to emulate the tendencies of the Elizabethans and ... he has done so in a free and independent manner without any suggestion of slavish imitation.[39]

The writer went on to suggest that the choral suite would be suitable for the Bristol Madrigal Society or the University Madrigal Singers. William Glock wrote in *The Observer*: '*Phyllida and Corydon* has few challenging phrases and few in which the two contrasting influences seem to have produced a truly original result' and called attention to what he saw as Moeran's dependency on *Hymns Ancient and Modern*, Delius and Peter Warlock.[40] When the suite received its first broadcast performance by the BBC Singers under Leslie Woodgate on the National Programme on 30 October 1939, the *Radio Times* printed a helpful programme note by Edwin Evans, which included detailed descriptions of each of the nine poems and the manner of their setting. Evans concluded:

> The settings vary considerably within the limits of the style. Through them all runs a sympathetic feeling for the pastoral convention which produced the poems. Some use is made of modal inflections suggesting the period, but it is the effect rather than the method that makes the Suite 'all of a piece'.[41]

The harmonic appositions in some of the songs of the suite do indeed sound unusual in the context of what are undoubtedly pastiche-madrigals. According to Hubert Foss, Moeran had told him that the extreme chromaticism derived from the influence of Bernard van Dieren.[42] The first song opens conventionally (music example 44). This is followed by an unexpected and at first disconcerting wrench into E flat minor (music example 45) and a similar pattern is followed in each of the other songs. Ultimately, the success or otherwise of *Phyllida and Corydon* can only be measured by the responses of performers and audiences. Since the first performance, the suite has been broadcast regularly both by the BBC Singers and other vocal ensembles. It has been recorded several times and it features occasionally on the programmes of concerts given throughout Britain by professional and good quality amateur choirs. Thus, despite the criticisms the mixed musical style

---

[39] 'Music and Drama – A Notable New Work for Unaccompanied Choir', *Western Daily Press*, (30 June 1939), 5.

[40] 'Music and Musicians', *The Observer*, (2 June 1940), 10.

[41] 'Phyllida and Corydon', *Radio Times*, Vol. 65, No. 839, (27 October 1939), 11.

[42] Hubert Foss, *Compositions of E. J. Moeran*, (Novello & Co., London, 1948), 15.

Music example 44. *Phyllida and Corydon* (No. 1): bars 1–10

Music example 45. *Phyllida and Corydon* (No. 1): bars 11–14

has attracted, it may be considered to stand as one of Moeran's most successful and enduring creations.

1939

Two performances of the symphony took place during the first few weeks of 1939. Malcolm Sargent conducted the London Philharmonic Orchestra in Nottingham on 10 January and the Hallé Orchestra in Manchester on 16 February. The press reviews of both performances were positive. In particular, the *Nottingham Evening Post* reported that the cheering and applause at the end of the symphony was 'spontaneous and enthusiastic'. At the end of February, Moeran travelled back to Ireland to attend a St Patrick's Day concert at the National Stadium, featuring Irish music of all kinds. The programme included two movements from the *Farrago Suite*, which Moeran had been engaged to conduct. Unfortunately, Moeran became ill and was unable to discharge his conducting task. Since the main concert director, Lieutenant J. Doyle, did not feel up to the job of conducting Moeran's difficult music, the *Fair Day* from Harty's *Irish Symphony* was performed instead.

In early April, Kenneth Wright telegrammed Moeran in Ireland to ask him if he had a new work that would be suitable for inclusion in the 1939 season of Promenade

Concerts. Moeran replied on 9 April to explain that he had not composed anything new for orchestra for some time. He said that he was still working on the piano concerto (piano rhapsody) but that he had no idea when it would be finished. He suggested the First Rhapsody or *In the Mountain Country* as orchestral works that Wright may consider including in the Proms. Moeran ended his letter by saying that he was likely to be remaining in Ireland for some considerable time. A further letter to Wright dated 22 May revealed the cause of Moeran's extended illness: 'the doctor thinks I had a gall stone and eventually passed it.' He further informed Wright that he would shortly be spending some time in hospital in Cork and that, consequently, he would be unable to complete any new orchestral works for the foreseeable future.

Moeran also wrote to May Harrison on Whit Sunday from Kenmare to explain the continuing delays in the composition of the violin concerto. His litany of excuses, while perhaps entirely valid, must have seemed a bit thin to the violinist, who may have been running out of patience: 'I have had a series of misfortunes. 1) 'flu ... 2) I ... was in a motor car collision, resulting in a dislocated elbow. 3) ... I developed strange symptoms ... I was very ill indeed ... It seems gallstone was the trouble.'[43] He had previously sent the violin and piano score of the first movement to Harrison, and he asked her to have it copied and the copy returned to him so that he could begin work on the orchestration. He also described his preliminary thoughts about the second movement: 'I am ... soaking myself in traditional fiddling with its queer but natural embellishments & ornamentations ... In the 2nd movement I am planning to work some of this idiom into concerto form.'[44] However, Harrison's initial enthusiasm had perhaps diminished during the two and a half years since Moeran had first offered to compose a work for her. Moreover, an episode the previous year had caused Harrison to regard Moeran in a much poorer light. On 7 February 1938, Moeran had accompanied her in a performance of his Sonata in E minor for Violin and Piano at the Wigmore Hall. The concert had been publicised as a recital by Harrison 'assisted by Cyril Scott and E. J. Moeran'. Unfortunately, it did not go well. The critic for *The Times* wrote that 'Mr E. J. Moeran seemed ... ill at ease at the piano on Monday night',[45] and Jack Westrup, writing in the *Daily Telegraph*, reported that '[Harrison] had to struggle against the composer's apparent inability to give a clear and intelligible account of the piano part'.[46] The reality was that, according to Suzanne Hughes, Moeran was drunk and could hardly play the accompaniment. It took all the soloist's exceptional musicianship to hold the piece together.[47] Harrison was furious, and it seems that she never fully forgave Moeran for making her look ridiculous. On the other hand, a new concerto is, after all, a new concerto, and she

---

43 Letter from Moeran to May Harrison, dated The Lodge, Kenmare, Whit Sunday 1939, transcribed in Lewis Foreman, *From Parry to Britten: British Music in Letters, 1900–1945*, (Amadeus, London, 1987), 214–215.

44 *Ibid.*

45 'Recitals of the Week', *The Times*, issue 47916, (11 February 1938), 12.

46 *The Daily Telegraph*, (8 February 1938), 10.

47 See reference to Suzanne Hughes' diary in Angela Hughes, *Chelsea Footprints: A Thirties Chronicle*, (Quartet Books, London, 2008), 172.

was evidently willing to overlook the Wigmore Hall disaster, provided he delivered
on his promise.

In the Whit Sunday letter to Harrison, Moeran had suggested that the concerto
could be ready for the 1940 Bournemouth Festival and that his influence with the
festival organisers was such that he could ensure that it would be included in the
programme. Unfortunately, Moeran was unwise enough to mention in the same
letter that while he was in Ireland, he was making preliminary sketches for a second
symphony:

> My other musical activity consists of going up the mountains & filling pages of
> notebooks with ideas I am working out for another symphony. I might actually
> commence the actual composition thereof in the winter when the [violin] con-
> certo & also the short pfte & orchestra work are, I hope, finished ... Please keep
> all this to yourself; I don't like being talked about, nor my activities either, as
> sometimes I go off at a tangent.

This is the first extant allusion Moeran made to composing a second symphony,
and the story of his attempts to complete it unfolded over the next eleven years. He
wrote again to Harrison from Kenmare in November, by which time Britain was at
war with Germany: 'I found I could do no work at all when the war started. I have
now steeled myself to the task and am pegging away. I was at the Violin Concerto
yesterday ... [Kenneth Wright] made a definite offer for you to do it next Proms.'[48]
The projected performance at the 1940 Bournemouth Festival had been quietly
forgotten. Indeed, Moeran may have assumed that due to the outbreak of war the
festival would be cancelled.[49] Harrison may well have wondered whether the work
would ever be finished, and it is possible that she did not believe Moeran's assurances. At some point during the next few months, Harrison withdrew her interest
in the concerto.[50]

Moeran had returned to Britain in late June to find that Leslie Woodgate of
the BBC Singers had evidently expressed an interest in performing *Phyllida and
Corydon*, and Moeran wrote to him in July with a few concerns:

> Brooke [of Novello & Co.] tells me you are thinking of doing my new Suite,
> *Phyllida & Corydon*, one of these days. While I have always enjoyed your perfor-
> mances of the *Songs of Springtime* with 8 singers, I do feel very strongly that more
> than 8 are desirable for the new work, owing to it's [sic] many chromaticisms. My
> experience has been that chromatic harmonies do not come off on anything less
> than 16 voices ... there are passages ... which I feel sure will sound odd unless

---

48 Letter from Moeran to May Harrison, dated The Lodge, Kenmare, 4 November 1939,
    transcribed in Foreman (1987), 224–225.

49 It was not, but it took place with a reduced programme.

50 As this book was being completed, it was brought to the author's attention that some
    correspondence may exist in the archive of the Harrison Sisters' Trust that clarifies the
    collapse of the arrangement between May Harrison and E. J. Moeran. The author has
    been unable to verify this.

there is a bit more 'body' ... I am merely throwing out a suggestion, but at the same time I think you may agree that I am right.[51]

The choral suite was performed by the BBC Singers under Leslie Woodgate in a performance broadcast on the National Programme on 30 October. In the meanwhile, Moeran had returned to Kenmare at the beginning of September and was therefore in Ireland as war was declared. Since the independent Éire had remained neutral, regulations were immediately imposed that restricted movement between the two countries, and Moeran found that he needed to apply for a permit to return to his parents' home for Christmas.

1940

Four Shakespeare Songs

After spending Christmas and New Year in Kington, Moeran took lodgings in Bristol, where he began work on a set of songs to words by Shakespeare. It is not clear why he chose to live in Bristol for a few weeks, but it may well have been due to the BBC having relocated their music department there shortly after the war began. Moeran returned to Ireland at the beginning of March and again took up residence in Kenmare, where he continued work on the Shakespeare song settings. Unfortunately, his health problems continued. During 1940 he first cut his right hand badly; he then fell, apparently while sleepwalking, and sprained his wrist and bruised some ribs. Then later in the year, he fell again, this time breaking his left wrist. These medical adversities had a severe effect both on his ability and motivation to work and on his capacity to write letters. However, he was able to write to Julian Herbage at the end of April following a broadcast performance of his *Farrago Suite* on the BBC Home Service the previous afternoon. Reception had been good in the west of Ireland, and Moeran said that he had 'never heard a better [performance]'.

The *Four Shakespeare Songs* were composed for solo female voice and piano. The first, 'The Lover and his Lass', was a re-working of a part-song setting that Moeran had composed in 1934 during his period of producing works for music festivals.[52] The tune is identical and the piano accompaniment mostly so. The song is a lively setting of a text from *As You Like It*, act V, scene 3, with an instantly memorable tune and an ebullient piano accompaniment reminiscent of the style of Moeran's piano piece *Bank Holiday*. However, Moeran's song recalls Warlock's 1925 setting of the same words *Pretty Ring Time*, and an ungenerous commentator – bearing in mind the composer's admitted occasional cribbing of the work of other composers – might simply dismiss it as Warlock-pastiche. The songs are in the same key and in an identical strophic form, although Moeran made more use of prolongation than

---

[51] McNeill, 390.

[52] Amongst other festivals, *The Lover and his Lass* part-song was selected as a test piece for the Girls' Choir section of the 1937 Portadown Festival, and for the Village Choirs (Division 2) section of the 1939 Stinchcombe Hill Competitive Music Festival.

did Warlock. They employ the same modulations at about the same points in the text and the harmonic vocabularies are indistinguishable. Its similarity to Warlock notwithstanding, the song is an attractive and jaunty opening number in a cycle of more original material. The other three songs in the set, 'Where the Bee Sucks', 'When Daisies Pied' and 'When Icicles Hang by the Wall' are less obviously derivatives of anything other than Moeran's own previous work. After its publication, Moeran made two arrangements of 'When Icicles Hang by the Wall' for Patrick Hadley and the choir of Gonville & Caius College, Cambridge.

Moeran completed the *Four Shakespeare Songs* during the late spring and early summer and on sending the manuscript to Novello & Co., they were immediately accepted for publication in the early autumn. Moeran wrote to Tilly Fleischmann on 24 October, enclosing a copy of the *Four Shakespeare Songs* and suggesting that he might return to England shortly for a visit to his parents whom he had not seen for several months. Unfortunately, wartime travel restrictions meant that while he could get a one-way visa to travel to England, there was no guarantee that he would be given authorisation to return to Ireland. There was also the question of work. As he wrote to Tilly Fleischmann from Kenmare: 'I don't want to be stuck over there [England], as I want to work. I can do so here in absolute peace and quiet, but my people have a house full of London friends and relations and it would be very noisy.'[53]

1941

Despite having connections in high places: 'I am in communication with the Irish Assistant High Commissioner in England … he is an old friend of mine', Moeran decided not to risk being unable to return to Ireland, and he stayed in his Kenmare lodgings working on the violin concerto. In early February, he received a telegram from Julian Herbage, asking about progress on the two concertos. Moeran sent a brief message in reply: 'Thanks for wire but can do nothing temporarily owing to broken wrist.' In May, he visited Dublin to act as adjudicator for the composition section of the *Feis Ceoil*. Amongst the other adjudicators on the syllabus were Herbert Howells (vocal, choral, organ and national music), Lionel Tertis (strings) and Gerald Moore (piano). Moeran eventually travelled to Britain in July, principally to get treatment for 'fibrocitis', as he described his condition in a letter to Herbage. In this letter, Moeran also gave some indication of how he had been spending his time in Ireland during the year. He had done 'various odd jobs' in Dublin – such as writing articles for the *Irish Times* – and had also been working on the violin concerto. In the letter to Herbage he wrote:

> I am in a bit of a quandery [sic] over the middle movement of my violin concerto. It is composed, but I must have a consultation with a conductor as to the most convenient way of writing out certain parts of the score. There is a combination of rythms [sic] … & it is a question of beats … whether 6/8, 3/4 or 9/8 etc.[54]

53 McNeill, 394.
54 McNeill, 395–396.

It is not known which conductor, if any, he was eventually able to consult. Moeran overcame the travel restrictions, and he returned to Ireland soon after a performance of the Symphony in G minor was broadcast by the London Philharmonic Orchestra conducted by Leslie Heward on 4 October. He remained there for the rest of the year working on completing the violin concerto.

1942

Moeran travelled back to Britain in mid-February. The first performance of the *Four Shakespeare Songs* took place at the Wigmore Hall at the end of that month, and an extended review was written by the music critic of *The Times*:

> Mr Moeran's songs are the work of a more experienced hand. They are none the worse for following the established tradition of English song, for they sound fresh without resort to any unusual devices. The two songs from *Love's Labour's Lost* ['When Daisies Pied' and 'When Icicles Hang by the Wall'] were the most successful. Ariel's song ['Where the Bee Sucks'] seemed too pensive to express the mood of joy at freedom regained.[55]

It is, perhaps, significant that the reviewer did not mentioned the Warlock-derived 'The Lover and his Lass'. Moeran probably did not read the review. He later remarked to his friend Lionel Hill 'I never read criticisms at all of my work unless they happen to occur in whatever newspaper I light on for other news after a concert.'[56] In Ireland, the Second Rhapsody for Orchestra was performed by the Radio Éireann Symphony Orchestra conducted by Michael Bowles at the Mansion House in Dublin on 12 March. 'Quidnunc',[57] author of 'The Irishman's Diary' column in the *Irish Times*, wrote:

> The work performed last night was [Moeran's] Second Rhapsody. This is, in a sense, a 'first performance'; for although the Rhapsody was originally commissioned for one of the famous Norwich Musical Festivals some years ago it has now been entirely re-written. The last time I met him he showed me the M.S. sketch of a violin concerto which he has since all but completed and which he has promised to the Radio Éireann Orchestra for its 'world première', as the film-people say. Moeran is at present staying in Herefordshire having taken leave for a few months of his beloved Kerry, where he has spent most of the past ten years, drawing inspiration from the local folk-music, which has left so deep a mark on his more recent compositions.[58]

The content of this piece would have originated in conversations with the composer, and it demonstrates a characteristic of the composer that has been high-

---

55 'Contemporary Music', *The Times* issue 49174, (3 March 1942), 2.

56 Hill, 11.

57 In 1942, the 'Quidnunc' column 'An Irishman's Diary' was written by the editor of the *Irish Times* Robert Maire Smyllie. The writer and humourist (and later television personality) Patrick Campbell took over the column in 1946.

58 'An Irish Composer', *Irish Times*, (13 March 1942), 2.

lighted repeatedly in this book: that many assertions that Moeran made about himself and his life were either what he wished to be true or what he believed others expected to be true. The suggestion that the Second Rhapsody had been rewritten to the extent that it was, effectively, a new work, was probably intended to establish Irish credentials for a composition that had originally been planned, conceived and created in Norfolk by a composer who was, at the time, thoroughly English.[59] While Moeran had made some modifications to the work, these related to a reduction in the instrumental forces and there were a few note changes to reflect this. There was certainly no extensive re-writing of the music, and Moeran had been considering such changes since as early as 1928. However, as a further attempt to obscure reality, the completion date on the manuscript was modified such that while 'Oct 20th' remains visible, the year, originally 1924, has been scratched out. As was shown in the earlier discussion of the first movement of the String Quartet in E flat, such manuscript history revisionism did not to trouble the composer.

Moeran invested time and effort during his adult life in constructing a persona, or a series of personas, that were intended to correlate with how he believed others perceived him, and this construction was founded on extensive dissembling. Clearly, he had not spent 'most of the past ten years' in Kerry, as stated in Quidnunc's piece, but he believed that the perception that he had done was to his advantage. He had certainly been in Ireland for extended periods during the previous few years, including one of more than a year between March 1940 and June 1941 when he had composed much of the violin concerto. While this could not alter his inherent English identity, did it inform his compositional nationality? After initially being a bit coy about any innate Irishness in his 10 February 1937 letter to Aloys Fleischmann, he strongly asserted an adopted Irishness. Moeran wanted to be perceived as Irish when he was in Ireland, and it may be that he believed that re-inventing some of his music as Irish would facilitate this. In an appreciation for Moeran that he wrote a few months after the composer's death, Sir Arnold Bax suggested:

> Moeran's life may be said to have been divided into two clearly cut parts. During his first thirty or so years he was an Englishman and a diligent collector of East Anglian folk-tunes, whilst for the remainder of his days he was almost exclusively Irish.[60]

While Moeran was certainly not 'almost exclusively Irish', his reaction to his rediscovery of the country at the age of forty-one indeed suggests that it had become, or had re-awakened, a crucial aspect of his personality that he subsequently went to great lengths to emphasise. Moeran believed that being physically present in Ireland was essential to his ability to compose as he wished, and that he needed what he described in his 24 October 1940 letter to Tilly Fleischmann as the 'peace and quiet' of Ireland to flush his mind clear of disruption and allow his creative energy to thrive. It is significant, perhaps, that between 1937 and 1941, Moeran's extended stays – mostly in County Kerry – were during the late spring and summer months,

---

[59] The supposed 'Irishness' of the Second Rhapsody had previously been questioned by the reviewer for the *Irish Press* after its first performance in Ireland in April 1938 (see p. 210).

[60] Bax, (1951), 125–127.

when the extreme westerly location ensured that the soft Atlantic coast daylight persisted long into the evening. Moeran's letters mention evening walks, and it is not too fanciful to imagine the composer standing on a hill overlooking Kenmare as the sun descended towards the north-west horizon and letting his mind fill with music. However, while the inspirational power of the landscape of the west of Ireland unquestionably expedited his inventiveness, the music he imagined and captured on paper was a synthesis of stimulations that had been recorded in his mind over his entire life, most of it with little association with Ireland.

It is interesting to discover that mapping Moeran's completed works between 1936 and 1950 against his physical locations reveals that the bulk of the composition was actually done in England. While he frequently professed to be working on his music in Ireland – his letters mention getting back to the country to walk the hills and think out themes and ideas – it is possible that the aspects of the country that he believed were essential to him actually functioned as distractions when it came to the real work of turning themes and ideas into coherent works of music. An extreme example, as will be seen later, was the ill-fated Symphony No. 2 in E flat major. Moeran was a regular drinker in the bar of the hotel where he stayed in Kenmare and in the public houses of south and west Ireland during his perambulations around the country. He was generally surrounded by people who did not worry about his music and who were not regularly badgering him for news about a score. Letters would eventually arrive in the remote west of Ireland, but these could be mislaid, forgotten, or otherwise ignored. Conversely, while he was at his parents' house, he could not drink much, and he could be easily contacted and asked about progress on the latest work he had promised for completion by a certain date. Social distractions had much less impact and so work was better enabled.

Concerto for Violin and Orchestra

The violin concerto was completed in mid-April in Moeran's composing studio at his parents' home at Gravel Hill, Kington. Although he could reasonably claim that much of the music had been conceived in Ireland, the work of committing it to paper and orchestrating it had been done in various locations. It had been more than five years since he first discussed the composition of the concerto with May Harrison and perhaps two years since Harrison's patience had eventually been exhausted. On 18 March, Sir Henry Wood wrote to Moeran to confirm that the concerto would be performed by Arthur Catterall during the forthcoming season of Promenade Concerts and that Wood would conduct. Engaging Catterall had been Wood's suggestion, and it seems that Moeran had agreed.[61] A month later, Wood wrote again to acknowledge that Moeran had confirmed that the concerto was finished. Wood suggested there was no hurry for the orchestral parts but that he would like to hear a run-through with Catterall as soon as he had finished his present concert commitments. The first performance of the concerto took place at the Promenade Concert

---

[61] No evidence has been found to indicate that Moeran had attempted any kind of reconciliation with May Harrison. However, see p. 218, note 50.

on 8 July and was (mostly) favourably reviewed. After some criticism of the unusual form of the work, the music critic of *The Times* wrote:

> [the concerto] gained immediate acceptance from last night's audience, who called the composer to the platform to receive their applause, and no wonder, for it is spontaneous and unaffected music in which are to be found many lovely details in the combination of the solo violin with the several elements of the orchestra. It is a work which one would hope to hear often.[62]

Having spent more than five years in gestation, the concerto was an undoubted success. There were repeat performances by Arthur Catterall in December at the Royal Albert Hall and in Birmingham the following March.

The form of the three-movement work: *Allegro moderato – Rondo Vivace – Lento*, is unusual in the repertoire, and one can find few similar models. Amongst these are Prokofiev's First Violin Concerto of 1923 and Britten's Violin Concerto of 1939, while Walton's 1939 concerto includes a *Scherzo* second movement and a slow final movement. Each of the movements presents memorable themes that, while original, nevertheless sound somehow familiar, with the jig-like third subject of the first movement played by the flute being especially evocative. With these themes, the listener is provided with reference points that guide the appreciation of the entire work. The soloist is prominent throughout, and there are several cadenza-like passages. However, the lyrical quality of the solo passages, during which the orchestration is frequently reduced, provides the work with an intimate quality that is characteristic of much of Moeran's music. His genius – if such a word may be used – lay in his ability to conceive musical forms that appear superficially to be simple yet reveal on closer examination an ingenuity that bestows aesthetic satisfaction. The listener is seized by the musical flow, teased by the presentation of memorable tunes and left both satisfied and wanting more. Those familiar with the music of Moeran's contemporaries and immediate predecessors will recognise features in the concerto that recall other composers. However, these are fleeting moments: no sooner heard than gone.

In early 1943, the musicologist and composer Wilfrid Mellers wrote a piece on modern English music for the literary magazine *Scrutiny*, and in it he subjected Moeran to withering criticism. Most particularly, Mellers bemoaned the 'stopping and starting' nature of the first movement of the Symphony in G minor.[63] It is certainly true that a feature of Moeran's orchestral music is an interrupted effect where a developed theme appears to collapse into a miasma of seemingly disconnected material before a further theme is stated and developed. For example, the first sixteen bars of the symphony state the main subject, after which the thick orchestral texture is dispensed with and a thematic fragment is flung from one instrument to another for a few bars before the full texture is resumed. The violin concerto also exhibits such discontinuities, and they can imbue a sense of anticipation – frustration even – before resolution is experienced. However, the gentle, almost soporific final bars of the concerto – based on a prolonged D major sixth chord – endow the

---

[62] 'Promenade Concerts – A New Violin Concerto', *The Times*, issue 49283, (9 July 1942), 6.
[63] 'New English Music', *Scrutiny*, Vol. XI, No. 3, (Spring 1943), 174.

work with a consummation that belies its unusual structure. As mentioned in the description of the Second Rhapsody for Orchestra in Chapter 10, Moeran's use of the major triad with added sixth to provide sweetness and complexity to his tonal harmony is evident from his earliest compositions, and his juxtaposition of this chord with sevenths and ninths varies the harmonic intricacy. According to Self, Delius used the added sixth to infuse 'serenity and repose' into the endings of movements.[64] However, Moeran's employment of the effects of such added note harmony predates his discovery of the music of Delius, and it is most probably a legacy of his early piano-based chord invention. However, the 'serenity and repose' of the coda to the final movement is briefly interrupted by a disconcerting harmonic departure in the brass before the concerto ends with a dotted crotchet rest (music example 46).[65]

Immediately after the first performance, Arthur Bliss wrote a brief note to Moeran: 'My dear Jack, A gorgeous work – full of poetry & passion and a lovely line throughout. My affectionate congratulations from your inferior colleague.'[66] Praise indeed from the director of music at the BBC, and Bliss wrote again to Moeran a few days later to suggest that he consider composing a work for the BBC Section C orchestra:

Music example 46. Concerto for Violin & Orchestra: final 7 bars

---

[64] Self, 142.

[65] This description of the concerto is an extended adaptation of a programme note the author provided for a BBC Promenade Concerts performance by Tasmin Little and the BBC Philharmonic Orchestra conducted by Juanjo Mena on 25 July 2014 at the Royal Albert Hall, London.

[66] McNeill, 687.

a classical-size ensemble intended primarily to perform such works as Mozart and Haydn symphonies and comprising the most competent players. Despite having the Harriet Cohen piano concerto (rhapsody) still in progress, Moeran seems to have seized the opportunity for a BBC commission, and he wrote back to Bliss in September to say that he was thinking about a sinfonietta-type work comprising four short movements for the size of orchestra specified. A few weeks later, Moeran wrote again to say that he was making good progress and that it would be in three movements, with the central movement combining the classical functions of slow movement and *scherzo* in a theme and variations form. He said that he was 'well on towards the end' of the first movement.

It was about this time that Moeran began a correspondence with Douglas Gibson, the Managing Director of publishers J & W Chester Ltd.[67] Chester had agreed to reprint the piano piece *Stalham River*, and Gibson wrote to Moeran on 2 October:

> I … am sending a copy of *Stalham River* to you for correction … I hope you will not forget my request that I might have an opportunity of considering the new orchestral work, of which you spoke to me. I am quite serious in my offer and hope that you will remember me when the time comes for discussing publication for your work.

This first letter of many from Gibson suggests that Chesters were looking to build on the success of the works that they had previously published.[68] Moeran replied from Gravel Hill: 'Thank you for your reminder about the orchestral work. As I do not work fast I shall not have anything ready just yet, but I fully hope to have something in the New Year which may interest you.' Following a further two letters from Gibson, mainly concerning the reprinting of *Stalham River*, Moeran replied on 14 December:

> I arrived back yesterday [from London] and got out the preliminary version of the piece for Piano and orchestra so far as it goes, and I hope to be able to get on with it, but now find I have no music paper except scoring paper. I wonder if you have anything in stock of about 12 to 14 staves[?]

The typed transcript of this letter in the publishers' archive has the note attached: 'Send 2 Royal MSS books gratis.' In one of his letters, Gibson had mentioned that he had spoken with Sir Henry Wood about the 1943 season of Promenade Concerts and specifically about the orchestral work that Moeran was composing. Moeran must have realised that he could never achieve a Promenade Concert deadline with a completely new composition, and the partially written work for piano and orchestra was a viable alternative. Thus, the focus of his attention switched abruptly from the sinfonietta to the piano concerto, or rhapsody, as

---

[67] R. Douglas Gibson (1894–1985) was noted for maintaining extended correspondences with the composers whose music he published, including Francis Poulenc and Lennox Berkeley.

[68] J & W Chester had published two piano pieces *Stalham River* and *Toccata*, the String Quartet in A minor, the Violin Sonata in E minor and the two songs *The Bean Flower* and *Impromptu in March*. Moeran was very fickle when it came to the publishing of his music, with works being taken by more than a dozen publishing houses during his lifetime.

he had by now reconceived it, and he confirmed this to Gibson: 'I cannot avoid calling it a Rhapsody, for it is that & nothing else, being the same form that I adopted in my two orchestral Rhapsodies.' Since Moeran could only concentrate on one major composition at a time, he had to decide which of the works currently in progress he was most likely to be able to complete, and which would bring him the greater amount of prestige. According to a letter that Moeran wrote to Anne Crowley in Kenmare on 14 December, Gibson's publishing house had been exploring performance possibilities for the piano rhapsody in the United States: 'I have arranged publication of [the piano rhapsody] with J & W Chester, & what is more, they propose fixing up it's [sic] first world performance not here, but in [the] U.S.A., at Cincinnatti [sic] under [Eugene] Goossens.'[69]

How did a planned three- or four-movement piano concerto metamorphose into a single movement rhapsody? While Moeran had first referred to the work as a 'piano rhapsody' in a letter to Kenneth Wright in 1938, description of the work had later switched back to 'concerto'. He probably realised that the concerto in its original conception would never be written, and that he could use what he had already composed to create a shorter work, thereby fulfilling both the original commission and the initiative from Wood and Gibson. While Gibson had asked for the opportunity to publish 'an orchestral work', his only concern was that Moeran would deliver the work as agreed. In fact, a piano rhapsody was well suited to Gibson's publishing plan. A multi-movement piano concerto would have relatively few opportunities for performances due both to it being a crowded genre and to the effort required by soloists to add the work to their repertoire. A shorter, virtuosic single-movement work could be placed in more concert programmes and would probably attract more soloists. Gibson was also interested in taking on the earlier orchestral rhapsodies as partner works.

Two other events dominated Moeran's time during the final months of the year, both in connection with the Symphony in G minor. Novello published a full orchestral and a miniature score, and the HMV record company, under the auspices of the British Council, recorded a performance with Leslie Heward conducting the Hallé Orchestra. The recording was the first sponsored by the British Council in a wartime initiative to promote British music around the world. Moeran attended the sessions and he was pleased about the level of commitment of both the orchestra and HMV. He explained that he was unable to get back to Kerry in his 14 December letter to Anne Crowley:

> I am at the moment & parhaps [sic] for always prevented from returning to Ireland & writing my 2nd Symphony, to be based on material I had started thinking out among the McGillicuddy [sic] Reeks & the Black Valley, because the Income Tax authorities make it impossible for me to do so ... I am told that having paid twice over I can claim & get 1/2 of it back eventually, but that doesn't help, neither do I see the justice of it.

---

[69] McNeill, 402–404. Moeran had befriended Anne Crowley during the early years of his visits to Kenmare and she adopted the unofficial role as his driver.

Since the facts of Moeran's double tax situation are not known, it is difficult to judge whether his bitterness was justified. However, it is reasonable to assert that 1942 marked the end of Moeran's seven years of spending extended periods in Ireland. Although he did make short visits to the country during his remaining eight years, the phase of his life during which he could identify Ireland as his second home was past.

PART 5

MATURITY, MARRIAGE
AND LAST YEARS

15
'Wonderful Things Together'
(1943–1944)

The British Council recording of the Symphony in G minor was reviewed in several newspapers and periodicals, perhaps most notably by Edward Sackville-West in the *New Statesman*:

> One must congratulate both the Gramophone Company and the British Council for their willingness to further the cause of English music; but, at the risk of seeming ungrateful, one must question the wisdom of spending a lot of money and precious shellac on so dubious a work as E. J. Moeran's enormous G minor Symphony ... the boneless and ornate romantic style which this composer affects is not representative of what is best in contemporary English music ... the impression made by each movement is in the last degree vague and imprecise. Instead of dealing a series of well-aimed blows, the symphony flops against the mind like a stingless jellyfish.[1]

Since taking up the position of music critic for the *New Statesman* in 1935, Sackville-West had established a reputation as a perceptive and discerning writer on music. *The Times* wrote that his articles: 'were distinguished not only for their command of the jewelled phrase but [also] for their zealous propagation of young British composers'.[2] However, the young British composers whose cause Sackville-West espoused were generally those – such as Benjamin Britten and Michael Tippett – whose musical style he believed looked forward and eschewed what he regarded as dated pastoralism. Whether jewelled phrases such as 'the symphony flops against the mind like a stingless jellyfish' were perceptive and discerning is questionable, but they reflected an agenda that went beyond strictly musical matters. Sackville-West's disparaging remarks on Moeran's music were not confined to the review of the recording of the symphony, and the context for them was probably his and Moeran's differing relationships with Benjamin Britten. Sackville-West was infatuated with Britten, while Moeran, having previously been close to the younger composer, was, by 1943, no longer a friend.[3] Nevertheless, the attacks did not seem to disturb Moeran. As he later wrote to Lionel Hill: 'I have been told that Sackville-

---

[1] 'Gramophone Notes', *The New Statesman and Nation*, Vol. XXV, No. 623, (3 January 1943), 82.

[2] 'Obituary – Lord Sackville', *The Times*, issue 56366, (6 July 1965), 14.

[3] For background, see Simon Fenwick, *The Crichel Boys*, (Little Brown Book Group, London, 2021).

West rarely misses an opportunity of having a hit at me.'[4] The *New Statesman* review excepted, however, most critics praised the recording of the symphony both for its purpose and for its content.

Regardless of the views of critics, Moeran's foremost musical concern was the completion of the piano rhapsody. Douglas Gibson wrote on 29 January to enquire about progress, and he asked that Moeran provide an indication 'as to when it might be completed'. He continued: 'I want to contact Wood and Herbage again and ... have some definite information to give them ... to be able to take the score with me would be a great advantage.' Moeran was under immense pressure to get the piece finished. Failure to do so in time for the publication and the Promenade Concert performance – events which it had been agreed would be coordinated – was no longer an option. Having previously withdrawn the work from the 1938 season, he probably realised that his credibility both at the BBC and with his new publishing best friend Douglas Gibson would not withstand a similar occurrence. Gibson wrote again to Moeran on 12 February:

> I have dictated [to Julian Herbage's secretary] ... a detailed statement of the position regarding your work, emphasising that there is no doubt whatsoever that it will be ready in good time for both Miss Cohen and also the orchestra ... Apparently H.J.W. [Sir Henry Wood] and Herbage are going to spend all next week in fixing dates, etc., for the Proms, so we are just in time.

Harriet Cohen had stipulated four months for practice. Therefore, for a mid-season concert, the piano part had to be available by early April at the latest. Unfortunately, Moeran had overcommitted himself by becoming involved with a project to provide the incidental music for a BBC Features Department propaganda film about Royal Navy destroyers operating in the Atlantic Ocean. Unable to manage his situation, he once again turned to Julian Herbage to resolve the problem, and it was decided that Moeran would be better employed getting his piano rhapsody finished and that another composer would be engaged for the Atlantic Ocean destroyers film. Thus, Moeran was saved from further embarrassment, and his schedule was cleared for completion of the rhapsody, delivering first a two-piano short score and the full score orchestration later. It is interesting to note that he asked Gibson to provide him with miniature scores of John Ireland's Piano Concerto and Rachmaninov's Second Piano Concerto.

At the end of March, Moeran travelled to Birmingham to hear Arthur Catterall perform the violin concerto with the City of Birmingham Symphony Orchestra, and on 3 April, he broadcast a tribute to Peter Warlock on the BBC Home Service from Bedford. On returning to Kington, he became ill, and it was during his convalescence that he received a letter from music enthusiast Lionel Hill, expressing appreciation for Moeran's work and asking if the composer shared his love for the music of Delius. This letter was the start of a correspondence and friendship that would endure until just a few months before the composer's death. Hill had heard a broadcast performance of *Lonely Waters* while in hospital awaiting an operation, and the music had affected him to the extent that he had felt compelled to 'make contact

4   Hill, 11.

with a mind so in tune with my own'. Moeran sent a somewhat reserved reply that was probably intended as a polite brush off. Nonetheless, Hill took Moeran's letter as encouragement, and he wrote again a few days later, mentioning that his father-in-law was the eminent violinist Albert Sammons. Moeran's reply to Hill's second letter was radically different in tone from that of his earlier letter. It is apparent that Moeran was actively encouraging continued correspondence and initiating the possibility of an eventual meeting with Hill. The agenda is not difficult to discern: it would be a major coup for Moeran if Sammons, widely regarded as the finest solo violinist in the country, could be induced to perform the violin concerto.

Rhapsody in F sharp major for Piano and Orchestra

In the meanwhile, Douglas Gibson was pushing ahead with plans for publishing the rhapsody in advance of its first performance, and his frequent letters and encouragement evidently focused Moeran's mind. The short score was completed by mid-March, and the orchestral score was ready by the end of April. There followed a period of proof production and checking that was managed by Gibson in a series of letters detailing what was expected of Moeran and when. This process culminated in a letter Gibson wrote on 30 July: 'I have a very pleasant surprise for you in sending by today's post two copies of your Rhapsody [two-piano version] which has just been received from the printers.' Gibson also informed Moeran that he would also be sending copies to some of the prominent pianists of the day, such as Cyril Smith and Clifford Curzon. Rehearsals were scheduled for July and August, and the first performance by Harriet Cohen with the BBC Symphony Orchestra conducted by Adrian Boult took place at the Royal Albert Hall on 19 August. The completion, publication and first performance of the rhapsody was the first time in Moeran's career that his work had, effectively, been managed by a third party. Although the rhapsody had its origins in 1935 in an informal arrangement to compose a piano concerto for Harriet Cohen, and the composition of the work during its eight-year gestation had been intermittent and haphazard, Douglas Gibson's involvement gave the project a level of professional organisation with which Moeran had hitherto been entirely unfamiliar. Most importantly, distracting administrative tasks were taken out of Moeran's hands and were managed by people whose job it was to do them. The production of the fair copies of both the short score and the orchestral score was contracted out to Arthur Willner – whose music handwriting was almost indistinguishable from printed music – with the result that Harriet Cohen and the engravers received legible music, rather than the composer's usual scrawl. All Moeran had to do was finish the composition, do the orchestration, check the proofs, attend the rehearsals and take his bow at the concert. The result was a huge success. Press reviews were complimentary, with some even suggesting that the confident tone of the work and its triumphant conclusion reflected an increasing national optimism regarding the eventual outcome of the war. The music critic for the *Liverpool Daily Post* wrote:

> Though only recently completed [the rhapsody] is contemporary in conception with the violin concerto, but, unlike that work, it is neither predominantly lyrical nor Irish in sentiment. It begins and ends in vigorous romantic vein, full

of life and colour expressed in a robust rhythm ... the work has much beauty of a romantic order.[5]

Regarding the music itself, given that the work was composed over a period of eight years and in several locations and that none of Moeran's notes, sketches or discarded ideas have survived, it is impossible to determine how many, if any, of his thoughts during that time persisted into the final score. The composer gave an idea of a possible programme for the piece when he told Nina Hamnett that it represented 'Saturday night in a four-ale bar in County Kerry',[6] and wrote to Anne Crowley that 'all the ideas were worked out ... on [Valentia] island'.[7] However, Moeran's probable locations during the period when he is known to have been working on the rhapsody suggests that very little of it could have been composed on Valentia Island, or anywhere else in Ireland. Moeran's remarks were clearly another attempt to establish retrospectively an Irish identity for one of his major works. In contrast to the violin concerto, there is little that is detectably Irish about the music of the rhapsody in the sense of conventional representational tropes, and the obvious influences of Rachmaninov and John Ireland – acknowledged in Moeran's request to Gibson for scores of their piano concertos – suggest that anything Irish about the rhapsody was an afterthought.

In the meanwhile, an event had taken place towards the end of June which would affect Moeran for the rest of his life. The cellist Peers Coetmore and the pianist Michael Mullinar had been engaged to give a recital in Leominster Priory under the auspices of the Council for the Encouragement of Music and the Arts (CEMA).[8] Moeran knew Mullinar very well – they had been contemporaries at the Royal College of Music some thirty years earlier – and Mullinar had also performed regularly at recitals of the Oxford & Cambridge Musical Club during the 1920s. Moeran and Coetmore had also been acquainted for some years through mutual musical connections.[9] According to the reminiscences of Coetmore's widower Maurice Walter Knott, Moeran's brother William Graham, who was Vicar of Leominster, entertained Moeran, their parents, Coetmore and Mullinar to tea on the day of the concert, and during the social gathering, a spark of mutual attraction had initiated what would shortly become a passionate liaison.

Little is known about Coetmore's early years. She was born Kathleen Peers Coetmore-Jones in 1905 in Skegness into an affluent family, and the household included a German governess, a cook and a housemaid. Her father, Stanley

---

5   'New Rhapsody', *Liverpool Daily Post*, (21 August 1943), 2.

6   Nina Hamnett, *Is She a Lady?* (Wingage, London, 1955), 141.

7   McNeill, 404.

8   The forerunner of the Arts Council of Great Britain. Coetmore and Mullinar were just two of many musicians and other artists engaged to perform around the country. By mid-1943, the war had been in progress for nearly four years and considerable efforts were made by the authorities to provide entertainment and cultural and educational stimuli, both to ameliorate the deprivations experienced by the public in general, and to maintain and enhance the perception that Britain would ultimately be victorious in the conflict.

9   Moeran later wrote to Coetmore: 'considering I had known you on & off for some time before without regarding you other than as a happy companion.'

Coetmore-Jones, was a local land agent, who was killed during the Battle of the Somme in September 1916, and Kathleen Peers spent most of her teenage years without a father. It was this, perhaps, that not only laid the foundation for an independent spirit and relaxed attitude to life, but may also have impelled her to seek some sort of father figure elsewhere. At the age of twenty-four, she met and married Arthur Davis, who was about forty-seven and thus not much younger than her father would have been had he lived. The marriage lasted less than two years until it was dissolved for medical reasons.[10] Coetmore was determined to succeed as a professional cellist. During her studies at the Royal Academy of Music, she had won the Piatti prize in 1924 and had been very highly commended for the Vallange prize in 1928.[11] After leaving the Academy, she studied with Emanuel Feuermann and Maurice Eisenberg – a pupil of Pablo Casals – and joined an informal group of young female cellists – all born during the first two decades of the twentieth century – each trying to make a career in a generally male-dominated profession.[12] She spent the next ten years giving recitals around the country and making frequent broadcasts. After the war began, Coetmore took her social obligations very seriously, spending time in the ambulance service during the Blitz and playing in numerous CEMA and Entertainments National Service Association (ENSA) concerts.[13]

During the three months after the afternoon tea at Moeran's brother's house, it seems that his mother and brother manoeuvred Moeran into considering Coetmore as a possible life partner. His mother may well have detected the rudiments of a mutual attraction during the social gathering at Leominster vicarage, and she would have made every effort to encourage it. According to the reminiscences of William Graham Moeran, their parents had been driven to some despair by Moeran's alcohol immoderations and their consequences, and they were desperate to find some solution. As suggested earlier, referring to his condition by such trivialising euphemisms as 'a tendency to drink' probably enabled them to encapsulate it as a problem that could potentially be resolved and to categorise it in their minds as a lifestyle choice which he could be induced to abandon. From their resolutely traditional social perspective, the solution was his marrying a good woman who would look after him. Thus, having conceived such a possibility with Coetmore, Moeran's parents may have endeavoured to keep her in his mind during the summer months of 1943. However, it is also possible that Moeran himself saw long-term possibilities in a closer relationship with Coetmore. He engaged her to return to Leominster

---

[10] A marriage might be dissolved were it to become apparent that one of the parties, usually assumed to be the wife, was unable to have children.

[11] 'Royal Academy of Music', *The Musical Times*, Vol. 65, No. 977 (1 July 1924), 642, and Vol. 69, No. 1023 (1 August 1928), 446.

[12] During the 1920s and 1930s, there were limited performing opportunities for a solo cellist as the repertoire was much smaller than that existing for the violin. Along with Coetmore were cellists such as Florence Hooton, Zara Nelsova, Helen Just, Norina Semino, Eleanor Warren and Raya Garbousova, all giving recitals in London and the provinces.

[13] See Stephanie Browne, *The life and career of Peers Coetmore, English cellist (1905–1976)*, (Melbourne Conservatorium of Music, Masters Research Thesis, 2012) for a detailed account of the life of Coetmore.

in early October to give several recitals in the area, one of which was arranged for Wednesday 6 October at the Priory. He also invited her to stay at his parents' house during the week in which she was performing.

Moeran's friendship with Lionel Hill had also been progressing, and he visited Hill's house in Seer Green several times. During one of these visits, he and Hill had met ENSA music director Walter Legge for lunch at The Cricketers pub, soon after which Moeran received a commission from Legge to compose a bright and extrovert overture appropriate for performing at morale-boosting concerts for wartime workers. Alongside Moeran, Legge commissioned similar works from several other composers, including Arnold Bax, Alan Rawsthorne, Ralph Vaughan Williams and John Ireland. After his visit, Moeran had returned to London where it is probable that he met Coetmore and that they travelled to Kington together, arriving on or about 30 September. During the week that Coetmore spent at the Moerans' house, she and Moeran were able to go for walks in the surrounding hills, and to the delight of his parents, a deeper attraction seems to have developed.

Although he later claimed not to enjoy writing letters, Moeran was nevertheless a prolific correspondent, and many of the letters, postcards, telegrams and airgraphs that he wrote to Peers Coetmore between October 1943 and March 1950 are extant. Unfortunately, the corresponding letters that Coetmore wrote to Moeran and which were returned to her after his death were probably destroyed during the 1950s. However, Moeran made sufficient references in his letters to her that at least the gist of what she had said to him can be deduced, and so the general course of two-way conversations may be followed. The letters enable the researcher to develop a form of acquaintanceship with Moeran (and to a lesser extent Coetmore), based on an intimate knowledge of his innermost thoughts, and they provide a detailed insight into both his developing relationship with Coetmore and the effect it had on his creative work. While Moeran's awkward, hesitating and at times embarrassing courtship-by-letter reveals that he was besotted with Coetmore from the start, his inelegance may be forgiven. His experience in affairs of the heart was limited, his sexuality was at the very least ambivalent, and he may in any case have long since resigned himself to life without an intimate personal relationship.

Moeran and Coetmore left Kington on the same train on 8 October, she travelling to Derby for an engagement at the Art Gallery the next day and he to Manchester en route to Dublin for a broadcast by Radio Éireann of the first performance of his recent Seumas O'Sullivan setting *Invitation in Autumn*. Moeran wrote to Coetmore that evening from the Haunch of Venison pub:

> I have a pleasant room here for the night … I will write to you again with news from cross-channel. And, be sure, I shall not forget our possible future arrangements and my trying to write a work for you, even if it is only a Sonata (to go on with). This has been a wonderful week in your company.

The only hint in this letter of anything more personal than a general concern for her welfare is the reference to a 'wonderful week' in her company. The conversations between Moeran and Coetmore in Kington had evidently touched on the possibilities both of some form of working relationship and of Moeran composing something for Coetmore. Moeran would not have been the first to use the device of writing music for the object of his affections as a mechanism to encourage an interest in him and to enable them to spend periods of time together. Moeran exploited this from the beginning, and in letters written during the next few days his offers became quite extravagant, suggesting the composition of a concerto and a sonata. While his motives may be seen retrospectively to be quite transparent, it is also probable that Coetmore had her own agenda. Moeran, with his influence in the musical establishment in Britain at the time, would have been an important net-working connection for Coetmore, and anything that he composed for her would enhance her professional position and reputation.

Moeran sailed from Holyhead to Dublin on 9 October, and he wrote a long letter to Coetmore from the Shelbourne Hotel the following day, having evidently changed his mind about the scale of the work that he planned to compose for Coetmore: 'my dear Peers, do let me try and show my appreciation of you by writing a really nice work for you ... please write & tell me you would like me to write a concerto espe-cially for you.' He continued by claiming that his influence both at the BBC and with the Royal Philharmonic Orchestra was sufficiently strong for him to insist on her being engaged to give the first few performances of the proposed concerto. The letter is the most significant of the dozen or so that Moeran wrote to Coetmore during the last three months of the year, in that it was written after his realisation of his feelings for her but before he had confirmation of any reciprocation. After finishing this long and rambling letter by saying that he loathed 'receiving long and rambling letters', he embarked on a long and rambling postscript. He asserted that if Coetmore accepted his proposal to compose a concerto for her, he would not be able to work simultaneously on the sonata or sonatina which apparently had been the focus of the discussions they had had during the previous week in Kington. As in the main letter, the tone was imploring: 'please write & tell me you would like me to go on with it ... only give me the OK, or your blessing on the project.' Moeran was expressing to Coetmore that in writing a concerto for her, he would be committing himself to devoting his entire creative potential solely to her for an extended period. Moreover, he went public with this declaration. In an interview published in the *Irish Times*, he asserted that 'after the broadcast, [he was] going to Kerry to write a concerto for cello and orchestra'.[14]

Invitation in Autumn

The broadcast took place on Friday 15 October. *Invitation in Autumn* was sung by Violet Burne and accompanied by Rhoda Coghill. The forty-minute progamme also included a reading of the poem by O'Sullivan, a performance of Moeran's *Rahoon* and a conversation on musical and literary matters. While *Invitation in Autumn* is representative of Moeran's evolved musical style of the mid-1940s exhibiting a harmonic kinship with the recently-completed Rhapsody in F sharp major for Piano and Orchestra and the soon-to-be-composed Concerto for Violoncello and Orchestra, it also harks back to his song-settings of the 1930s, particularly *The Day of Palms* (1932) and *Rahoon* (1938). It begins with an example of Moeran's eco-

---

[14] 'Composer Comes for Broadcast', *Irish Times*, (14 October 1943), 3.

nomic re-use of material. Bars 1–4 of the piano introduction (music example 47) are musically almost identical to bars 46–49 of the piano piece *Stalham River* (music example 48). The intentional nature of this self-plagiarism is exposed not only by the correspondence of the notes, but also by the appearance of a triple quaver rest in the first bar of the song. Since there is no vocal line interest until bar 7, the inclusion of a full bar with rests instead of using a three-quaver anacrusis suggests that Moeran began with the *Stalham River* bars and simply erased the first three quaver beats. These bars are not the only self-references in the song, with Moeran re-using fragments of the piano accompaniments of several earlier song settings. These, together with the inclusion of typical Moeran song setting features – such as delaying by half a beat the accompaniment of a significant melodic highlight or the modified repeat of structural sections – endow *Invitation in Autumn* with familiar stylistic characteristics.

Moeran had still not heard anything from Coetmore, so he took the further step of sending her a telegram to inform her that he had begun work on the concerto: 'Have started Cello concerto. Hope you don't mind. Writing.' Moeran travelled on to Kenmare by train, and on 19 October he received a letter from Coetmore that sent him into a state of great excitement. The first paragraph of his immediate reply reveals that something significant had happened:

> I got your exceptional letter to-day: it stirred me up to the extent of sending you a further wire. It is a little difficult to know how much you really mean in your last sentence, but if it should be what I hope & fervently think you mean i.e. that you have a personal regard for me … it would alter my whole idea of life.

Moeran clearly understood an implication that she reciprocated his feelings for her. Although the emotional state conveyed by Moeran's previous letter was transparent, he did not actually say anything that specifically declared his intent, beyond the desire to compose for her. Had any kind of romantic involvement been out of the question for Coetmore, she would have been able to reply to what Moeran wrote about the composing without encouraging the poorly concealed personal agenda. Nevertheless, it is reasonable to wonder what Coetmore wanted to achieve. Why would she have been considering a personal relationship with Moeran, expressing it in such a way as to prompt Moeran to write 'Do you mean there is the bare possibility of your linking up with me for good & all?' Her principal motivation could well have derived from a realisation of the advantages that were to be gained from having her own personal composer, both to supply her with new music and to prevent it being composed for anybody else.[15] However, she could have accomplished this without insinuating that she and Moeran become life partners. Other reasons must therefore be sought. Coetmore was in her late thirties and possibly subject to family pressure to settle down with a husband. While her surviving correspondence suggests that she had numerous male (and female) admirers, she seems to have

[15] Few new cello concertos were being composed and having a composer write one for a cellist was a significant career move. One of Coetmore's close friends, the Russian cellist Raya Garbousova, had been the dedicatee of Bohuslav Martinů's First Cello Concerto, composed in 1931.

Music example 47. *Invitation in Autumn*: bars 1–6

Music example 48. *Stalham River*: bars 46–51

been reluctant to enter deep relationships. One such, known only as 'Fernando', poured out his heart to her in 1933:

> Every day I remember … the wonderful night under the light-house beams, where for the first and last time I have pressed you between my arms and kissed you … Should you ever come back [to Oporto] don't forget to advise me as I will be very happy meeting you again … Many ardent kisses from your sweet boy, Fernando[16]

[16] Letter to Coetmore from 'Fernando', dated Oporto 21 August 1933; part of the Coetmore Archive at the Performing Arts Museum, Melbourne.

There may also have been a subconscious seeking of a father figure. Although Moeran was not as much older than Coetmore as her first husband had been, he was certainly considerably her senior and had gained an avuncular disposition that she may well have found appealing. It is also possible that Moeran's air of vulnerability may have stirred her maternal instincts. While she later proved incapable of looking after him in the way that his parents had hoped, this does not necessarily mean that the basic urge was absent. By providing a form of controlled encouragement to Moeran perhaps to express his feelings and intentions further, she may have been testing the water without necessarily making a definite commitment. This is evident from Moeran's statements that it was 'a little difficult to know' what she had meant in her last sentence.

Whatever it was Coetmore wrote in her letter, Moeran regarded it as encouragement and responded clumsily:

> it was just during the final Thursday on Bradnor & the next day in the several trains we had to take that this feeling changed to one of complete & absolute adoration … for an individual for her superb beauty as a person and for her integrity as a human being … But, Peers dear, I was too tongue-tied to say anything at such short notice.

This is typical of numerous blundering, schoolboy-crush-like phrases in the letter. Moeran continued in a similar fashion in this and his next two letters, begging and cajoling Coetmore not to go on a planned ENSA tour to the Middle East and continually seeking reassurance that she meant what he believed her to have said. Moeran also outlined potential difficulties that the progress of their relationship might face. He wrote, 'Now here is a snag, which really did make it awkward for me to say anything of my real feelings towards you (2 snags in fact) (a) I am middle aged, & you are young and lovely, (b) Your career & ambitions as a "cellist."'

In fact, the disparity in age between Moeran and Coetmore was not that great. At the time, he was forty-eight and she about thirty-six, but he clearly felt some degree of insecurity about even a relatively small age gap. More interesting was his proposal for the resolution of the second snag. Moeran suggested that they could join forces and 'write music together'. He returned to this idea several times in subsequent letters, and it seems to have been one of his ploys for convincing Coetmore to maintain and increase her commitment to the relationship. Regarding a possible creative collaboration, Moeran did not mean just his composing for Coetmore. Peers had taken composition in addition to her main cello study during her time at the Royal Academy of Music, and Moeran seems seriously to have been proposing the creation of joint works. On 21 October he wrote, 'there are wonderful things we could do together in creating music, not only concertos & orchestral work, but chamber music. When I say creating music, I mean writing it, as I know that since I hurt my wrist, I am no player.' However, Moeran's practices would have rendered the collaborative composing proposal totally impractical. Had they ever attempted it, working with Moeran would very soon have become impossible.

In her next letter, Coetmore confirmed her intention of going to the Middle East, and Moeran again tried to persuade her to reconsider. His principal argument was that her cooperation in the composition of the cello concerto was essential for its successful completion and eventual performance. He implied that if she were unable to get over to Ireland, he could return to England and they could meet again in Kington to work on the concerto. He included hints that his parents had taken 'a wonderful fancy' to her. He also referred to his periodic excessive drinking and wrote the first of countless promises that he would no longer so indulge:

> This is now a thing of the past, so far as I am concerned. Let me blurt it out & say I mean excessive liquor. I have done too many pub crawls in past years, but with you at my side, I can definitely & finally promise that I won't any more want to step off the deep end.

His letters to Coetmore over the next seven years contained many such resolutions. Ultimately, he was unable to keep to any of them.

In early November, Moeran travelled back to Britain, and he spent a few days in London with Coetmore, taking lodgings near her flat in Belsize Lane. In particular, he introduced her to a Prelude for Violoncello and Piano that he had evidently composed during his fortnight in Kenmare the previous month. These few days were the first opportunity for Moeran and Coetmore to discuss the nature of their relationship face to face, and it is apparent from the more relaxed tone of the letter Moeran wrote to Coetmore from Kington on 12 November that a heightened degree of connection had been reached. The casual conversational mood of the letter is in sharp contrast to the infatuated blundering characteristic of Moeran's October correspondence, and the almost manic seeking of reassurance about Coetmore's commitment to the relationship is entirely absent. Moeran had evidently gained confidence that Coetmore was as committed as Moeran believed himself to be, and he seems to have felt comfortable about discussing general topics, such as Coetmore's mother, the resolution of some short-term financial difficulties and his own parents' regard for Coetmore. Letters that each of Moeran's parents wrote to Coetmore the same day provide some background. His father wrote:

> The good news Jack sent in a letter a few days ago was not a surprise to two old people here. Independently, we had a suspicion of what might come. And I would like you to know how very glad we both are. In his letter Jack gave us to understand that you have decided there is to be no definite engagement until you return home with the concert party. But from his manner since he returned, I gather that there is no doubt in his mind![17]

In Moeran's next letter to Coetmore dated 14 November, he talked about being 'frantically busy'. Although he did not provide details, it is likely that he was completing the Prelude. He also mentioned the work that became the *Irish Lament*: 'I am most colossally hard at work. At the moment I am on a somewhat elaborate and exceedingly free arrangement for cello & piano of the Irish Tune "Johnny

---

[17] The location of the original letters written by Moeran's parents to Peers Coetmore between 1943 and 1950 is unknown, although they are probably in the Coetmore Archive at the Performing Arts Museum in Melbourne. The quotations in this book have been taken from photocopies in the Barry Marsh Collection.

Asthore"'.[18] However, the claim that he was 'most colossally hard at work' must be regarded more as an attempt to impress her with his dedication than a statement of fact. Moeran's piano work *Irish Love Song* of 1926 was also an arrangement of 'Johnny Asthore', and his 'elaborate and exceedingly free' piano accompaniment for the new cello piece was almost the same as the *Irish Love Song*. Moreover, both works are fifty-seven bars long with identical formal structures. While Moeran's memory in later life was questionable, it is inconceivable to suggest that he had forgotten *Irish Love Song* to the extent that he could unknowingly re-compose the same music from scratch. What his colossal hard work really amounted to was extracting the tune from the piano piece bass line as the cello part and copying out what remained as the accompaniment. It cannot have taken him long to do and was probably finished by the end of November.

Moeran travelled from Kington to London on 18 November and remained there for the next few weeks until Coetmore's departure for the Middle East concert tour. He again took lodgings close to her flat, giving him ample opportunity to spend time with her. Although he had repeatedly pleaded with her not to go on the tour, eventually he had accepted that it was inevitable and had decided that his attitude was selfish. He had to content himself with her reassurance that she would not forget him, and, as a means of cementing the relationship, they became engaged. This news sent Moeran's mother into a frenzy of excitement, and she immediately wrote a short note to Coetmore:

> I must tell you how very pleased & thankful I am to get Jack's good news & to think that I am really to have a daughter of my own & it will be the making of him – to have a wife who will be a real friend & comrade … My husband is so very glad too & so is Graham.

Moeran and Coetmore had decided to get married shortly after Coetmore's planned return in June 1944. However, in late November, Moeran received news that his elderly father was ill, and he was torn between wanting to remain in London and spend as much time as he could with Coetmore before she left and feeling compelled to return home to support his mother.

Coetmore embarked for the Middle East on 11 December. The character of the letters Moeran wrote to her during December indicates that he was desolated by the suddenness and extent of the separation. A week after her departure, he received two short letters written aboard ship and presumably posted at ports where they docked en route. Nevertheless, he became increasingly worried as the days passed without hearing about her safe arrival in Egypt, even though he knew it would be several weeks before there was any chance of receiving a communication of any kind. The dangers of sea voyages during wartime were very real, and the chances of attack by submarine were high. Moeran distracted himself by pottering about for a few days doing various errands in connection with the sub-letting of Coetmore's flat before he returned home on 14 December. His father's illness worsened considerably, and the worries about Coetmore continued. He wrote to Coetmore on 16 December

[18] An Irish folksong otherwise known as '*Jimmy Mó Mhíle Stór*' ('Jimmy, my thousand times beloved').

with perhaps an element of under-statement: 'Please forgive me for this bleak epistle, but it would be dishonest if I were not to admit to you that since we separated I have been feeling very down in the dumps.'

Prelude for Violoncello and Piano

Coetmore had taken the manuscripts of both the *Irish Lament* and the Prelude for Violoncello and Piano on her Middle East concert tour, presumably with a view to including them in her recitals. While the *Irish Lament* was simply a recasting of an earlier piano piece, the Prelude was a new work, its fifty-six bars encapsulating Moeran's formidable compositional technique in perhaps the smallest scale possible. The effect is of a concentrated emotional outpouring that belies the creative ingenuity of the piece. Moeran employed classical sonata form in miniature to create a tight and compelling structure that urges the listener forward to a climax that, when it eventually happens, seems effortlessly inevitable. The theme is a ballad-like melody reminiscent of folksong. Indeed, it resembles such traditional melodies as 'O Waly, Waly' and a 'Londonderry Air', and it can be readily imagined as a vocal setting. Whether Moeran had a poem or text in mind when he created his tune is speculative, but his innate sense of word-setting, refined through the practice of composing dozens of songs, resulted in an unmistakeable 'song without words'. The piano accompaniment comprises a four-beat per bar chordal pulse throughout most of the work, gently underpinning the solo line (music example 49).

Moeran indulged a harmonic richness that is the principal element providing the piece with its individuality of style. Structurally, the tasks of the solo and accompanying parts are clearly delineated throughout the piece. Except for two bars, the cello solo carries the entire melodic burden, and the piano provides the harmonic rhythm.

Music example 49. Prelude for Violoncello and Piano: bars 1–11

It is probable that Coetmore provided technical assistance in the composition of the piece, and this was discerned by the *Musical Times* reviewer of the published work, who remarked that it 'exploits ably the genius of the solo instrument'.[19] The notational precision and its tonal effect is fundamental to the work, for example, the direction to play the first phrase on the G string. This is an indication of the close cooperation between composer and dedicatee. The five-minute Prelude has been dismissed as inconsequential, but, in the opinion of the author, it crystallises the intense feelings of a man who believed himself to be in love, probably for the first time for decades. Moeran had extreme difficulty in communicating his regard for Coetmore whether in conversation or by letter, and he was fearful either that it may not be reciprocated, or that she would cast him aside when she got to know him better. Nonetheless, the first weeks of their relationship may have been his happiest days since his time at Uppingham, and it is possible that he crammed every nuance of his mental state into this short piece. The seemingly innocuous Prelude is, through its immensely powerful symbolism, one of Moeran's most significant works.[20]

The latter months of 1943 had been momentous for Moeran, and he found himself at the beginning of his fiftieth year in the unfamiliar position of having developed a dependency upon another person. In a matter of weeks, Moeran had come to rely upon Coetmore to provide a focus both for his creative efforts and for his life in general. This contrasts sharply with the self-reliant and fully occupied composer who had begun the previous year in confident mood. The text of his letters shows that after Coetmore's departure he was bereft, and he began to experience a new sensation: that of anxiety. He appears to have reasoned to himself that work was probably the only palliative measure to which he could resort. On 16 December, he wrote to Coetmore, 'I am missing you terribly. I suppose the only antidote is work.' However, he was hit by a further blow two days later when his father succumbed to his final illness. The conditions in the Moeran household seem rapidly to have become oppressive: 'The atmosphere in the house is one of continuous anxiety and depression.' Moeran's plan had been to remain just a short time in Kington and then return to London for a while before embarking on a trip to Ireland, but his father's death meant that he was obliged to stay longer, both to deal with funeral arrangements and to support his mother at her time of loss. Writing to Coetmore seemed to help, and this enabled him to spend several hours each day in her company.

---

[19] 'New Music', *The Musical Times*, Vol. 86, No. 1227 (1 May 1945), 150.

[20] For a more detailed examination of the Prelude, see Ian Maxwell, 'Moeran and Coetmore', *BMS News* 126 (June 2010), 287. It should be noted that in this paper, the author suggested that Moeran and Coetmore may have consummated their relationship during their few days together in London in mid-November 1943 and that the Prelude was a token of this. In the light of more recent consideration of Moeran's sexuality and behaviour, this now seems improbable.

1944

Moeran celebrated his forty-ninth birthday at Kington under the muted circumstances occasioned by his father's death and in a state of continuing depression over both his enforced separation from Coetmore and not having heard anything from her. It is difficult when writing in the context of instant global communications in a generally peaceful Western world to understand the mind-set that appreciated the very real dangers of overseas travel during wartime and the uncertainty and constant worry that accompanied each day that did not bring a letter or telegram from a loved one. Although much of the population would have been sharing his worries and anxieties – and in countless cases their worst fears would have been realised – for Moeran it was entirely new. For decades, he had lived an insulated and privileged life with few emotional ties beyond those to his immediate family, and the suddenness of his new state must have been almost overwhelming. Even following his normal daily routine provided opportunities for his worry to increase. The act of reading a newspaper for example: 'last Friday there was certain news in the *Daily Telegraph* relative to the claims of the enemy at sea, & this thoroughly un-nerved me.'

It is unsurprising, therefore, that composition was the last thing on his mind. Despite having accepted the commission for the ENSA overture in September, several months later Moeran had made no progress: indeed, it is probable that he had not yet even begun to think about the piece. In late December, he received a communication from Walter Legge, informing him that his overture had been programmed in a concert for workers at a north London factory on 25 February, just eight weeks away. Thus, summoning the vestiges of objectivity with which his parlous emotional state had left him and doing his best to be positive, he began work. He wrote to Coetmore, 'I have started off the morning of New Year's Day on Legge's overture, and if all goes well, I shall have it ready for him ... After all, it is by nature of being war-work & it has got to be done.' However, his heart was clearly not in it: 'Oh, how I would much rather be writing something for you now,' but even when he was planning music for Coetmore his thoughts were unclear. Since he had first stated his intention to compose for her, the priorities (whether sonata followed by concerto, or concerto then sonata) had changed several times.

In several of his January letters, Moeran referred to the problems he would have in composing a concerto without Coetmore being there to help and advise him: 'I don't feel equal to the complications of the cello concerto in your absence ... In the meantime, I can be getting my hand in with the idiom of the cello by writing a sonata.' Finally, on 5 January, after nearly a month of increasing trepidation, Moeran received a cable from Coetmore confirming that she had arrived safely, and he immediately wrote to tell her how excited and relieved he was. Due to wartime censorship, she was not able to give her location, but Moeran's anxiety was ameliorated somewhat and he felt himself able begin serious effort on the ENSA overture. He wrote: 'Now my work will go ahead like a house on fire. Today I have actually approached my ENSA overture with zest,' and three weeks later on 26 January he was able to write, 'Now that overture is so nearly finished, when I go for my walk today ... I am going to let myself go in my thoughts of music for you, my darling, for the cello sonata which I am going to do first before the concerto.' Despite this assertion, Moeran was struggling to get the work ready in time for the London concert. He wrote to Coetmore on 20 February:

> I have run it decidedly close in the time I have left myself to copy out the score of the overture – 8 more pages which must be done tomorrow at all costs. I think it turns out to be quite a good little work, what you might call athletic in style. Consequently, it has reams of long string passages in semi-quavers, & the consequences is [sic] it takes the devil of a time to write out

The next day, he travelled to London, writing a letter to Coetmore on the train in which he mentioned that he planned to stay with the Hills in Seer Green. Apart from attending the performance of the ENSA overture – now titled *Overture to a Masque* – he was also going to the Red Army Day Festival at the Royal Albert Hall during the afternoon of 23 February, which was to open with a short fanfare for three military brass bands that Moeran had been asked to compose for the occasion.

Fanfare for Red Army Day

February 23 had been celebrated as Red Army Day in the Soviet Union since 1923, and, after that country became a wartime ally in 1941, it was also marked in Britain as a gesture of solidarity. Moeran regarded the offer of a commission for an opening fanfare as part of his 'war work' and had felt obliged to undertake it, although he faced numerous difficulties in composing and scoring a work in a genre in which he had previously never worked. Nonetheless, the composition had been essentially complete by 12 February, as he wrote to Coetmore:

> I gave Willner the job of making a fair copy of the full score of the Fanfare. It has no accidentals in it at all, being diatonic throughout, but even in that he made so many mistakes that we missed the post with it yesterday and only got it off this morning.

Moeran had also requested help with the instrumental ranges and characteristics: '[Michael Mullinar] came to my rescue last week by lending me a handbook on military band instrumentation when I was hard put to it to know how to set about my fanfare.' On 21 February, he expressed his worries to Coetmore about how the piece would sound: 'I can't help feeling a bit nervous about my fanfare, as I trust to instinct rather than knowledge that it is scored for the instruments correctly in such a way that it will sound well.' The festival concert programme comprised patriotic music – mainly by contemporary British composers – and the items were linked together by a blank-verse narrative written for the occasion by the poet and author Laurie Lee. The massed musical forces of the London Symphony Orchestra, the Royal Choral Society and the bands of the Royal Marines, the Royal Air Force and the Coldstream Guards were conducted by Dr Malcolm Sargent. However, the newspaper reports of the concert published the next day – while including reviews of each of the other programmed works – did not mention Moeran's fanfare, and it seems that the piece was omitted. In a letter to Coetmore written on 27 February, Moeran did not talk about either the fanfare or the ENSA overture, and the only reference to his visit to London was: 'having finished what I had to do in town.'

According to Lionel Hill, Moeran had travelled from Seer Green to London to attend the Red Army Day Concert and returned late in the evening in an extreme drunken state.[21]

Why would the fanfare have been dropped from the programme? There are at least two plausible scenarios: either the parts were not available in sufficient time, or the work failed in rehearsal. According to Moeran's 12 February letter, the full score had been sent to London by post that morning, which would have left limited time for a copyist to extract the individual parts for the players in each of the three brass bands. The bandsmen would therefore have first seen the music no more than a day or so in advance, and possibly not until the day of the concert itself. Moreover, Moeran's inexperience with the genre – despite his obtaining a handbook on military band instrumentation – may have led to his writing music that was at best too difficult or at worst impossible for some of the instruments. It is thus likely that the work was found to be unplayable and was removed from the programme.[22]

Overture to (for) a Masque

Moeran's tribulations in London did not end with the failure of his fanfare. His overture was not included in the 25 February factory workers concert and was replaced by Arnold Bax's imaginatively titled commission *Work in Progress*. Again, it is probable that late delivery of the score made it impossible either for the parts to be copied in time or for the work to receive sufficient rehearsal. The evidence from Moeran's letters to Coetmore during January and February suggests that he had been working on the overture intermittently, having again discovered that trying to adhere to a rigid schedule compromised his usual *modus operandi*. He wrote, 'It is a commissioned work, as you know, and it is not my top notch. The fact is I am doing it as a duty engendered by the war and, working to a timetable, I am not able to follow my normal method of extreme self-criticism.' In the same letter, he explained how he planned to address the time constraints problem:

> This time next month, the actual composition of it should be finished for good or ill, and I shall be in the thick of the entirely enjoyable task of orchestration and writing out the full score. The Professor [Arthur Willner] will then come into action as amanuensis, making a fair copy for the copyists of the parts day by day from my original score as I do it in pencil. Normally, I like making my own final score, but in this case, time presses.

Moeran's optimism was misplaced, and as the days went by, composition of the music got further behind, partly because he could not prevent himself from being distracted by other ideas. In addition to composing the *Fanfare for Red Army Day* and thinking about the cello sonata for Coetmore, he was also probably working

---

21 Hill, 30–32. Moeran had apparently spent the evening 'drowning his sorrows' in May Mukle's Mainly Musicians club. According to Hill, it remained a mystery how he made his way in the blackout from there to Marylebone railway station, caught the correct train and managed to alight at Seer Green.

22 Speculation about the fate of the score of *Fanfare for Red Army Day* is presented in Chapter 20, pp. 320-322.

on his settings of poems by Seumas O'Sullivan: a song-cycle later known as the *Six Poems by Seumas O'Sullivan*. Moeran had previously mentioned composing these songs in his first extended letter to Coetmore dated 10 October:

> As soon as I shall have had a day or two at a piano there will be a whole cycle of [O'Sullivan's] verse ... There are two more poems I want to set, & actually I have got the music of them in my head, so it will be mainly a matter of committing it to paper.

Determining exactly when the *Six Poems* were originally composed is problematic, since the dating evidence from Moeran's letters and known activities is contradictory. Moeran declared on at least three separate occasions that he had finished the set, but the only reliable evidence of their eventual completion is an anecdote from Lionel Hill in which Moeran gave an impromptu recital of the original seven songs – including the later omitted *If There Be Any Gods* – at Seer Green shortly before their first performance in Dublin in October 1944.[23] It is reasonable to believe, therefore, that Moeran was working on them sporadically until at least September 1944 and that his several assertions about having finished them earlier probably included elements of wishful thinking.

As a short cut to get the composition of the overture completed to schedule and perhaps in some desperation, Moeran once again resorted to self-plagiarism. The music of the overture includes sections that were lifted and adapted from earlier works, including the First and Second Rhapsodies and two of the songs in the choral suite *Phyllida and Corydon*.[24] As with the examples presented earlier of Moeran's re-use of material, the extent and exactness of the duplication eliminates any possibility that this was anything other than deliberate. It is, perhaps, a tribute to Moeran's strength through adversity that he was able to incorporate the music from his existing compositions into something that nevertheless sounds like a coherent Moeran work. Regarding the title of the piece, *Overture to a Masque* had been Moeran's first thought, but on discovering that William Alwyn had composed an orchestral piece with that name a few years earlier, he modified the title slightly to *Overture for a Masque*.[25]

---

[23] According to Hill, Moeran had arrived at Seer Green drunk, and had immediately attempted to play and sing his Seumas O'Sullivan song-cycle: 'This unexpected treat was most exciting, and as his fingers moved over the introductory arpeggio in the piano part I wondered what would happen when the voice entered. The result was beyond description. To the words 'I will go out and meet the evening hours' he produced a wailing, tuneless drone that went on and on, continuing thus right through the seven songs. Betty [Hill's wife] and Judy [Hill's daughter] ... were convulsed with suppressed laughter'. Hill, 86.

[24] At least a third of the music of *Overture for a Masque* appears to have been sourced directly from Moeran's earlier compositions.

[25] Alwyn's *Overture to a Masque* was composed in 1940 as a tribute to Sir Henry Wood in what was intended to have been Wood's final season as conductor of the Promenade Concerts. It was programmed for inclusion in Prom 39 on 24 September. Due to German bombing, the 1940 Proms season was curtailed earlier that month, and Alwyn's overture was not performed.

Despite having missed its first intended performance on 25 February, *Overture for a Masque* became one of Moeran's most performed works during the mid-1940s, but it was several years before the composer was able to attend a performance. As he wrote somewhat plaintively to Aloys Fleischmann in April 1945:

> I have not yet heard [the overture] properly performed. The L.S.O. did it at a Sunday concert in London in February but I had 'flu & couldn't go to town for it. I now hear that it was performed last week at several concerts in the north of England ... but nobody told me ... indeed, it has had many performances, only I don't happen to have heard it as they always forget to tell me.[26]

Musically, the overture successfully fulfils its commission brief. It begins and ends brightly with alternating extrovert and introspective episodes during its approximately ten-minute duration. Despite being a patchwork of new and re-composed music, the piece holds together principally through its imaginative orchestration. Moeran even included a glockenspiel in the extensive instrumentation, and the varied sound palette provided the possibility of widely contrasting textures, serving to disguise the derivativeness of much of the music. The review of the first performance by the Liverpool Philharmonic Orchestra in Hanley Victoria Hall appreciated this: 'There was also a new work, E. J. Moeran's *Overture to a Masque* specially written for these concerts. This, full of pomp and bustle, brilliantly scored, and with a pleasant pastoral interlude, gave an impressive start to the concert.'[27] However, the reviewer of the second performance a few days later in Birmingham was not so sure: '[The concert] included ... a rather forbidding novelty, E. J. Moeran's bleak but bracing *Overture to a Masque*'.[28]

[26] McNeill, 502.
[27] 'Symphony Concert for War Workers', *Staffordshire Sentinel*, (6 April 1944), 3.
[28] 'Music in Birmingham: E.N.S.A. Concert', *Birmingham Daily Post*, (8 April 1944), 2.

16

Muse
(1944–1945)

Having returned to Kington on 27 February, Moeran had to prepare immediately for a short visit to Ireland. The first Irish performance of the Concerto for Violin and Orchestra was to take place in Dublin on 5 March with Nancie Lord as soloist and the Radio Éireann Symphony Orchestra, and Moeran had been invited to attend the concert. He travelled to Dublin on 1 March, with his plan being to stay in Ireland for about ten days, making a brief trip to Kenmare after the concert. On arriving in Dublin, Moeran found that the Irish authorities would not allow sealed airmail letters to be sent from Ireland to any address in British-controlled territory, the consequence being that Moeran could contact Coetmore only by expensive telegram. Furthermore, when he arrived in Kenmare, he became ill and was confined to bed for two weeks. He was obliged to remain until he was well enough to return to Dublin to convince the authorities to grant him special permission to go home, his original two-week visa having expired in the meanwhile.

Unfortunately, from early 1944, public travel between Britain and Ireland was becoming increasingly restricted, and it became virtually impossible after the beginning of April.[1] Ireland, while officially politically neutral, was nevertheless viewed with suspicion by the British authorities, and extensive precautions were taken to prevent the movement of possible German agents. One of Moeran's fellow members of the Oxford & Cambridge Musical Club during the 1920s had been the talented cellist Guy Maynard Liddell. Several of the club programmes show that Moeran accompanied him, and so they must have known each other. In 1940, Liddell had been appointed Director of B Division in the British Security Service (MI5) responsible for all aspects of counterespionage. He would have been particularly interested in travelling British citizens, especially those whose names were familiar to him. Moreover, Liddell's brother Cecil Frederick Liddell had been director of the MI5 Irish Section since the outbreak of the war. Moeran's previous associations with the Irish Republican Army would probably have been known to Liddell, and – while it is unlikely that Moeran was considered to be a major security risk – his being a suspected Nationalist sympathiser would have compounded his difficulties in obtaining a travel permit at a time of heightened sensitivity. When Moeran's efforts to return to Britain would have brought him to the attention of the security services, Liddell and

---

[1] This was due to the preparations for the still top-secret Operation Overlord ('D-Day' invasion).

his colleagues may have thought it best to keep him out of the way in Ireland. There is no evidence from Moeran's letters that he suspected that he was being singled out, and he seems to have put the problems down to bureaucracy.

Moeran's recovery from his illness took several weeks. While by the middle of April he was again mobile, he was marooned in Ireland with no travel permit and no prospect of getting one. For the first month of his stay in Kenmare, the rules forbidding the sending of private airmail letters had frustrated his attempts to write at length to Coetmore. He resorted to expensive and unreliable cables, none of which she received. The earliest extant communication from him in Kenmare is a long telegram dated 13 April, in which he said that he had, 'given up the sonata idea' and was, 'in the thick of your concerto'. Shortly after this, Moeran discovered the Airgraph service, and he was subsequently able to use this to post longer letters more economically. His first airgraph was dated 15 April:

> My darling Peers, I got your letter from Syria dated March 29th, in which you said you were anxious because you had no letter from me. But, as I warned you, there is no air-mail letter-card service from Eire. This wretched epistle is just to say that I have sent frequent cables to you at your original address; you may pick them up; also, that I shall continue trying to cable, but, meanwhile, I am attempting to pick up the inspiration for our own 'cello concerto in Kerry. Darling, beloved Peers, I am trying to work for you: you as an artist & as my dear love are all that matters, Jack.

Since his letters up to this point had focused on composing a sonata for Coetmore, and since he had explicitly ruled out embarking on the complicated task of composing a concerto without her technical assistance, Moeran's abrupt change of mind is curious. However, a second airgraph, written a couple of days later, included the assurance: 'Whatever work I can do is for you & you alone,' and this, together with the reference in the first airgraph to working on 'our own cello concerto', provides a possible clue to the sudden change of priority. Moeran's words may have been a response to a request – possibly even a demand – from Coetmore that he compose a concerto for her, and that he should not compose anything for anybody else. While this deduction may initially seem over-thought, it is supported by other evidence. Coetmore was undoubtedly ambitious as a solo cellist and would have realised the career-boosting effect of being the dedicatee of a new concerto. In early 1944, her friend and professional rival Raya Garbousova was in the process of commissioning a new concerto – funded through the Koussevitsky Foundation – and, since the two cellists were in regular correspondence, it is very probable that Coetmore would have been aware of this.[2] While it is unlikely that Garbousova, who was resident in the United States of America at the time, would have considered Moeran as the composer of her new concerto, even the thought of her friend approaching Coetmore's 'own' composer would have concentrated her mind.[3] Under these cir-

---

[2] Letters from Garbousova to Coetmore in the Coetmore Archive at the Performing Arts Museum in Melbourne confirm this correspondence.

[3] This scenario is rendered plausible by the probability that Garbousova knew Moeran through having met him at May Mukle's Mainly Musician's club. Although Garbousova

cumstances, Coetmore sending an urgent request to Moeran essentially to drop everything else and get on with composing her concerto is a reasonable scenario, and Moeran's extant responses are consistent with this.

Also consistent are his subsequent attempts to extricate himself from other commitments that he had made. Earlier in the year, he had accepted an invitation from the BBC to provide a work for the 1944 season of Promenade Concerts. Rather than begin an entirely new composition, he had intended to revive and complete the sinfonietta that he had begun the previous year as a commission for the BBC Symphony Orchestra Section 'C', and he had agreed with the BBC Concert Manager, W. W. Thompson, that it would be ready for inclusion in the Promenade Concert on 23 June. Unfortunately, Moeran had left the partly completed manuscript in Kington, having planned to work on the piece when he returned after his short trip to Ireland. By the end of April and with the performance date less than two months away, he would have realised that there was no possibility of completing the commission, even if he could arrange to have his manuscript sent to him. On 22 April, Moeran wrote to Thompson, 'I am very much afraid that the Sinfonietta will not be finished in time', and he provided a litany of excuses, ending with the suggestion that his *Overture for a Masque* be programmed instead. He also stated very clearly that he was 'under Doctor's orders' not to work or to travel, and he enclosed a medical certificate signed by his doctor so that Thompson would know 'that the affair is genuine' and that he 'was not backing out from carrying out the work'. On the same day, however, Moeran sent an airgraph to Coetmore in which he reiterated that he was working on the concerto: 'remember this, I am all the time working out your concerto, and I never cease thinking of you.'

Having made the decision to begin work on a cello concerto, Moeran was faced with the problem of how to tackle the technical difficulties of an instrument with which he was relatively unfamiliar. The hour-long sonata that he had composed for Roland Perceval Garrod was thirty-five years in the past and the manuscript long since lost. In any case, it is unlikely that the standard required to play Garrod's sonata was anywhere near that necessary for a concerto. His eventual solution was to use his enforced stay in Ireland to get the inspiration for thematic material and to delay any actual composition until he could once again discuss things with Coetmore. As he wrote to her: 'I shall return home as soon as possible ... I must be there at all costs for your home coming.' In the event, even the plan to wander the Kerry hills and be inspired had to be abandoned. Moeran accepted an engagement to judge the composition section of the annual *Feis Ceoil*, and he travelled to Dublin at the beginning of May. He decided to break his journey in Cork and spend a few days with the Fleischmanns going through the package of scores that had been sent to him as competition judge.[4] While these activities left little time for composition, he wrote to Coetmore to say that he had been 'sketching out various ideas for our

---

initially asked Czech composer Bohuslav Martinů for a concerto, which he agreed to consider, the work that eventually emerged from the commission was Samuel Barber's Concerto for Violoncello and Orchestra, completed in early 1945.

4   Aloys and Anne Fleischmann lived at *Oileán Ruadh* near the Rochestown district of Cork City.

concerto' and that he longed 'for our life together when we can work it out together as a composition'. He also said that he had arranged for Coetmore to give the première of the as yet uncomposed concerto at the Capitol Theatre Dublin, with the concert being broadcast by Radio Éireann. However, shortage of coal during the war years had led to the gradual reduction in the frequency of train services on the largely steam-hauled Irish railways, and by 1944 there were just two passenger trains each week between Cork and Dublin. This meant that Moeran had to wait for the next train the following Tuesday.

A cable had informed Moeran that Coetmore had agreed to remain on the Middle East tour for a further month, expecting to return to Britain in early July, but he remained optimistic about his chances of getting back to Kington, thus facilitating better communication with her regarding the composition of the concerto. Nonetheless, some sense of the reality of his situation also appears to have dawned on him, and in an airgraph he qualified his optimism: 'it is on the cards I may not be allowed to leave Eire yet awhile.' While he was waiting in Dublin to hear from the authorities about his travel permit, his time was occupied both with the *Feis Ceoil* adjudication and with some journalistic work he had agreed to undertake: the reviewing of some of the festival concerts for the *Irish Press*. On 8 May he wrote claiming to have been 'working out the thematic & harmonic scheme' of the concerto, but it is difficult to see how and when he would have been able to do this during the previous week or so. He ended his airgraph: 'My wonderful, beloved Peers, please never go away from me again. I will devote my whole life & my music to trying to make you happy. Thank God I met you at last. Nothing else matters.'

Inevitably, Moeran failed to obtain a permit to return to England, and on 12 May he was back in Kenmare. Awaiting him was a letter from W. W. Thompson, expressing concern about Moeran's illness and disappointment in his inability to complete the Proms commission. Moeran replied reiterating his original excuses, but suggesting that if Thompson or the BBC or Sir Henry Wood could use their influence to persuade the 'authorities at that end' to grant him a travel permit, he would be able to guarantee to have his sinfonietta ready for a Proms performance if it was rescheduled from its June date to a concert at the end of the season. However, his mood of depression had returned. He wrote several airgraphs to Coetmore during the month, and these communicate both an increasing frustration at his continuing involuntary sojourn in Ireland and mounting worry resulting from his not having heard anything from her for some time. His dejection was ameliorated to an extent when a letter dated 3 May arrived from Coetmore having been forwarded from Kington, and on 30 May, he received a long cable that reassured him sufficiently about her welfare and intended return to England, and he was able to reply to her in a more optimistic mood: 'I heard from Walter [Legge] today to the effect that ENSA are applying for my return.' While Moeran could not have known that there was still no possibility of his being granted a travel permit until well after D-Day had taken place, having the belief that things were beginning to move for him and that Coetmore would be returning home shortly was clearly sufficient to elevate him somewhat from the low state into which he had descended. Coetmore had also raised the question about when the couple would get married. Moeran immediately replied in an airgraph:

You … wonder when the great date will be. Dear Peers, all I can reply to that is that my ambition in life is to be with you, to work with you and for you at our music, and to do everything in my power to try and make our two lives, which might become mutually one life, happy for you. I think you happen to have come into my life like a gift from the gods. Beloved, I am agreeable to anything you like. Let's get married soon, & I will get my brother Graham to give us a quiet wedding in Leominster Priory.

At the beginning of June, Moeran visited Mount Melleray Abbey in County Waterford. He had been invited there to listen to the Gregorian chant, and although he seems to have enjoyed the music, the spartan lifestyle did not appeal to him. He remained at Mount Melleray for a few days and then returned to Kenmare where he spent the rest of the month, variously writing airgraphs to Coetmore and letters to all and sundry in London who he hoped might be able to influence the decision of his application for a special travel permit. There is no mention of progress on the concerto in any of this correspondence, and it is possible that Moeran had quietly dropped the project until he could get back home. It is also possible that Coetmore had heard that Garbousova had finalised a commission for Samuel Barber to compose her concerto, thus removing any residual risk that Moeran might be approached, and she had consequently relaxed the pressure.

Towards the end of June, Moeran was finally granted permission to travel, and he returned to Kington in early July. Correspondence with Coetmore was now easier and quicker, but the situation remained unsatisfactory. He was torn between wanting to encourage Coetmore to advance her career ambitions – by extending her stay in the Middle East – and needing her to return to him, both to consult on the concerto and to continue the development of their personal relationship. In the end, he left her to make her own decision. On 11 July, he wrote, 'I should never be happy if I thought you would be spoiling the chance of being in those lovely surroundings a little longer because you thought you ought to come back on my account.' Most of this letter was newsy trivia about mundane aspects of his life and that of Coetmore's mother, much in the manner he had written after Coetmore had first departed for the Middle East tour. Moreover, he seemed to feel that it was no longer necessary to keep reassuring her that he was working on her concerto. In fact, he mentioned having composed 'a song cycle to Irish poems'.[5]

On 14 July, Moeran attended a Promenade Concert in Bedford at which his violin concerto was performed by Audrey Catterall[6] and the BBC Symphony Orchestra conducted by Adrian Boult. He wrote again to Coetmore on 24 July, mentioning that he was studying other cello concertos as examples: 'Since writing to you last, I have played over the Piatagorsky [sic] records of the Schumann Concerto; they are really excellent & I long for you to be here to listen to them.' While this may have been intended to reassure Coetmore that he was still working on the concerto, progress had stalled, and Moeran was concentrating on other projects. He eventually

---

[5] The *Six (or Seven) Poems of Seumas O'Sullivan* that Moeran had begun composing in mid-1943.

[6] Daughter of Arthur Catterall.

confessed as much to Coetmore, and her response seems to have been reasonable. On 10 August, he wrote, 'You are good in what you say about my other work, apart from the cello concerto. You evidently fully understand the necessity for following to a certain extent where fancy happens to lead.'

Sinfonietta

Moeran wrote to Lionel Hill on 26 August: 'I am busy finishing off my sinfonietta; nearly done now,'[7] and the final page of the manuscript score in the Royal College of Music Library bears the message: 'Finished, September 23rd, 1944, Kington.' He also wrote at the end of September to Julian Herbage, perhaps with a hint of triumphalism:

> I have finished my sinfonietta, the work that was suggested for the Proms for June 24th last, but which I was unable to finish then. It has actually turned out to be rather more of a major work than I thought it would be when I first started it.[8]

It was almost exactly two years since Moeran had written to Arthur Bliss to say that he was 'well on towards the end' of the first movement of the work. Moeran had written again to Bliss a month later to say that he had 'hit on what [he thought was] a good tune for making the middle movement a theme and variations'.[9] As is almost always the case with Moeran, no working material has survived, so it is impossible to determine whether the 'good tune' persisted into the finished Sinfonietta. However, his letters provide some clues to his thought processes during the composition of the work. Particularly interesting was his assertion that the reason he could not complete it while he was isolated in Kerry was that he had begun its composition in Herefordshire. His letter to Herbage continued: 'It was started here [Herefordshire], & owes its initial inspiration to this district, and had I attempted to continue to carry it out in the entirely different surroundings and atmosphere of Co. Kerry it might have become too much of a hybrid.'[10] While Moeran's belief in the importance of place was clearly at the front of his mind, it will be recalled that he had originally given other reasons for his inability to make progress with the composition. These reasons were his doctor having ordered him not to work and his having left the partly completed manuscript at his parents' home.

Musically, the Sinfonietta recalls principally the style of the piano rhapsody, which is perhaps only to be expected, given that the composition of the two works partly overlapped. There is little similarity with the violin concerto and no evidence that Moeran ever attempted to attribute Irish influences in the work. According to Nicholas Temperley, the sinfonietta genre is a largely twentieth-century concept, having probably originated with Joseph Joachim Raff in 1874.[11] Examples

---

7   Hill, 34.

8   McNeill, 482.

9   McNeill, 399–400.

10   Geoffrey Self wrote that Moeran's friend Dick Jobson had asserted that the Sinfonietta had been conceived 'while Moeran accompanied him on his daily rounds in Herefordshire'. Self, 59.

11   Temperley, Nicholas. 'Sinfonietta' *Grove Music Online*. 2001; https://www. oxfordmusiconline.com/grovemusic/view/10.1093/gmo/9781561592630.001.0001/omo-

with which Moeran may well have been familiar in the mid-1940s would have included Leoš Janáček's Sinfonietta of 1926, the Sinfonietta by Arnold Bax and that by Benjamin Britten (both composed in 1932) and Albert Roussel's Sinfonietta for String Orchestra of 1934. According to Temperley, a sinfonietta is defined as 'an orchestral piece on a smaller scale, or of more modest aims, than a symphony'. These are, of course, relative terms, and so it is interesting to compare the scale and aims of Moeran's Sinfonietta with those of his earlier Symphony in G minor. In the case of scale, the contrast is clear: while the instrumentation of of the symphony includes a large brass section and a harp, that of the Sinfonietta is comparable with that for a Mozart or Haydn symphony but with the addition of two trumpets and percussion. Moreover, the duration of the four-movement symphony is about forty-five minutes, while that of the three-movement Sinfonietta is about twenty-four minutes. However, the two works are less distinct when their respective aims are considered. Moeran's commission had been for a work for the 'Section C' orchestra, as a platform to display the ability of the BBC's most competent instrumentalists. Moeran could therefore have been confident that in writing technically demanding music it would be played correctly. The Sinfonietta features instrumental parts of considerable difficulty: most particularly rapid and extended quaver and semi-quaver runs in strings and woodwind and extreme upper register brass notes. Moeran did not compose difficult music for its own sake. The textures that result from the musical devices utilised are fundamental to the overall effect. In no sense may the Sinfonietta be regarded as musically more modest than the symphony. Its aural impact – while necessarily constrained by its instrumentation – is nonetheless the equal of its larger-scale predecessor. Moeran's ability to juggle and juxtapose sonorities was such that the result could be an almost *gestalt*-like musical effect, and this is evident in sections of the Sinfonietta, where the apparent texture belies its relatively limited instrumentation.

Writers on Moeran hitherto have assessed the Sinfonietta as outstanding in the composer's oeuvre. Rhoderick McNeill asserted that it represented 'one of the peaks in Moeran's creative output and is perhaps the composer's most flawless work',[12] while Geoffrey Self hailed it as 'marvellously concise' and demonstrative of Moeran's 'structural and technical skill'.[13] Critical reception was also favourable, with Eric Blom of *The Observer* noting:

> E. J. Moeran's Sinfonietta is about as bucolic as anything Beecham, the most urban and civilised of conductors, would care to touch, one imagines. To a fairly robust taste it is most attractive. It does not present folky material only to leave it in the raw for want of resource. There is a real art of composition in it. Moeran can both expand and construct, though he does it unconventionally.[14]

9781561592630-e-0000025862 (Accessed 24 Sep. 2020).

12 McNeill, 274.

13 Self, 184–185.

14 'The Pick of Concerts', *The Observer*, (5 February 1950), 6.

McNeill and Self in their extended technical and formal analyses of the work heap praise upon both Moeran's compositional skill and what they perceive as an attempt to inject modernism – in the form of Neo-Classicism – into a musical style that had, perhaps, 'passed its sell-by date'.[15] McNeill and Self both trace this to an origin in the Sonata for Two Violins. However, it is difficult to avoid concluding that their reasoning has more to do with Moeran's adroit deployment of limited resources than any specifically musical aspects of either work. Twentieth-century Neo-Classicism in music is conventionally defined as being a reaction to the perceived excesses of Romanticism, in the same way that the Classical movement was assumed to be a reaction against the Baroque. While, as a general concept, this broad definition may stand, it is difficult to apply it to an individual piece of music. Moeran's Sinfonietta does indeed exhibit stylistic elements that could be regarded as consistent with Neo-Classicism, but it also includes features that inhabit most of the composer's creations: primarily pentatonic melodic constructs that recall folk music; lush secondary harmony and broad instrumental textures that bear the listener away to the landscapes of Moeran's rural inspiration. If the Sinfonietta is Neo-Classical, it is also Romantic, and, in that juxtaposition, it is definitively Moeran. As an example, consider the lyrical second subject of the first movement as played on the strings (music example 50). As this develops over several bars, it is almost as if the years have fallen away and the young Moeran is sitting at the piano playing the lush chords with which he harmonised the songs in *Ships, Sea-songs and Shanties*. Then, suddenly, the listener is transported to bustling London with a 'Big Ben'-like statement, again on strings (music example 51). Moeran wrote no programme notes for the Sinfonietta, neither did he ever say it was 'about' anything, but, perhaps more than any of his other works, it drew together the influences and inspirations that had informed his original creations during the previous twenty-five years.

Coetmore returned to England in late September and it is apparent from the gap in the correspondence that Moeran and she must have spent some time together. Moeran did write letters to other people from which can be deduced some of his activities and movements around the country. In a letter to Julian Herbage dated 29 September, he mentioned the song-cycle of *Seven Poems of Seumas O'Sullivan*, which he said would be given its première in Dublin in October. Moeran was presenting the cycle for possible broadcast, going so far as to suggest Kathleen Ferrier as a possible singer, although he suspected that the songs may be a bit high for her. Moeran followed up this letter with a second a couple of weeks later in which he stated that he had spoken with John Barbirolli in Manchester about the sinfonietta and that Barbirolli 'took a liking to it'. Moeran claimed that Barbirolli had suggested it be performed in a BBC broadcast the Hallé Orchestra would be undertaking in November. Herbage had long been an admirer of Moeran's music – perhaps more so than other senior music staff at the BBC – and Moeran was clearly directing his self-promoting onslaught where he felt it would be most effective. Eventually, he travelled to London to show Herbage the score of the Sinfonietta, and he stayed with the Hills at Seer Green for a few nights. With his other work out of the way, and with

[15] See McNeill, 260(a)–274, and Self (186), 175–185.

Music example 50. Sinfonietta, first movement: second subject

Music example 51. Sinfonietta, first movement: 'Big Ben' theme

Coetmore back in England – albeit fulfilling numerous concert and recital engagements around the country – it might be expected that Moeran would have resumed
work on the cello concerto. However, he seems to have spent much of the time until
the end of the year continuing his self-promoting activities and travelling around the
country to attend performances, including two weeks in Dublin in mid-October for
the first performance of the *Seven Poems of Seumas O'Sullivan* by dedicatee Violet
Burne and a second performance by Nancie Lord of the violin concerto. However,
he did eventually resume serious work on the cello concerto. He wrote to Coetmore
from Kington on 24 December:

> I am very deeply immersed again at last in the cello concerto and have reached the
> end of the expositionary section of the 1st movement. There will be more inter-
> ruptions to-morrow and Boxing Day, but I may do a bit more this coming week. I
> shall also have from Jan 16 – 26th.

1945

Christmas and New Year for Moeran was quite different from the miserable festive
season he had experienced the previous year. During the first few months of 1945,
his work on the cello concerto can be followed in detail as he conveyed news of its
progress to Coetmore by letter. The letters provide an insight into Moeran's composing process. His haphazard approach to getting things down on paper from the
ideal solutions he had in his head is confirmed, his 'last-minute' strategy is demon-

strated, and his almost manic tendency to destroy material which failed his own standards of quality is revealed. Moreover, his continuing desperation to please Coetmore by creating a work for her that would establish himself permanently in her affections is also indicated. Moeran was also juggling his time amongst several other requirements. It was a major exercise trying to keep up with Coetmore's concert engagements and arranging to be in her vicinity whenever possible, and he was concerned about his elderly mother who was suffering from increasing ill-health. Moeran also had many corrections to make to the score and parts of the Sinfonietta as rehearsals revealed shortcomings in the orchestration, and he continued to promote himself with the regional orchestras and elsewhere around the country. However, he endeavoured to keep the cello concerto uppermost in his mind whenever possible. On 17 January he wrote to Coetmore:

> Apart from having you here for something more than a rushed weekend just for the sake of being with you for country explorations & yourself, I had been reckoning on being at the end, or very near, of the first movement of the concerto by about that time, so that having you here with your cello, we could have gone into it thoroughly & put it into final shape in detail as to the solo part. You must let me know where you will be in Wales for the week ending Feb 17th.

He also mentioned the scoring problems with the Sinfonietta:

> I have the whole of the string parts of the 2nd & 3rd movements of the Sinfonietta to correct, & I find I must re-score the last 3 or 4 pages of the finale entirely. After several days experience of listening in Liverpool to a full sized orchestra ... I have learnt a certain point of technique, namely that an important wood-wind passage as I now have it will almost certainly be inaudible against a full body of strings such as I shall have at Bedford with the BBC Symphony Orchestra. I am now going to ring up Novello to accordingly hold up the copying of the woodwind [parts].

His next letter, dated 26 January and written from Liverpool where he was attending rehearsals for a performance by the Liverpool Philharmonic Orchestra of the Symphony in G minor, suggests that he was coming under pressure from Dublin concerning the première of the cello concerto:

> I have just had a letter from Dublin to know whether I can have it ready for you to broadcast in the autumn from a Sunday Symphony concert at the Capitol Theatre. Well, I can't: it will take me longer to write it, apart from you learning it: not that you won't do that quickly. Anyhow, we can perhaps arrange to have it produced a little later in the season.

Although Moeran's discussions with Radio Éireann the previous year had not fixed a date, they would have needed to plan their schedules some time in advance, and they were clearly looking for Moeran to commit to a more definite date. By 8 February, Moeran was back in Kington and had clearly been working hard on the cello concerto. He wrote:

> I have been at work again on the concerto and have been getting on well ... The cello has been plugging away for 60 bars on end and now I am at a big climatic

'Tutt-eye' … much easier to write than for your wretched instrument in combination with orchestra! The cello is the devil in this respect on account of its middle & bass register … you must be so careful not to put too much on top. Hence, I believe, the scarcity of cello concertos owing to the technical difficulty in writing them.[16]

This suggests that Moeran's awareness of the register problems in composing for cello and orchestra was acute. As has been shown, he had studied other concertos as models to determine how other composers had resolved the problem, and the solution he devised was to split the overall sonic texture responsibility between cello with reduced orchestration and full orchestra alone. Moeran demonstrated awareness of the impact the soloist and even the instrument itself has on the overall effect of the performance. Coetmore had apparently been talking about replacing her instrument, and Moeran was eager to know how that would make her sound change:

I hope that it is an instrument with a big tone suitable, apart from anything else, for putting over a concerto in a large hall. I notice in listening to cellists (Pini for one) in concertos that they don't 'come over' and dominate the proceedings like Casals does in the Dvorak records.

Again, Moeran shows a perceptive appreciation of Coetmore's own characteristics as a performer, and he clearly wanted to ensure that she provided herself with an instrument that could help accommodate the requirements of standing up to orchestral accompaniment. Moeran's approach to the balance problems of the concerto was to customise it for Coetmore's instrument and playing style: so much so that he refused to countenance a performance by anybody other than Coetmore during the remainder of his life.

A gap during March and April in the sequence of letters written to Coetmore is accounted for by the fact of their being able to spend more time together, and this led to Moeran making significant technical progress with the cello concerto. He also continued the promotion efforts on behalf of the Sinfonietta in letters that he wrote to Julian Herbage and the conductor Clarence Raybould at the BBC and to Aloys Fleischmann in Cork. Interestingly, in the letter to Fleischmann dated 28 April, he mentioned, 'I may be over [in Cork] in June for a brief visit prior to my marriage sometime in July.'[17] Clearly, Moeran and Coetmore had finally set at least a target date for their wedding.

Unfortunately, London was not conducive for serious composition, and neither were frequent return railway journeys from Kington. At the beginning of May, Coetmore joined a party organised by the singer Walter Widdop to tour Belgium and Germany giving concerts for servicemen in units of the British Liberation Army,[18] and Moeran returned to stay in Kington in order to try to complete the concerto.

---

[16] In fact, there is and was no scarcity of cello concertos: more than 500 were composed between 1700 and 1945, but the great majority of these would probably have been unknown to Moeran as they were not in the standard repertoire.

[17] McNeill, 503.

[18] The British Liberation Army (BLA) was the generic name under which the British forces that served in Western Europe between the invasion of Normandy and the end of the war

It is apparent that Coetmore was also becoming frustrated with Moeran's frequent alterations and discarding of material from the solo part that she had already learned. With a wedding and honeymoon to plan, a full schedule of concerts and recitals to fulfil and a première now set for late November in Dublin, Coetmore could perhaps be forgiven for losing some patience with Moeran's disorganised working processes. However, the composer himself seemed to be regarding the work as progressing well, as he wrote to Coetmore on 4 May:

> The concerto is in a position which requires no more work today but sleeping on tonight, plus a lot of thought as to what is to happen. I am back again to tonic (in the major) after a section which contains probably what is best in the whole work & ends in soliloquy but the thing is how to round it off so as to make a satisfying ending. It will either require a little or a lot so far as I can see at present. It has got to be a brilliant finish ... I shall have to summon up energy to go up to the hills & think out a finish.

Moeran also kept up his correspondence with Lionel Hill, and these letters provide interesting background to the composition of the concerto. On 12 March, Moeran had written:

> The only new records I have acquired lately are Elgar's Cello Concerto. It is a wonderful study in orchestration of a very tricky kind i.e. how to accompany the cello on [sic] the orchestra without submerging it; that is what I got it for, but the playing of Beatrice Harrison in the solo part is not my ideal.[19]

Moeran and Coetmore had decided to get married in Kington Church, rather than Leominster Priory, and William Graham Moeran conducted the ceremony. The best man was Moeran's doctor and friend, Dick Jobson, who, according to Hill, later related that Moeran had confided to him the night before the wedding that he believed the marriage would be a disaster. When Jobson had asked Moeran 'Why go on with it?' Moeran had apparently said, 'I have given her my word as a gentleman. I cannot break my word.'[20]

There were few guests – neither Moeran nor Coetmore had much family – and apart from Moeran's brother and mother and Coetmore's mother and sister, the attendees at the ceremony and celebration lunch were a half-dozen or so local friends. Amongst these was Arthur Willner, whose description of the occasion in a letter to his wife Cecile provides a personal perspective:

> Dearest, Finally I find the time to let you know that the wedding went very well. We had an intimate supper in Burton's hotel on Wednesday evening – only ten people; I sat between the two mothers. We had soup, chicken and plums in cream – no alcohol was served! Today the ceremony was just as intimate,

---

were known. As its role changed in mid-1945 into one of managing occupation, the BLA was renamed the British Army of the Rhine.

[19] Hill, 44. Hill mentioned in his commentary to this letter that Moeran had told him that he was also studying the Dvořák cello concerto, again to see how the orchestration problems had been addressed by another composer.

[20] Hill, 52 and 114.

Figure 8. Moeran-Coetmore Wedding, Kington Church, 26 July 1945

with only the Jobsons, the Ensleys and a cousin, Peers' sister and Mrs Edwards' daughter. [William] Graham performed the ceremony and Potter gave the address. Since there was no music at all, I went to the organ after the celebration and played (improvised) *Mein glaübiges Herze, Frolocke, sing, scherze*. Mr Potter was happy to drive me to the lunch, which was excellent: sandwiches, pate, fruit salad, trifle, chocolate cream, coffee and champagne. I talked the whole time with Peers, who was delighted about the lace collar. The sonata and the wine were also appreciated.[21]

---

[21] Extract from letter from Arthur Willner to Cecile Willner dated 26 July 1945, translation by the author. Willner had composed his Sonata for Violoncello and Piano, Op.97 as a wedding gift for Coetmore and Moeran. The manuscript of this work is now part of the *Moeran-Coetmore-Knott Collection* archive in the Performing Arts Collection at the Arts Centre, Melbourne. Willner himself, with his luxurious moustache, can just be seen in the wedding photograph peeping out from behind the group of four in the doorway on the left.

17

'My Word as a Gentleman' (1945–1946)

After the lunch, the newly-weds departed for a short honeymoon in Bala in north Wales, where 'they found sunshine and fair weather'.[1] According to Lionel Hill, their transport was Coetmore's unreliable old Wolseley Hornet.[2] At the beginning of August, they returned to London to begin their life together in Coetmore's flat in Belsize Lane. In the meanwhile, Moeran's mother moved out of the Gravel Hill house in Kington and went to live with William Graham at his rectory in Ledbury.

Until he met and became besotted with Coetmore, Moeran had been a confirmed bachelor. He had reached the age of fifty having given little thought to what conventional married life entailed, and so it may reasonably be asked why he had allowed himself to get into this situation. Nothing about Moeran's life hitherto suggests that he was in any way suited to be a husband for anybody. However, it is clear not only that he had been coerced by his mother and brother and manipulated by Coetmore herself, but also that he had failed to consider objectively the reality of what was happening to him. While his letters reveal that he had divined Coetmore's underlying motivation, he was undoubtedly flattered by her attention, and this, together with pressure especially from his mother – who clearly had no understanding of Coetmore whatsoever – was evidently sufficient for Moeran to disregard any niggles of common sense that may have been trying to make themselves apparent.

Over the years since the ending of the Eynsford cottage *ménage*, Moeran had evolved for himself an itinerant existence in Britain and Ireland – variously living with his parents, staying with friends and acquaintances, taking occasional lodgings, or residing in hotels or boarding houses – which suited a composing process in which place was a key aspect. Moeran had convinced himself that to compose successfully, he needed an appropriate environment that was determined by the character of the music. Essentially, it was as if a composition that was begun or first imagined in a certain location became bound to that location, the effect being that he subsequently found it difficult to work on it anywhere else. Whether Moeran had considered the effect that married life would have on his ability to be where he

---

[1]   From a letter dated 29 July 1945 from Grace Jobson to Betty Hill, quoted in Hill, 53.

[2]   Moeran and Coetmore visited the Hills on 26 August and recounted their adventures with the car: 'Over lunch they gave us a graphic account of their journey through Wales, and of some amusing incidents that had occurred. One of these was the way the Wolseley Hornet, once stopped, would not re-start until someone had given her bonnet a sharp blow'. Hill, 53.

needed to be in order to work is not clear, but it is evident from the reminiscences of Lionel Hill and from Moeran's testimony as revealed in his letters that 'settling down' to a 'normal' married life – particularly in Coetmore's London flat – would be impossible for both Moeran the composer and Moeran the man. It is also apparent from the Dick Jobson anecdote quoted at the end of the previous chapter that Moeran realised this before he was faced with his final curtain – so to speak – on 26 July 1945.

Thus, it may reasonably be asserted that, where the marriage was concerned, Moeran was partly the agent of his own subsequent misfortunes, in as much as he missed the opportunity to prevent at the outset the psychological disintegration that he would eventually experience as a result of his relationship with Coetmore. However, he had given her his 'word as a gentleman', and that was that, although it may have been equally the case that failing to go through with the marriage would have deeply disappointed his mother and brother. Perhaps Moeran was optimistic about their future – an assertion that is supported by the content and tone of letters he wrote during the first year or so of his marriage – and he simply hoped they would be happy. Of course, marriage is more than just living as a couple in a flat in London, and it is interesting to speculate how their lives progressed after their return from honeymoon. Moeran's domestic arrangements had always been taken care of – either by the housekeeping staff at his parents' home, or by landladies or hotel or other laundry services – and it is unlikely that, since he left the army, he had ever been in a position of having to wash his own clothes or to cater for himself. It would have gone without saying that he would have expected this to continue. Coetmore's position would have been similar: her professional life required that such arrangements be taken care of in the form of a laundry service or daily domestic help. It is probable that Coetmore made it clear from the start that she had no intention of adapting her previous regime to accommodate any of Moeran's personal or working requirements. As an active career solo cellist, she needed both to maintain a base in London and to be available to travel around the country or possibly even abroad for engagements without hindrance and sometimes at short notice. A pattern of mostly living apart was soon established, with either Coetmore being away on a concert or recital tour, or Moeran travelling about the country attending performances or staying with his mother and brother. Sufficient evidence exists in the form of letters, reliable contemporary accounts, and newspaper concert reviews to make it possible to construct a timeline of Moeran's and Coetmore's relationship, and it can be calculated with some precision how much time they spent together. Regarding the conjugal aspects of the marriage, Coetmore's own testimony provides a vivid description of an unsatisfactory or even non-existent sexual relationship. In *Lonely Waters*, Hill recounts a visit by Moeran and Coetmore:

> I was able to show Jack my new 'OO' gauge model railway layout that was beginning to take shape in the back bedroom … Jack was naturally fascinated, and I had difficulty in tearing him away when Betty [Hill's wife] said tea was ready … While we were enjoying ourselves upstairs, Peers was talking in a frank manner to

Betty about her relationship with Jack. She told my wife that 'It is like living with an uncle – you don't know how frustrated I feel.'[3]

Coetmore's statement serves both to verify Moeran's lack of interest in a physical relationship with her and to provide a basis for her undoubted liaisons with other men. Other writers have described Moeran's and Coetmore's marriage as 'ill-fated', 'uneasy', 'not a happy one' or even 'a disaster'.[4] However, the evidence presented by the letters that Moeran wrote to Coetmore between 1945 and 1950 suggests an alternative analysis, and this will become apparent in the final chapters of this book.

Concerto for Violoncello and Orchestra

While the testimony of Lionel Hill suggests that the concerto was complete by the date of Moeran and Coetmore's wedding, evidence from Moeran's letters suggests that he was still working on it until at least the middle of October, and the manuscript itself is dated 'Oct 22/45': some eighteen months after he began work the previous April in Kenmare. Moeran had soon found that it was impossible to compose in the confines of the Belsize Lane flat, and after having done nothing for about a month, he travelled back to Ledbury at the beginning of September, seeking the tranquillity he needed to finish the composition. During this time, Coetmore continued with her solo and chamber ensemble engagements. One letter survives from this period, and it supports the notion that Moeran's ability to work was tightly bound with his environment:

> I thought of a lovely bassoon thing this morning that wasn't there before & I am longing to see what other ideas crop up as I forge ahead. I think working in bright daylight has more to do with it than anything, together with a pleasant outlook from the window facing me on to the green lawn. I work in the dining room, & if, which is only very occasionally, I need the piano, I nip into the next room. I do hope you are not too terribly lonely. I do miss you & wish you were here so much. But for the sake of making your concerto as good as I possibly can, the present temporary arrangement for me to finish it here is obviously turning out for the best.

The 'present temporary arrangement' of Moeran working in an environment apart from Coetmore would soon become the norm. While the first performance of the concerto had been agreed more than a year earlier, the date of 25 November 1945 had only been decided during the summer. As with other deadlines with which he had previously been faced, the effect of a fixed date had been to raise Moeran's level of tension and anxiety. This time, however, failure did not just mean for himself, it would compromise and embarrass his wife. As suggested in the letter extract above, Moeran applied himself as he rarely had, and the concerto was completed in October. He returned to Belsize Lane, and he and Coetmore spent a few weeks

---

3 Hill, 73.

4 See Hill, 115, and Self, 156 and 247. As shown earlier, the suggestion that the marriage was a disaster was asserted by Dick Jobson to have been made by Moeran himself. See Hill, 52 & 114.

going through the solo part. Lionel Hill wrote that he visited the flat during this time: 'It is a treasured memory that on several occasions I was able to hear [Coetmore and Moeran] playing the Cello Concerto before the first public performance.'[5] At the beginning of November, the couple took a few days holiday in Southsea, and, on the 19th of the month, they travelled to Ireland.

Their arrival was noted in the press: 'Mr. E. J. Moeran, the well-known composer, accompanied by his wife, Miss Peers Coetmore, also arrived at Dun Laoghaire.'[6] 'Quidnunc' of the *Irish Times*, wrote a gossipy piece about the coincidence of the 'oe' diphthong in both their names:

> Most people seem to believe that Mrs Moeran – Peers Coetmore that was – must be Dutch … [she], in fact, comes from Wales. In Welsh, the letters "oe" frequently come together … Moeran himself, of course, is Irish, and has done most of his best work down in Kerry … In spite of the trouble which the 'oe' business has caused them, the Moerans can still be objective about it. They remember with pleasure the occasion of a party, the invitations for which they headed: 'The Coetmoerans invite you …'[7]

The fact of the first performance of the cello concerto being in Ireland was regarded as something of a coup in Irish cultural circles. Few British composers – even those with genuine Irish connections – had made any great effort to support music in Ireland during the war, and Moeran's regular visits and the fact that he did some of his compositional work there had not gone un-noticed. His perceived dedication to the art music of Ireland was appreciated in a manner that was not possible in the much more cosmopolitan and congested musical milieu of London. The fact that he was now married – and to a glamorous and talented cellist for whom it was believed he had very romantically composed a concerto as a wedding present – only served to enhance further his standing in the country. The press lost no time in also elevating Coetmore to a position in Irish society. The gossip correspondent of the *Evening Herald* wrote at length following a news conference with the couple:

> Peers Coetmore [Mrs Moeran] extracted a cigarette case from her handbag. Three men made belated efforts to supply her with a cigarette, but only succeeded in providing her with a light for her own. I noticed that she had just one more in the case. 'I hope you will have no difficulty in renewing your supply while in Dublin,' said I, making polite conversation. The tall young woman raised her eyebrows. 'Is there a great shortage?' she asked … I assured her that there was.

---

5   Hill, 55.

6   'Social and Personal', *Irish Independent*, (20 November 1945), 2. The *Irish Independent* had, over the years, staunchly asserted and defended Moeran as an Irishman and composer. In 1940, it was suggested that Moeran 'had been living in Kenmare for the past five years'. In August 1943, the newspaper published an almost entirely fictional biographical piece: 'E. J. Moeran is the son of a one-time Cork parson. He himself was born in Norfolk. Now in his middle fifties, still a bachelor, he lives with his father in the latter's Yorkshire Rectory. Very tall, brusque and of military bearing, he was a dispatch rider in the last war, and got severely shell-shocked. His work has been a triumph of mind over matter, as are his hobbies: mountaineering in Kerry, motor-cycling at home.'

7   'An Irishman's Diary', *Irish Times*, (21 November 1945), 3.

'However,' I said, 'your hotel should be able to save you from destitution. Or,' I added, glancing across at the Musical Director of Radio Éireann, 'Captain Bowles might be able to come to the rescue.' She flashed a smile at Captain Bowles ... The other *Herald* man present asked a question about music. He and Captain Bowles and composer E. J. Moeran discussed concertos ... When I heard that [Mrs Moeran's] experience of this country hitherto had been confined to recitals in the Six Counties, I hastened to assure her that it was only now that she was beginning to meet the real Ireland. She seemed politely incredulous, but forbore comment save to say how charming the people of the North had been to her. I did not see how it could be otherwise. I began to think that I would like to hear the 'cello concerto that she inspired her husband to write ... we know that a good deal of the brilliant work which has made him famous was done in his cottage in Kenmare, where he spends six months every year. Mrs Moeran has not yet met the County Kerry cottage, but she should find it an ideal holiday home.[8]

This extraordinary piece paints a wholesome, attractive but quite illusory picture of Moeran and Coetmore as a devoted musical couple, whose relationship appears quite natural – inevitable even – and soon to be continued in their (non-existent) holiday and working cottage in Kerry. Nonetheless, this article, together with several other similar pieces, achieved its objective, and the concert at the Capitol Theatre, Dublin on Sunday 25 November was well-attended. While press reviews of the concerto were mixed, Coetmore's playing of it was widely praised. J. O'Neill in the *Irish Independent* wrote:

The composer appreciated that the violoncello is heard to best advantage in broad and flowing melody, and in both the first and second movements the soloist, Peers Coetmore, was given many opportunities to display power, beauty and variety of tone in smooth melodic playing. There is a very fine cadenza at the end of the second movement, well in character, which was excellently played. The last movement has a strong flavour of Irish folksong but is rather jumpy and was the least impressive movement. The work forms a welcome addition to the small list of significant works for 'cello and orchestra.[9]

'P. T.' of the *Irish Press* was concerned that the orchestra did not seem to have been very well rehearsed and felt that the 'Moeran' and 'Irish' elements of the work were, perhaps, too distinct.[10] The music critic of the *Irish Times* averred that the slow movement 'with its quiet dreamy atmosphere ... was one of the loveliest things that have been produced in recent years'.[11]

Moeran's cello concerto has previously been the subject of several technical and formal analyses, and these are in broad agreement about the underlying structures of each of the three movements.[12] However, there are other aspects of the concerto

---

8   *Evening Herald*, (21 November 1945), 4.

9   'First Performance of New Concerto', *Irish Independent*, (26 November 1945), 4.

10   'Moeran's New Concerto', *Irish Press*, (27 November 1945), 5.

11   'First Performance of New Concerto', *Irish Times*, (26 November 1945), 4.

12   See McNeill, 275–284, Self, 187–199, Bruce Polay, *Selected Orchestral Compositions by Ernest John Moeran*, (unpublished DMA Thesis, Arizona State University, 1989), and

that warrant a closer examination. Before the beginning of his relationship with Peers Coetmore, Moeran had almost certainly not considered the composition of a cello concerto. His selection of compositional ideas was necessarily capricious as he reacted to stimuli rather than sought them out, but he would not have envisaged writing for forces with which he had little or no familiarity. As has been shown, as his career progressed Moeran became increasingly commercially minded, and he tended to compose works that he believed would have a good chance of being performed, usually as the result of having certain performers or ensembles in mind. Thus, the existence of the cello concerto is attributable entirely to Coetmore having come into his life. While the offer to compose a concerto was part of Moeran's awkward courtship process, from Coetmore's perspective it was like manna from heaven. Although the repertoire contained several hundred cello concertos composed before 1945, only a few were well-known and frequently performed: Dvořák, Elgar, Schumann, Haydn and Boccherini being the most popular. Cellists were keen to find obscure or forgotten works, or to get new ones composed. The opportunity to have a work composed for and dedicated to her at no expense other than that of a personal relationship was evidently compelling for Coetmore. Moreover, hearing that her friend and rival Raya Garbousova was commissioning a new work was a further impetus.

In comparison with Moeran's other large-scale works, eighteen months is a remarkably short time to complete a similar scale piece, especially in a genre with which he was unfamiliar. However, this is unproblematic to explain. Firstly, Moeran made extensive use of existing models, both formally and musically. The fundamental parameters of the concerto betray indebtedness to the concertos of Dvořák and Elgar (see figure 9).[13] Moeran had realised that the cello would be unable to compete with the orchestra in the way a solo violin could, and he turned this apparent disadvantage to good effect. He deployed symphonic textures for the *tutti* sections and limited the instrumental forces where the soloist was playing, thus simplifying the compositional process. Despite assertions of the restricted nature of the cello concerto repertoire, an exhaustive search of published and manuscript music databases returns more than 500 concertos for the instrument that were composed up to 1945. Of these, just nine are in the key of B minor, and of those, most are by composers who were cellists themselves and were created as exhibition works to showcase their own virtuosity. The principal reason for the small number in B minor is probably the tuning to C_2 of the lowest string of the instrument. Selecting B (minor or major) as the key leads inevitably to the lowest octave lacking its tonic. This in turn means that all melodic structures residing in that register must resolve upwards, and the composer is faced with a self-imposed constraint from the outset. So why did Moeran choose B minor as the principal key for the concerto?

Christopher Pidcock, *An Exploration of the Compositional Idiom of E.J. Moeran with Specific Focus on his Cello Concerto*, (Unpublished M.Mus. Dissertation, University of Sydney, 2010).

[13] For the purposes of this comparison, the second movements of the four-movement concertos have been ignored.

Composer	Cellist	Concerto	Composed	Movements	1 Key	1 TS	2 Key	2 TS	3 Key	3 TS	Other Concertos
Moeran		Cello Concerto in B minor	1947	3	B minor	9/8	B flat major	3/4	B minor	2/4	0
Dvořák		Cello Concerto in B minor	1895	3	B minor	9/8	G major	3/4	B minor	2/4	1
Elgar		Cello Concerto in E minor	1919	4	E minor	9/8	B flat major	3/8	E minor	2/4	0
Vivaldi		Cello Concerto in B minor			B minor	4/4	B minor	4/4	B minor	2/4	27 (at least)
Servais	Y	Cello Concerto in B minor	1834	3	B minor	4/4			B minor	2/4	4 (possibly)
Davydov	Y	Cello Concerto in B minor	1859	3	B minor	4/4	A major	3/4	B minor	6/8	3
Vieuxtemps		Cello Concerto in B minor	1884	3	B minor	4/4			B minor	6/8	1
Tchaikovsky		Cello Concerto in B minor	1893	3	B minor	9/8	G major	3/4	B minor	2/4	0
Popper	Y	Cello Concerto in B minor	1900	4	B minor	3/4	B minor	1/4	B minor	2/4	3
Goltermann	Y	Cello Concerto in B minor	1915	3	B minor	4/4	G major	3/4	B minor	2/4	7

Figure 9. B minor Cello Concerto Table of Comparative Structures.

Firstly, selecting B minor is the best resolution to the register problem in a tonally-based work. By forcing the cello line as high as possible, increased sonic power is available to help overcome the orchestral accompaniment. Secondly, he may have asked Coetmore which keys she preferred. For the cellist, B minor (and its related D major) is straightforward from a technical and fingering perspective, the scales from B_3 and D_3 lying easily under the fingers on the upper three strings. These strings: A, D and G, also lie on the B minor scale and are available to the composer to provide open string tonal contrast with the stopped equivalent notes. Moeran, as a former violinist, would have been able to appreciate this. However, much of this argument could also apply to E minor – the key of the Elgar concerto – with the further advantage of the availability of a fourth string tonic. The main influencing factor was probably that Dvořák's B minor Concerto was the most readily available model, and, perhaps even more significantly, it was in Coetmore's repertoire and she had performed it many times.[14] Moeran would have begun work by listening to the Dvořák concerto, and the key would have imposed itself in his mind. Given the distant key of B flat major for the central movement and its coincidence with the Elgar cello concerto, it is likely that this decision originated with his later becoming familiar with the Elgar work. Moeran usually adopted a linear compositional process, in that he started at the beginning and composed through to the end. He rarely considered later parts of a work before he had established most of the music for what would come before. The second movement dates from late 1944/early 1945, and Moeran's correspondence suggests that towards the end of 1944, he had discovered the Elgar cello concerto through a recording made by cellist Anthony Pini. As far as is known, Coetmore did not add the Elgar concerto to her repertoire until the late 1940s.

Each movement of the concerto exhibits Moeran's expert use of orchestral colour and texture, deployed such that it never overwhelms the soloist. Orchestral *tuttis* break up the more delicate flow of the solo passages, providing a contrast. The only occasions where the soloist is in competition with the full orchestra, it is playing in an upper register where the tone has the intensity to cut through even the orchestral

---

[14] Two examples of the score of the Dvořák cello concerto exist in the Coetmore-Moeran archive in Melbourne and each has been heavily annotated with performance notes.

fortissimo power. The first movement, cast in a modified sonata form,[15] incorporates an example of Moeran's re-use of earlier material: the principal theme of the second subject group recalls the tune of 'Donnycarney', from Moeran's *Seven Poems of James Joyce* (1929). The harmony underpins the tonality suggested by the solo cello melody and eliminates the natural expectation of a modulation to the sub-dominant (music example 52). Since the listener's attention is concentrated on the solo line, the murmuring accompaniment on *sotto voce* strings achieves an almost subliminal effect. Moeran emphasised the lyrical, pastoral impact by adding short flowing descending runs from the flute and then the clarinet. In this case, the actual notes played are less important than the instrumental colour, although the runs heighten the pentatonic force powering the solo line.

In *Lonely Waters*, Lionel Hill asserted that Moeran had told him that the opening second movement was influenced by Beethoven and that he had eventually seen a similarity between the orchestral opening of the movement and that of the slow movement of Beethoven's Ninth Symphony.[16] However, the author is unconvinced of any musical similarity and suggests instead that Moeran's claim of Beethoven influence is more likely to have been his use of lower register note clustering: a defining characteristic of Beethoven's style. Regardless of this, the opening of the second movement performs an adroit but undeniably Sibelius-sounding modulation from the B minor of the first movement to the B flat major of the second. After a short introduction, the solo enters (music example 53).

This is one of Moeran's most sublime themes, and while the opening bears a resemblance to the tune of the *Irish Lament* – which was itself an arrangement of the Irish traditional song '*Jimmy Mó Mhíle Stór*' (or 'Johnny Asthore' as Moeran referred to it) – the harmonisation and development of the theme differentiates it. The movements ends with the only cadenza in the concerto, which leads directly into the Rondo form third movement which begins with a jig-like theme played by the solo with minimal accompaniment. The similarity of this theme to the opening of the third movement of Dvořák's B minor Concerto is clear, and Moeran's debt to Dvořák cannot be denied. However, all music owes a debt to what has gone before, and it would surely be overly pernickety to castigate the entire concerto on the basis that parts of it sound like something else. The author's opinion is that the concerto works particularly well because it was customised to Coetmore's playing: composer and soloist worked on the composition together. She was not the most techncially accomplished cellist of her time – and Moeran knew this – so the concerto is demanding only to the level of her ability. Her tone was more lyrical than powerful – although her higher register playing was commanding – and so Moeran balanced the orchestral forces such that the solo line was always prominent.

---

[15] Moeran had written to Coetmore early in their relationship, 'I hope you don't mind sonata form, in spite of the dicta of our Sibelius, but I was so imbued with it for many years that I find it natural to think that way,' and again a year or so later during the composition of the work: 'I am very deeply immersed again at last in the cello concerto and have reached the end of the expositionary section of the 1st movement.'

[16] Hill, 49–50.

Music example 52. Concerto for Violoncello and Orchestra,
first movement: second subject

Music example 53. Concerto for Violoncello and Orchestra,
second movement: bars 14–23

Given Moeran's self-imposed requirement for a consistent environmental background for his composition, the cello concerto perhaps falls between two stools. Much of the original thinking was done during his enforced stay in Kenmare between April and June 1944. However, after his return at the end of June, he was working either in London or Kington, and it is likely that most – if not all – the music of the concerto was composed in Britain. Thus, while the influences of Irish traditional music are clearly apparent, particularly so in the second and third movements, Moeran did not attempt to assert an Irish identity for the work, in the way that he had done for the violin concerto.

Following the first performance of the concerto, Moeran and Coetmore travelled to Cork, where Coetmore had been invited to give a recital accompanied by pianist Charles Lynch in the Aula Maxima of University College. They played the Prelude for Violoncello and Piano, which the reviewer for the local newspaper described as 'quiet and lyrical and left a most pleasant impression',[17] and Arnold Bax's *Legend-Sonata*. A cello sonata by Beethoven and a series of Chopin piano works completed a programme that was well-appreciated by audience and reviewer alike. Moeran and Coetmore stayed with the Fleischmanns at *Oileán Ruadh* for a few days before Coetmore returned to Dublin for a second performance of the concerto on 14 December. Moeran travelled on to Kenmare, from where he wrote to Coetmore the day after having listened to the concert on the radio:

> Your playing last night was just wonderful. I loved every minute of your performance ... I gather this morning that the whole of Kenmare tuned in to you last night, & they all say what a wonderful wife I have! ... I am staying aloof up at the Lodge & getting on with the symphony.

This letter is the first evidence for several years that Moeran had begun serious work on a second symphony.

1946

Moeran remained in Kenmare over Christmas and New Year, and on 7 January, he wrote again to Coetmore, 'The E flat symphony progresses, but I am a bit stuck over the slow movement, also about the finish of the first ... I have all the material for it & it will be only a matter of time working it out.' However, letters written to Coetmore in January indicate that he had spent most of the Christmas and New Year period carousing and over-indulging with friends in Kenmare.[18] Although he had (yet again) promised Coetmore that he would henceforth refrain from such excesses, she did not believe him, and she wrote a letter in which she suggested that he should not travel to Liverpool in mid-January to attend a series of three Philharmonic concerts featuring the cello concerto, with Coetmore giving the English première, the Symphony in G minor and the Sinfonietta. Moeran was incensed, and he wrote back to her:

---

[17] 'Cork Concert of a Type That Is All Too Rare', *Kerryman*, (8 December 1945), 3.

[18] Kenmare reputedly was home to thirty-six public houses at the time.

I am afraid I have offended you sometimes ... but there are limits in the things you should say to me, e.g. that I should parhaps [sic] not come to Liverpool in case I do not 'behave myself' ... you should not say things like that to me – they hurt.

This long letter included several variations on this theme. Coetmore had apparently also suggested that Moeran seek medical assistance, and, in one of many postscripts, he replied, 'As for your talk about seeing doctors & having a cure, that will surely not arise so long as I carry out my New Year's pledge of going dry?' Coetmore had not realised the extent of Moeran's problems with alcohol until she had discussed it with his doctor Dick Jobson in a series of letters the previous October. Jobson had explained Moeran's condition as best he could – within the constraints of the exaggerated First World War injury details that Moeran had given him – and these letters have subsequently contributed significantly to the hitherto generally accepted portrait of Moeran as a long-term victim of his First World War injuries, with his susceptibility to alcohol being at least partially excused. While Jobson wrote about Moeran as he knew him, his knowledge was based on a constructed reality, although he would have had no reason to doubt the truth of what the composer had told him.[19]

Moeran left Ireland for Liverpool on 17 January. His *Irish Independent* gossip-columnist friend wrote an extended piece:

Jack Moeran, renowned British composer, is leaving Ireland to-day for a week in Liverpool, where the Philharmonic will be giving three concerts of his works. I met him earlier this week in his beloved Kenmare in the throes of creation, working one night right through until six in the morning. In his spacious first floor room at the Lodge – more properly describable as the O'Donnell Castle – he has his own Bechstein, on which his late great friend, Peter Warlock composed his last songs. Welsh composer Peter Warlock was the father of Dublin producer-turned-medical-student, poet and man about town Nigel Heseltine – or 'Michael Walsh' of stage fame. To return to Jack Moeran, he is now working on a great symphony in E flat. As he tramps the hills, he has his notebook with him for the sudden inspiration of a tune or a theme. Thus, a sunset over the McGillicuddy Reeks inspired the last movement in his concerto for cello and orchestra, of which a Radio Éireann Capitol concert gave the world première before Christmas.[20]

Fantasy Quartet for Oboe and Strings

After the Liverpool concerts – during which period Moeran and Coetmore were together – Moeran returned to Ledbury, while Coetmore resumed her concerts and recitals schedule around the country. However, he found himself unable to work. Having begun the second symphony amongst the hills and landscapes of County Kerry, his requirement for place became manifest. As he wrote to Lionel Hill on 10 February:

I started work on a new symphony [when I was in Kenmare], but I see no prospect of going on with it, nor with any composition in the immediate future. I have

---

[19] See McNeill, 245–6.
[20] 'Kenmare Inspiration', *Irish Independent*, (17 January 1946), 4.

nowhere to work. I can't do anything at all in London, and until I can find some pied-a-terre in peace and quiet, I can't compose.[21]

Moeran's time over the next few months was spent travelling between Ledbury and London, occasionally meeting Coetmore and attending performances of his works. Coetmore included the Prelude in a recital in Ledbury on 6 February, Laurance Turner played the violin concerto with the Hallé Orchestra in Bradford on 16 March, the BBC Singers broadcast the *Songs of Springtime* towards the end of March, and the cello concerto received another performance by Coetmore with the BBC Symphony Orchestra under Adrian Boult on 10 April. Three months of performances of Moeran's music culminated on 28 April with a long-awaited concert with Albert Sammons playing the violin concerto with the BBC Symphony Orchestra, again under Adrian Boult. Moeran had also been travelling around the country, spending time in Manchester, Sheffield and Oxford. During this period, he had received and accepted a commission through Douglas Gibson to compose a chamber work featuring the oboe-player Leon Goossens. Since composing a work to commission required concentrated and extended effort in a congenial environment – clearly not to be found in London or Ledbury – Moeran took a room on extended terms at The New Inn in Rockland St Mary – a village to the south-east of Norwich – not far from his parents' former home in Lingfield. Despite it having been more than ten years since he had last frequented the area, it remained familiar to him, and he lost no time in renewing his acquaintance with former neighbours, such as Audrey Alston in nearby Framlingham Earl. He spent May and June based at The New Inn working on what he eventually decided would be an oboe quartet, but he made occasional visits to London. Another letter to Coetmore described his return journey:

> I changed trains at Norwich & reached Brundall exactly at 6.40 – then a half mile walk to the river [Yare]. I couldn't make anyone hear this side to [ferry] me across. However, Tom Trett, a Rockland farmer then appeared on the scene & ... pinched a boat that happened to be nearby ... and we set off ... It was a pleasant walk back over the fields from the ferry.

Another letter mentioned that although The New Inn was not furnished with a piano, Moeran had been given the use of an instrument at a nearby farm. With relatively few distractions, work on the quartet proceeded apace, and at the beginning of July he returned to Ledbury to complete the writing out of the fair copy of the score, which was completed on 8 July. Moeran wrote to Douglas Gibson that night: 'I have been all day on the oboe 4tet & have finished the fair copy this evening.' Later in the month, Moeran spent a couple of days visiting Leon Goossens at his smallholding in Sussex, and composer and soloist went through the work in detail. To Moeran's delight, 'Leon only wanted to alter one phrasing mark in the whole quartet,' as he later wrote to Coetmore.

The genre of the Oboe Quartet is that of the English Phantasy that was originally devised by Walter Willson Cobbett and which Moeran had used in earlier works, such as his two orchestral rhapsodies. For this reason, he called the work *Fantasy*

---

[21] Hill, 57.

Quartet. Like the cello concerto, the composition of the work took much less time than might have been expected, given Moeran's usual highly self-critical working process. This may be attributed principally to his having deployed a formal structure with which he was intimately familiar, effectively acting as a blueprint into which he placed the music. Moreover, the musical material throughout the thirteen or so minutes of the duration of the piece derives from a folksong-like pentatonic theme that is stated in the solo line at the outset (music example 54).

While the string trio oscillating accompaniment is similar to many such functions throughout Moeran's oeuvre – from the String Quartet in A minor to the opening of the Symphony in G minor – the opening of the work establishes a stylistic impression that is soon found to be misleading. The effect is that the listener is challenged with the juxtaposition of Moeran's attempts to inject a modernistic element into a work in which he cannot help reverting to his natural pastoral and lyrical character. The quartet begins in F minor and ends in F major, but in between it progresses through a variety of key signatures. It seems that the composer used the key direction more for visual effect than anything else. An extreme example is a section where the oboe is playing in E minor, the violin and viola are in F minor and the cello key signature is C# minor. As with the Sinfonietta, writers on Moeran hitherto have been split on the success of the *Fantasy Quartet* as a coherent piece. Self suggested that while the quartet is 'an accomplished score … the work as a whole does seem [to be] a stylistic regression',[22] with its reversion to the familiarity of Norfolk folksong. McNeill acknowledged the 'technical mastery of the oboe quartet medium' and Moeran's achievement of 'an extraordinary fullness of sound and a rich variety of textures and effects from [the] strings',[23] but he implied that the contrasting stylistic features of the work did not combine as effectively as he believed they had in the Sinfonietta. Reviewers of the first few performances of the work all concentrated their attention on its lyrical and folksong-inspired aspects and ignored entirely the more stylistically adventurous sections. Moeran himself seems to have had second thoughts about the *Fantasy Quartet* after he had heard the first few performances and was preparing the work for publication. He wrote to Coetmore later in the year:

> I have here the proofs of the oboe quartet. This does on reflection, seem a bit naive and childish. I liked it well enough when I heard it last Saturday, but it certainly does seem to hark back to the idiom of before the Sinfonietta & it is, very likely, not the music of a grown-up person.

The author's opinion is that the *Fantasy Quartet* is successful as an example of its genre, but that the conflicting musical style renders the listening experience unsatisfactory. Nonetheless, the work proved popular, if only due to the relatively limited repertoire, and it was performed and broadcast many times during the two or three years after its publication in 1947.

Moeran spent the remainder of the year living in Ledbury with his brother and mother, but also making frequent visits to London and around the country.

---

[22] Self, 200.
[23] McNeill, 289.

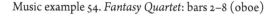

Music example 54. *Fantasy Quartet*: bars 2–8 (oboe)

Tracing his movements is possible to some extent through his letters, and the fact that so many of these were written to Coetmore suggests that they spent little time together. However, Moeran frequently used writing paper printed with the 55 Belsize Lane address, and it is not certain where he was when some letters were written. He returned for a week to Rockland St Mary to write an article on folksong for the *Countrygoer* magazine,[24] lodging with the Chamberlains who had provided him access to their piano while he was living at The New Inn earlier in the year. Towards the end of August, he made a brief visit to Dublin for a concert by the visiting Hallé Orchestra at which his violin concerto was performed by Laurance Turner. Coetmore played the cello concerto at a BBC Promenade Concert on 2 September at the Royal Albert Hall, and a week later, Moeran was at the Three Choirs Festival at the Kemble Theatre in Hereford for a performance of the Sinfonietta. Moeran had been engaged to conduct the work, but at the last minute he withdrew due to illness. At the end of October, he and Coetmore were in Manchester for another performance of the cello concerto. November and December were occupied with, amongst other things, attending concerts at the London Delius Festival, correspondence with Douglas Gibson about the contract for publication of the *Fantasy Quartet* and arrangements for the quartet's first performances.

Despite these perambulations around the country, Moeran must also have been working steadily on the Sonata for Violoncello and Piano. Although the composition of a sonata had been promised – and begun – as early as October 1943, it had been abandoned a few months later in favour of the cello concerto. There is no mention of further progress on the piece in Moeran's correspondence until November 1946, when he wrote to Coetmore from Ledbury, 'I hardly know how to express things to you, but when I was all set to get on with the next movement of the cello sonata your letter of Tuesday came & literally stopped the clock as regards the composition of that work.' Coetmore had written to Moeran and suggested that his behaviour was that of a spoilt child. The exact context of this accusation is unknown but most probably connected with his drinking: Moeran wrote later in the letter about perhaps visiting Mount Melleray Abbey again. However, the letter verifies that Moeran had been working again on the cello sonata for some time, probably since the completion of the *Fantasy Quartet*.

---

[24] E. J. Moeran, 'Folksongs and some Traditional Singers in East Anglia', *Countrygoer*, No. 6 (Autumn 1946).

18

Masterpiece?
(1947–1948)

Moeran spent Christmas with Coetmore in Ledbury, and he remained there over the New Year period after she returned to London. He began the year by writing to her, once again expressing regret for his alcohol-fuelled behaviour and suggesting possible avenues for the 'cure' that Coetmore evidently hoped would be possible. In this, and several later letters, he mentioned either visiting Coetmore in London, or travelling to wherever her recital schedule took her. He spent a few days at 55 Belsize Lane in early February, but the première of the still uncompleted cello sonata had been arranged to be given in Dublin in May, and pressure to complete it was mounting, most especially from Coetmore who needed time to learn the solo part. In a letter to Victor Hely-Hutchinson dated 10 February, Moeran mentioned that he was 'now writing the finale of a new sonata for cello and piano', which he hoped to have 'finished soon – within the next month or so'.[1] He returned to Ledbury at the end of February, having found it impossible to work in the flat. He wrote to Coetmore that he was expecting to have the final movement completed in a few days and that he would then travel back to London so they could 'spend some time together working out it's [sic] interpretation', but he would not let himself be 'rushed and spoil the finale' of the sonata.

Sonata for Violoncello and Piano

The manuscript of the cello sonata bears no completion date, but it may be assumed from Moeran's end of February letter that the work was finished during the first or second week of March. Having delivered the final solo part to Coetmore in London and worked through it with her for a few days, Moeran travelled to Cork via Fishguard and Rosslare on 22 March to stay for a few days with the Fleischmanns, before journeying on to Kenmare to work on the symphony. Coetmore followed him to Ireland at the beginning of May, and the first performance of the sonata – by Coetmore and Charles Lynch – was broadcast by Radio Éireann on 9 May. Moeran and Coetmore were then able to spend a few days together in Dublin before she had to return to London, where she gave the first English performance of the sonata on the BBC Third Programme on 5 June. Moeran 'listened-in' in Kenmare and wrote to her the following day, 'You & Freddie played marvellously. That is all there is to say about it, except that I think F was more sympathetic & satisfactory in the piano

---

[1]   McNeill, 542.

part than Charles.'² It was probably during these few days in Dublin that Moeran was interviewed by Eamonn Andrews for Radio Éireann.

While twenty-five years separate the composition of Moeran's two solo instrumental sonatas, with some eighty-five works coming in between, there is much that links them. The violin sonata is the work of a young composer at the outset of his career – created when the foundations had been laid for a glittering future that was there for the taking – and it embodies the promise of what might have been. The cello sonata represents the culmination of musical recovery from the wreckage of the possibilities that were squandered, but it also distils the vagaries of a meandering stylistic evolution into a bravura finale, which, nonetheless, retains the personality of the violin sonata. Writers on Moeran have commented on the quality of his achievement in the cello sonata.³ Self wrote, 'The Sonata is remarkable for the sustained intensity of its mood and for the perfection of its structural proportions,' while McNeill remarked, 'In the [cello sonata] Moeran links all the various idioms evident in his instrumental music from 1921 to 1947 ... [it] thus sums up his instrumental output ... arguably his best chamber work.' Moeran also regarded it as his best work. In a letter to Coetmore dated 4 February 1948, he was to write:

> I have just spent all yesterday on cello sonata proofs. You know I don't usually boast, but coming back to it, going through it note by note, & looking at it impartially, I honestly think it a masterpiece. I can't think how I ever managed to write it.

It is in the thematic material and the development of it that the similarity with the violin sonata becomes apparent. Consider the first few bars of the first movement solo parts (music example 55). Not only are the melodic shapes similar, but the tension-building function is identical: small intervals are juxtaposed with larger leaps. Moreover, when the piano accompaniment is included, there is the same tonal ambivalence that characterises much of Moeran's oeuvre: in this case, E minor and A minor. The relationship between the sonatas is also apparent both in the similarity of purpose of the second movements and the dynamic shape of the third movements with their extravagant and aggressively confident codas.

As an early work, the violin sonata received numerous performances throughout Moeran's lifetime, becoming part of the standard twentieth-century British violin repertoire until the 1950s. In contrast, after Coetmore's few performances during the two years before she left Britain permanently in early 1949, the cello sonata languished forgotten, until it was revived by a new generation of British cellists fifty years later. Just one contemporary press review of the work has been found. Following a performance in Cheltenham in October 1950, the reviewer wrote:

> A grim and intense work, E. J. Moeran's *Sonata for 'Cello and Piano* ... gave [the performers] scarcely any chance for rest or relaxation throughout its three

---

² Coetmore's accompanist for the broadcast was Frederic Jackson, Professor of Pianoforte at the Royal Academy of Music.

³ See respectively Self 202–216, and McNeill 291–298 for the source of these quotations, and for detailed formal analyses of the sonata.

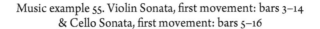

Music example 55. Violin Sonata, first movement: bars 3–14
& Cello Sonata, first movement: bars 5–16

movements, which are unrelieved by any lighter passages to offset its forbidding character. Both players deserved the enthusiasm with which the audience hailed their performance of a by no means easy or straightforward work.[4]

It seems hardly fair to judge the reception of the sonata on a single critical review, particularly one that (in the opinion of the author) so spectacularly missed the point. If the work does, as McNeill put it, 'sum up' Moeran's instrumental oeuvre, perhaps it deserved a more discerning critique. Reviews of recent recordings of the sonata have been better-informed and have considered the work in the context of Moeran's entire oeuvre. The author's opinion is that the cello sonata indeed does represent a culmination of compositional achievement, and it does this by embodying the nebulous characteristics that define a personal creative style within a coherent and aurally satisfying whole. By revisiting – whether consciously or unconsciously – the youthful individuality that produced the violin sonata some twenty-five years earlier and imbuing it with greater maturity, Moeran successfully defined a personal voice that stands apart from his contemporaries. He regarded the cello sonata as his masterpiece, and perhaps that should be the final word on it.

On 12 May, Moeran had written to Coetmore, informing her that he was planning to travel back to Cork the following morning and suggesting that the few days they spent together in Dublin had been enjoyable:

4 'New Sonata by Moeran Performed', *Gloucestershire Echo*, (26 October 1950), 3.

I miss you very much – somehow, I feel things have been different this trip, & I think you & I really did enjoy ourselves together. Anyway, I know I did, & I am afraid I have to confess to you that I am terribly lonely thinking of you & wishing you were here to share this lovely spring with me.

Moeran and Coetmore had been married for nearly two years, during which time they had spent about four months in total in each other's company. Although Moeran had ostensibly moved into Coetmore's flat, he spent most of his time elsewhere. Moreover, even when he was resident in Belsize Lane, Coetmore was often away, and their long and frequent periods of separation place the above quotation into context.[5] While Moeran's words are susceptible to several interpretations, perhaps the most obvious is that neither had really adapted from years of living single, professional lives. It seems unusual indeed that, even after two years of marriage, he should emphasise that he thought that they had enjoyed their time together in Dublin and that things were now somehow different, but the usual conventions of marriage did not apply in the case of the 'Coetmoerans', and it is difficult to form a coherent impression of their life together: when they were together. Fortunately for the Moeran biographer, their unconventional married life provided a singular benefit, in the form of the numerous letters that Moeran wrote while they were apart which have enabled the gaining of a unique perspective.

Moeran wrote several more letters to Coetmore during May and early June in which the subject of their taking a holiday together recurs. This idea was probably initiated by Moeran following the enjoyable time they had spent together in Dublin. Several possibilities were considered, including house-sitting for the Hills in Seer Green, taking a flat in Lewes, or even Moeran remaining in Ireland and Coetmore joining him there for a fortnight. Moeran returned from Ireland in late June, after which he and Coetmore spent a few days at the Cheltenham Festival where the violin concerto was performed by Laurance Turner with the Hallé Orchestra. After this, they travelled to Ledbury, where they stayed for two weeks, both needing to recuperate from health conditions. According to a letter Moeran wrote to Lionel Hill at the beginning of August, Coetmore had injured herself pushing their car, and Moeran had stayed too long out in the Herefordshire sunshine and was recovering from sunstroke. In a letter to Arnold Dowbiggin, Moeran also mentioned a gastric upset. Hill also recorded that following their stay in Ledbury, Moeran and Coetmore – and possibly Coetmore's mother – spent a week in August staying in a 'cottage in Sussex'.[6]

---

5   According to the testimony of Lionel Hill, Hill would occasionally visit Moeran at Belsize Lane: 'I always enjoyed these visits because music was usually discussed or played. Peers was not always there for she had many engagements … so Jack and I used to go out for our meals.' Hill, 62.

6   Hill, 68. The 'cottage' was a substantial property in Piltdown. Nearby was a private school (now closed and re-used), of which it seems Moeran and Coetmore had been given the use during the summer vacation. According to the reminiscences of Peers Coetmore as stated in the Introduction she wrote to Stephen Wild, *E J Moeran*, (Triad Press, London, 1973): 'One of my happiest summers was spent in Sussex where we had the loan of an empty school. Ensconced in the music room Jack worked on the Sinfonietta, whilst I was

At about this time, Moeran had negotiated the use of a studio at a house in Harben Road that belonged to Frederick Jackson, chorus master of the London Philharmonic Choir. The studio was a fifteen-minute walk from the Belsize Lane flat and was intended as a solution to the composer's problems in finding it difficult to work in London. According to Lionel Hill, he visited Moeran there many times during the eighteen-month tenancy. He wrote:

> [The studio] was hidden at the far end of a large garden, access being gained by a pleasant walk along a gravel path flanked by shady trees … Dominating the room was a Bechstein grand piano. On the left a settee stood against the wall under the only window. A pretty brick fireplace took up most of the wall opposite the door, on the hearth of which stood a gas fire. A large glass-fronted bookcase was set against the wall to the left of the chimney breast and was full of Jack's music. Several Indian rugs lay on the parquet floor.[7]

This seemingly idyllic location might be thought to have been the appropriate setting for stimulating Moeran's creativity, and indeed he was able to work on the second symphony there. However, even in 1947, there would have been the background noise of traffic on the nearby Finchley Road. Moreover, the apparent rural nature of the garden was enclosed by tall walls, and when Moeran walked out of the front gate, he was on a street, not in the countryside. According to the reminiscences of Lionel Hill, on 4 September Moeran played the short score of the symphony to him.[8] While Hill was unable to recall how much of the work was played, he remembered that it was not complete. Later in September, Moeran and Coetmore took up the offer to house-sit in Seer Green while the Hills took a family holiday. On their return, Moeran showed Hill the score of the Serenade in G for Orchestra on which he had also been working.

Serenade in G for Orchestra

Since the completion of the cello sonata in March, Moeran's erratic compositional effort had been directed primarily towards his second symphony. During the publication process for the cello concerto, he had become acquainted with Gustave de Mauny of the Novello publishing company, and it seems that de Mauny had suggested the composition of an orchestral suite – in a mood lighter than the Sinfonietta – which was also being published by Novello. Moeran appears to have decided to expand his *Farrago Suite* of 1932 into a larger work. To the original four movements (*Prelude, Minuet, Rondino, Rigadoon*), he added a *Prologue, Air, Galop* and an *Epilogue*. The *Prelude* was renamed *Intermezzo*, the *Rondino* became *Forlana*,

---

able to practise in some remote room without disturbing him and when work was over, we had the swimming pool to ourselves.' While this must be filtered through the prism of Coetmore's unreliable and selective memory – clearly Moeran could not have been working on the Sinfonietta in 1947 – the Piltdown geography accords with both Hill's and Coetmore's testimony, although it is most probable that, since the purpose of the stay was a holiday, neither spent much time working.

7   Hill, 69.

8   Hill, 70–71.

and an eight-movement suite lasting some twenty-three minutes was the result. Having ostensibly begun work on the suite in the summer, it was essentially complete by the end of September, which was unusually quick for Moeran. However, the music of the four original *Farrago Suite* movements remained mostly unchanged, the most significant modifications being the omission of the xylophone part at the end of the *Prelude* (*Intermezzo*) and some dynamic marking changes throughout. Nonetheless, this still implies that Moeran composed four additional movements over a relatively short period.

Amongst Moeran's letters written to Coetmore after she had returned to London following the Dublin première of the cello sonata was one dated, 'By the banks of the Blackwater, 30 May.' Moeran was out for a day's fishing with Patrick Little and his family,[9] and he wrote:

> I have my music paper with me, & have put in a couple of hours composition out here in the sunshine. I can always work out my ideas best when out in the open … I think I have succeeded in writing some quite exceptionally (for me) good music this morning, & I hope to do some more after our picnic lunch … this trip is the birth of 2 more works, apart from the Symphony, one a movement for string orchestra (possibly a la [sic] Barber) & the other a completely mad & wild Scherzo for Orchestra

It is not difficult to identify the 'a la Barber' work as the *Air* from the Serenade and the 'wild Scherzo' as the *Galop*. Thus, with these movements completed during the summer, his work during the two weeks spent in the Hills' house was the composition of the *Prologue* – a task made relatively straightforward by its rondo form – and the *Epilogue*, which was essentially a repeat of the final 'A' section of the *Prologue*. The composition of the new movements was further simplified by re-use of some material previously heard in the violin concerto and the Sinfonietta. Despite these limitations and the fact that the work was composed over more than fifteen years, the movements of the Serenade hold together consistently, and the overall effect is satisfying. The sequence of the melancholy but beautiful *Air*, followed by the mad and frantic *Galop*, immediately contrasting with the sublime *Minuet* is, in the opinion of the author, some of Moeran's most inspired music. The Serenade is also significant in that it is Moeran's last completed major work, but far from progressing the stylistic evolutionary path recently marked by the Sinfonietta and cello sonata, Moeran returned to the world of *Whythorne's Shadow*, which itself had influential roots in Warlock's *Capriol Suite*. Of course, Moeran could not have known that it would be his last major work. While his current project was the composition of a second symphony, it is possible that other ideas were in his head: perhaps a second concerto for Coetmore, or a full-scale piano concerto. However, for the remainder of the year, much of his time was occupied with attending performances of his music, including travelling with Coetmore to a recital in Trowbridge at which she played the Prelude for Violoncello and Piano. Moeran's correspondence with Coetmore had ceased in early June, and there are no surviving letters written to

---

9   Patrick John Little (1884–1963) was, at the time, Minister for Posts and Telegraphs in the government of Taoiseach Éamon de Valera.

her for the rest of the year. This suggests that they spent most of the period July to December together.

Thus, after having been mostly living apart for the first two years of their marriage, circumstances seem to have led to a closer relationship over these six months. This was due partly to Coetmore's injury having led to her cancelling or postponing some of her concert and recital schedule and perhaps partly to the greater pleasure they found in each other's company, about which Moeran had remarked in his 12 May letter. It may even have been that their activities together served to dampen Moeran's propensity to over-indulgence in alcohol and to limit his opportunities so to do. They had taken two holidays, lived together for a while at the Belsize Lane flat, visited Moeran's mother and brother in Ledbury, and each had accompanied the other to professional engagements. It seems as if a marriage of sorts was finally developing. However, set against this are the observations of Lionel Hill. While these must be considered in the context of his unconditional fondness for the man and composer, by this time Hill probably knew Moeran better than anybody, and his testimony provides an astute insight into the reality of the Moeran-Coetmore relationship. According to Hill, the 'Coetmoerans' visited Seer Green on 19 October. After describing the conversation Coetmore had with Hill's wife about the physical aspect of their relationship,[10] Hill wrote:

> We had already sensed that things were not quite as they should have been between [Moeran and Coetmore]. For some time, we had felt that they behaved more like brother and sister, accentuated by Peers' tom-boyish and forthright manner. Jack's was a reserved nature, and he seldom showed his feelings, but even so Betty and I were intuitively sure that the marriage was a curious one, and not helped by constant separation due to Peers' playing engagements at home and abroad. Jack was very much a lone spirit yet restless in his habits, but I still think that if he and Peers could have settled down in the country there might have been more happiness for both of them, and a greater likelihood of regular composition from Jack.[11]

Hill perceived the basis of the problem. Moeran's and Coetmore's professional lives were incompatible with a 1940s conventional marriage and their personalities were poles apart, but his proposed solution – that they settle down somewhere in the country – only addressed Moeran's side of the problem. His assumption was that Coetmore should adopt the role of dutiful wife, supporting and looking after her creative husband and, if necessary, abandoning her own aspirations. While this was undoubtedly the lot of countless career-minded women of that period when they married, it was not a future that Coetmore would have accepted. The foundations of Moeran's and Coetmore's adult personalities may be deduced from what is known about their respective growing-up years, and this reinforces Hill's assessment of the 'curious' nature of the marriage. Nonetheless, it is possible to read into the six months from July to December a definite effort by both to build a form of compatibility, and each would have had a compelling motive for so doing. For Moeran, it

10 See pp. 264–5.
11 Hill, 73–4.

was that stabilising his life and emotional state was essential to his ability to compose. For Coetmore, it was that the professional advantages from having an eminent and respected composer-husband remained significant.

Moeran featured twice in BBC radio programmes towards the end of the year. In late October, he had spent a few days travelling around East Anglia with the producer Maurice Brown, resulting in a feature broadcast on the BBC Third Programme called *East Anglia Sings*. The *Radio Times* published a short article: 'Maurice Brown, BBC Features Producer, and E. J. Moeran, composer, musician and noted collector of folksongs, made an interesting journey recently into North-East Anglia [sic] to capture at first hand some of the many folk songs that can be heard in the villages.'[12] The programme presented recordings of songs made in the public houses of Norfolk and Suffolk, interspersed with conversation between the presenters. On 13 December, Moeran was the focus of a programme in the Contemporary British Composers series, again broadcast on the BBC Third Programme. It included Coetmore performing the cello sonata and Parry Jones singing *Invitation in Autumn* and the *Six Poems by Seumas O'Sullivan*.

Moeran and Coetmore spent Christmas in Ledbury with Moeran's mother and brother, visiting Bristol on Boxing Day so that Coetmore could examine and test a possible replacement instrument. The next day, she returned to London, but Moeran stayed on for a few days in Ledbury to catch up on correspondence. After the success of his programme on East Anglian folk songs, the BBC had asked him to recommend other parts of the country where similar recordings could be made, and Moeran had suggested Co. Kerry, perhaps stretching somewhat the definition of 'other parts of the country'. However, the BBC had agreed, and Moeran hastily arranged a visit to Ireland, crossing by ferry from Fishguard to Rosslare on New Year's Eve. Moreover, W. W. Thompson of the BBC had asked Moeran for a work for the 1948 season of Promenade Concerts and the Serenade in G for Orchestra seemed to be appropriate, if a little long. Moeran replied on 29 December:

> I know you like to fix things up early &, in any case, I shall be back some time in February or early March. In the meantime, I am hanging on to my score [of the Serenade] as I might want to touch it up 'here & there' when I am working in the peace & quiet of my room in Kenmare &, as I told you, if you want it for the Prom season, I shall not in the meantime show it to anyone else.[13]

1948

Aside from the BBC commission to collect and document County Kerry folksongs for the proposed feature programme, Moeran's intention in Ireland was to make solid progress on the composition of the symphony, and this can be followed through the content of the letters he wrote both to Coetmore and to others. His first letter to Coetmore was dated 14 January, and while it made no mention of compos-

---

12 'Folk Songs are not Dead', *Radio Times*, Vol. 97, No. 1257, (14 November 1947), 9.
13 McNeill, 555.

ing work – being entirely concerned with practical matters – the tone is that of his letters from the first few months of the previous year and is liberally scattered with phrases such as 'My darling' and 'all my love'. His next letter, dated 17 January, was similar in content but suggested that he would be unable to continue writing such long letters as he was 'getting really Symphonic minded'. Unfortunately, he could not compose that day, because he needed to get ready for his being presented to Éamon de Valera, who was making an election visit to Kenmare. A few days later, Moeran wrote again mentioning their summer holiday: 'When we were in Sussex together, we lived such a happy life of work & country walks in the evenings. Can't you possibly come here ... & let us walk the Kerry mountains together.'

At the beginning of February, Moeran was asked by John Lowe of the BBC concerts department whether he had any new works that would be suitable for scheduling in forthcoming concerts. Moeran replied, apologising for not having anything available and mentioning that his recently completed Serenade had been promised for the forthcoming season of Promenade Concerts and that the symphony that was currently in progress was a commission by the Hallé Orchestra.[14] About this time, Coetmore had written about the possibility of going to Cape Town for an extended period. She had determined that there would be ample opportunity for teaching and concert and recital work for her and that there was a music lecturing post at the university becoming available in February 1949, which she thought might suit Moeran. The terms of the position included three months' annual leave, which she suggested he could devote to composition. This was the first of several such initiatives by Coetmore over the next two years, and it provides a possible clue to understanding her approach to and intentions for their marriage. It was suggested earlier that Coetmore's motivations for embarking on a relationship with Moeran had been partly professional and partly psychological, but it may also have been that she had at first seen his family as a more attractive alternative to her own. Coetmore's mother was in poor health, both physically and psychologically, and her sister Sheila was not sympathetic with Coetmore's ambitions as a musician, perhaps understandably since Sheila undertook the main responsibility for looking after their mother. From their first meeting, Moeran's parents had made it abundantly clear how much they liked Coetmore. Ada Esther Moeran wrote to her:

> I would like you to know this, that I quite fell in love with you myself, the very first evening you were here! And when I watched you & Jack together, I could not help wishing that you might be drawn nearer together. My hope & prayer will be that after due deliberation you may both feel that you will do well to spend your lives together. I hope that in the future we shall see a great deal more of each other.

However, following this initial declaration of affection, it is possible that Coetmore gradually felt smothered by Moeran's mother's attention. After the announcement of the engagement, Ada Esther had written, 'I must tell you how very pleased & thankful I am to get Jack's good news – & to think that I am really to have a daughter of my own.' While Moeran's mother's devotion to Coetmore

---

[14] This letter is the only documentation to suggest that the second symphony was a commissioned work.

remained steadfast until the end of her life – there are other letters with similar sentiments expressed – it may have been that this was not reciprocated, or rather it was reciprocated with Moeran's mother, but not with his brother, in whose house Ada Esther Moeran now lived. By suggesting that she and Moeran leave Britain for South Africa, Coetmore may have been thinking of putting considerable distance not only between him and his drinking companions, but also between both of them and his family. Moeran had been financially dependent on his mother for much of his working life, and this had left him with a profound sense of obligation to her, which Coetmore may have seen as excessive. Perhaps she believed that if he could no longer return regularly to his mother's house, such ties would be severed, or even transferred to Coetmore herself.

Moeran's reply reveals that he was torn between wanting to support her in her career ambitions and not wishing to compromise his own. He implied that taking a job as a teacher – while this may prove interesting in itself – would necessarily mean giving up being a composer. Her suggestion of spending a few months each year composing could not work for him. He explained that the Hallé orchestra symphony would be completed by the end of the year and that the first performances would be in the spring of 1949. He also mentioned the publication process for the violin and cello concertos which he foresaw would entail his having to take time to correct the engraved proofs, again during the spring of 1949. He wrote:

> I am very sorry on your account, because I was really wondering whether we could not have afforded to live in S. Africa (Cape Town) without my taking such a full-time job, & you could have had your 20 cellists & parhaps [sic] formed a 4tet. But you see, my dear, Feb 1949 is literally impossible for me owing to my commitments here.

Coetmore's reaction to this cannot be deduced from Moeran's subsequent letters, other than that the South Africa proposal was shelved, at least for the time being. In a sequence that runs from 10 February to 19 April, the principal topic of their correspondence concerns a possible recital tour for Coetmore in Ireland during early April, followed by her taking an extended holiday with Moeran in Kenmare. There are occasional glimpses of progress on the symphony: 'I do so much want to make the most of my time here on the symphony' (10 February), 'I did a very good morning's work to-day' (12 February), 'I am at the moment in a state almost amounting to stupor [sic] at the point I have reached in the Symphony. It may be imperfect in its present form, but … it is rather luscious & spring-like – or so I hope it will sound' (8 March), 'New E Flat Symphony going strong' (11 March: letter to Hill), 'This Symphony is a devil of a job … the question of form and construction is causing me some trouble, as I am arriving at a single-movement work' (18 March: letter to Hill) and, finally, 'the Symphony is going fairly well' (19 April). For whatever reason, Coetmore's recital tour did not take place, although she did travel to Cork at the end of March, and she and Moeran spent a weekend with the Fleischmanns and then went to Kenmare for a short holiday.

While in Ireland, Moeran had resumed his occasional bouts of heavy drinking, after each of which he was profoundly apologetic. His regrets and assurances of non-repetition and declarations of love became increasingly wretched. On 10 March he had written somewhat enigmatically:

> I do feel in my solitudes & lonelinesses here that I am being drawn closer & closer to you in my thoughts for you, & it is my daily & nightly wish that even now, if I am spared & kept in health, I might be such that I could feel that I had not let you down. It might even happen here if I can keep my health. You know what I am talking about & I know how much I have hurt you. I did not mean to do it & it was selfish of me because I loved you, (& still do & could never still my love & adoration for you, which I try to put into notes & staves) but I did not parhaps [sic] realize you were young & ardent & I was hopelessly middle-aged. But still I cannot help in my queer way going on loving you, & always will.

and on 19 April:

> I shall not be able to write much to you these next few days, as I fell in the woods behind the Lodge & damaged my right wrist again. Now, my darling, I did not do this by having too many drinks. Actually, I am completely 'on the dry' as I promised you I would be when I got here. Please trust me. You have all my love, if you are willing to accept it.

Nonetheless, in between his drinking sessions, he was able to work on both the symphony and the final score of the Serenade which it had been arranged would be performed at a Promenade Concert on 2 September. It is not clear how much of the BBC commission to research folk songs in Ireland Moeran had been able to undertake. While there is no record of a follow-up programme to *East Anglia Sings* having been broadcast or made, later in the year, Moeran contributed an article to the *Journal of the English Folk Dance and Song Society* based on the experiences of recording the sessions for *East Anglia Sings* and, in a footnote at the end, the editor wrote:

> Note. – It is hoped that in a later number of the Journal, Mr Moeran will tell of his travels in Eire and contribute some of the songs he collected there – particularly those peculiar to the calling of the tinkers, among whom, and in their tents he lived in the spring of 1948.[15]

This suggests that Moeran had informed the editor that he had spent time living with the Irish traveller[16] community at that time located in Kerry. While the editorial comment implies that Moeran spent an extended period with the travellers, the dates and locations of his letters render it problematic to see how this could have been true. As with many of the unsubstantiated claims of activity by Moeran the origins of which can only have been the composer himself, it is probable that a minor event has subsequently been exaggerated into one of more significance. It is likely that Moeran came across and befriended members of the traveller community during his years in Ireland. It is known that they stayed in and around Cahirciveen

---

[15] E. J. Moeran, 'Some Folk Singing of Today', *Journal of the English Folk Dance and Song Society*, Vol.5, No.3, (December 1948), 152–154.

[16] Use of the word 'Tinker' to refer to Irish Travellers is now regarded as pejorative.

– which Moeran knew well through his visits to Valentia Island – and they were active at the Killorglin Puck's Fair, which, again, Moeran had visited. Regardless of whether the putative *Ireland Sings* programme was ever made, the existence of Moeran's set of arrangements *Songs from County Kerry* verifies that he found and collected local folk songs, at least one of which, 'The Tinker's Daughter', was an Irish traveller song.[17]

Moeran journeyed back to London in late July to find that the studio in Harben Road had been let to another tenant from September, and so what passed for a composing retreat in London would shortly no longer be available. He called on Lionel Hill for assistance in locating alternative working accommodation within reasonable travelling distance of the Belsize Lane flat. Together, they explored around the Chiltern Hills north-west of London, looking at several possibilities, but none was suitable. Examined objectively, the plan to find a working studio outside London made little sense, other than as a placation for Coetmore. Perhaps having vetoed her suggestion for their emigration to South Africa, Moeran had felt obliged to try to accommodate her working requirements as far as possible. However, living with Coetmore at Belsize Lane and commuting regularly to whatever country retreat he eventually found was hardly practical, and if he had decided to live in the place, it may as well have been anywhere.

Coetmore seems not to have understood Moeran's working needs. She perhaps believed that since composing clearly required nothing more than a pen, manuscript paper and a quiet desk to sit at – and, perhaps, a piano – surely Moeran would be able to find these anywhere. While it is evident that he had attempted to make his environmental needs known to her, she may have simply dismissed them as idiosyncrasies and assumed that he could manage without them if necessary. During the next few months, she continued to raise the subject of her going abroad as the next step in her career. Her engagement calendar had been getting less busy over the previous year or so, and her perception was that in the post-war re-thinking of art music in Britain, local musicians were being passed over in favour of foreign talent. Whether this was true or not is less important than the fact that Coetmore believed it to be true, and her solution was to relocate herself to where she thought that she would be better appreciated. With so many instrumentalists and composers flocking to London from both Commonwealth and foreign countries, possibly Coetmore imagined that there would be more opportunities in the locations from which they had come. The effect on Moeran of this pressure from Coetmore was to deepen his depressive state. Trying to resolve the seemingly unresolvable problems, first, of finding a way to live with Coetmore but also provide himself with a suitable working environment, and second, to reconcile her career ambitions with his own

---

[17] There is considerable blending between music labelled 'Irish Traveller Music' and other forms of traditional Irish music. Apart from twentieth-century influences, a recent study which shows that the Irish Traveller community became a distinct Irish sub-population during the seventeenth and eighteenth centuries would probably account for this. See Gilbert, E. *et al.* 'Genomic insights into the population structure and history of the Irish Travellers', *Sci. Rep.* 7, 42187; doi: https://doi.org/10.1038/srep42187 (2017) (accessed 8 October 2020). It is noted that Irish Travellers are not related to European and British Romani, although the word 'Gypsy' is commonly applied to Romani and Traveller alike.

composing needs was driving him to despair. Lionel Hill perceived Moeran's problems but could do little to help, other than provide moral support and a welcoming refuge when needed. He wrote:

> There is no doubt that things were now becoming desperate … Jack found himself in a cleft stick. He was married to someone who found relations with him difficult, and who for several reasons was not in a position to make a proper home for him … Jack had always been used to complete freedom … Every note of his music had been inspired by contact with Nature, and without that stimulus he was a lost spirit.[18]

Again, these observations must be considered in the contexts of Hill's devotion to Moeran and his somewhat traditionalist view on the status of the wife in a marriage. However, while his assessment was precise, there was clearly no easy answer to Moeran's (and Coetmore's) problems. Unfortunately, as had been the case on previous occasions, and, with nobody in London to turn to for help or support, Moeran sought refuge in pint beer glasses and whisky bottles. The Serenade in G for Orchestra had its first performance at a Promenade Concert given by the London Symphony Orchestra conducted by Basil Cameron on 2 September, and according to a letter that composer Christopher Le Fleming wrote to Rhoderick McNeill in 1981, Moeran arrived at the final rehearsal for the concert intoxicated. He spent the rehearsal and concert asleep in the artists' room, 'waking just in time to take his bow at the end of the performance'.[19] A profile published at the time in the *Irish Independent* asserted that Moeran was 'torn between rival musical loyalties … he likes to put in several hours a day practising – but he also likes writing about musicians.'[20] A practical instance of his 'writing about musicians' had been an invitation by composer and BBC music producer Humphrey Searle to contribute a programme to a series called *Musical Curiosities* to be broadcast on the BBC Third Programme on 8 September. Searle wrote in his memoirs about the series:

> The Third Programme was becoming somewhat solemn and esoteric – one Planner is reputed to have deleted Brahms' 4th Symphony from a proposed programme as being a 'repertory work' – so I thought I might brighten it up by introducing some programmes of absurd or comic music.[21]

Searle recalled that Moeran had written 'an excellent script' for the half-hour programme, which included a song, *Forget me not*, by his former Eynsford cottage housemate Hal Collins and excerpts from the oratorio *Ruth* by George Tolhurst.[22] However, Searle continued:

---

18 Hill, 93–94.

19 McNeill, 307.

20 'London Letter', *Irish Independent*, (2 September 1948), 4.

21 Humphrey Searle, *Quadrille with a Raven – The Memoirs of Humphrey Searle*, published online at http://www.musicweb-international.com/searle/titlepg.htm, accessed 1 November 2020.

22 George Tolhurst (1827–1877), born in Kent but resident in Melbourne, Australia between 1852 and 1866. *Ruth* was unkindly dubbed the worst oratorio composed. See Sarah Kirby,

In these programmes the authors of the scripts usually read their own texts. I had a date to meet Jack Moeran at the George shortly before the preliminary rehearsal and was alarmed to be told by Constant [Lambert] that Jack was in another pub down the road 'three sheets in the wind'. The rehearsal was at 2[pm], and the programme was due to go out live at 6pm, so I thought we would have four hours to sober him up. I hadn't reckoned, however, that he would be carrying a flask in his hip pocket. To let him go on the air in that state would have been disastrous. Fortunately, we managed to lose his spectacles temporarily, and the continuity announcer read the script.[23]

Moeran's movements between the evening of 8 September, when he would have left Broadcasting House in London and 25 October, when he wrote a letter to Coetmore from Mount Melleray Abbey in County Waterford, are difficult to determine. The only evidence is the content of the 25 October letter and that of a second letter written a few days later. What emerges is that Moeran had been drinking heavily, and he had decided – or been persuaded – to try the regime at Mount Melleray, which claimed some success in the 'drying out' of alcoholics.[24] Although the timeline of the events described in Moeran's letter is difficult to discern, it seems likely that after the *Musical Curiosities* debacle, Moeran spent the remainder of September on his own at the Belsize Lane flat – Coetmore was away on a recitals tour of Yorkshire – and went out drinking with his London friends. When his wife returned at the beginning of October, it would have been to find him in a sorry state. She lacked both understanding of and sympathy for the causes of Moeran's over-indulgences, and it is likely that she reacted in a way unlikely to have improved matters. Whether she told him to leave or that he left of his own accord is unknown, but he returned to Ledbury, where it is probable that his welcome was also somewhat restrained. Treatment for his drinking problem may have been discussed, with the result that he decided to travel to Ireland and put himself in the hands of the monks at Mount Melleray. Before his departure, Coetmore telephoned to inform him flatly that she would be leaving soon for an extended concert tour overseas – probably to South Africa or Australia and New Zealand – that she had arranged despite his unwillingness (or inability) to accompany her. She also told Moeran that his friend, the composer Herbert Murrill, had been diagnosed with terminal cancer.[25] Moeran's own words provide the best description of his actions and state of mind and health following these emotional upsets:

"'The Worst Oratorio Ever!'": Colonialist Condescension in the Critical Reception of George Tolhurst's *Ruth* (1864)', *Nineteenth-Century Music Review*, (May 2017), 1–29.

[23] Searle, Chapter 10 'BBC Bedlam'. Moeran's *Musical Curiosities* script now resides in the *Humphrey Searle Collection*, Add.MS 71829 f.23, British Library, London.

[24] Moeran had previously suggested a visit to Mount Melleray in response to Coetmore's agitation about his drinking some two years earlier. See p. 276.

[25] Herbert Murrill (1909–1952) was married to Coetmore's cellist friend Vera Canning, for whom he composed his Second Cello Concerto. Murrill lived with his cancer diagnosis for several years, eventually succumbing in 1952 at the age of forty-three.

I have been very ill otherwise apart from the liquor question but originally induced by it ... The news you gave me about Herbert Murrill had the effect of knocking me on the head as if with a crowbar & I did what I should not have done otherwise, I took a lot of drink on the journey. Coming so soon after the shocks of the previous week when I was barely over that awful binge I could not face up to things ... when I got to Ireland I was not in my really right mind & I decided to wait till the Monday before coming up here & went to Fermoy near here where I have friends [the author and poet Niall O'Leary Curtis] ... the result of all this was a complete nervous breakdown, partial loss of memory, absolute insomnia day & night & other symptoms of a mental nature ... that several times I went to the river when it was in flood with the idea of going in and ending things ... I have been to a doctor as I felt I was going off my head ... it is just a pity you sprung that bombshell on me over the phone at that particular time when I was just after a series of upheavals & shocks otherwise. Don't think for a moment I blame you in the least.

This quotation is only a small part of Moeran's rambling 25 October letter, which ends with him complaining how cold it was with snow falling but that the monks were not intending to run any heating in the abbey. Even allowing for exaggeration, Moeran's physical and mental condition sounds alarming in the extreme, most especially his admission to thoughts of 'ending things' in the river, and it must be considered how a conventionally loving and concerned wife would probably react on reading such a letter from her husband. Moeran wrote a more optimistic letter on 29 October, and it is possible that Coetmore read both of Moeran's letters on the same day. In the second letter, he wrote, 'I hope & really trust that after what has happened here at Mt. Milleray [sic] I may go through life for the future as a normal person so as not to cause so much anxiety.' Despite not having any religious convictions, he also wrote that he had 'taken a vow before the altar never to touch spirits again except medicinally'.

While Coetmore's intention to go abroad for an extended period undoubtedly contributed much to Moeran's apparent breakdown, it is interesting that he emphasised in the letter that he did not blame her. It is noticeable, however, that Moeran's greeting at the head of the letter, 'My dear Peers', was significantly different from the tenderer 'My darling Peers' that had been his custom for several years. This more formal phrase was maintained for several more letters, together with the non-committal sign-off 'Love Jack', which also contrasts with more demonstrative variations on 'All my love Jack', that had been more usual up to that point. While it is important not to read too much into words sometimes written in haste, a seeming change of emotional declaration must signify some change in Moeran himself. It is noteworthy that he did not resume the intimate form of address in letters to Coetmore until several months later.

In his 29 October letter, Moeran wrote that he planned to return to Ledbury the next week. After discussion with his mother and brother, he decided to consult a specialist in the treatment of alcohol-related conditions, who was based in Cheltenham. Accompanied by his mother, he visited Dr Hazlett for an initial examination. Following this, Moeran wrote to Coetmore to explain that Hazlett had taken him on as a patient. He had recommended that Moeran should take lodgings near to his surgery so that he was available locally for an extended course of treatment. In a sequence of letters to Coetmore written between 22 November and 30 November, Moeran provided more details of the treatment, and he asserted that after having undergone this he would be in a fit state to look confidently towards the future:

> I must set myself to try & get permanently right & with the settled habit of righter living & at the same time not to be idle. As I should not be able to be with you in London yet awhile, if ever at all in London, it is right for you to make this trip, although I hate you going so far away & I staying behind. But we must look to the future & hope that I shall become such that we can be together again always whether it is in some other country or here.

While Moeran had evidently accepted the inevitability of Coetmore's intentions, his use of the word 'trip' – and that of 'tour' in an earlier letter – indicates his expectation that she would be returning. Indeed, an overseas concert tour of many months' duration may well have been Coetmore's original plan. In the late 1940s, most journeys to the southern hemisphere were undertaken by ship, intercontinental air travel being still uncommon and expensive. Since travelling to South Africa or Australia would have involved a four to eight week voyage – with a similar time commitment at the end of the tour – it would not have been worth doing for anything less than a stay of at least three months. Thus, the minimum duration of Coetmore's absence was likely to have been between six and nine months, and this is probably the 'bombshell' to which Moeran referred in his 25 October letter from Mount Melleray Abbey. Nonetheless, by the end of November, Moeran had apparently reconciled himself to the extended separation, perhaps reassured by the prospect that his forthcoming treatment by Dr Hazlett would turn him into a new man ready for Coetmore's return later in the year. The couple spent some time together at Belsize Lane in early December. In a letter to Percy Grainger written from there on 13 December, Moeran said that he and Coetmore would be spending Christmas together with her family in Devon and that after her departure for Australia in January, he would be moving to a flat in Cheltenham where he would be receiving treatment for 'arthritis in the knee joints'.[26]

As the year ended, the future of the 'Coetmoerans' appears to have been in the balance. Coetmore was determined to pursue her career as a cellist by taking opportunities abroad, albeit hoping to persuade Moeran eventually to join her. Moeran was similarly determined to put an end to his alcohol excesses and to prove himself to be a fit and reliable partner. However, part of Coetmore's rationale for embarking on a relationship with Moeran – and marrying him – had been his career-promoting value to her both as a composer and as a facilitator in British and Irish music circles. Five years later, although he had composed two major works for her, there appeared to be little prospect of any more concertos or sonatas in the foreseeable future, and Moeran's increasingly embarrassing alcohol-fuelled behaviour was reducing his

---

[26] The original of this letter is in the Grainger Museum at the University of Melbourne. A copy in the Barry Marsh Collection was made available to the author by Rachel Marsh. It is interesting to note what Moeran claimed as the condition for which he would be treated.

usefulness as a contact in the music establishment. She probably realised that unless there was some intervention, this situation could only deteriorate. Whether or not it was true that Coetmore was finding it more difficult to secure engagements than she had before and during the war,[27] it was certainly convenient for her as a reason for going abroad, and her strategy (or perhaps gamble) was that if she could entice Moeran either to go with her or to follow her later, he would – as suggested earlier – be removed both from social drinking temptations and the suffocating bosom of his close family. All he would have in the new environment would be Coetmore, and she could exploit this to encourage him to be the composer-husband she believed that she had married. Coetmore clearly found some of his behaviour to be unacceptable but had this been a deal-breaker regarding their relationship and marriage, she could simply have left him and decamped to the southern hemisphere without any suggestion that he come with her. It is probable, therefore, that Coetmore really did love Moeran – or at the very least had come to love him in her own way – and that she did not intend to leave him permanently. Thus, she may have seen getting him away from Britain (and Ireland) as the only chance of their relationship surviving.

Determining Moeran's interest in keeping the marriage going is unproblematic. Apart from the endless declarations of love and statements of missing her that he included in his letters, his mother's devotion to Coetmore was such that he could never have contemplated the possible effect on her of informing her that his marriage was over. Coetmore was also providing the status that being married to a person of some significance in his professional world conferred. Thus, the assurance in his 25 October letter that he did not blame her for his mental and physical health problems, despite her springing on him that she was going to leave him for an extended period to travel around the world giving concerts, has a convincing rationale.

[27] Evidence from Moeran's letters during late 1948 appears to contradict this assertion. For example, in a letter to Lionel Hill dated 25 August 1948, Moeran wrote, 'Peers is on an Arts Council tour in Yorkshire and I hear that she is having great success and they want her to go again.' Hill, 93.

19

'No More Partings'
(1949–1950)

O n 14 January, Coetmore embarked for her planned concert and recital tour of Australia and New Zealand. She and Moeran had spent a month or so together over Christmas and New Year, partly at Belsize Lane, partly in Devon with members of Coetmore's family and partly in Ledbury. According to a letter Moeran wrote to Percy Grainger dated 3 March, much of December and early January was spent dealing with the acquisition and occupation of lodgings in Cheltenham and selling Coetmore's Belsize Lane flat, with the attendant requirements to relocate its contents to storage or to Moeran's new lodgings.[1] The fact that Coetmore had decided to sell the flat is significant, given that she had let it during her previous extended absence between December 1943 and September 1944. Although not conclusive, her action supports the assertion that she had no intention of returning for some considerable time. Equally significant is the equanimity with which Moeran seems to have accepted the fact of the sale of the flat. He clearly regarded it as a positive move, perhaps in that when Coetmore eventually returned, the two of them would then be able to find a home together that would accommodate each of their working needs. He had never settled into Coetmore's flat, and during the years of their marriage – except for July to December 1947 – he had stayed there only for infrequent short periods.

Songs from County Kerry

By the beginning of February, Coetmore's liner was approaching Port Said in Egypt, and Moeran was settled in his lodgings at Park House West in Cheltenham. He wrote to Herbert Murrill at the BBC, 'thanks to good doctoring here, my insomnia & other disabilities have been disappearing and I am able to work much harder.'[2] It seems that Dr Hazlett's treatment regime was proving efficacious. Moeran also mentioned a collection of settings of *Songs from County Kerry*: the culmination of his folksong collecting trip in Ireland the previous year. However, when the set of songs was published in 1950, Moeran included a Composer's Note:

---

[1] The original of this letter is in the Grainger Museum at the University of Melbourne. A copy in the Barry Marsh Collection was made available to the author by Rachel Marsh.

[2] McNeill, 584. It is interesting that the principal reason for Moeran's treatment was presumably included as 'other disabilities'.

These arrangements are taken from a much larger collection I noted in Co. Kerry at odd times during a period roughly between 1934 and 1948. They were sung to me by Kerrymen in Cahirciveen, Sneem and Kenmare. The verse by verse variants in some of the tunes are exactly as I heard them from the singers themselves on a number of occasions.[3]

While none of Moeran's writings dating from prior to 1948 mention working on County Kerry folksong arrangements, if Moeran is taken at his word it is possible that some of the arrangements date from as early as the 1930s. Thus, accounting for the apparently sudden appearance of a collection of seven songs in early 1949 becomes less problematic. The Swiss soprano Sophie Wyss had sung three of the *Songs from County Kerry* arrangements, including 'The Lost Lover' and 'The Roving Dingle Boy', during a series of recitals in several venues in Britain and Ireland under the auspices of CEMA during the early part of 1948. Moreover, in a letter to Coetmore dated 7 February, Moeran wrote that Wyss had 'sung "The Roving Dingle Boy" all over Australia & elsewhere with success'. This evidence indicates that at least these two song arrangements must have been composed considerably earlier than January 1949.

More problematic is the identification of the sources of the texts and melodies of each song. Searches of folksong databases have revealed variants – of both tunes and lyrics – with origins all over the British Isles, but none with the exact words and melodies in Moeran's arrangements. In the article that Moeran had published in the December 1948 edition of the *Journal of the English Folk Dance and Song Society*,[4] he had written:

> In my recent researches on the sea-coast of SW Ireland, I have come across songs that seem to be more prevalent in England among the East Norfolk people near the port of Great Yarmouth … The Yarmouth trawlers used to fish frequently in Irish waters. In bad weather, the crews would go ashore and meet the local people in the back kitchens of Cahirciveen. Then they would spend a convivial evening singing songs and telling stories.[5]

The article continued with Moeran presenting some examples of songs that had both English and Irish versions, such as 'O Father, Father, build me a boat' and 'The Raggle Taggle Gypsies'. Given the former geographical remoteness of County Kerry, it is probable that some of the songs that Moeran collected represent evolution in isolation of songs brought from elsewhere through cross-fertilisation with locally created songs in a purely oral process. Nevertheless, a consideration of some of the texts raises doubts about the genuineness of Moeran's blanket claim to have collected all this material from 'Kerrymen in Cahirciveen, Sneem and Kenmare'. The lyrics of the first song in the set, titled 'The Dawning of the Day', are more characteristic of a poem than a folksong text. The first verse runs:

---

3   E. J. Moeran, 'Composer's Note', *Songs from County Kerry – Collected & Arranged for Voice & Pianoforte by E. J. Moeran*, (Augener, London, 1950).

4   See p. 287, note 15.

5   Moeran, (1948), 153–154.

In winter's gloom and dreary blast, I must retract my flight,
Through mountain roads, through snow and frost, all alone in the dark of night,
Thought or news, no time to lose, I cannot long delay,
I must be there each morning fair, by the dawning of the day.

The melody is a derivation of the tune of the song 'Skibbereen', which recalls the aftermath of the Irish famine in the village of Skibbereen in County Cork. 'Skibbereen' was published by Herbert Hughes in his 1915 collection *Irish Country Songs*, and it is possible that Moeran knew it. Extensive searches of British and Irish poetry databases have not located a poem with the text of 'The Dawning of the Day', but the mention in the final verse of 'Sweet Derreen, Oh lovely vale, Oh noblest seat on earth,' suggests that the text was written by a poet local to the Kenmare area. It is not possible to determine how and by whom the text and the tune were combined into a song, other than by Moeran himself. The arrangement – which incorporates some word painting – accompanies the sense of the text without overwhelming the delicacy of the tune. Being entirely distinct from the emotive force of the original 'Skibbereen' words, the setting of the somewhat florid and elaborate poem depicts an evocative representation of the Kenmare Bay landscape (music example 56).

The second song, 'My Love Passed Me By', is an arrangement of a variant of 'Going to Mass Last Sunday', which is itself a variant of the English (probably Norfolk) folksong 'Loving Hannah'. It is likely that this song is another example of exporting folksong by means of the trawlermen, although it is not known whether the Irish or the Norfolk version is the original. Moeran's arrangement includes just three of the many verses that form the original songs. The accompaniment is simple for the first two verses and first part of the third, comprising mainly quaver parallel sixth oscillatory figures. In the second part of the third verse, the accompaniment changes to a more chordal texture, with the song terminating with a *pianissimo* enigmatic superimposition of a G major triad on a D minor seventh chord (music example 57).

'The Murder of Father Hanratty' evidently had three different titles before Moeran settled on his final choice. The manuscript copy (not in Moeran's hand) in the E. J. Moeran Collection at the Southbank Library of the University of Melbourne bears the title 'The Death of Father Hegarty', but the final line of the song has the original words 'Father Hermity' struck out. 'The Murder of Father Hanratty' (originally titled 'The Sorrowful Lamentation on the Most Awful Murder of the Revd. Father Hanratty') was a Broadside ballad published in several variants during the nineteenth century. Original examples are held in several libraries, including Cambridge University Library and the Bodleian Library in Oxford. The modification of the title suggests that Moeran originally heard a variant ('Father Hegarty' or 'Hermity') in Ireland and corrected it after he examined an original broadsheet example in Cambridge in March 1950. The origin of the melody is unknown.

The fourth song in the set, 'The Roving Dingle Boy', poses some interesting questions. No other evidence of a song with this title has been found anywhere, and it is likely to be a highly localised variant of the well-known 'The Roving Galway Boy'. Both are probably variants of the English folksong 'The Handsome Cabin Boy', the text of which originated as a Broadside ballad in the nineteenth century. However, the traditional tune of 'The Roving Galway Boy' (music example 58) bears

Music example 56. *Songs from County Kerry*, 'The Dawning of the Day': bars 1–10

Music Example 57. *Songs from County Kerry*, 'My Love Has Passed Me By': final 5 bars

no resemblance to that used by Moeran in his arrangement, and no similar melody has been found in any folksong database.[6]

The opinion of the author is that the tune of 'The Roving Dingle Boy' was composed by Moeran himself. The arrangement sets four verses of the many that comprise 'The Roving Galway Boy' variant. The accompaniment of the first two comprises flowing arpeggiated figures across the two hands. The arrangement of the

6   If any reader is familiar with this tune, the author would be interested to hear from them.

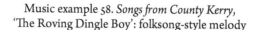

Music example 58. *Songs from County Kerry,*
'The Roving Dingle Boy': folksong-style melody

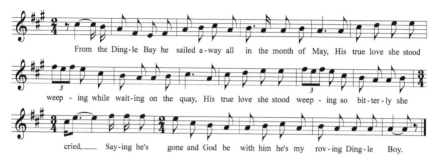

third verse, which begins 'Now he'd gone away past six months clear when a letter he sent home', provides a contrast reflecting the questioning emotional tone of the text. The fourth verse accompaniment is harmonically richer, with a rhythmic complexity that provides a fitting vehicle to carry the moralistic nature of the text. 'The Roving Dingle Boy' is the strongest and most satisfying of the seven songs, which, if the suspicion about the origin of the tune is correct, is probably due to it being an original song by Moeran rather than a folksong arrangement.

The text of 'The Lost Lover' seems to be a variant on the traditional Irish song *'Tiochfaidh an Samhradh is fásfaidh an féár'*, ('The summer is coming and the grass will grow'), variants of which have been collected across Ireland.[7] Many variations of the tune exist, but none has been found that exactly matches that of Moeran's version. The texture of the arrangement increases in harmonic and rhythmic intensity across the three verses of the setting, culminating in an arresting D flat/D natural collision at the climactic point (music example 59).

The text and tune of the sixth song, 'The Tinker's Daughter', have not been found in any folksong database. It is probable that this song was collected by Moeran during his time visiting the Irish traveller community in and around Cahirciveen the previous year, and that he is the only folksong collector to have recorded it. The references in the text to Kilgarvan and Kenmare would support its specific locality, and the pseudo-Romani amphigoric refrain 'With my gumshilla, an a goushilla, an me gashilla like a Leary' convincingly link it to the traveller community. Similarly, the melody is probably an authentic Irish traveller song. In Moeran's arrangement, the accompaniment is sparse, frequently acting more as musical punctuation than functional harmony. The mood of the text is highlighted by extensive use of stacked fourths and false relations at the key climactic points. The style of the arrangement

---

[7]   One researcher has suggested that the text originated in the English Broadside Ballad 'The Croppy Boy'. See 'Glimpses into the 19th Century Broadside Ballad Trade: No. 11: The Croppy Boy', https://www.mustrad.org.uk/articles/bbals_11.htm (accessed 12 October 2020).

Music example 59. *Songs from County Kerry*, 'The Lost Lover': bars 25–29

recalls some of Moeran's earlier folksong arrangements, such as 'The Pressgang', *High Germany* and 'A Seaman's Life'.

Like 'The Tinker's Daughter', no source for the tune and text of 'Kitty I Am in Love with You' has been discovered, although the local reference to Mount Brandon again probably ties the song to the Kerry Irish traveller community. The mood resembles 'The Tinker's Daughter' although the sense of the text is different. The blatant sexual connotations in the middle verse: 'I have a foot for a stocking and I have a leg for a shoe | I have a kiss for the ladies and maybe some other thing too', are typical of folk verse and may well not have escaped Moeran's notice. The musical style of the accompaniment is similar to that of 'The Tinker's Daughter', and it supports the text well, although in performance the manic patter-song-like solo line requires precise diction to deliver convincingly.

Commentary on the *Songs from County Kerry* has observed that while the set is stylistically consistent, it poses problems in performance in that not all the songs are equally suitable for either a male or a female singer. The perspective of 'The Lost Lover' is that of a girl pining for her boyfriend, while the texts of 'My Love Passed Me By' and 'Kitty I Am in Love with You' are expressed from a male point of view. Moeran's reasoning for deciding to gather these songs into a collection in early 1949 is not known, but given the apparent success of the Sophie Wyss performances and interest from the Irish singer Robert Irwin, he may have perceived an opportunity, and he wrote in his 4 February letter to Herbert Murrill, 'I … have just had a most enthusiastic letter from [Robert Irwin] in which he suggests he should broadcast the whole set [of County Kerry songs] at a later date as the [BBC] 3rd Programme people have asked him for some Irish songs.'[8] Moeran's efforts to have the set published can be followed in letters he wrote to Coetmore during the next few weeks, culminating on 23 April with his being able to write, 'Augener's have accepted my new Irish song-cycle.'

Some detail of Moeran's life in Cheltenham can be traced through the letters that he wrote during his stay at Park House West. He mentioned to Coetmore

8   McNeill, 584.

the possibility of his visiting her in Australia or New Zealand for a time: 'I wonder whether there may be some way of my getting out to Australia later on in some capacity or other.' While he realised there would be practical and personal difficulties, he seemed very positive about the prospect:

> What you say about New Zealand, & Wellington in particular, makes my mouth water. Darling, the only thing that makes me hesitate about coming later & eventually to settle there with you is the older generation. My Mother has been so good to me for many years past & she has this dread of my going astray & never seeing her again.

The letters also show that Moeran continued to work on his E flat symphony and on other compositions. Apart from the *Songs from County Kerry*, he created choral arrangements of *The Jolly Carter* and *The Sailor and Young Nancy* at the request of T. B. Lawrence, conductor of the Fleet Street Choir, with whom Moeran had had a close association since their concert performance of *Phyllida and Corydon* in 1940.

Candlemas Eve

In a letter to Coetmore dated 25 May, Moeran wrote that, as he was 'stuck with the Symphony', he was working on a madrigal. This was the same letter in which he mentioning describing his profession as a 'Madrigalist' if he was ever arrested by the police (see Chapter 13). The madrigal was *Candlemas Eve* and was dedicated to the Cheltenham Male Voice Choir. However, it does not compare well with Moeran's earlier madrigal-style compositions, such as *Phyllida and Corydon*. Having been composed for a male voice choir, Moeran overlooked the necessity for clear and well-separated vocal lines, especially in the two bass parts. Moreover, the upper tenor part reaches a top B flat, which is beyond the comfortable range of most singers in amateur choirs, although it may be that the Cheltenham Choir tenors could sing that high. The work was published in 1950, but the author has found no record of any performance.

Moeran was also interested in the possibility of composing some film music. In mid-May he wrote to Coetmore, 'There is a proposition that I write the film music for a production of one of the Somerville-Ross stories. I shall know next week. The fee suggested is £500.'[9] This would have provided Moeran relatively quickly with a substantial sum, which he proposed he could spend on a passage to visit Coetmore in Australia. He wrote, 'I met a man from Bank House at the British Council party on Wednesday & he said that if I wanted to go to Australia any time he could fix me a passage either by liner or cargo boat at very short notice.'[10] Moeran wrote about the possibility of the film work in letters during the following two weeks, after which it

---

[9] Equivalent of about £3,750 in 2020. Somerville and Ross were an Anglo-Irish writing team, best known for their series of three books chronicling the adventures and misadventures of an Irish R[esident] M[agistrate]. Moeran provided no information about on which Somerville and Ross story the film was to be based.

[10] Moeran's ability – which has been mentioned before – to develop advantageous acquaintanceships very quickly was a characteristic that served him well throughout his life.

disappeared from his correspondence. Assuming that the contract opportunity was genuine, it is possible that Moeran's well-known aversion to working to deadline eventually deterred the film company from proceeding.

String Quartet in E flat

In a letter to Coetmore dated 31 May, Moeran mentioned that he was 'hung up with the [second] Symphony' and that he was 'seriously considering [Coetmore's] idea of trying to concoct another quartet.' The use of the word 'concoct' suggests that he wanted to create a new work without the necessity to compose it all from scratch. The circumstances of the discovery of the manuscript and eventual publication of the String Quartet in E flat were presented in Chapter 7, where it was suggested that the two-movement quartet was a composite work, with the first movement dating from 1918 and the second – together with a short linking passage – having been composed later. For this to have been true, it must also be true that Moeran had retained the manuscript of what became the first movement for more than thirty years. While Moeran's tendency to lose or deliberately destroy manuscripts renders it unlikely that a work composed in Ireland in 1918 would have survived, it has been shown that a few of Moeran's early manuscripts did escape his periodic self-censoring; it is also possible that some of his early compositions remained in the keeping of his mother. Thus, having either recently rediscovered or recalled the existence of the E flat string quartet movement, Moeran may have decided to expand it into a larger, multi-movement quartet. The reason for the dating evidence vandalism then becomes apparent, with Moeran having intended to represent the work as coherent and recently composed.

It was shown in Chapter 7 that the first movement is consistent with the composing style of Moeran's late juvenile period, being cast in a straightforward unmodified sonata form, and it lacks the structural and harmonic sophistication that underpinned the music composed after 1920. In contrast, the published second movement is an English Phantasy – a genre employed by Moeran in several works over his mature career – and it exhibits the formal and harmonic ingenuity that pervades his oeuvre. However, there is no other evidence to suggest when it was composed, and it could be a string quartet movement dating from any time during the previous twenty years. The most probable 'concocting' scenario is that these two existing movements were coupled with a new seven-bar linking passage (music example 60). The final movement then begins with a statement of its principal theme in D major, played by the first violin. The other three instruments provide an accompaniment, the flowing lines of which combine to produce an interesting and satisfying harmonic effect. The theme itself comprises a sequence of five two-bar sub-phrases (music example 61).

Elements of this theme resemble other tunes. For example, the first four bars are reminiscent of such songs as 'Loch Lomond', 'The Minstrel Boy' and 'Shenandoah', and this endows the theme with both Scottish ballad and Irish song characteristics. Features of folksong are identifiable: a sequence of rising phrases each of which reaches a higher top note than the previous one; the use of an imperfect cadence to conclude the first melodic phrase, followed by modulation first to the relative minor and then to the sub-dominant, and the inclusion of idiomatic motifs, such

Music example 60. String Quartet in E flat: 7-bar link passage

Music example 61. String Quartet in E flat, second movement: first subject

as the triple reiteration of the tonic at the end of the theme. It will also be noticed that the viola motif in the seven-bar link portends the final two bars of the theme. Moreover, by stating it clearly and with increasing emphasis at the start, this motif is established as a recognisable marker that subsequently punctuates the sections of the movement. The structure follows the principle of Cobbett's English Phantasy form in that it comprises a series of clearly defined sections which vary in tempo and rhythm. Following an *andante* section based on the theme above, the tempo changes to *vivace* for a two-subject fugue in E minor, the exposition of which comprises entries in turn on cello, viola and violin two (music example 62).

The first violin enters with a contrasting eight-bar Dorian mode subject derived from the theme of the *andante* section. The fugue is followed by an *allegretto* section in E major based on a modified version of the opening *andante* theme. This section functions as a conventional development which merges into a recapitulation of the second part of the opening section with the original key raised by a perfect fourth. The movement ends with an extended coda incorporating elements from each of the preceding sections, beginning with a restatement of the *andante* melody harmonised modally (Dorian). This harmonisation, together with the instrumentation – the melody is played on the viola – imbues an impression of a wistfulness that

Music example 62. String Quartet in E flat, second movement:
fugue section (beginning)

provides a starting point for an increasingly energetic and frenetic tumble towards the end of the movement. The publication of the work as the String Quartet in E flat was largely due to it having been discovered amongst Moeran's papers as apparently complete. Nevertheless, it fails as a coherent quartet due to the difference in musical style between the two main movements and the lack of a consistent central movement. On the other hand, as a 'concoction' it has interest, as it has ensured that an early example of Moeran's composing style has survived.

Moeran's principal task was the completion of the E flat symphony. The originally planned first performance in the spring of 1949 had clearly become impractical, and Moeran suggested to Sir John Barbirolli that the Cheltenham Festival in the summer of 1950 would be possible. Even with that performance, Moeran would have had to finish the composition by the end of 1949 at the latest. On 5 May he wrote to Coetmore, 'you asked me what my views were about coming out there later on … I can't stir until after the Cheltenham Festival of next year with my new symphony.' A few days later, he wrote, 'I am sorry to say I am by no means satisfied with my E flat symphony, well on towards the finish … I fear it may have to be scrapped *in toto*.' It had been nearly two years since Moeran had played through a short score version of part of the symphony to Lionel Hill in his Harben Road studio, and he was now contemplating abandoning all the work he had thus far completed. The next day he wrote again to Coetmore, 'I am still worried about my symphony … I may have to put it aside & start again with entirely different material.' However, a few days later – after a short trip to London – he was able to write, 'After my little change of air I feel happier about finishing the E flat symphony.' Unfortunately, his optimism was short-lived. On 31 May, he wrote that he was 'hung up' with the symphony, and by mid-June had decided that it was a hopeless case. In a long letter to Coetmore he wrote:

> This Symphony which I started perpetrating in Eire & which I have been working on here simply will not stand ... there are only 3 alternatives, one is to tear up & abandon the E flat Symphony & the other is to go to Ireland & complete it, & the 3rd is to write something else.

The letter was a rambling outpouring of conflicting emotions, ranging from optimism about the possibility of travelling to New Zealand or Australia to see Coetmore, to the despair occasioned partly by his belief that the symphony was a failure, partly by his deteriorating financial position,[11] and partly by his continuing to miss Coetmore. He concluded the final postscript of his letter with the inadvertently portentous phrase, 'surely ... we can't be separated for ever.' A month later, after receiving a series of letters from Coetmore extolling the distinctions of life in New Zealand and Australia and encouraging Moeran to consider seriously the idea of his travelling there to join her, his optimism returned, to an extent. On 26 July (their fourth wedding anniversary), he wrote, 'I am determined to get the Symphony written and produced at Cheltenham ... I had a good morning on it here, having written 30 odd bars before lunch.' He mentioned that he had been asked to compose works both for the planned Festival of Britain and for the Norwich Festival: both in 1951. On the basis that he needed to remain in Britain until after the 1950 Cheltenham Festival performance of the E flat symphony, he suggested that Coetmore return home for engagements in the autumn of that year, after which they would both travel to Australia to 'do my lectures or broadcasts there, at the same time see the lie of the land for a possible permanent home for the future', and then return to Britain in mid-1951 for the Festival of Britain and the Norwich Festival, prior to their emigrating together.

The tenor of Moeran's wedding anniversary letter strongly supports the assertion made earlier – that Coetmore was urging him to consider coming to Australia to be with her – but with her letters to him having been destroyed it is impossible to be certain. In writings hitherto about Moeran, it has generally been suggested that Coetmore deserted Moeran for a better life in Australia. However, the only evidence quoted to support this has been anecdotal, deriving solely from the undoubtedly biased testimony of Moeran's family and friends. In a letter to Colin Scott-Sutherland, William Graham Moeran wrote:

> As you know he married Peers Coetmore the cellist ... she caused him great unhappiness. Eighteen months before his death she left him and went to Australia. She has since married again and lives in Melbourne. She is a woman for whom her profession comes first, and her home seems to play second place.[12]

This, together with similar statements from others, has served to place Coetmore squarely in the frame of blame, not only for the supposed end of the marriage, but

---

[11]   His full board Park House West lodgings were luxurious and expensive.

[12]   Letter from William Graham Moeran to Colin Scott-Sutherland, dated 24 August 1962; quoted in Talbot (2009), 8.

also for contributing to Moeran's decline and eventual death. In the absence of Coetmore's direct testimony, it is problematic to contest this conclusion with primary evidence. Nonetheless, as has been suggested, had her intention been to leave Moeran, it is unlikely that she would have maintained such close contact with him and particularly unlikely that she would have so encouraged him to think about how he could come to Australasia to join her. Her reasoning may have been that if she had managed to separate Moeran from the stale routine in which she perhaps perceived him to be, it would invigorate his personal and creative lives to the benefit of both their marriage and his ability to compose new music for her.[13] If this speculation is correct, then Moeran's elaborate scheme to accommodate his composing plans, her professional career and their future lives together must have been heartening for Coetmore. In each of Moeran's letters written during his time in Cheltenham, he included declarations of love for Coetmore and how much he missed her. He even wrote about their unsatisfactory physical relationship, acknowledging that this was his fault but expressing a hope that this could be better in the future:

> I think that, with all my failings, & I know I have failed very badly, you do still love me, otherwise you wouldn't have written as you did. Dr H[azlett] tells me that, with his treatment I should be able to love you more as a husband than in the past. Wouldn't it be splendid if this were to happen? ... it would be lovely to come out, & you & I be the dear companions (& now that I am better, perhaps lovers) that we always planned.

In the meanwhile, Moeran was trying to find an alternative place to live. He could no longer afford the expense of the Park House West flat and had enquired about lodgings in the village of Painswick in Gloucestershire, which is where his friend the composer Charles Wilfred Orr lived. On 2 August, he wrote to Coetmore, reporting that his visit to Painswick had been fruitless but that he still had hopes of finding somewhere. He mentioned that after the performance of his Serenade in G for Orchestra at the Promenade Concert on 12 August, he would be staying a few nights 'with some people I have got to know in Wimbledon'. He wrote that he planned to attend the Hereford Festival at the beginning of September, and after that he would be spending ten days with his mother and brother on holiday at Overstrand in Norfolk.

---

[13] The testimony of third-party observers of the 'Coetmoerans' both supports and contests these conclusions. For example, Sheila Varley (Coetmore's sister) wrote two letters to Lionel Hill in 1984 with her memories: 'Peers didn't know about alcoholism ... the only hope was to have no drink in the house and no drinking parties ... she was horrified at the reality before she went to Australia and went off saying she would make a home for him if he was cured. After the honeymoon she threw one of her usual parties and of course started him off on a bout ... We always had a feeling that he didn't really want to get married.' Pauline Jobson (wife of Dr Dick Jobson) wrote to Hill in 1980: 'Peers swore she knew nothing about [Moeran's] drinking habit before their marriage. Pat Ryan [clarinettist in the Hallé Orchestra and Moeran's friend] said she must have known; all the musical world knew, and Peers moved with these people. But she was quite determined to marry Jack to promote her position as a musician.' Hill, 154 & 114.

The sequence of events during the next few months is far from clear, but what is certain is that Moeran suffered a major mental breakdown shortly after he wrote his 2 August letter. Although the Serenade in G for Orchestra had been programmed for the Royal Albert Hall Promenade Concert on 12 August, none of the newspaper reviews of the concert mentions it – although they mention all the other works – and it is probable that it was not performed. Moeran had written to the BBC on 20 July, indicating his intention to attend the morning rehearsal of the Serenade. Thus, had he not been informed beforehand, he would have arrived at the Royal Albert Hall at 10am on the day of the concert to find that – due to time constraints – his work had been dropped from the programme.[14] Moeran's reaction to his music being removed from a programme on the day of the concert has previously been observed when his *Fanfare for Red Army Day* was dropped in February 1944 – he spent the rest of the day drinking – and it is possible that this was again his course of action. Whether he then went to stay with his new friends in Wimbledon is not known, but a few days later, he was back in Cheltenham. William Graham Moeran wrote to Coetmore to explain that he had travelled to Cheltenham on 16 August to accompany Moeran to a cricket match, and he found him in the company of a man called Gordon (surname not known), who seemed to be a close friend. During the next two weeks, Moeran was in regular contact with both his brother and mother but had apparently been away from Cheltenham for a few days, possibly in Cardiff. On 30 August, he sent a telegram to his mother to the effect that he would be coming back to Ledbury the following day, but, according to William Graham, he did not arrive.

A few days later, William Graham drove over to Moeran's flat in Cheltenham to discover that he had disappeared and was in arrears with his rent. By the end of September, Moeran had not returned, and William Graham was obliged to go back to Cheltenham to clear the flat, which had been let to other tenants on the assumption that Moeran had left permanently. William Graham was able to meet Gordon again and found that Moeran had been staying with him until a few days earlier but that he had left Cheltenham without leaving a forwarding address. William Graham wrote in his letter to Coetmore:

> [Gordon] said that Jack was pretty bad at first, especially at night when he was noisy, but was much better during the latter part of his stay. He had suggested getting in a doctor, but Jack wouldn't hear of it, nor would he make up his mind to return to his flat. He told him that he missed his wife terribly and that it was no use his trying to get on with his composition … Jack seems to have spent his days lolling about in the mornings, going for a walk in the afternoons, and going out in the evenings with Gordon to a pub.[15]

---

[14] The original programme was inordinately extended – even for the norms of BBC Promenade Concerts in the 1940s – comprising two Beethoven symphonies (No. 1 and No. 8), Beethoven's Piano Concerto No. 2 in B flat and the London premiere of William Alwyn's Oboe Concerto, in addition to the Moeran Serenade. Since Moeran's piece came at the end of the programme and required none of the engaged soloists, it was probably considered to be the most expendable.

[15] McNeill, 312.

The identity of 'Gordon' is likely to remain a mystery. According to William Graham, Moeran had been living with him for several weeks. While the possibility that he was a sexual partner must be considered, he may have been simply a temporary drinking companion that Moeran had met casually. While Moeran's movements during October and November are unknown, he returned to Ledbury in mid-December. His next letter to Coetmore was dated 22 December, and he mentioned only hints about his life during the previous three months. He wrote:

> As you know, things went wrong in Cheltenham & remained so for a very long time both there, Cardiff & London. I may say that after the initial bout of drinking, Gloucester Perry started the trouble, I got hold of a doctor in London who put me on to Paraldehyde to make me sleep. This did infinite harm as I took to taking too much of it, not knowing the danger. I am temporarily under Dr Groves, who when one gets to know him turns out to be much more up-to-date, sympathetic & sound than I formerly thought him. There is a brand new treatment for my complaint about which I will tell you when my hand permits me to write more. You know how sorry I am if I caused you anxiety, but I did not mean to do it. Your very unhappy Jack.

There are several factors, in addition to the stress he was already under concerning the E flat symphony, that would have contributed to Moeran's breakdown: 1) his reaction to the removal of the Serenade in G for Orchestra from the Promenade Concert programme, 2) his meeting with 'Gordon' and 3) his eviction from his Park House West lodgings. An additional consideration may be found in the reminiscences of Lionel Hill. In *Lonely Waters*, Hill wrote only very briefly about the period under consideration. It is apparent that something had taken place – perhaps financial concerns with his building business – that necessitated Hill selling his house in Seer Green and relocating his family to London. He devoted just a short paragraph to this: 'Shortly after this concert [Pierre Fournier and Francis Poulenc recital at Jordan's Village Music Club] my family was engaged in a major upheaval. For several reasons we decided to sell "Woodfield" and move to London and on September 16th we left Bucks for ever.'[16] While Hill not going into any detail about his possible business problems is understandable, it may have been that these distracted him for a period. Consequently, he may have lost sight of Moeran at perhaps exactly the time that his friend needed his support most urgently. Again, this is speculation, but Hill's later mention of having met Moeran in London during this time and of having lent him £10 suggests that Hill must have had some awareness that all was not well with his friend.[17]

Moeran's state of physical and mental health had reached a parlous state, and – whatever the degree to which this had been self-inflicted – one can only sympathise with him. Hill had been precise in his earlier analysis of Moeran having been driven further and further into a cleft stick, with the options for resolving his problems becoming more and more limited. Coetmore's solution that he could follow her to Australasia may objectively have been his best prospect, and he was evidently

[16] Hill, 99.

[17] Hill, 100.

enthusiastic about this, but doing so immediately – or even in the short term – was quite impractical, given his commitments. Unfortunately, it was exactly these commitments that were placing the greatest strain on his mind. Thus, he was in a vicious circle where the mechanisms for resolving his problems were themselves partly the cause. Having been blessed (or cursed) with a strong intellect, he would not have been able to prevent himself from continually running things through in his mind, desperately trying to find a course of action that resolved everything. His inevitable failure to do so, and the lack of anybody that understood his situation and to whom he could turn for support, adequately explains the desperation that drove him to drown his problems in Gloucester Perry.[18] It is to his great credit that he eventually found the physical and mental strength again to consult the doctors that he mentioned in the letter to Coetmore.[19]

1950

Moeran spent Christmas and New Year in Ledbury, gradually recovering in the company of his mother and brother. In early January, he received a letter from Coetmore together with a Christmas present of a pullover that she had knitted for him and a studio portrait of her with her cello. She was naturally concerned about Moeran's behaviour, and she listed in her letter the aspects of his life which she believed could be improved. Although her letter is not extant, Moeran's reply – dated around 14 January – contains sufficient detail to determine the essence of its content. She had asked him to consider the effect drinking had on his ability to work and his productivity. Moeran replied the same day in a long letter:

> I need hardly tell you that the questions you enumerated are very constantly present in my mind but, without anyone with whom to discuss such things, there are some things which make difficult answering, e.g. how many more works would I have written if I had kept off the booze? My own opinion is that, as it is, I have written too many & would gladly scrap a lot that is in print, in fact practically all up to 1937, barring a few of the songs & the string quartet.

Coetmore had also suggested that his behaviour was selfish. His somewhat irritated response was:

> Selfishness is hardly the word when you wait to consider. Just stop & realize all that I missed or looked-forward-to far happier events which didn't happen, Hereford Festival, Norfolk holiday with sea-bathing, a week's invitation to friends in Rye, not to mention the agony of mind & consciousness of a temporarily warped & changed mentality & personality which actually do occur during a bout in lucid moments. I can assure you that if you knew the periods of extreme misery & mental & physical exhaustion suffered during such a period of what is really a kind of mania caused by alcoholic poisoning, selfishness is the last word

[18] A strong variety of pear cider.

[19] Although a letter written by Moeran's mother to Coetmore dated 17 November 1949 makes it clear that Moeran faced immense family pressure to undergo urgent treatment. See Hill, 147.

to be employed in that 'Self' suffers hell far worse beyond compare with any other injuries, illnesses or wounds ever experienced, & I have had a share.

This detailed, if rambling, account of the effects of Moeran's excessive drinking provides a vivid and distressing image, Coetmore's reaction to which can only be imagined. However, her accusation of selfishness pertained to his drinking – which caused all the unpleasantness he so graphically described – and it may reasonably be argued that, since the indulgences were his choice, she had some justification. Hitherto in writings about Moeran, there has been debate about whether the composer was an alcoholic. Considered in overview, Moeran's periodic overindulging was more consistent with his having been unable to control his occasional drinking than his suffering from an alcohol dependency. Moeran never exhibited the classic symptoms of alcoholism. The remainder of Moeran's letter was devoted to an explanation of the new treatment, supervised by his local doctor in Ledbury, Dr Groves. Moeran would be undergoing chemical aversion therapy by taking a recently developed drug that in combination with alcohol induced unpleasant physical symptoms.[20] His next few letters track the course of this treatment, which was also being tested by Dr Groves on himself, and it appears initially to have been successful. Moeran wrote on 29 January:

> I hope you will be glad to know that last evening (Saturday) Dr Groves & I had another drop of Scotch, one medium-sized measure each, in order to verify the effects of the tablets after a daily 1/2 gram over a week or so, & the effect this time was almost immediate with both of us. We both agreed we couldn't have faced another drink ... now the thing to do is to persevere. To that end he has procured for me a large supply of tablets.

Moeran also wrote about his plans for the immediate future, addressing particularly the problem of completing the composition of the E flat symphony. He had been making enquiries about possible lodgings in Ireland – he mentioned Dalkey as a possibility – where it would be 'quiet for work & be on the sea & at the foot of the mountains & the air is good & invigorating'. He added that he had not 'actually committed any more [of the symphony] to paper', but he had 'spent a fair amount of time in thought over it'. He asserted that he needed the Irish environment for the completion of the work, even if it was not Kerry, to which Coetmore was averse given the temptations presented by his drinking companions there. Moreover, he had negotiated more time, with the first performance of the symphony having been further postponed until the Festival of Britain in 1951. Interestingly, Moeran included a direct quotation from Coetmore's letter: 'you say "A clearer future will then have to be planned – As soon as you feel then able to make up your mind I shall know better what to do."' While this could be interpreted in several ways, these

---

[20] The drug was Disulfiram, which had been developed as tetraethylthiuram disulfide in the nineteenth century for the rubber 'vulcanisation' process. It was noticed that the rubber factory workers who were exposed to the chemical had negative reactions to alcohol, and in the mid-1940s the chemical began to be produced as a drug useful for alcohol aversion therapy. It remains in use today. Moeran and his doctor would have been some of the first patients in Britain to try the treatment.

are not the words of a wife who does not care about her husband and has abandoned him, although a trace of running short of patience may be detected. Moeran's response was to assure her again about the effectiveness of his treatment and his determination to persist with it until the induced aversion became permanent.

During the last week of January, Moeran went to stay with the Hills in their new house in Brondesbury, and he and Lionel Hill attended a performance of the Sinfonietta conducted by Beecham at the Royal Albert Hall. Hill related an anecdote in which at the end of the performance Sir Thomas Beecham located Moeran in the audience and applauded him personally.[21] Shortly after returning to Ledbury, Moeran crossed from Liverpool to Dun Laoghaire and took lodgings in Dublin at 125 Lower Baggott Street. He remained there for three weeks, catching up with acquaintances and examining various possibilities for a long-term property rental. Having rejected Dalkey and neighbouring locations, he found through a friend that there was a room available in a remote country cottage at Coolagad, near Delgany, some seventeen miles south of Dublin. He spent a day visiting the area and the cottage and, as he wrote to Coetmore, found that it was 'ideal' with 'the house full of books & culture – nobody in it all day from breakfast till dinner except the housekeeper or maid who will give me lunch & tea … essentially a place for anyone who wants to work in peace'. The cottage was owned by one Sheila O'Mahoney, who was the sister of Pope O'Mahoney, with whom Moeran was well acquainted.[22]

By 25 February Moeran was back in Ledbury, where he found a letter from Coetmore that included several questions about the future. Moeran wrote back at considerable length, mentioning that he had been fielding several enquiries about engagements for her in Britain, restating his need to remain there until the performance of the symphony and asserting that his much reduced drinking was saving him considerable money. He also wrote about the beneficial effect his new lodgings would have on his work: 'My 3 weeks in Eire seems to have done me great mental good, as I now see what was wrong with [the symphony] & I feel sure that in the lovely air, congenial home and beautiful scenery of Delgany, I shall forge right ahead.' The letter also contained more detail about possible plans for their future together, including possible visits to Britain and Ireland: 'how lovely if you were to come back & for a month or so we were to take a furnished cottage in Co. Wicklow,' and reiterating Moeran's preference for New Zealand over Australia.

At the beginning of March, he spent a day in Cambridge consulting a resource in the University Library concerning one of the *Songs from County Kerry* and visiting his friend Patrick Hadley. He stayed for the weekend with the Hills in Brondesbury. In between returning to Ledbury from London and departing again for Ireland, he wrote a further letter to Coetmore, packed with news about his activities, musical experiences in London and his plans and in no way whatsoever giving any hint or sense of dejection or depression. His letters from these

---

21 See Hill, 101.

22 Eoin O'Mahoney (1905–1970), Irish barrister, politician, wit and 'fighter for hopeless causes' – according to his obituary in *The New York Times*. His nickname, 'The Pope', was commonly thought to have derived from his having been asked as a child what he wanted to be when he grew up.

few weeks are the writings of a man with purpose and energy. As he wrote to Coetmore after returning to the Lower Baggott Street lodgings in Dublin: 'Dr Groves at Ledbury vetted me & said since my return from Ireland I looked a new man.' Moeran arrived at his Coolagad cottage during the weekend of 11/12 March and began to settle in. He immediately began work and wrote to Coetmore that he had 'put in some satisfactory hours on my symphony'. He wrote again on 16 March with detail about the other work he was doing:

> I have 3 works on the stocks ... *The Oyle of Barl[e]y*, an orchestral fantasia on this tune from Playford, 1675, at the instigation of Barbirolli & Francis, Day & Hunter. It is going well & should be finished & off to the publisher by the end of this month ... Then (April) I shall get back to the Symphony, on which I have put in 2 solid days this week to the end of a section. For the Norwich 1951 festival I am setting some Seumas O'Sullivan poems for Parry Jones & orchestra. I am working like blazes here in this lovely & peaceful place; also getting plenty of exercise walking & climbing.

He ended the letter by reporting that he had been to an eye specialist who had said that Moeran's eyes were good but that he needed new glasses. By 20 March, he had received these, and he wrote two letters that day to Coetmore. The first acknowledged that he had received hers of 8 March in which she had given reasons for not making a trip to Europe during the next year – the principal of which was cost – and rejecting the plan for their future that he had put forward the previous July and which he had been mentioning in most of his letters since January. However, it seemed that she was still very hopeful that he would join her in Australia. She had evidently suggested that he could travel after the Cheltenham and Norwich Festivals in the summer of 1951. While he noted that a further year of separation was hardly ideal, he wrote that he would be willing to do this, perhaps by getting a passage on a fast cargo ship or even buying an airline ticket. His last letter to Coetmore was written that afternoon following an invigorating walk, and he wrote in perhaps the most optimistic and relaxed way of any of his letters during the past two years:

> After the wet weekend, everything is bursting out; lovely green shoots in the hedges, the purple heather on the mountain side, & to the East the perfect blue of the sea. Darling, this makes me think the more of you & how you would love it. And here I am in this peaceful cottage in the thick of composition & finding things come easy to me. There has been nothing like it for writing purposes since our happy time in Sussex. Everything is perfect except that you are not here. I find that now I am working again amid the kind of country that is most dear to me, & living with kind people, Sea, heather & Mountains, that you, Peers, always seem to be not very far away. Actually, I feel you with me when I am walking the hills. I love to think, & I believe &, in fact, know that you are with me spiritually, though so many miles separate us.

He ended:

Goodbye, my own darling. With this lovely spring, the birds singing, & everything day-by-day coming out (& I hope my music) you are always in my thoughts & I long to be with you again & no more partings. J.

A few days later, after having lived in the cottage for just two weeks, Moeran unexpectedly and apparently inexplicably left Coolagad and disappeared.

20

Last Days and Death

The atmospheric pressure and temperature charts for the afternoon of Friday 1 December 1950 indicate that the weather on the south-west coast of Ireland was poor and that in Kenmare, Co. Kerry, it was especially bad.[1] Despite the cold, wet and very windy conditions, at about four o'clock Moeran evidently left his lodgings at the Lansdowne Arms Hotel for a walk down to the town pier: a distance of about half a mile. By the time he reached the river estuary, the light would have been fading, but he was a well-known and recognisable figure. According to the report in the *Irish Times*:

> There was a strong gale blowing when [Moeran] was standing on the Pier and, shortly afterwards, he was seen to fall over the edge into the water. The alarm was raised immediately, and Sergt McCabe, Kenmare, with Mr Thomas Palmer, farmer, Mr John Fitzgerald, manager of the Kenmare Creamery and Mr Richard Aldwell, Press correspondent, went out in a boat and brought Mr Moeran to the pier. The Bay was so rough that they were unable to get Mr Moeran into the boat, and one of the men held his head out of the water while he was brought in.[2]

By the time they returned, a doctor had been summoned and resuscitation was attempted unsuccessfully. Moeran's body was taken to the local mortuary, and an inquest was opened and adjourned until the next day. The report of the composer's death was quickly communicated by telephone and telegram from that remote corner of Ireland and was printed in many newspapers in Britain as early as the following morning. Lionel Hill recalled: 'We received the shock of [Moeran's] sudden death in the morning papers.'[3] Within a few days, the composer's life and career had been summarised and celebrated by obituary writers in Britain, Ireland and around

---

[1] The weather details have been extracted from contemporary reports and historical data provided by Met Éireann and the Deutscher Wetterdienst.

[2] 'Composer Drowned In Kenmare Bay', *Irish Press*, (2 December 1950), 1.

[3] Hill, 103. Moeran's death was reported on page 2 of the edition of *The Manchester Guardian* dated Saturday, 2 December 1950: 'Mr Ernest John Moeran, the composer, whose death in Kenmore, [sic] Country Kerry, at the age of 55 is announced, came of Irish parentage', and on the same day in several English and Scottish regional newspapers, including *The Scotsman*, the *Aberdeen Press & Journal*, and the *Yorkshire Evening Post*. *The Times* published its obituary in the edition dated 4 December 1950 under the headline 'MR. E. J. MOERAN – A MODERNIST WITH HIS ROOTS IN THE PAST': 'Mr. E. J. Moeran, whose body was found in the River Kenmare on Saturday, was a composer who, if a nationalist school had arisen in England after our musical emancipation from the Continent, would have been one of its prominent members.'

the world. The news of his death was received in Ledbury by telegram and similarly by Coetmore in Australia. Ada Esther Moeran wrote to her on 3 December:

> My darling Peers, I don't know how to write to you. You will have received the cable with the tragic news. It came as a dreadful shock to me, as I had actually had a letter from Jack only a few days ago – I expect you had one too. Graham has gone to Kenmare. I have no details at all, so can tell you nothing yet. What to say to you, my poor daughter, I do not know, or what to advise you. I can only pray for you, that you may be comforted & guided. As soon as Graham returns, I will write again. Your broken-hearted Mother.

Popular opinion in Kenmare was divided. Some believed that Moeran had taken his own life by deliberately jumping into the river, while others thought that he must have fallen off the pier while intoxicated and had drowned. The inquest established that he had died before entering the water, since the post-mortem examination found there was no water in his lungs, and the cause of death was officially recorded as a cerebral haemorrhage. Moeran was buried in the churchyard at nearby Killowen the following Monday. His popularity in Kenmare ensured that his funeral was well-attended, and, according to Sir Arnold Bax, he was mourned locally for some considerable time.[4]

Almost all the testimony pertaining to the eight months between Moeran's disappearance from Coolagad in late March and his death in Kenmare on 1 December was written or collected after and in the knowledge of the composer's death. None of Moeran's personal documents written at the time have survived, neither is there any mention of him in newspapers or journals. Tracing his movements after his disappearance and determining the reasons for them is, therefore, problematic. The only evidence is a letter written to Coetmore on 29 May 1950 by Larry Morrow, the friend who had recommended the Coolagad cottage and who was also resident there at weekends. Morrow wrote that after Moeran's arrival at Coolagad on 11 March he had 'seemed thoroughly happy'.[5] Then, soon after writing the two letters to Coetmore on 20 March, he had 'broken out' and drunk excessively for a few days. Morrow said that the landlady Sheila O'Mahoney had spoken to Moeran 'quite frankly' and that he had resumed taking the alcohol aversion medication. Morrow continued: 'That weekend (the last in March) he went off – with a small attaché case – to stay for three days at Dunleer, Co. Louth, with Brian Easdale.'[6] However, Moeran did not return after the planned break in Dunleer. 'After a week I became worried,' wrote Morrow, 'since all his belongings (besides a hired piano), bags, MSS were still all here, and his correspondence … was beginning to pile up.' It is unknown whether Moeran ever arrived in Dunleer, and there is no indication that Morrow contacted Easdale. Moeran was in Dublin on 3 April, from where he sent a birthday greetings telegram to his brother in Ledbury, but he still did not return to Coolagad. Nothing was heard

---

4   See Bax, (1951), 125–127.

5   McNeill, 316–317.

6   Composer Brian Easdale (1909–1995) lived in Cheltenham near Moeran's former lodgings at Park House West. Moeran had been an admirer of Easdale's music since hearing his piano concerto in 1938.

until 1 May, when he sent a telegram to his mother in Ledbury in which he said that he had been 'very ill but was recovering'.[7] Moeran also sent telegrams to Coolagad, followed by what Morrow called 'a very abject letter' from the Rothesay Hotel in Dublin. This letter mentioned that Moeran had been beaten up and robbed and that he needed help. On receipt of this, Morrow and O'Mahoney visited the hotel, only to find that Moeran had moved to another in Dun Laoghaire. It took Morrow several days to locate this hotel, by which time Moeran had again moved, this time to an undisclosed destination. When Morrow wrote his letter to Coetmore, Moeran's location was still a mystery. William Graham wrote to Coetmore on 3 September to say that he had been in contact with Sheila O'Mahoney at Coolagad several times over the summer, but that she had no information about where Moeran had gone.[8] It was not until mid-October that his family in Ledbury received a letter from Bridget O'Donnell at the Lansdowne Arms Hotel in Kenmare to inform them that Moeran was staying there. On 13 October, Moeran's mother wrote to Coetmore:

> I have heard of Jack, but not from him. He is in Kenmare, & is now fairly well, & doing some work. Why he does not write to me or to you I cannot imagine. The mystery will get cleared up in time. But it is something to know where he is.

Moeran, a previously reliable correspondent, wrote very few letters during the five months he spent in Kenmare, and one of these was to his mother shortly before his death. Writing to Coetmore on 3 December, William Graham mentioned that Moeran had written 'an affectionate letter to Mother',[9] and further details were later provided by Ada Esther Moeran to Lionel Hill:

> After months of silence I had a letter from him about two weeks before he passed away – which told me the great dread he had that his brain was growing weak … The rest of the letter was just full of his usual loving way of writing.[10]

William Graham Moeran travelled to Kenmare immediately on hearing of his brother's death, and during his few days there made extensive enquiries about Moeran's activities and state of health. He discovered that Moeran had appeared in Kenmare in mid-June and had lodged in his usual room at the Lansdowne Arms Hotel. He found that Moeran had spent the next few months there living 'very quietly … he pottered about, listened to the wireless, gave … some music lessons, [and] played the piano to his friends'.[11] Anecdotal evidence from others – most particularly from Moeran's Hallé Orchestra clarinettist friend Pat Ryan and his Irish poet friend Niall O'Leary Curtis – confirms that Moeran stayed in Kenmare for the last few months

---

7   This information is in a letter written by Ada Esther Moeran to Peers Coetmore dated 8 May 1950. The original letters from Larry Morrow and Ada Esther Moeran are in the Coetmore Archive at the Performing Arts Museum in Melbourne.

8   Letter from William Graham Moeran to Peers Coetmore dated 3 September 1950.

9   Letter from William Graham Moeran to Peers Coetmore dated 3 December 1950. The original letters from William Graham Moeran are in the Coetmore Archive at the Performing Arts Museum in Melbourne.

10   Hill, 109.

11   Hill, 152–153.

of his life.[12] Other than this, there is no evidence to indicate how he spent his time. If the precedent of the 1948 and 1949 breakdowns can provide any indication, it is probable that by the time he arrived in Kenmare, he would have recovered from the worst aspects of this latest one. Significantly, in contrast to the previous occurrences, he did not write to Coetmore to say that he had recovered. The dearth of any letters written after 20 March 1950 is perhaps the strongest indicator that Moeran's personality had undergone a significant change. The reason he stopped writing can only be speculated, but it is possible that for the final few months of his life Moeran felt abandoned by his wife, family and colleagues.

Moeran's brother also visited Coolagad and interviewed Larry Morrow and Sheila O'Mahoney. The results of his investigations in Kenmare and Coolagad were two letters that he sent to Coetmore in which he presented what he had found out about Moeran's last months and death in a manner and tone that he perhaps intended would place his brother in the most positive light. Unfortunately, these letters – the content of which was either speculation or selective and reinterpreted third party testimony – have subsequently been taken to be authoritative factual accounts. They have been the basis of several sensational stories of the end of Moeran's life that have been written over the years. As with other episodes in the composer's life, separating fact from more compelling fiction has been rendered difficult both by the lack of verifiable evidence and the very existence of the dramatic alternative. Based on testimony from Sheila O'Mahoney, William Graham wrote that Moeran had consulted a specialist in Dublin. He wrote, 'we imagine he was warned in some way of the danger of something pressing on his brain, or of the state of his heart.'[13] While William Graham was probably endeavouring to establish a blame-free explanation for Moeran's behaviour, his entirely unsupported speculation, conceived in the knowledge of Moeran's subsequent death, has since been used – in a form of circular reasoning – as authoritative medical evidence to explain the composer's death. In fact, as Moeran wrote to Coetmore on 16 March, he had indeed consulted an eye specialist, but he had been told that his eyes were 'v. good' and had been given a prescription for new glasses. There is no reason to add further speculation to this. William Graham also exaggerated the content of the single letter that Moeran wrote to his mother shortly before his death. According to William Graham, Moeran had written that 'his lucid moments were very limited and that his main dread was that he would be certified insane and shut up in an asylum'.[14] This suggestion is inconsistent with Ada Esther Moeran's own summaries of the letter content sent to Coetmore and Hill. Fuel has subsequently been added to this fire of speculation over the years, such as the assertion that William Graham had found chains and padlocks in Moeran's jacket pocket, the implication of which was that

[12]   See 'Missing Symphony', *The Irish Times*, (23 January 1951), 6.

[13]   Hill, 152.

[14]   McNeill, 319.

Moeran feared being taken away and locked up in an asylum.[15] All these claims lack both evidence and plausibility.

While the dearth of primary evidence hinders determining what caused Moeran to act the way he did, his final 20 March letter to Coetmore – when read with the knowledge of what happened – reveals some clues that enable reasonable and less sensational speculation. The letter is in many senses hopeful and positive, but it is nonetheless enigmatic in some of its phrasing. For example, 'Goodbye' as a sign-off could bestow a sense of finality. However, it is the sentence 'Everything is perfect except that you are not here' that perhaps provides the most significant clue to Moeran's mood and subsequent actions. He had just received Coetmore's letter in which she said that she had decided not to make the trip to Europe that he had suggested. It may be that having found an ideal location for his work and built up an expectation that his wife would be coming back in a few months and spending time with him there, his hopes were mercilessly dashed. All he could look forward to for the next year or more was a perfect place rendered hollow and empty due to her absence. It is reasonable to assert that this had the effect of driving Moeran into such miserable despair that he felt that his only recourse was the whiskey bottle and, eventually, to run away.

Coetmore's reasoning for deciding against travelling back to Britain was partly cost, partly not wishing to put her newly established teaching practice at risk, but probably mainly that it would compromise her agenda to persuade Moeran into joining her in Australia. If this is true, then she was gambling everything on the success of that agenda, but it is probable that she had no other option. Returning to Britain would simply set everything back to how it had been eighteen months earlier. While Moeran was apparently being conscientious with his alcohol aversion therapy, it would take many months before he could be said to have been in any way cured, while in the interim, there was still the danger of his finding himself in situations where he could return to his old drinking habits. It would have been impractical for Coetmore to supervise him permanently, even if she had been willing to do this. Her solution for their marriage problems was 'all or nothing': either Moeran joined her in Australasia or he remained in Britain or Ireland on his own. While in Coetmore's mind, this may simply have been a matter of his booking a passage, packing his bag and waving goodbye to Britain, for Moeran, it was an agonising choice between abandoning his family and friends and his established musical life in the British Isles to be with his wife on the other side of the world, or abandoning his wife to remain with his family and attempt to continue his British and Irish career. Consequently, Moeran's mental state must rapidly have become desperate. It has already been suggested that his intellect would have driven him to seek solutions to problems, and this unresolvable situation could well have pushed beyond breaking point his ability to cope. As suggested, his precipitous disappearance from Coolagad bears a similarity to the sequences of events that characterised his breakdowns in the summers of 1948 and 1949. If the testimony of Larry Morrow is reliable, soon after writing to Coetmore Moeran began drinking again, and a few days later he left the

---

15 See letter from Sheila Varley (Coetmore's sister) to Lionel Hill dated 24 September 1984, partially transcribed in Hill, 154–155.

Coolagad cottage never to return. Despair over the possibility of not seeing his wife again for at least another eighteen months, compounded by increasing worry about his having overloaded his composing schedule and desperate not to disappoint the various conductors, orchestras and performers to whom he had promised works during the next year or so, seems to the author to be sufficient explanation for the onset of yet another alcohol-fuelled personal crisis.

What is known or suspected about Moeran's behaviour after leaving the Coolagad cottage at the end of March and until his death in Kenmare on 1 December is consistent with his having suffered another mental breakdown. Extending the consideration of his behaviour to the previous few years even suggests the possibility that Moeran had developed bipolar disorder.[16] If these assertions are correct, then Moeran was in a dark and dreadful place, and his prospects for help were extremely limited. It is probable that, as had been the case in his September 1948 crisis, he considered suicide. That he did not end his life and that he again recovered – at least to an extent – testifies to an underlying emotional strength that had reliably supported him through numerous personal ordeals and which may have had its roots in the death of Roland Perceval Garrod in May 1915. However, it is unproblematic to discern a convincing clinical explanation for Moeran's premature death, without resort either to supposed pressure on his brain or heart trouble, or to long-term effects of his First World War injury, or even to long-delayed Post Traumatic Stress Disorder. While no medical records for Moeran after his army days exist that could provide details of his state of health, the fact that he took regular exercise in the form of long and strenuous walks suggests that his basic fitness was probably good. Nevertheless, years of periodic heavy drinking and his frequently mentioned ruddy complexion are good indicators of hypertension. Before the 1950s, this was rarely diagnosed or treated, and it is likely that Moeran had had this condition for at least the previous two decades. Suffering a stroke in one's late fifties or early sixties was a common fate at that time – particularly for men – and it may have been that Moeran had been living with this danger for many years. This being the case, his having died from a cerebral haemorrhage at the age of fifty-six in 1950 was, sadly, unexceptional.

Symphony No. 2 in E flat

Moeran's death snatched away a composer with, perhaps, much more to contribute to human culture. It was the final act in a concatenation of increasingly ill-fated circumstances that had begun decades earlier, but which had nonetheless played a significant part in defining the music that he composed during the last twenty years of his life. His private means had enabled him to compose mostly what and when he wanted, with little interruption from the burden of commissions or otherwise having to compose to order. Thus, his surviving corpus of works is a more personal creation than might be usual for a professional composer. Consequently, it may be supposed that more of the man himself may be found distilled in his music. While

---

[16]   In the 1940s, the condition was known as manic depression, but it was rarely diagnosed, principally because sufferers seldom sought treatment. In-depth discussion of the possibility that Moeran was bipolar is beyond both the scope of this book and the expertise of its author.

Moeran's works were often inordinately long in both gestation and time to completion and were as near perfect as their creator felt able to achieve, this aspiration to
perfection eventually fatally hindered his ability to compose. At the end of his life,
several major works in progress remained uncompleted, including the E flat symphony and the commissions for the Festival of Britain and the Norwich Festival. In
January 1951, the *Irish Times* published correspondence concerning the fate of the
manuscript of the second symphony. Pat Ryan wrote that he had spent a month in
Kenmare during the summer, and he asserted that Moeran had been working quite
diligently on the symphony.[17] According to Ryan, '[Moeran] said he was working
as hard as he could, but was feeling depressed because there did not seem to be
any music in him.'[18] However, while Ryan wrote that 'The symphony was almost,
if not wholly, finished',[19] his authority for making such an assertion is suspect.[20]
Moeran's landlady at the Lansdowne Arms Hotel, Bridget O'Donnell, mentioned in
her October letter to Moeran's mother that she believed that Moeran was working
on composition, although she also suggested that Moeran was 'not quite himself' for
a while after his arrival in Kenmare.[21] Moeran's peripatetic lifestyle and increasingly
chaotic personal organisation ensured that some of his manuscripts were mislaid
during the days and weeks after his death, and these may have included the full
score of the E flat symphony. William Graham and Pat Ryan diligently but unsuccessfully searched Moeran's lodgings in Kenmare, the local places he was known
to frequent and the cottage at Coolagad, in the hope of finding any of the music on
which Moeran had said that he had been working. Unfortunately, it is quite possible
that irreplaceable material may have simply been thrown into the dustbin by an
over-zealous housekeeper. The surviving seventeen pages of the second symphony,
the possible composition of which Moeran had first mentioned in 1939, eventually
became part of the E. J. Moeran Collection at the University of Melbourne.

Moeran had made his will a fortnight or so after his and Coetmore's wedding
by filling in a standard pre-printed Last Will and Testament form which was witnessed by two employees of the Kington Branch of Barclay's Bank. He appointed
his brother as Executor and Sir Arnold Bax as Literary Executor. The text of the
document was simple: 'I give and bequeath unto my wife Peers Moeran all my possessions.' Probate was granted on 24 January 1951, and the net value of Moeran's
estate was calculated at a modest £847.4s.9d.[22] Coetmore travelled to Britain in
September 1951, staying for just a few months before she returned to Australia the

---

[17] Anecdotal evidence suggests that Ryan had taken a cottage in Tuosist (near Kenmare)
on a long rental, having been captivated by the area on a previous visit to Moeran in
Kenmare.

[18] 'No Sign of Symphony Manuscript', *The Irish Times*, (6 January 1951), 9.

[19] 'Missing Symphony', *The Irish Times*, (22 January 1951), 6.

[20] See p. 72, note 17 of Fabian Huss, 'E. J. Moeran's Symphony No. 2 in E Flat'. *Journal of
the Society for Musicology in Ireland* 6 (June):67–85, https://doi.org/10.35561/JSMI06102
(accessed 1 November 2020). This paper presents a comprehensive examination of the
extant material of the Second Symphony and includes a transcription of the manuscript.

[21] McNeill, 317.

[22] Equivalent to about £30,000 in 2020.

following January. During these few months, she spent some time with William Graham and Ada Esther in Ledbury deciding what to do with Moeran's remaining former possessions, which were now hers. Amongst the items that she took with her to Australia were all the manuscripts that Moeran had left in his room in Ledbury. However, these did not include anything that Moeran had taken with him or had created during his final visit to Ireland.

According to a letter that Moeran's mother wrote to Lionel Hill dated 14 October 1953, William Graham returned from Ireland with a 'bundle of MSS, which were done up in a parcel ... and sent to Sir Arnold Bax'[23] in his capacity as literary executor. The context of the October 1953 letter was that Bax had recently died, and Moeran's mother and brother were wondering what should be done with the bundle of Moeran's manuscripts that they believed must still be amongst Bax's papers. Hill had previously written to Ada Esther Moeran mentioning that he believed that the completed (more or less) manuscript of the second symphony was included in the package that had been sent to Bax. Moeran's mother added that she would be happy for the package to be sent to Hill, 'giving [him] a free hand to deal with them as [he thought] best'. Unfortunately, Hill was unable to take on the responsibility of dealing with Moeran's manuscripts, and, together with Bax's own papers and manuscripts, they were sent to Bax's literary executor Julian Herbage. After separating out what he believed was Moeran's work, Herbage wrote to Hill in March 1954, also offering him the possibility to take possession of and arrange what was to be done with the material. Herbage provided a list of what he had found:

> The two most important works appear to be sketches in short score of (a) an Overture, and (b) a Symphonic movement, of which the first page is dated '11/2/48'. There is also part of a movement scored for String Quartet, some Part Songs, including a setting of the folksong *It was happy and delightful*, several songs, the words only (with space for tunes) of what was evidently intended to be a collection of Ballads, a short score of the Rondo from the Violin Concerto, the full score of a *Fanfare for Red Army Day 1944* and several other odds and ends.[24]

Thus, by mid-1954, the music manuscripts that Moeran retained until his death were in two groups: 1) those from Ledbury which Coetmore had taken to Australia, and 2) those which Moeran had with him in Ireland and were now in the keeping of Julian Herbage. However, Hill was again unable to take responsibility for the manuscripts, and they remained with Herbage until he arranged to send them to Coetmore in Melbourne some years later.[25] Of the works mentioned by Herbage, only the Overture, the Symphonic movement and the Rondo from the violin concerto can be definitively identified as manuscripts presently in the E. J. Moeran Collection held in the Southbank Library of the Faculty of Fine Arts and Music (formerly the Victorian College of the Arts) at the University of Melbourne. The Symphonic movement corresponds to the seventeen-page manuscript collection item number VCA 25, labelled as Sketches of Symphony No. 2. The date men-

---

23   Hill, 111–112.

24   Hill, 112–113.

25   See Hill, 113.

tioned by Herbage '11/2/48' appears very faintly in the upper left corner of page 1 verifying its identity. Regarding the other works detailed in Herbage's letter, there is nothing in the E. J. Moeran Collection in Melbourne that corresponds either to 'part of a movement for String Quartet',[26] or to a 'collection of Ballads'. Neither is the score of *Fanfare for Red Army Day* extant. This was mentioned by Coetmore's widower Maurice Walter Knott in a letter he wrote to Colin Scott-Sutherland dated 3 April 1978:

> Quite recently I found a MS which I have passed on to the Victorian College of the Arts ... it is a fanfare for Red Army Day ... scored for 4 horns and 2 trumpets. The large envelope it was in had the name of Gus de Mauny & address on the front cover and on the back.[27]

Coetmore had died in July 1976, and she had bequeathed the Moeran manuscripts in her possession to the Victorian College of the Arts (VCA) where she had taught since 1959. Rhoderick McNeill created the first catalogue of these manuscripts in about 1979, and this does not include the *Fanfare for Red Army Day*. Since there has been no trace of either this work or the other missing items from Herbage's list for the past forty years, it is presumed that they were mislaid from the VCA E. J. Moeran Collection on some date unknown between April 1978 and late 1979.

So, what may have happened to them? The trail of evidence presented above indicates that on Coetmore's death in 1976, she was in possession of all known Moeran manuscripts that were not in private hands, including all those mentioned by Julian Herbage in his 2 March 1954 letter to Lionel Hill. Over the next two years, these were transferred according to her instructions to the college library, placed into storage boxes on arrival, and catalogued by Rhoderick McNeill. The numbering system adopted by McNeill indicates that the manuscripts were in no special order: he assigned VCA numbers starting from one as he examined each item. The present contents of the boxes still accord with McNeill's catalogue, which indicates that the *Fanfare for Red Army Day* and the other missing manuscripts were either removed from the boxes before McNeill compiled his catalogue or they were never there in the first place. While several plausible explanations for their apparent disappearance may be devised, the most probable seems to be that either they were mislaid on arrival or were subsequently removed from the boxes for examination and, for whatever reason, never returned. In any case, determining their present location, if any, would appear to be a forlorn hope.[28]

Ada Esther Moeran died in 1956 and William Graham in 1967, and on Coetmore's death in 1976, Moeran's immediate family was extinguished. While most of his and Coetmore's musical material – manuscripts and printed music – went to the

---

[26] Unless this is the link passage between the two extant movements of what was published as the String Quartet in E flat.

[27] Letter dated 3 April 1978 from Maurice Walter Knott to Colin Scott-Sutherland, now part of the Barry Marsh Collection, which was made available to the author by Rachel Marsh.

[28] The author is indebted to Georgina Binns, Librarian of the Faculty of Fine Arts and Music at the University of Melbourne, for her assistance in investigating the missing Moeran manuscripts.

Victorian College of the Arts, their legacy of personal items passed into the keeping of Coetmore's widower, Maurice Walter Knott, and he also inherited the copyright for Moeran's music. On his death in August 2003, the copyright and a few
personal items were bequeathed to Wesley College: Knott's former school in
Melbourne. The collection of letters, diaries and other documents pertaining to both
Moeran and Coetmore were gifted to the Melbourne Arts Centre, and these now
form the Coetmore, Knott, Moeran Collection at the Performing Arts Museum.
Over the years since Moeran's death, manuscripts of individual works have been
found or have emerged from private collections, and these are now secured in the
British Library, the Grainger Museum at the University of Melbourne, the Fleisher
Collection in Philadelphia, and the libraries of the Royal College of Music, Britten
Pears Arts and Trinity College Dublin. While some items are in private collections,
the fate of the manuscripts of nearly half of Moeran's published compositions is
unknown. Some of these were probably lost through destruction of property during
the Second World War, and Moeran himself disposed of the manuscripts of some
of his earlier published works with which he had become dissatisfied. His own care-
lessness and that of some publishers also accounts for several missing items, and the
consequences of his mental and physical breakdowns also probably ensured that
material was mislaid. Nevertheless, a significant number of Moeran manuscripts
may well have survived these upheavals, although – as is the case with the missing
VCA manuscripts – their present whereabouts are unknown.

Afterthoughts

Although it is evident that Moeran was highly regarded and widely performed during
much of his lifetime – most particularly during the periods 1920–1925 and 1935–1945
– for the two decades following his death, his music was neglected. However, from
the mid-1970s, Moeran came to the attention of British music enthusiasts, whose
championing of the music of a wide range of nineteenth and early twentieth century native composers had been prompted by the perception of excessive emphasis
on modernism by academia and influential art music promoters such as the BBC.
Alongside these enthusiasts, organisations including the British Music Society
and the pioneering record label Lyrita worked to perform and record the work of
Moeran and that of other neglected British composers. Subsequently, over the past
forty years, his tuneful, well-crafted and approachable music that is cast in a harmonic language firmly rooted in a post-Romantic tonal genre has attracted a new
audience. However, Moeran's place in British and Irish music has remained predicated on his moderately small surviving corpus of works representing a life-long
struggle – ultimately lost – against apparently unassailable adversity. His relatively
minor position as a composer has inevitably ensured that any apparent similarities
in his music to the work of more highly regarded composers has been explained as
his absorbing of their influences. However, this book has presented evidence that
must cast doubt on both these perspectives, and therefore Moeran and his music
must now be considered in a different way. There has been a tendency – deriving from his supposed experiences during the First World War and reinforced by
such testimony as that of Lionel Hill – to regard Moeran sympathetically and as a
victim. This has resulted in the creation of a stoutly defended edifice of belief that

has strongly resisted evidence-based assault, and the possible causes of this require some consideration. Moeran's minor status has ensured little rigorous scholarly examination, and previously accepted assumptions based on unsupported assertion have rarely been subjected to effective challenge. As will have become apparent throughout this book, there exists an unusually limited amount of direct documentary evidence pertaining to Moeran, and most especially relating to his childhood and youth. It has thus been necessary to subject to scrupulous examination each rare fragment of evidence that has survived, not only for what it validates, but also for what it may render as either plausible or implausible.

Moeran's life in overview exhibits some critical aspects that are central to a full understanding of the man and the music that he composed. Born towards the end of the nineteenth century, his early life was spent in the sheltered environment of a late-Victorian and Edwardian middle-class household that was the product of intellectual and financial privilege, while frequent family relocations led to an unsettled childhood. Moeran's early education was conducted at home by his mother and a governess, and he had little opportunity to associate with children of his own age. Nonetheless, he benefitted from an artistic, creative and intellectual legacy from members of both sides of his family. He was exposed to music-making – probably in the form of his mother playing and singing – and his own music lessons began early. At the age of ten, he was sent as a weekly boarder to preparatory school where his formal music tuition began. Four years later, he proceeded to Uppingham where he received both a public-school education and an extensive exposure to music that provided the basis for the life as a musician that he eventually chose. He involved himself in music-making in many forms, participating in chamber music ensembles and the school orchestra. It is probable that his sexuality imposed itself on him during his time at Uppingham, and he formed a close relationship with one of the other pupils: cellist Roland Perceval Garrod.

Moeran was intelligent and well-educated and may have proceeded to Cambridge – following his father and elder brother – had not the lure of continuing his musical studies at the Royal College of Music been so strong. Eventually coming under the tutelage and influence of Sir Charles Stanford, Moeran had instilled in him the importance of form which, together with the legacy of an extensive classical repertoire he had acquired during his years at Uppingham, later enabled him to devise inventive and convincing structures for his own compositions. While in London, the chance discovery of the possibilities inherent in folksong melodies led to a lifelong commitment to preserving the traditional musical heritage of England and, later, Ireland. Suspending his studies on the outbreak of the First World War, he enlisted, and he spent the first two years of the war on light duty in East Anglia, during which time he was able to continue to compose and participate in musical activities in London. Soon after his friend Garrod was killed in action, Moeran volunteered for front-line duty. He was eventually deployed to France early in 1917 and was wounded leading an attack on German lines at Bullecourt, after which he was repatriated for medical treatment. His injury was not serious, and a few months later he was sent to Ireland with his regiment. While there, he developed the beginnings of a love for the country that would ultimately lead to his spending much of his time there.

After his recovery and discharge from the army in 1919, Moeran's mother established him with a private income that enabled him to devote his life to composition, and she also provided the financial resources that facilitated the promotion of his music more intensively than could many of his contemporaries. As a result of both this and the networking opportunities afforded by his membership of the prestigious Oxford & Cambridge Musical Club – within the opulent rooms of which he made the acquaintance of some of the most important members of the British Establishment – Moeran rose rapidly to prominence as a composer in the musical London of the 1920s. This culminated in the commissioning by Sir Hamilton Harty of a symphony for the Hallé Orchestra. In mid-decade, Moeran developed a friendship with Philip Heseltine, and he eventually joined Heseltine in his artistic commune in Eynsford. The hedonistic lifestyle of the commune led to creative barrenness, failure to complete the symphony and lifelong inability to control the consumption of alcohol.

Heseltine's death in 1930 was a release for Moeran. He gradually recaptured his ability to compose, although he never recovered the facility and productivity that characterised his achievements of the early 1920s. From 1930, his life was circumscribed by periodic excessive drinking, which led to accidents, periods spent in nursing homes and encounters with the police. Musical London in the mid-1930s was different from his experiences of a decade or so earlier, and the importance of the BBC was much greater. However, Moeran made use of influential connections to re-establish himself back in the centre of musical life. While he was never in any sense wealthy, neither was he ever really short of funds, and he had a wide circle of acquaintances – many of whom were his drinking companions – that were willing to accommodate his peripatetic lifestyle, and he regularly returned to his parental home. In the mid-1930s, Moeran visited Ireland again and re-discovered the country that eventually became his second home, and his symphony was completed there in 1937.

By mid-1943, and despite frequent periods of ill-health, Moeran had again achieved a level of eminence, recognition and success. He had several large-scale works receiving repeat concert and broadcast performances, and he was composing as part of the war effort. His time was mostly his own, and – within the restrictions of wartime Britain – he was able to travel and visit as he pleased. In June 1943, he met the cellist Peers Coetmore. In some desperation over his continued and worsening alcohol over-indulgences, Moeran's brother and parents engineered a situation where he and Coetmore were thrown together for a while, and the most unlikely of relationships began. Until then, he had either shied away from or not had the opportunity for romantic liaisons. Since Garrod, the only experiences he is known to have had were in the orgiastic milieu of the Eynsford cottage. While these appear on occasion to have led to aborted pregnancies, none resulted in an extended relationship.

The impact of Coetmore on Moeran's life was far-reaching.[29] His comfortable existence and the freedom to compose what he liked when he liked was fatally compromised, and Coetmore's presence seems to have compelled him – at least for a

---

[29] The coincidence of both Garrod and Coetmore having been cellists is noted.

time – to want to compose only for her. Other work that he had shortly before found congenial became a nuisance or a chore, and the desire to buttress the relationship by the creation of numerous works for Coetmore inhibited his previously improving productivity. Nonetheless, Moeran was inspired by his muse to compose music that was possibly some of his finest. Sadly, during the final three years of his life, his creative capacity diminished, and he struggled and ultimately failed to complete a second symphony. Years of alcohol over-consumption, together with increasing depression over his inability to resolve the professional and personal conflicts in his life, led to deteriorating health, a series of mental breakdowns and death.

It is evident that Moeran did indeed struggle against adversity, and there can be no doubt that the final twenty years of the composer's life were defined by debilitating physical and mental ordeals. Nevertheless, the fact that his problems were largely self-inflicted must be accounted for in the perception and reception of the music. While one is naturally sympathetic to his plight, Moeran cannot be regarded solely as a victim of uncontrollable circumstances, and the unconditional and all-excusing admiration and respect that has characterised some writings about the composer hitherto may now be seen to have been misplaced. Moeran's life to 1926 demonstrates a determination to succeed as a composer and musician. Almost half of his extant compositions were completed between 1920 and 1926, and the final twenty years of his life account for just over one third of his music. These statistics testify strikingly to the contrast between these two phases of Moeran's career. That he succumbed to the temptations afforded during his years in the Eynsford cottage is beyond doubt, and recourse to possible effects of his wartime experiences cannot provide sufficient justification to regard such temptations as having been beyond his capability to resist.

Does Moeran's removal from a pedestal of unreserved admiration affect the appreciation of his music? To answer this, it must be considered generally whether creative work may only be fully appreciated if the details of the life of its creator and the circumstances of its creation are known. Does the discovery that an artist has failed in some way as a morally-praiseworthy person degrade or devalue that artist's work, or should his or her creation, once brought into being, lead an existence entirely isolated from its creator? According to Kurenkova and Kurenkova:

> You cannot separate an artwork from the artist. It was only Tolstoy who could create *War and Peace* and it was only Prokofiev who could compose a namesake opera and it was only Bondarchuk who could make the film of the same name ... The personality of an artist is never outside a work of art; on the contrary it infuses all its subject-matter and structure. But you should distinguish a real everyday personality of an artist and his poetic personality, which Pushkin called the soul of a poet.[30]

Whether one agrees with this or not, it is the undoubted tendency to perceive innate beauty in a creator of beauty that explains the indignant outrage that can accompany

---

30 R. A. Kurenkova & N. E. Kurenkova, 'Creative Process as a Factor and Condition of the Phenomenology of Life' in Anna-Teresa Tymieniecka (ed.), *Analecta Husserliana: The Yearbook of Phenomenological Research*, Vol. 83, (2004), 88.

the discovery that an artist failed to achieve the pinnacle of virtue that the lovers of their creation have themselves assumed for him or her. It is also undoubtedly the case that many people that appreciate art in any of its forms have little detailed knowledge of the artists' lives, and it may therefore be supposed that, outside of philosophical debate, the answer is not relevant. The creation endures unchanging, irrespective of what may be discovered about its creator. Musical biography and the determination of its importance as an adjunct to the complete study of the work of a composer has been the subject of much debate since Guido Adler suggested in 1885 that it was 'low in the hierarchy of the proper subjects for musical study'.[31] In the Karenkova and Karenkova quotation above, it was suggested that the personality of the creator of a work of art is an inherent part of its structure, and thus it may be thought that the identification and understanding of as many as possible of the constituents of that personality is required for a fuller understanding of the creation. There has been much deliberation about whether or not this is the case, and what part biography – or the mapping of a composer's life – contributes to the understanding of the music.[32] According to Jolanta T. Pekacz, 'in the case of artistic lives [biography] is supposed to provide a framework within which the creative output can somehow be related to the artist's life.'[33]

Regardless of the facts, assertions and speculations that comprise Moeran's re-considered biography, not a single note of his music has been changed, and its intrinsic aesthetic properties are unaffected by any alteration in the perception of the composer. What has been illuminated is the knowledge of the circumstances under which the music was composed. Consequently, its reception must be subject to review. It is now known that Moeran did not have a metal plate in his skull (nor pieces of shrapnel embedded near his brain), that he did not spend years in the First World War trenches, that he embodied an ambivalent sexual identity that compromised his building of satisfying personal relationships, and that he acquired an inability to control his consumption of alcohol. However, it is possible that the improved and enhanced knowledge of the composer's life could reinforce the sympathy for a victim narrative. As stated at the very beginning of this book, Moeran was simply a human being, and like all of us capable of succumbing to temptation, of making injudicious decisions, of being pleasant or unpleasant, of sometimes succeeding and sometimes failing: in short, of being imperfect. He undoubtedly made decisions during his life that, with the benefit of hindsight, may be considered to have been injudicious. Perhaps he should not have volunteered for front-line active service in 1916, although his decision to do so is understandable in the context of the deaths of so many of his friends. He should not have had such a close association with Heseltine and the Eynsford cottage commune, although this is again understandable through his desire to maintain a close friendship that he had once again made. Once in the cottage, he should perhaps have found the willpower to resist the

---

[31] Hans Lenneberg, *Witnesses and Scholars: Studies in Musical Biography*, (OPA, Amsterdam, 1988), 1.

[32] See, for example, Lenneberg, (1988), and Jolanta T. Pekacz (ed.), *Musical Biography: Towards New Paradigms*, (Ashgate Publishing, Aldershot, 2006).

[33] Pekacz (2006), 1.

hedonistic temptations to which he succumbed, again through his need to maintain his friendship. It is also easy to assert that he should not have married Coetmore, although he was powerless to stand firm against the influence of his mother and his own determination to keep to his word as a gentleman. Finally, and perhaps most significantly, he should have taken the opportunity to join Coetmore in Australia, but he could not abandon his family and friends and put aside what he saw as his responsibilities. Nevertheless, Moeran repeatedly overcame his personal demons – at least until the final one – and that can only be admired.

While Moeran the man now exists only in biography, Moeran the composer continues in his music, and if the author has one hope for this book, it is that the reader will have become sufficiently interested in both man and composer to listen to the music. Whether or not it is the product of a flawed personality, it holds a value beyond that of reflecting a single life, and it stands as a significant contribution to human culture.

Appendix I:
The Moeran Mythology

A list of commonly-believed misconceptions has long existed pertaining to Moeran's life, labelled collectively as the Moeran mythology. While each of these has been discredited, it may be wondered how and when they originated. The most dramatic of them was that the treatment for Moeran's seemingly serious injury at Bullecourt in May 1917 required the insertion of a metal plate to replace a damaged part of his skull. This story was in circulation by the late 1930s, as attested by Maureen O'Shea, daughter of the former proprietors of the Lansdowne Arms Hotel in Kenmare, Jim and Bridget O'Donnell.[1] More recent dissemination of the narrative began with its inclusion in Geoffrey Self's 1986 book *The Music of E.J. Moeran* and it subsequently became one of Moeran's most distinguishing characteristics. Self had relied for his biographical information on anecdotal evidence provided by people who had known Moeran, most particularly the former director of the Radio Éireann orchestra Michael Bowles. Since the source of Bowles' information can only have been Moeran, it is reasonable to suggest that the composer himself invented the metal plate story. A plausible scenario is that it was concocted by Moeran – possibly in conversation with Philip Heseltine – as an excuse for his behaviour under the influence of alcohol.[2]

Alongside the metal plate, Moeran's other legacies of the First World War were believed to have been fragments of metal embedded too close to his brain to be removed safely, a disability pension and the trauma induced by several years of experience of the horrors of the trenches. Again, the modern propagation of each of these began with speculations that were based on anecdotal evidence – chiefly that of Michael Bowles – in *The Music of E.J. Moeran*, and again, the ultimate source must have been Moeran himself. In Self's defence, it must be said that he would have had

---

[1]   In an interview with Barry Marsh recorded 12 May 2011. A transcription by the author of Mrs O'Shea's testimony was published as part of the author's paper 'A Composer Goes to War: E. J. Moeran and the First World War', *Journal of the Society for Musicology in Ireland*, No. 14, (2018–2019), 83–109 (94n45). https://doi.org/10.35561/JSMI14195 (accessed 28 November 2020). The audio recording is part of the Barry Marsh Collection, access to which was provided by Rachel Marsh.

[2]   This idea was adopted as a plot element in the BBC Radio Play *Moeran's Last Symphony*, written by Martyn Wade, and first broadcast in December 2010 as part of the BBC's marking of the sixtieth anniversary of the composer's death. The play is a fictionalised account of the last few months of Moeran's life in Kenmare, and it features a scene in flashback where Heseltine suggests that Moeran should claim to have a metal plate disability – resulting in a low alcohol tolerance level – as a convenient way to excuse any alcohol-related misdemeanours.

no reason to disbelieve the evidence of Moeran's former friend, and since the archival material to which the author has had access was not available in 1986 – indeed even its existence was not known until many years later – Self would have had no means of either verifying or challenging Bowles' assertions.

Other aspects of the mythology grew from biographical inventions most of which were originally perpetrated by Philip Heseltine, such as the notion that Moeran spent his childhood in Norfolk, that his family had no musical connections, that his ambition was to be an engineer and that his First World War injury was sustained carrying out duties as a motorcycle dispatch rider. Again, however, the origin of each of these must have been Moeran. Further misunderstandings led to the beliefs that Moeran spent time as a music teacher at Uppingham School, that he retreated to the Cotswold Hills in 1930 to re-appraise his compositional style and that his undeniable behavioural foibles were the natural consequences of his compositional genius and creative and artistic temperament, with those that could not be so explained being attributed to his war wound exacerbating the effect of small amounts of alcohol on his system. All these assumed characteristics and narratives have resulted in a compelling portrait of Moeran that has been shown in this book to have had little basis. However, the author would argue that the facts that have replaced the fiction are at least as compelling and dramatic, with the decided advantage that they are true. Surely Moeran's involvement in front-line action in May 1917 and that he was wounded going 'over the top' is more dramatic and sensational than the story that he was hit accidentally while riding a motorcycle?

The concept of the composer myth is, of course, not confined to Moeran. Musical biography abounds with exaggerated or invented accounts of the activities and accomplishments of composers and musicians. Christopher Mark Wiley has written a comprehensive examination of the phenomenon, showing how apocryphal stories – such as the fourteen-year-old Mozart's apparent memorisation of Allegri's *Miserere* – have become part of canonical biography.[3] However, when the fascinating or sensational mythology is eventually superseded by (usually) more mundane fact, it must be discarded, regardless of its appeal. Since much of Moeran's mythology was created by the composer himself, it is perhaps appropriate to end by quoting his own words. From a letter he wrote to Coetmore in January 1945:

> Perhaps I am not a composer at all. I had my suspicion of that some time ago, but I veered round & on the strength of finding myself in certain surroundings I wrote a couple of big works which have got me into the position of being 'reckoned' as being a writer of something worth-while. But I have been so badly stuck fast lately that I wonder whether it may not be a myth.

---

[3]   Christopher Mark Wiley, *Rewriting Composers' Lives: Critical Historiography and Musical Biography*, (Royal Holloway, Unpublished PhD Thesis, 2008).

Appendix II:
List of Works

Assembling and collating the list of works has been hindered by the fact that original manuscripts have survived for fewer than half of Moeran's published compositions, and of these, only a small number bear reliable dating evidence. The dates for some works can be deduced from Moeran's correspondence and from data extracted from articles in newspapers and music periodicals, and in some cases the titles of the works suggest possible dates. However, in many cases, no evidence for a precise date has been found, and an approximate date has been extrapolated from the date of publication. Since almost all Moeran's work was published during his lifetime, this has enabled the creation of this list, which is as chronologically accurate as possible.

Individual works are ordered by their known or deduced completion date. Works that were grouped as a set are ordered by the date of the collection.

Chronological list of Completed Works

M	Title	Genre	Composition Date
1	*Dance*	Piano	May 1913
2	*Fields at Harvest*	Piano	23rd Dec [1913]
3	*The North Sea Ground*	Song	04 April 1915
4	*Four Songs from A Shropshire Lad*	Song	Midsummer 1916
4.a	'Westward on the High-Hilled Plains'	Song	Midsummer 1916
4.b	'When I Came Last to Ludlow'	Song	Midsummer 1916
4.c	'This Time of Year, a Twelvemonth Past'	Song	Midsummer 1916
4.d	'Far in a Western Brookland'	Song	Midsummer 1916
5	String Quartet in E flat (first movement)	Chamber	April 1918
6	*The Lake Island*	Piano	1918
7	*At a Horse Fair*	Piano	1918
8	*Mantle of Blue (A Cradle Song)*	Song	1918
9	*Autumn Woods*	Piano	1919
10	*Ludlow Town*	Song	1920
10.a	'When Smoke Stood Up from Ludlow'	Song	1920
10.b	'Farewell to Stack and Barn and Tree'	Song	1920
10.c	'Say, Lad, Have You Things to Do?'	Song	1920

M	Title	Genre	Composition Date
10.d	'The Lads in their Hundreds'	Song	1920
11	*Spring Goeth All in White*	Song	1920
12	Theme and Variations in F minor	Piano	1920
13	*A Dream of Death*	Song	1920
14	*In the Mountain Country*	Orchestral	1920
15	*Twilight*	Song	1920
16	*On A May Morning*	Piano	1921
17	String Quartet in A minor	Chamber	1921
18	*Stalham River*	Piano	1921
19	*Toccata*	Piano	1921
20	First Rhapsody for Orchestra	Orchestral	1922
21	Sonata in E minor for Violin and Piano	Chamber	Summer 1922
22	*Three Fancies*	Piano	1922
22.a	*Windmills*	Piano	1922
22.b	*Elegy*	Piano	1922
22.c	*Burlesque*	Piano	1922
23	Two Songs	Song	1923
23.a	*The Bean Flower*	Song	1923
23.b	*Impromptu in March*	Song	1923
24	*When June Is Come*	Song	16 April 1923
25	*Two Legends*	Piano	1923
25.a	*A Folk Story*	Piano	1923
25.b	*Rune*	Piano	1923
26	*The Monk's Fancy*	Song	1923
27	*High Germany*	Folksong	1923
28	*Robin Hood Borne on his Bier*	Partsong	1923
29	*Can't You Dance the Polka?*	Folksong	1924
30	*Weep You No More, Sad Fountains*	Partsong	1924
31	Six Norfolk Folksongs	Folksong	1924
31.a	'Down by the Riverside'	Folksong	1922
31.b	'The Bold Richard'	Folksong	1920
31.c	'Lonely Waters'	Folksong	1923
31.d	'The Pressgang'	Folksong	1920
31.e	'The Shooting of his Dear'	Folksong	1922
31.f	'The Oxford Sporting Blade'	Folksong	1923
32	*Commendation of Music*	Song	1924
33	*Gather Ye Rosebuds*	Partsong	1924

M	Title	Genre	Composition Date
34	*Sheep-Shearing Song*	Folksong	1924
35	*Under the Broom*	Folksong	1924
36	*Mrs Dyer the Baby Farmer*	Folksong	1924
37	*Bank Holiday*	Piano	1924
38	*The Sailor and Young Nancy*	Folksong	1924
39	*Gaol Song*	Folksong	1924
40	*The Jolly Carter*	Folksong	1924
41	*O Sweet Fa's the Eve*	Folksong	1924
42	Second Rhapsody for Orchestra	Orchestral	20 October 1924
43	*Christmas Day in the Morning*	Folksong	1924
44	*'Tis Time, I Think, By Wenlock Town*	Song	1925
45	*Far in a Western Brookland*	Song	1925
46	Piano Trio in D major	Chamber	1925
47	*The Merry Month of May*	Song	1925
48	*In Youth is Pleasure*	Song	1925
49	*Troll the Bowl*	Song	1925
50	*The Little Milkmaid*	Folksong	1925
51	*Come Away, Death*	Song	1925
52	*Summer Valley*	Piano	1925
53	*Irish Love Song*	Piano	1926
54	*The Blossom*	Song	1926
55	*Maltworms*	Song	1926
56	*The White Mountain*	Piano	1927
57	*Seven Poems of James Joyce*	Song	1929
57.a	'Strings in the Earth and Air'	Song	1929
57.b	'The Merry Green Wood'	Song	1929
57.c	'Bright Cap'	Song	1929
57.d	'The Pleasant Valley'	Song	1929
57.e	'Donnycarney'	Song	1929
57.f	'Rain Has Fallen'	Song	1929
57.g	'Now, O Now, in this Brown Land'	Song	1929
58	*Rosefrail*	Song	1929
59	*The Sweet O' The Year*	Song	1930
60	Te Deum & Jubilate in E flat	Church Music	1930
61	Magnificat & Nunc Dimitis in D	Church Music	1930
62	*Praise the Lord, O Jerusalem*	Church Music	1930
63	*Blue Eyed Spring*	Song	1931

M	Title	Genre	Composition Date
63.a	*Blue Eyed Spring* (Choral Version)	Partsong	1931
64	String Trio in G major	Chamber	1931
65	*Whythorne's Shadow*	Orchestral	May 1931
66	*Lonely Waters*	Orchestral	1931
67	Sonata for Two Violins	Chamber	1931
68	*Loveliest of Trees*	Song	June 1931
69	*Oh Fair Enough are Sky and Plain* (1)	Song	June 1931
69.a	*Oh Fair Enough are Sky and Plain* (2)	Song	1931
69.b	*Oh Fair Enough are Sky and Plain* (3)	Song	26 December 1934
70	*Tilly*	Song	1931
71	*Six Suffolk Folksongs*	Folksong	1931
71.a	'Nutting Time'	Folksong	1931
71.b	'Blackberry Field (Blackberry Fold)'	Folksong	1931
71.c	'Cupid's Garden'	Folksong	1931
71.d	'Father and Daughter'	Folksong	1931
71.e	'The Isle of Cloy'	Folksong	1931
71.f	'A Seaman's Life'	Folksong	1931
72	*Parson and Clerk*	Folksong	1931
73	*The Day of Palms*	Song	1932
74	*Farrago Suite*	Orchestral	Summer 1932
74.a	*Farrago Suite* (piano duet arrangement)	Piano	Summer 1932
75	*Alsatian Carol*	Folksong	1932
76	*Ivy and Holly*	Folksong	1932
77	*Songs of Springtime*	Partsong	1933
77.a	'Under the Greenwood Tree'	Partsong	1933
77.b	'The River-God's Song'	Partsong	1933
77.c	'Spring, The Sweet Spring'	Partsong	1933
77.d	'Love is a Sickness'	Partsong	1933
77.e	'Sigh No More, Ladies'	Partsong	1933
77.f	'Good Wine'	Partsong	1933
77.g	'To Daffodils'	Partsong	1933
78	*Two Pieces*	Piano	1933
78.a	*Prelude*	Piano	1933
78.b	*Berceuse*	Piano	1933
79	*The Echoing [Ecchoing] Green*	Partsong	1933
80	*Weep You No More, Sad Fountains*	Song	1933
81	*Green Fire*	Partsong	1933

M	Title	Genre	Composition Date
82	*Nocturne*	Choral	1934
83	*To Blossoms*	Partsong	1934
84	*Weep You No More, Sad Fountains*	Partsong	1934
85	*Four English Lyrics*	Song	1934
85.a	'Cherry Ripe'	Song	1934
85.b	'Willow Song'	Song	1934
85.c	'The Constant Lover'	Song	1934
85.d	'The Passionate Shepherd'	Song	1934
86	*The Lover and his Lass*	Partsong	1934
87	*Cherry Ripe*	Partsong	1934
88	Symphony in G minor	Orchestral	22 January 1937
89	*Rosaline*	Song	1938
90	*Diaphenia*	Song	1938
91	*Rahoon*	Song	1938
92	*Blessed are Those Servants*	Church Music	1938
93	*Phyllida and Corydon*	Partsong	1939
93.a	*Phyllida and Corydon*	Partsong	1939
93.b	*Beauty Sat Bathing by a Stream*	Partsong	1939
93.c	*On a Hill There Grows a Flower*	Partsong	1939
93.d	*Phyllis Inamorata*	Partsong	1939
93.e	*Said I That Amaryllis*	Partsong	1939
93.f	*The Treasure of my Heart*	Partsong	1939
93.g	*While She Lies Sleeping*	Partsong	1939
93.h	*Corydon, Arise*	Partsong	1939
93.i	*To Meadows*	Partsong	1939
94	*Four Shakespeare Songs*	Song	1940
94.a	'The Lover and his Lass'	Song	1940
94.b	'Where the Bee Sucks'	Song	1940
94.c	'When Daisies Pied'	Song	1940
94.d	'When Icicles Hang by the Wall'	Song	1940
94.a(a)	'When Icicles Hang by the Wall'	Partsong	1940
94.a(b)	'When Icicles Hang by the Wall'	Partsong	1940
95	Concerto for Violin and Orchestra	Concerto	1942
96	Rhapsody in F sharp major for Piano and Orchestra	Concerto	1943
97	*Invitation in Autumn*	Song	1943
98	*Prelude for Violoncello and Piano*	Chamber	1943
99	*Irish Lament*	Chamber	1943

M	Title	Genre	Composition Date
100	*Overture for a Masque*	Orchestral	1944
101	*Six Poems by Seumas O'Sullivan*	Song	1944
101.a	'Evening'	Song	1944
101.b	'The Poplars'	Song	1944
101.c	'A Cottager'	Song	1944
101.d	'The Dustman'	Song	1944
101.e	'Lullaby'	Song	1944
101.f	'The Herdsman'	Song	1944
102	*If There Be Any Gods*	Song	1944
103	Sinfonietta	Orchestral	23 September 1944
104	*I'm Weary, Yes Mother Darling*	Folksong	1944
105	Concerto for Violoncello and Orchestra	Concerto	22 October 1945
106	Fantasy Quartet for Oboe and Strings	Chamber	1946
107	Sonata for Violoncello and Piano	Chamber	1947
108	Serenade in G for Orchestra	Orchestral	1947
108.a	*Prologue*	Orchestral	1947
108.b	*Air*	Orchestral	1947
108.c	*Galop*	Orchestral	1947
108.d	*Minuet* (Farrago 2 *Minuet*)	Orchestral	1947
108.e	*Rigadoon* (Farrago 4 *Rigadoon*)	Orchestral	1947
108.f	*Epilogue*	Orchestral	1947
109	*Songs from County Kerry*	Folksong	1949
109.a	'The Dawning of the Day'	Folksong	1949
109.b	'My Love Passed Me By'	Folksong	1949
109.c	'The Murder of Father Hanratty'	Folksong	1949
109.d	'The Roving Dingle Boy'	Folksong	1949
109.e	'The Lost Lover'	Folksong	1949
109.f	'The Tinker's Daughter'	Folksong	1949
109.g	'Kitty I Am in Love with You'	Folksong	1949
110	*The Jolly Carter* (choral version)	Folksong	1949
111	*The Sailor and Young Nancy*	Folksong	1949
112	*Candlemas Eve*	Partsong	1949
113	String Quartet in E flat (second movement)	Chamber	1949
114	String Quartet in E flat	Chamber	1949
115	*Rores Montium (Mountain Dew)*	Folksong	??
116	*Whisky, Drink Divine!*	Folksong	??
117	*One Morning in Spring*	Folksong	??

List of Lost or Uncompleted Works

It is estimated that the list of surviving works represents less than half of the completed music that Moeran composed during his lifetime: many works were lost, destroyed or otherwise misplaced. This list comprises surviving uncompleted works and the pieces for which there is reasonable evidence of their former existence.

M	Title	Status	Genre	Date
0.a	String Quartet 1	(lost)	Chamber	1911
0.b	String Quartet 2	(lost)	Chamber	1911
0.c	String Quartet 3	(lost)	Chamber	1912
0.d	Cello Sonata	(lost)	Chamber	1912
0.e	Violin Sonata 1	(lost)	Chamber	1912
0.f	Violin Sonata 2	(lost)	Chamber	1912
0.g	Violin Sonata 3	(lost)	Chamber	1912
0.h	*Looking Back*	(lost)	Song	1918
0.i	*The North-West, Canada*	(lost)	Song	1918
0.j	*The Captain's Apprentice*	(lost)	Folksong	1920
0.k	*Piano Trio in D major* (original)	(lost)	Chamber	1921
0.l	*Lonely Waters* (original)	(lost)	Orchestral	1924
0.m	Overture	(uncompleted)	Orchestral	1924
0.n	*Whythorne's Shadow* (original)	(lost)	Orchestral	1925
0.o	*An April Evening*	(lost)	Piano	1930
0.p	*Fanfare for Red Army Day*	(lost)	Orchestral	February 1944
0.q	Serenade: *Intermezzo*	(deleted)	Orchestral	1947
0.r	Serenade: *Forlana*	(deleted)	Orchestral	1947
0.s	The Oyle of Barley	(uncompleted)	Orchestral	1950
0.t	Symphony No. 2 in E flat	(uncompleted)	Orchestral	1950

Select Bibliography

Unpublished Sources

Individual items from archive sources are referenced in the text. The following are general references for collections of Moeran material:

Archives

Barry Marsh Collection (uncatalogued)

Coetmore, Knott, Moeran Family Collection, Collection ID 1M27, 1M49, Library of the Arts Centre Melbourne, Melbourne, Australia

E. J. Moeran Collection, Southbank Library, University of Melbourne, Melbourne, Australia

Ernest John Moeran Military Record, WO 374/48245, United Kingdom National Archives

Julian Herbage Papers, catalogue JH at the Britten Pears Arts Library, Aldeburgh

Papers of the Oxford and Cambridge Musical Club, 1899–1954, Dep. C 958-68, e. 487, Department of Special Collections and Western Manuscripts, Bodleian Library, University of Oxford

2/8 Battalion West Yorkshire Regiment: War Diary, WO 95/3082/3, United Kingdom National Archives

Uppingham School Magazine, Uppingham School, Uppingham, Rutland

Unpublished Theses

Blosser, Cyril Andrew, *Ernest John Moeran: Seven Poems of James Joyce. A Singer's Guide to Preparation and Performance*, (Ohio State University, DMA Thesis, 2009)

Browne, Stephanie, *The life and career of Peers Coetmore, English cellist (1905–1976)*, (Melbourne Conservatorium of Music, Masters Research Thesis, 2012)

Huss, Fabian Gregor, *Inspiration, Influence and Stylistic Development in the Symphonies and Concertos of E.J. Moeran*, (Mary Immaculate College, University of Limerick, MA Thesis, 2007)

Marchman, Judy O., *Peter Warlock (1894–1930): A Contextual Analysis of his Art Songs Related to Symptoms of Mental Illness*, (University of Miami, DMA Thesis, 2013)

Maxwell, Ian, *The Importance of Being Ernest John : Challenging the Misconceptions about the Life and Works of E. J. Moeran*, (University of Durham, PhD Thesis, 2014)

McNeill, Rhoderick, *A Critical Study of the Life and Works of E. J. Moeran*, (University of Melbourne, PhD Thesis, 1983)

Polay, Bruce, *Selected Orchestral Compositions by Ernest John Moeran*, (Arizona State University DMA Thesis, 1989)

Pidcock, Christopher, *An Exploration of the Compositional Idiom of E. J. Moeran with Specific Focus on his Cello Concerto*, (University of Sydney, MMus. Thesis, 2010)

Yenne, Vernon Lee, *Three Twentieth Century English Songs Composers: Peter Warlock, E. J. Moeran and John Ireland*, (University of Illinois DMA Thesis, 1969)

Published Sources

Some individual items from published journals and newspapers are referenced in the text.

Books

A Pictorial and Descriptive Guide to London and its Environs, (Ward, Lock & Co, London, 1919)

Crockford's Clerical Directories, volumes for 1905 to 1940, (Horace Cox, London)

Marlborough College Register: from 1843 to 1904 inclusive, (Oxford, 1905)

Register of the Alumni of Trinity College Dublin, 9th edition, (Trinity College, Dublin, 1970)

Uppingham School Roll 1853–1947, (H. F. W. Deane, London, 1948)

Allinson, Helen, *The Story of Gore Court House and Estate, Tunstall*, (Sittingbourne Heritage Museum, 2006)

Banfield, Stephen, *Sensibility and English Song*, (Cambridge University Press, Cambridge, 1985)

Bishop, Alan & Bostridge, Mark (eds), *Letters from a Lost Generation: First World War Letters of Vera Brittain and Four Friends: Roland Leighton, Edward Brittain, Victor Richardson, Geoffrey Thurlow*, (Abacus, London, 1999)

Blom, Eric, (ed.), *Leslie Heward*, (J. M. Dent, London, 1944)

Brady, W. M., *Clerical and Parish Records of Cork, Cloyne, and Ross, Vol 3*, (Alexander Thom, Dublin, 1864)

Brittain, Vera, *Testament of Youth*, (Victor Gollancz, London, 1933)

Britten, Beth, *My Brother Benjamin*, (Faber & Faber, London, 2013)

Campbell, Sir Malcolm, *My Thirty Years of Speed*, (Hutchinson & Co., London, 1922)

Caulfield, Richard, *Annals of St Fin Barre's Cathedral, Cork* (Purcell & Co., Cork, 1871)

Charlton, Anne & William, *Putting Poetry First: A Life of Robert Nichols 1893–1944*, (Michael Russell Publishing, 2003)

Copley, Ian A., *The Music of Peter Warlock: A Critical Survey*, (Dobson Books, London, 1979)

Cunningham, Joseph & Fleischmann, Ruth, *Aloys Fleischmann (1880–1964): An Immigrant Musician in Ireland*, (Cork University Press, Cork, 2010)

Dibble, Jeremy, *Hamilton Harty: Musical Polymath*, (Boydell & Brewer, Woodbridge, 2013)

Dillistone, F. W., *Charles Raven: Naturalist, Historian, Theologian*, (Hodder & Stoughton, London, 975)

Douglas, Norman, *Looking Back: An Autobiographical Excursion*, (Chatto & Windus, London, 1933)

Evans, John, (ed.), *Journeying Boy: The Diaries of the Young Benjamin Britten 1928–1938*, (Faber & Faber, London, 2009)

Fenby, Eric, *Delius As I Knew Him*, (G. Bell & Sons, London, 1937)

Fenwick, Simon, *The Crichel Boys*, (Little Brown Book Group, London, 2021)

Fleischmann, Ruth (ed.), *Aloys Fleischmann – A Life for Music in Ireland Remembered by Contemporaries*, (The Mercier Press, Cork, 2000)

Fletcher, Ivan Lyrle, *Ronald Firbank: A Memoir*, (Duckworth, London, 1930)

Foreman, Lewis, *From Parry to Britten: British Music in Letters, 1900–1945*, (Amadeus, London, 1987)

Foreman, Lewis and Foreman, Susan, *London: A Musical Gazetteer*, (Yale University Press, New Haven CT., 2004)

Foreman, Lewis, *Music in England 1885–1920*, (Thames Publishing, London, 1994)

Gibbings, Robert, *Coming Down the Wye*, (Robert Gibbings, London, 1942)

Gray, Cecil, *Peter Warlock*, (Jonathan Cape, London, 1952)

Hamnett, Nina, *Is She A Lady? A Problem in Autobiography*, (Wingate, London, 1955)

Hanley, Brian, *The IRA: 1926–36*, (Four Courts Press, Dublin, 2002)

Heseltine, Nigel, *Capriol for Mother: A Memoir of Philip Heseltine*, (Thames Publishing, London, 1992)

Heseltine, Philip, *Miniature Essay: E. J. Moeran*, (J & W Chester, London, 1926)

Hill, Lionel, *Lonely Waters: the diary of a friendship with EJ Moeran*, (Thames Publishing, London, 1985)

Hold, Trevor, *Parry to Finzi*, (Boydell & Brewer, Woodbridge, 2002)

Holloway, Mark, *Norman Douglas: A Biography*, (Secker & Warburg, London, 1976)

Holroyd, Michael, *Augustus John, Vol.2 The Years of Experience*, (William Heinemann Ltd, London, 1975)

Howes, Frank, *The English Musical Renaissance*, (Secker & Warburg, London, 1966)

Hughes, Angela, *Chelsea Footprints: A Thirties Chronicle*, (Quartet Books, London, 2008)

Hugh-Perks, Richard, *George Bargebrick Esquire: The Story of George Smeed, the Brick and Cement King*, (Meresborough Books, Rainham, 1981)

John, Augustus, *Chiaroscuro; Fragments of Autobiography*, (Jonathan Cape, London, 1954)

Kendall, Paul, *Bullecourt 1917: Breaching the Hindenburg Line*, (The History Press, Stroud, 2010)

Lenneberg, Hans, *Witnesses and Scholars: Studies in Musical Biography*, (OPA, Amsterdam, 1988)

Lindsay, Jack, *Fanfrolico and After*, (The Bodley Head, London, 1962)

Lloyd, Stephen, *Constant Lambert: Beyond the Rio Grande*, (Boydell & Brewer, Woodbridge, 2014)

Lloyd, Stephen, *William Walton: Muse of Fire*, (Boydell Press, Woodbridge, 2001)

Lloyd, Stephen, Sparkes, Diana, Sparkes, Brian, (eds), *Music in Their Time: The Memoirs and Letters of Dora and Hubert Foss*, (Boydell & Brewer, Woodbridge, 2019)

Longmire, John, *John Ireland: Portrait of a Friend*, (Baker, London, 1969)

Matthews, Bryan, *By God's Grace: A History of Uppingham School*, (Whitehall Press, London, 1984)

Mitchell, Donald (ed.), *Letters from a Life: The Selected Letters and Diaries of Benjamin Britten 1913–1976, Volume I 1923–1939*, (Faber & Faber, London, 1991)

Nevinson, Christopher Richard Wynne, *Paint and Prejudice*, (Methuen, London, 1937)

O'Higgins, Rachel (ed.), *The Correspondence of Alan Bush and John Ireland 1927–1961*, (Ashgate Publishing, Aldershot, 2006)

Pekacz, Jolanta T., (ed.), *Musical Biography: Towards New Paradigms*, (Ashgate Publishing, Aldershot, 2006)

Phoenix, Eamon, Ó Cléireacháin, Pádraic, McAuley, Eileen & McSparran, Nuala (eds*), Feis na nGleann A Century of Gaelic Culture in the Antrim Glens*, (Ulster Historical Foundation, Belfast, 2005)

Powell, Neil, *Benjamin Britten: A Life for Music*, (Hutchinson, London, 2013)

Raven, Charles E., *A Wanderer's Way*, (Martin Hopkinson & Co. Ltd., London, 1928)

Rawnsley, Eleanor, *Canon Rawnsley: An Account of his Life*, (Maclehose, Jackson & Co., Glasgow, 1923)

Richards, Fiona, 'An Anthology of a Friendship – The Letters from John Ireland to Father Kenneth Thompson', in Fuller, Sophie & Whitesell, Lloyd, *Queer Episodes in Music and Modern Identity*, (University of Illinois Press, Urbana IL., 2002), 245–268

Richards, Fiona, *The Music of John Ireland*, (Ashgate, Aldershot, 2000)

Rowland, Peter, *Raffles and his Creator: The Life and Works of E. W. Hornung*, (Nekta Publications, London, 1999)

'Rus, Urban', *Old Faces in Odd Places*, (Wyman & Sons, London, 1882)

Searle, Humphrey, *Quadrille with a Raven – The Memoirs of Humphrey Searle*, (Online Publication, http://www.musicweb-international.com/searle/titlepg.htm)

Self, Geoffrey, *The Music of E.J. Moeran*, (Toccata Press, London, 1986)

Sherwood, John, *No Golden Journey: A Biography of James Elroy Flecker*, (Heinemann, London, 1973)

Smith, Barry, *Frederick Delius and Peter Warlock: A Friendship Revealed*, (Oxford University Press, Oxford, 2000)

Smith, Barry, *Peter Warlock: The Life of Philip Heseltine*, (Oxford University Press, Oxford, 1994)

Smith, Barry (ed.), *The Collected Letters of Peter Warlock, Vol.4 1922–1930*, (Boydell & Brewer, Woodbridge, 2005)

Tertis, Lionel, *My Viola and I*, (Paul Elek, London, 1974)

Thorne, Graham (ed.), *The Oxford & Cambridge Musical Club: An 80th Anniversary History*, (Oxford & Cambridge Musical Club, London, 1980)

Underwood, Peter, *Horror Man: The Life of Boris Karloff*, (Leslie Frewin, London, 1972)

Venn, J. A., *Alumni Cantabrigienses*, (Cambridge University Press, Cambridge, 1974)

Warner, Philip, *Horrocks: The General Who Led from the Front*, (Hamish Hamilton, London, 1984)

Westrup, Jack A., 'E. J. Moeran', in Bacharach, A. L., (ed.), *British Music of our Time*, (Penguin, Harmondsworth, 1951)

Whall, William Boultbee, Whall, Roughton Henry, Whall, Veronica (illus.), *Ships, Sea Songs and Shanties*, (James Brown & Son, Glasgow, 1910)

Wild, Stephen, *E.J. Moeran*, (Triad Press, London, 1973)

Wright, David C. H., *The Royal College of Music and its Contexts: An Artistic and Social History*, (Cambridge University Press, Cambridge, 2019)

Journal articles

Bax, Arnold, 'E. J. Moeran: 1894–1950', *Music & Letters*, Vol. 32, No. 2 (April 1951), 125–127

Cockshott, Gerald, 'E. J. Moeran's Recollections of Peter Warlock', *The Musical Times*, Vol. 96, No. 1345 (1 March 1955), 128–130

Heppa, Christopher, 'Harry Cox and his Friends – Song Transmission in an East Norfolk Singing Community c.1896–1960', *Folk Music Journal*, Vol. 8, No.5 (2005)

Heseltine, Philip, 'E. J. Moeran', *The Music Bulletin*, Vol.6, No.6, (June 1924), 170–174

Heseltine, Philip, 'Newcomers: E. J. Moeran', *The Chesterian*, No. 36, (January 1924), 124

Maxwell, Ian, 'A Composer Goes to War: E. J. Moeran and the First World War', *Journal of the Society for Musicology in Ireland*, 14, (2018–2019), 83–109

Moeran, Ernest John, 'Folk Songs and some Traditional Singers in East Anglia', *The Countrygoer*, Issue 7, (Autumn 1946)

Moeran, Ernest John, 'John Ireland as a Teacher', *Monthly Musical Record*, (March 1931)

Moeran, Ernest John, 'Obituary: Sir Charles Villiers Stanford, Mus. Doc., D.C.L.', *Journal of the Folk-Song Society*, Vol.7, No.28, (December 1924)

Moeran, Ernest John, 'Some Folk Singing of Today', *Journal of the English Folk Dance and Song Society*, Vol.5, No.3, (December 1948), 152–154

Moeran, Ernest John, 'Songs Collected in Norfolk', *Journal of the Folk-Song Society*, Vol. 7, No. 26, (December 1922), 1–24

Self, Geoffrey, 'E. J. Moeran – Unpublished Letters and Songs', *British Music*, Vol. 16, 1994, (British Music Society, London, 1994), 33–44

Senior, Evan, 'E.J. Moeran', *Australian Musical News and Digest*, (1 May 1950), 30–31

Talbot, John, 'Memories of Jack', *British Music*, Vol. 31, 2009 (British Music Society, London, 2009), 6–21

Articles in various issues of:

BMS News
British Music
Chamber Music
Delius Society Journal
Journal of the English Folk Dance and Song Society
Journal of the Folk-Song Society
Monthly Musical Record
Music & Letters
Musical Opinion
Punch
The Chesterian
The Listener
The Music Bulletin
The Musical Standard
The Musical Times
The New Statesman & Nation
The Radio Times
The Royal College of Music Magazine
Tempo
Uppingham School Magazine

Reports and articles in various issues of the following newspapers:

Belfast Newsletter
Cork Southern Reporter
East Kent Gazette
Irish Independent
Irish Press
London Gazette
Maidstone Journal & Kentish Advertiser
Norfolk Chronicle & Norwich Gazette
Norfolk News
Pall Mall Gazette
Saunder's Newsletter
Southern Reporter & Cork Commercial Courier
The Cork Examiner
The Cork Mercantile Chronicle
The Daily Telegraph
The Guardian
The Irish Times
The Kerryman
The Observer
The Scotsman
The Times
Yarmouth Independent

Index of Works

Orchestral Music

Concertos

Chamber Music

Piano Solo

Solo Songs

Part-Songs

Choral Music

Church Music

Folksong Arrangements

Lost or Uncompleted Works

General Index